amar • Ashrey • Az Yashir
Mo … ifices • Barukh
chanun … eridat Hashefa •
Minchah • … a al Hamitah •
• Hallel • Modeh Ani • Morning Blessings •
ishtabach • Shema • Amidah • Tachanun • Kr
food • General Blessings • Minchah • Maariv
Rosh Chodesh • Yom Tov • Hallel • Modeh A
rifices • Barukh She'amar • Pesukey d'Zimra •
HaTorah • Yeridat Hashefa • Aleinu • Birkh
• Kriat Shema al Hamitah • Kiddush Levan
ning Blessings • Sacrifices • Barukh She'ama
Chodesh • Yom Tov • Hallel • Modeh Ani • Mo
Yishtabach • Shema • Amidah • Tachanun •
upon food • General Blessings • Minchah • M
bos • Rosh Chodesh • Yom Tov • Hallel • Mod
mra • Ashrey • Az Yashir • Yishtabach • Shem
Birkhat Hamazone • Blessings upon food • G
vanah • Sefirat HaOmer • Shabbos • Rosh C
Modeh Ani • Morning Blessings • Sacrifices • B
hema • Amidah • Tachanun • Kriat HaTorah
Minchah • Maariv • Kriat S

The Potency of Prayer

Rebbe Nachman

How to understand the power that lies behind the words of prayer.

Chaim Kramer

BRESLOV RESEARCH INSTITUTE
JERUSALEM / NEW YORK

ISBN 978-1-944731-46-5

First edition

For further information:

Breslov Research Institute
POB 5370
Jerusalem 91053, Israel

Breslov Research Institute
POB 587
Monsey, NY 10952-0587
USA

internet: www.breslov.org
e-mail: info@breslov.org

Printed in Israel

The Breslov Research Institute
gratefully acknowledges
the generosity of the

Schonfeld Family

of Beachwood, Ohio

who dedicate this book
in memory of

ר' יצחק אייזיק בר' חיים אלעזר ז"ל

ר' חיים אלעזר בר' יהודה שונפלד ז"ל
מרצפרד (אופהערטו), הונגריא

ציפורה פייגא בת ר' אברהם ע"ה
ממונקטש, אוקראינה

ר' אברהם בר' סלומון פיליפ ז"ל
מקמה, רומניה

ר' ברוך בר' משה מוזס ז"ל
מבטח, רומניה

This book is dedicated to
finding the way for all those souls that are lost,
in search of, downtrodden and in despair,
those that have lost true faith, those in the dark,
those sleepwalking, those that have forgotten,
those entrapped in lusts and illusions,
those in danger or illness,
those in need of salvation and blessing,
and those that need renewal and elevation

May this book open all the
gates of Prayer and Blessing
in the merit of
Rebbe Nachman of Breslov

May the commentaries reveal the concealed
and open the eyes of those who do not understand
the power of Jewish prayer

*What nation is so great that they have God so close to it,
as God our Lord is, whenever we call out to Him?*
(Deuteronomy 4:7)

**Akiva Betzalel Gavriel
& Frimet Tziporah
Hannan**

The Breslov Research Institute
extends heartfelt thanks
to

Diana Korzenik

Whose generosity has
showered upon us the ability
to continue to bring
Rebbe Nachman's teachings
to the world

May God shower upon her
all the blessings found in the
Torah and Prophets for
a long, healthy and
successful life, Amen

With immeasurable gratitude to HaShem
and the Breslov Research Institute for
giving us the opportunity and ability
to support the printing of these
life changing books that share the
light and wisdom of Rebbe Nachman

Daniel & Lauren
Zahavi

Table of Contents

Preface

As for me, I offer my prayer to you, HaShem, O merciful God, at this time of Divine Favor. Elohim, O just God, in the abundance of Your loving kindness, answer me with the assurance of Your deliverances (Psalms 69:14).

Prayer has been with us since creation. Adam prayed, Noah prayed, as did the Patriarchs. Perhaps their connection to God was a given, due to their high level of spirituality, but what has that got to do with us? Their prayers were their own words, flowing from their hearts. Our prayers are the established prayers from the time of the second *Beis HaMikdash* (around 350 B.C.E.) some 2,400 years ago. Are they still relevant today?

When introduced to prayer as children, we were taught, 'The prayers were established by our Sages. We rely on them, so this is the way we do things.' But a quick overview of organized prayer tells us that we have no explanation as to why we say this chapter, why this verse, why this idea, or why this particular order. What is the correct order of the prayers? What is the purpose of this or that prayer? And more importantly, what are we expected to accomplish with our prayers?

Prayer is extremely powerful. Our Matriarch Sarah had no womb, yet she and her husband Avraham prayed for children and Sarah conceived. Yitzchak and Rivkah were barren, yet they prayed and had children as well. Simply put, their prayers transcended nature. Can we pull this off too? The answer is a resounding, "Yes!" We too, with our prayers, can transcend nature.

When a person is ill, we pray for their healing. But if the illness is a fatal one, are we asking for a miracle? Well, yes. Can we expect a miracle? We've seen it happen! Maybe not always, maybe rarely, but it does happen. And when our prayers aren't answered, we have to ask ourselves whether we really prayed for the cure for that person. The Talmud teaches, "A person's prayer is not accepted until he places his soul into his hands" (*Taanit* 8a). This means that we should place our very thoughts and souls and our entire energy into our prayers. This is called praying with *kavanah* (concentration). When we pray with *kavanah*, there is a far greater likelihood that we will see wonders with our prayers.

When we pray with *kavanah*, the prayers become all-powerful, potent enough to cause changes in nature. I have merited in my lifetime to see answers to many of my prayers, and I'm sure many readers have also witnessed replies to their requests. What is lacking when we feel our prayers are lackluster, that we are missing meaning in our prayers? Perhaps it is the actual *meaning* of the prayers.

The idea behind *The Potency of Prayer* is the search for meaning. In these pages, you will find that there are definite reasons why a prayer is recited, why the prayers are arranged in this specific order, and what we can hope to accomplish with our prayers. With a blend of straightforward commentary and Kabbalistic insights, you will discover the power that lies behind the words and realize the potency of your efforts.

The commentaries chosen for this collection are ones that we have found most enlightening and accessible. For the most part, we have drawn our explanations from *Otzar HaTefillot*, an incredible collection of commentaries on the siddur, written predominantly by HaRav Chanokh Zundel of Salant, who authored various commentaries on Midrash, *Ein Yaakov* and other works. *Otzar HaTefillot* is a truly remarkable siddur commentary and is recommended for those who really want to understand the prayers (albeit it is in Hebrew). We have also drawn ideas and inspiration from the *Matok MiDvash* siddur, whose commentary is based on the *Zohar* and Kabbalah. Where no source is cited, the material can be found in either of those two works. The sources for other insights, especially from the writings of Rebbe Nachman and Reb Noson of Breslov, are cited by name.

The Breslov Research Institute extends a heartfelt thank you to all those who worked on this project. To Yonina Hall, *a"h*, who, due to corona, left us in the middle of her work. Yonina was our editor for some twenty years and had worked with self-sacrifice to help produce our publications in the highest quality possible.

To Bonnie Weinberg who picked up the project and turned out an excellent editing job, deepest thanks and accolades. To Becky Aber for another amazing typesetting job. Kudos to all.

And deepest thanks to Louie Schonfeld, Brian Hannan, Diana Korzenik and Daniel and Lauren Zahavi for their support for this book, which made its printing possible.

I pray that this collection will awaken us to pray more efficiently to the point that we can see the answers to all of our prayers. *Amen.*

CHAIM KRAMER

Elul 5781

September 2021

Introduction

Prayer.

A measure of one's heart's longing and yearning.

A release of one's bottled-up emotions.

An expression of one's internal conflicts, woes and joys.

Prayer. It is all of the above, and yet so much more.

It can move mountains — it can move Heaven — and it can move us!

Prayer has been with us since the days of our forefathers. Actually, it predates the Patriarchs, from the time of Adam and the Creation. However, it was Avraham who established *Shacharit* (the morning prayer); Yitzchak who established *Minchah* (the afternoon prayer); and Yaakov who established *Maariv* (the evening prayer).

The Exodus

Most people view the Exodus as the deliverance of the Jewish nation from slavery to freedom. A little-known fact is that speech, which was trapped in Egypt, was also freed, as in "freedom of speech." The Torah states that when Pharaoh died, "The Jewish people groaned from their labor and cried out, and their outcry from their subjugation went up before God" (Exodus 2:23). But we do not find that they prayed. Why not?

It was due to a combination of factors. One was the enslavement and distress they were going through. The second was that their belief in God and in prayer was weak. The mixture of both factors combined made praying to God an almost impossible task. They didn't have the strength to speak with God and to express what they were feeling (*Shelah*).

The ARI[1] explains that the Hebrew word for Egypt, *MiTZRayim*, is from the same root as *MeiTZaR* (narrowness) and represents the neck of a person, the narrowest part of the human body. We find that Pharaoh had three important ministers: the chief baker, the chief wine steward, and the chief butcher. These three "ministers" correspond to the neck: the baker represents the esophagus, where food is absorbed; the wine steward parallels the trachea, as it allows for fluids to be absorbed in the body; and the butcher parallels the carotid arteries and veins, which bring the blood to the brain. This teaches us that Pharaoh and his ministers subjugated the Jewish nation to such an extent that even their necks, through which the vocal cords deliver speech, were under their control.

After the Exodus, the Jews were finally able to pray. And when pursued by Pharaoh and his army, they indeed turned to God and cried out in prayer. When they found themselves trapped by the sea — impassable cliffs on one side, a forest with wild animals on the other, the Egyptians pursuing them from behind, and of course the Red Sea before them — they felt they had no chance of survival. Still, they prayed, and God caused the sea to split before them. As the commentaries explain, they "grabbed the craft of their ancestors" and prayed.[2]

Praying Today

How many times have we found ourselves facing similar circumstances? Maybe our circumstances are not as extreme, but they certainly brought on feelings of being trapped with no apparent way to escape or survive the problem. How many times have we let out a *krechtz* (groan or moan), a scream of

1 The ARI refers to Rabbi Yitzchok Luria (1534-1572). Many consider the ARI the greatest of all Kabbalist.

2 Rashi on Exodus 14:10; *Rabbeinu Bachya* on Exodus 14:11.

anguish, or a woeful cry: "Help! Help me!" And how many times afterward have we seen a solution to the problem? We find ourselves in a bind, then the problem is solved, then another problem comes along, *ad infinitum*. Do we ever entertain the idea that prayer itself is the key to our salvation?

Why not? Why don't we pray and pray again? Why don't we exert ourselves even just a little bit more to pour out our hearts in prayer and supplication?

Perhaps it's because we don't grasp the potency of prayer. Is it reasonable that we can open our hearts and reach out to an unseen God who hears and listens to every word we articulate? Do we find it so hard to understand that there is a God who created us and wants us to turn to Him for help in every difficulty we experience?

God is the One, Who, aside from His blessings, sends illness, financial strain, and other types of suffering (such as floods, earthquakes, or tornadoes) upon people. If so, asks Reb Noson, how can we pray to God to remove that suffering, since it is His will that dictates our anguish? Reb Noson answers that God is not seeking to have His creations endure pain. He just wants us to turn to Him. He wants us to look up and beseech Him to cancel His decrees and make us well (LH, *Cheilev v'Dam*).

In the following pages, we will glimpse the power of prayer, to where it ascends, how much it can accomplish, and how we can involve ourselves in prayer to the extent that we, too, can witness the answers to our prayers. Using the siddur as our guide, we will take the reader from a casual look at the daily prayers to an incredible comprehension of what we, as corporeal human beings, can achieve with prayer. Nothing is beyond us; nothing is out of reach! It's all in our mouths and hearts, as the Torah states, "It is very close to you; with your mouth and your heart you *can* do it" (Deuteronomy 30:14).

PART I

The Potency of Prayer

CHAPTER 1

The Siddur: Order and Unity

Before God created the world, He had everything. He was not in need of anything. Still, He decided to create the universe. What was His purpose? Considering the way the world exists today—with all its wars, catastrophes, illness and poverty—why did He bother?

The Kabbalists explain that God created this world with an intentional fault. He formed it without any assistance from anyone or anything. The Kabbalists call this manner of creation *i'taruta d'l'eila,* an awakening from Above. Since man had no part in creating the world, God made it man's mission to complete and perfect the world. Man's part in creation would be known as *i'taruta d'l'tata,* an awakening from below. The Midrash explains that the intended purpose for mankind was to irrigate and till the land, tend animals for food, skins and clothing, and perform other acts which would enable them to survive and lead productive lives. Most important, human beings would realize that they could not accomplish anything without God, and they would be beholden to God for His aid. This completes the plan of creation, because it would be a joint effort from Above and below.

Making man the supreme entity on the planet, God granted him two things that distinguished him from all other aspects of creation: a creative and thinking brain, and the power of speech (Rashi on Genesis 2:7). When God formed the world, He created everything in its final form, but He also left everything in a state of suspended animation. For example, all vegetation was ready to sprout but remained at the tip of the ground and did not grow. What was lacking? Man.

The verse states, "All the wild grasses had not yet sprouted, because God had not yet caused it to rain upon the earth, and there was no man to work the land" (Genesis 2:5). As Rashi explains, "When man was created, God hoped man would recognize the need for rain and would pray for it. Only then would the system of irrigation and rainfall be implemented" (Rashi, loc. cit.). The partnership between man and God in the running of the world would turn the world into its most ideal and perfect state.

We find that the first man, Adam, was given the necessary tools to put the earth's needs in motion. He understood the necessity for rain, and he prayed for his needs. The concept of Prayer originated from the beginning of time. However, it wasn't until Avraham, some 2,000 years after Adam, that the regular daily prayers were established. As our Sages teach, "Avraham established *Shacharit*" (*Berakhot* 26b).

Avraham didn't have a set siddur. He used his mind, his heart and his mouth, and he composed his prayers daily, according to his needs *at that moment*. As we know from our own lives, each moment is different. From the time that Avraham discovered there is a God, he turned to Him in prayer, beseeching God to help him draw close to Him. Following Avraham were Yitzchak (who established *Minchah*, the afternoon prayer) and Yaakov (who established *Maariv*, the evening prayer). Rebbe Nachman calls this practice of prayer "*hitbodedut*," which translates as "self-seclusion." *Hitbodedut* refers to private, secluded prayer before God, where one expresses his needs and yearnings in his own words. This was the form of prayer handed down to us from the Patriarchs and the way people prayed generation after generation until they returned from the Babylonian exile, when they dedicated the Second *Beis HaMikdash*.

As explained in the Rambam,[3] when the Jews returned from the Babylonian exile, they were an admixture of nations. They spoke several languages and they no longer were able to converse and express themselves in the Hebrew language. At the consecration of the Second *Beis HaMikdash*, an assembly of 120 leaders of the nation was held. Among them were prophets (i.e., Ezra, Nehemiah, Haggai, Zekhariah, Malakhi) and the leading scholars of the generation. When these members of the Great Assembly saw the mishmash of people before them, they were astonished and dismayed: How would they ever be able to pray to God as one people? That was when they established the siddur, the prayer book which has kept the Jewish nation on a common ground for thousands of years, no matter where they spent their exile. The siddur was written in Hebrew, and although it is a set text, it wondrously contains all the needs and requests of every Jew for each day.

Unique Paths

The Hebrew word *SiDduR* (סידור) derives from the root word *SeDeR* (סדר, order). As Jewish communities became established throughout the diaspora, each community developed its own personal style of prayer. This caused the siddur to be available in several different *nuscha'ot* (formulations or versions).

The *Zohar* (III, 170a) teaches that each of the Twelve Tribes of Israel has its own unique path via which its prayers enter Heaven. This is understood from the four letters of the Tetragrammaton, the Holy Name of God, which has twelve permutations.[4] The *Zohar* (II, 251a) also tells us that this is the reason for the custom of having twelve windows in a synagogue.

3 *Yad HaChazakah, Hilkhot Tefillah* 1:4.

4 Permutations result from rearranging the order of the letters in a word. For example, God's Holy Name *YHVH* can be written *YHVH, YHHV, YVHH, HHYV,* and so on. A four-letter name would normally yield twenty-four permutations,

Just as in the 'synagogue' above there are twelve gates through which prayers enter, so too, in our synagogues, there should be twelve openings through which the prayers ascend.

Regarding these unique paths, "All the *nuscha'ot* are holy and are rooted in exalted places" (*Kitzur Shulchan Arukh* 18:5). However, although each is equally acceptable, one should pray in the *nusach* of his family. Today there are several main *nuscha'ot* of the siddur as we know it: Sephardic communities pray in the *nusach* known as *Eidot HaMizrach* (Eastern Communities); European Jewry pray in *Nusach Ashkenaz* (the *nusach* of Dutch and German Jewry); and chassidic communities pray in *Nusach Sephard* (similar to the *nusach* used by Sephardic Jewry but at the same time very much like *Nusach Ashkenaz*). There exist minor differences within each *nusach*, but for the most part, these varying formulations are quite similar. It is actually incredible that the prayers themselves are so very much alike, considering that all siddurim were hand-copied from handwritten manuscripts generation after generation until the invention of the printing press in around 1450, a little over 500 years ago.

It is important to note that the ARI considered *Nusach Sephard* to be the most comprehensive *nusach* which includes all the others (*Tosafot Chaim* on *Chayey Adam* 23:1). This is why our commentary in this book is based on the order of *Nusach Sephard*.

What was the reason the members of the Great Assembly introduced a common siddur with the established prayers? One of their goals was to bring about a unity between Jews. With everyone speaking a different language, how were they ever supposed to explore the commonality between themselves? With a common tongue, unity can be achieved.

but since there are two of the same letters (*Heh*, ה) in *YHVH*, only twelve permutations can be formed.

Unifications and Unity

Unity is essential for prayer. This is the reason we seek to pray with a quorum of ten men, so they can pour out their hearts together, as one, before God.

One of our prayers is "*L'Shem Yichud Kud'sha Brikh Hu u'Shekhintei*" (For the sake of the Unity of the Blessed Holy One and His *Shekhinah*). This prayer is said prior to performing a mitzvah, such as before putting on *tallit* and *tefillin*, reciting the *Birkhat HaMazon*, counting the Omer, and so on. What is this "unity" that we articulate with our intentions? After all, God is One, a Single Unity. What are we trying to unite?

A person must recognize that God is One. There certainly does not exist a separation between God and His *Shekhinah*, His indwelling presence. They are always One. The commentaries explain that the Blessed Holy One is the unseen God, the One we always refer to, the One whom we speak of but have no idea who or what He is. His *Shekhinah*, on the other hand, is the individual experience of God that each person can sense and feel. There are times we feel distant from God, and then there are times we feel God's presence. The performance of any mitzvah is meant to make that connection. God commanded us to pray or perform the *mitzvot*. However, do we feel the significance of the mitzvah or do we perform it by rote? Reciting the *L'Shem Yichud* places us into the mindset that our good deeds *can* affect this unity between God and His *Shekhinah*.

Moreover, Rebbe Nachman says, our very words of Torah and prayer create unity and peace in the world. He explains:

Where there is a trait of *nitzachon* (victory; i.e., always having to win), there is also conflict and strife. Each person must eliminate his having to always win and argue, and instead pursue peace; for God found no suitable vessel to contain blessing other than peace (*Uktzin* 3:12). This peace is attained by reciting many words of Torah and prayer.

For at the time of Creation, the "Shattering of the Vessels" caused worlds to fall below and descend to very low levels.[5] These worlds correspond to letters, which were shattered into many sparks. Speech is the act of joining these sparks and letters together to create words and sentences. By speaking the holy words of Torah and prayer, one rectifies and renews all the fallen worlds, and it is considered as if he has created them anew. As the letters combine, their joining together creates unity and peace (LM I, 75-B:1, 3).

The idea of a united community was the intention and goal of the Great Assembly, and it is the reason for the siddur. Indeed, the *Zohar* teaches that if any community would truly unite and join together, that power of unity could bring the *Mashiach*! (*Zohar Chadash, Noach*, p. 40a).

Reb Noson expands on this idea. He writes that this is the reason that a synagogue, a place for Torah study and prayer, is called a *Beis Knesset* (בית כנסת, house of gathering). For it is there that we gather and join the letters and words together in prayer, which unite to create and build worlds. Reb Noson also points out that when we engage in idle chatter in a synagogue, we are shattering the vessels instead of reconstructing them. Conversely, speaking Torah and prayer builds worlds. The term *Beis KNeSset* also implies that we are *KoNeS* (gathering together) the scattered sparks[6] and infusing them with fresh life and unity.

Reb Noson adds that our Sages established a certain order for the synagogue prayer service to maintain peace and unity.

5 The Shattering of the Vessels is a Kabbalistic teaching about how God created and formed the worlds. See below Chapter 4.

6 Scattered sparks. See below Chapter 4.

For example, the order people are called to the Torah — first a Kohen, then a Levi, then a Yisrael — is to keep peace between the attendees. When there is unity below, this generates a unity Above, which filters down to us on earth to enable us, in the form of blessings, to experience God.

Therefore, we find that the siddur is meant to maintain order in one's prayers, to maintain order in the synagogue, and most importantly, to establish and maintain peace and unity among the congregants!

CHAPTER 2

Service of the Heart

Like everything else, prayer needs the proper tools to make it happen. You wouldn't think about raking a lawn without a rake or entertain the idea of flying from New York to Israel without an airplane. Nor would you attempt to store data and work out complex mathematical equations without a computer. If you want to pray, which tools do you require?

The Torah speaks of serving God "with your mouth and your heart" (Deuteronomy 30:14). The Talmud speaks of prayer as the "service of the heart" (*Taanis* 2a). Simply put, this is because when one turns in prayer to God, he obviously has something in his heart that he wants to say to God. That something—be it a deep feeling of gratitude or a painful ache from which he seeks relief and salvation—is the expression of his heartfelt emotions that cause those words to be said.

Furthermore, our heartfelt prayers express our yearning for a connection to God. Does God need our prayers? He has myriads of angels who serve Him! But He created us, and He wants us to turn to Him. Just as we seek the connection to Him, He desires our connection too. So yes, He awaits our prayers.[7] But how can we pray if God is so exalted above us?

7 See *Yevamot* 64a: "Why were the Patriarchs and Matriarchs barren? Because God *desires* the prayers of the righteous." The *Eitz Yosef* explains that the tzaddikim can mitigate decrees. Throughout his *Likutey Halakhot*, Reb Noson teaches that the same applies to each individual. Anyone who prays with deep intention for God can also turn a harsh decree into kindness and effect healing and salvation.

What can we give Him? The answer is: We can give over to God our heart.

The prophet Isaiah rebukes us, "With your lips you honored Me, yet your hearts are distanced from Me" (Isaiah 29:13). Often when we pray, our minds and hearts are elsewhere. "With your mouth and your heart" you can serve God, but are your words pouring forth from your hearts or being recited by rote? The important thing is to make that connection between the heart and the mouth so that you truly mean what you say.

Rebbe Nachman (as do many others) asks, "Why do we need to pray? God, after all, knows our thoughts. Why must we articulate our prayers?" The Rebbe explains that God wants to bestow blessing upon each person at all times. But when you receive God's bounty, do you have a place to put it? Imagine pouring a delicious drink without a cup to receive it. If you pour it, as God does with His blessings, where are you going to put that drink? You need some type of vessel to receive God's blessings. We have mentioned previously[8] that when praying we are able to join letters and words together. These prayers repair the Shattered Vessels, which creates the necessary vessels within which we can receive God's blessing (LM I, 34); hence, the necessity for prayer.

Kavanah: The Sincere Prayer

Now that we understand our need to pray, the question naturally follows: How can we know whether our prayers have any effect?

Rebbe Nachman points out the conflict between two verses in Psalms. One verse states, "God is my light and salvation" (Psalms 27:1), while a second verse states, "God is near to all

8 See Chapter 1.

who call Him, to all who call Him in truth" (ibid. 145:18).[9] When we say our prayers, we are calling upon God. If we recite our prayers with honesty and sincerity, then we connect with God, who *is* Truth. Obviously, since we connect with God, we also connect with His light and His salvation. As Rebbe Nachman mentions, the greater the degree of sincerity and truth in our prayers, the greater the degree of connection we will have with God. Understanding this, we can understand that if we reach out in prayer, it will be received, and we will be answered. It all depends on the sincerity of our prayers and the concentration of our heart.

Therefore, it's important to make the effort to concentrate on what we're saying to God. This is called praying with *kavanah*. Praying with *kavanah* requires effort, but it's what makes the prayers meaningful. Rebbe Nachman teaches that the main *kavanah* is to understand the simple meaning of the words we are enunciating. He also teaches about the beauty of prayer, comparing each letter to a most beautiful flower. When we join the flowers together, they create a most beautiful bouquet. So too, our prayers are beautiful combinations of letters and words. Making them meaningful by saying the words with emotion and *kavanah* will have a most incredible impact (LM I, 65:2).

Four-Part Harmony

Creation was intended for the world and its inhabitants to be harmonious. Unfortunately, it doesn't always seem to work. Wars disrupt peace between people; greed wrecks the environment; poaching and other cruelties can decimate animal species, and so on. The cure for this discordance is prayer, which brings unity into the world.

9 LM I, 9:3; ibid. I, 112:1.

The Tetragrammaton, God's holy name *YHVH,* has four letters. The name *YHVH* stands for *HaVaYaH,* meaning "to be," and in Hebrew it stands for *HaYaH, HoVeh, v'YiHiYeH* (He was, He is and He always will be). These four letters are the origin of creation and sustain everything within it. The Kabbalists teach that there are several ideas or concepts of "four," and they all reflect, in one way or another, the harmony that should be present in the world. We will now introduce some of the ideas of what harmony can attain and where our focus should be during our prayers.

The Four Elements

The four letters of God's name are the origin of the four elements, which are the building blocks of creation. In Hebrew, they are known as the four *Yesodot* (foundations). These are not the chemical elements that are commonly spoken about, but four distinct concepts of which everything in the world is comprised. These four elements are: fire (hot and dry), air (hot and damp), water (cold and damp), and earth (cold and dry).

For example, a human being is comprised of fire (his digestive system which consumes all that he devours), air (what he breathes), water (the bodily fluids), and earth (the substance from which he was formed). When these elements are in harmony, the person is in good physical condition and can go about his daily routines in a healthy manner. Should any of these elements be out of sync, then illness sets in. Thus, the purpose of prayer is for us to focus on unity. We should, for example, pray that the elements with which we survive should be in harmony so that we can lead productive lives.

The four elements also manifest in human characteristics. Fire represents the characteristic of arrogance and haughtiness. Just as fire always rises, an arrogant person feels he is above others, as if people should pay homage to him. Likewise, anger is an offshoot of arrogance since the person feels he should be listened to and thus his anger flares when people do not do his bidding. On the positive side, when a person displays humility, he controls his "fire."

The element of air is present in one's manner of speech. It can be used for good, such as to encourage and support others, or it be used for bad, such as to speak slander, profanity, or falsehoods.

Since water brings pleasure to people, water represents sensual pleasures as well as one's control over his inclinations. And just as the sea never stops moving, water represents a person's emotions which are forever flowing and changing (e.g., love or hate, admiration or jealousy, and so on.)

The element of earth represents laziness and depression. On the positive side, a person can take hold of himself and learn how to energize himself when things turn against him so that he can still be creative and productive.

The Four Realms of Existence

Another idea of four is found in the four realms of this world: mineral, vegetable, animal and man. God put Adam into the Garden of Eden "to tend it and to guard it" (Genesis 2:15). He could eat from its fruits and enjoy its cool shade, but he must also take care of the environment. Everything in this world was made for man's benefit, but he is not allowed to abuse the planet and its environs.

The Torah speaks of the sacrifices that were brought in the *Beis HaMikdash*. A careful study shows that all four levels were present in these sacrifices. A human would bring an animal sacrifice to the altar. Together with that sacrifice, there were wine and oil libations (the vegetable realm), water libations, and a salt offering (the mineral realm). The *Zohar* teaches that the sacrifices were meant to elevate the entire physical world to God, since the sacrifices ascended to the most exalted levels in Heaven. Thus, each of the four levels of this material world had its place in the sacrifices (and the prayers parallel the sacrifices).

The Four Levels of Torah Study

The Torah, too, entails the concept of four. There are four levels of interpreting the Torah, known as *PaRDeS* (פרדס), an acrostic which refers to *Pshat* (פשט, simple meaning), *Remez* (רמז, allusions or hints), *Drush* (דרוש, homiletics and discourses) and *Sod* (סוד, mysteries, the Kabbalah). By studying these four parts of Torah, man can attain perfection in the corresponding parts of his body and soul.

Additionally, the Talmud (*Eruvin* 54b) and Midrash (*Shemot Rabbah* 40:1) both speak of the importance of learning and reviewing one's studies at least four times. Similarly, a person should never try to teach a lesson to others until he has reviewed his ideas four times. God Himself, as it were, reviewed the Torah four times before delivering it to Moshe!

The Torah laws we have today in the *Shulchan Arukh* are grouped into four sets of laws: *Orach Chaim* (laws of observance of daily routines as well as Shabbos and holidays), *Yoreh De'ah* (laws applying to oneself, such as what constitutes kosher food, family purity, usury, mourning, etc.), *Even HaEzer* (laws of marriage and divorce), and *Choshen Mishpat* (civil and financial law).

The Four Worlds

Yet another manifestation of the four letters of God's Holy Name is seen in the spiritual realms. The Kabbalah teaches that there are four worlds: *Atzilut* (Nearness), *Beriyah* (Creation), *Yetzirah* (Formation) and *Asiyah* (Action). The world of *Atzilut* is "adjacent" to God; no evil exists there. The world of *Beriyah* is used to describe the Throne of Glory, upon which God "sits." It is below that of Nearness yet still within the realm of the Divine; however, a minute bit of evil exists there. The next lower world, *Yetzirah,* is cited as the angelic world, where the angels dwell. Within it exists an equal mixture of good and evil. The lowest world, *Asiyah,* includes the physical universe and the world we live in. It contains both good and evil, but evil is more dominant.[10]

The Four Sections of the *Shacharit* Prayer

The *Shacharit* prayer is also divided into four parts. The first part is called *Korbanot* (קרבנות, sacrificial offerings) and contains the Torah passages of the sacrifices. The second part is called *Pesukey d'Zimrah* (פסוקי דזמרה, Verses of Song). This part is a collection of verses, mostly from Psalms, and includes other verses from the Torah, the Books of Prophets, and the Books of Writings (כתובים, Hagiographa) which praise God and recount His creation and miracles. The word *zimrah* also translates as "cutting" or "pruning" since the praise we offer to God is a means to cut and tear away the *kelipot* (forces of evil) that oppose our prayers. The third part comprises the *Shema,* our declaration of faith, and its accompanying blessings. The fourth part is the *Amidah* (Standing Prayer), also known as the *Shemoneh Esrei.*

The prayers are intended for us to connect with God and thereby unify all aspects of four that are in the world. Doing so invokes God's blessing and causes Him to send down His bounty and blessing.

10 By way of comparison, *Atzilut* corresponds to *Chokhmah, Beriyah* to *Binah, Yetzirah* to *Zer Anpin,* and *Asiyah* to *Malkhut.* See Appendix, p. 456. The terms are explained in Chapter 4.

After the Amidah, there are four remaining parts of the morning prayers, which are meant to act as the channels to bring down God's blessings and bounty to us. These are: *Tachanun*, *Ashrey*, the Song of the Day and *Aleinu*.

Through prayer, we in this lowly, corporeal world can join with all realms of the physical and spiritual worlds to access the loftiest of places Above. The idea of prayer as a means of elevating oneself to the highest of levels is beautifully illustrated by Rebbe Nachman's famous tale, "The Exchanged Children," which will be discussed next.

CHAPTER 3

The Exchanged Children

Last chapter, we discussed how the four parts of prayer elevate us to the highest of levels. In this chapter, we will illustrate this concept with one of Rebbe Nachman's famous stories, *The Exchanged Children*.[11] The story, as explained by Reb Noson, describes the ongoing battle for supremacy between a princely mind and a servant's attitude. The story appears in its entirety in Appendix B; however, the highlights are presented below as they apply to the Morning Prayer of *Shacharit*, followed by Reb Noson's commentary.

The Exchanged Children

Synopsis

Once there was a queen who had a servant woman. Both women gave birth at the same time. The midwife exchanged the babies to see what would happen. She placed the king's son beside the servant woman and the servant's son beside the queen.

The boys grew up. The one raised by the queen was called "the king's son" and was given greater and greater status. The king's true son, growing up in the servant's house, was called "the servant's son," although by nature he was drawn to ways of nobility and royalty.

One day the midwife admitted to someone in confidence that she had exchanged the babies. The secret got out and people started talking about it privately since they didn't want the king to find out. One day the secret was revealed to "the king's son." It was beneath the king's son's dignity to investigate this rumor. But in case it were true and one day rebels might challenge the king

11 *Rebbe Nachman's Stories* #11.

and claim they were bringing the king's true son to the throne, he was advised to do away with "the servant's son."

"The king's son" attacked and afflicted the true prince until the true prince was forced to flee. Frustrated and challenged, the true prince lapsed into a "loose life," visiting bars and brothels. Whenever he began to regret his lifestyle, he would grieve over his evil deeds and then get drunk again. Yet since he had already begun to have thoughts of regret and repentance, these thoughts constantly bothered him.

He began having a recurring dream. He envisioned a fair in a certain place and was told to go there and take the first job that was offered to him, even if he felt it was beneath his dignity. Finally, he realized that he had to obey the dream and went to the fair. There he encountered a merchant and agreed to drive cattle for him. When they passed a thick forest, the prince's animals wandered away and the merchant screamed at him to follow them. The prince chased them deep into the forest, but they kept eluding him. He was terrified to return to the merchant empty-handed, so he kept chasing them.

Night fell. He heard the sounds of wild animals growling and decided to spend the night in a tree. All night he heard the sound of wild animals roaring. At daybreak he saw his cattle standing right next to him. He climbed down from the tree but when he tried to catch them, they ran further away.

Night fell again, and when he heard the wild animals roaring, he was terrified. He found a huge tree and climbed up into it. He was surprised to find another person there. He told the stranger that he had ended up in the forest because he had been chasing the cattle. The stranger said he had come because his horse had wandered away and he couldn't catch it. They decided to remain together.

At daybreak, they saw the prince's cattle and the stranger's horse standing there next to the tree. They each began to give chase, one after the cattle, and the other after the horse, but the animals kept running further away.

Meanwhile, the true prince found a bag of bread. He took the bag and continued chasing the cattle. Suddenly he encountered another stranger. The stranger asked him how he'd come to be there. The true prince replied that he was chasing his animals.

When he returned the question, the stranger said, "My father and my father's father grew up here. But no one from a civilized area ever comes here." The true prince realized that the stranger was not a human being.

"Stop chasing your sins," said the stranger. "These are not animals at all. They are your sins, and they are leading you around. But it is now sufficient. You have already received your punishment. Now you can stop chasing. Come with me, and you will attain what is coming to you."

As he followed the forest man, the prince saw his companion who was chasing his horse. The other man eyed the bag of bread and pleaded with the prince to give him some. At first the prince refused, since bread is very valuable in a forest, but the other man kept begging. Finally, the man offered to sell himself as a servant in return for bread. The true prince agreed.

The forest man took them to his house and gave them food and drink. The other man was very upset that he had sold himself for an hour's worth of food. When asked about this, he replied he had once been a king who was rumored to be exchanged at birth. And now he has become a servant.

The forest man brought them more food and drink that night. Again, they heard the roars of the wild animals at night but, listening closely, they realized it was the sound of music, a beautiful and wondrous chant. All the joys in the world were insignificant compared to the wondrous enjoyment of listening to this song.

The forest man told them that he had a special instrument that he had received from his ancestors. When this instrument was placed on any animal, the creature would sing this song. After he had brought the prince and the stranger back to civilization, the forest man gave this instrument to the king's true son. He then directed the prince toward a land where, he promised, "you will attain your greatness." The land was presently known as "The Wise Land with the Foolish King."

The guards at the gate did not want to let them in because the king of that land had died. When a man would undertake to restore the original name of the land, "The Foolish Land with the Wise King," they would crown that man king.

A man on a horse appeared. The king's true son placed the instrument on that horse and it began to play the melodious tune. The king's true son then traded the instrument for the ability to understand one thing from another. The ministers of the land gave him two tests which he successfully solved, and he was given the kingdom. Then the king's true son, who was now crowned king, said to the son of the servant woman, "Now I understand that I am actually the king's son, and you are actually the servant's son."

Reb Noson's Commentary

Reb Noson discusses the story of *The Exchanged Children* in a most incredible discourse found in his *Likutey Halakhot, Birkhot HaShachar* 3. Following are excerpts applicable to the morning prayers.

The story reflects the Biblical stories of Yitzchak and Yishmael, and Yaakov and Esav. Yishmael, the son of the slave woman Hagar, was the first son of Avraham and claimed the birthright and inheritance. Yitzchak, however, was the true son and prince. Similarly, Yaakov was born second to Esav, who claimed the birthright. But Esav had sold his rights, and Yaakov became the true prince. Throughout history, this battle constantly takes place: Who is the true ruler and who is the nation to be pushed around and tortured? In the end of days, though, the truth of who is the real prince will emerge.

Reb Noson takes this analogy a step further and discusses which organ rules over a person's body and decides how a person should act. Mankind is engaged in a constant battle: which organ is the master? Is it the body and its desires, or is it the soul, mind and brain, which can differentiate between good and evil, right and wrong? A person's mission in life is to become master of their destiny, as the true prince did. But similar to the prince, one must overcome obstacles and pitfalls in order to attain their true destiny.

Next, Reb Noson compares the four parts of the story to the four parts of the *Shacharit* prayer: sacrifices, *Pesukey d'Zimrah, Shema,* and the *Amidah.*

The animals the prince had to chase were his sins. Reb Noson parallels these animals / sins with the first part of *Shacharit,* the sacrifices. When a person sins, he debases himself and becomes animalistic. By bringing a sacrifice, he symbolically exchanges his base characteristics that led him to animalistic behavior and re-elevates himself to a human level. The prince visited brothels and indulged in drinking. Therefore, he was punished, and he had to "chase the animals." Paralleling this, we recite the passages of the sacrifices, recalling that we have erred in life and wish to repent and draw close to God.

The prince and the servant heard the howling in the forest, which they later recognized as beautiful music. When they were ensconced in the forest man's home, the forest man gave them the instrument that could reproduce the same melody that the animals sang in harmony each time. This corresponds to the *Pesukey d'Zimrah,* the second part of *Shacharit.* While sacrifices were brought in the *Beis HaMikdash,* the *Leviim* would sing and play musical instruments. When the forest man's instrument was placed on an animal, the creature sang the most wonderful song. So too, when we sing and praise God after reciting the sacrifices, we subdue our animalistic tendencies and elevate ourselves to the human level.

When the prince exchanged the instrument for the power to understand one thing from another, he acknowledged that he could now ascend to levels of intellect previously withheld from him. This parallels the third part of *Shacharit,* the *Shema* and its blessings. According to the Kabbalists, the *Shema* represents receiving great spiritual intellect.

Once the prince passed the two tests with which he was challenged, he rectified the land to its original name, "The

Foolish Land with the Wise King." Afterwards he became king. The kingdom discussed in this story is a parable for the Kingdom of God. The prince rectifying the land represents the *Amidah*, because with prayer, one rules and extends authority over all the worlds. This is the reason the prince became king. When a person prays and his prayers are answered, it implies that he has assumed control over the worlds, for they are doing his bidding.

Reb Noson displayed to us how the various aspects of life in this world can be very confusing and challenging, even to a true prince. Mistakes are made, sometimes intentional errors, which change the course of a person's life. What choice do we have? Are we compared to the servant's son, becoming immersed in jealousy and revenge? Do we stand up to evil, do we succumb to our desires and characteristics? Perhaps we run away from our troubles, drowning them in drink, drugs, or some other temporary escape, as the true prince was doing? Do we end up "chasing our sins," spending our days running after unattainable goals?

The forest man represents the true tzaddik with clear vision. He is the one who seeks each person's true and long-term rectification. The true tzaddik tells us, "Stop chasing your sins. You are a prince, and you have a wonderful future before you. Elevate yourself to new heights, great heights. Recognize the potency of your prayers. You can ascend beyond your base traits. You can merit to hear the song of the forest, the harmony and beauty of melodies and songs to God. You can raise your intellect to recognize the wonders that abound in this world. You can rise to the greatest heights through your prayers, and gain control of your destiny!"

CHAPTER 4

The Heights of the World

"Prayer stands at the heights of the world; yet people make light of it" (*Berakhot* 6b, Rashi).

Reb Noson was once talking about the greatness of prayer, referring to the Midrash which states: After the prayers have been received in Heaven, an angel ... then sends the prayers upward, to the *Keter* (Crown) that adorns the Holy One's head (*Shemot Rabbah* 21:4). "Take note," said Reb Noson, "even angels cannot rise to the level that prayer can reach!" (*Aveneha Barzel*, p. 88).

What is that "Heights of the World"? What is the *Keter*? The Kabbalists explain:

In the holy writings, God is referred to as *Ein Sof*, the Infinite One. A person simply cannot grasp the concept of infinity, for the human mind is, by definition, finite. Therefore, when we speak of God, we use the phrase *Ohr Ein Sof* (Light of the Infinite). This is a very abstract definition of God, but nevertheless is the best way of describing Him. His Light is so awesome that nothing can withstand it directly. Therefore, God had to create a system of filters to constrict His Light in stages until human beings in a corporeal world could relate to Him.

Think of the sun. A person gazing at such an intense light will damage his eyes, so he requires a filter to enable him to see that light. And the sun is but one of God's servants. So too, we require filters to be able to "see" God and to experience Him.

It is beyond the scope of this book to explain the entire system of filters and stages. We provide just a brief commentary to understand the connection with the potency of prayer.[12]

The *Partzufim* and the *Sefirot*

The Kabbalah explains that God designed five *Partzufim* (Divine Persona) and ten *sefirot* (energies) as filters to diffuse His awesome Light so that we may benefit from Him and receive His light. These *sefirot* (singular, *sefirah*) represent the characteristics of intellect—to think and to know—as well as the characteristics to either give or restrain, and to advance or retreat. The *sefirot* are the basic modes of God's creative power and providence with which He guides creation towards its ultimate perfection.[13] The five *Partzufim* are: *Arikh Anpin* (extended countenance), *Abba* (father), *Imma* (mother), *Zer Anpin* (son, groom or diminished countenance), and *Malkhut* (daughter, bride, Kingship or Authority). These five *Partzufim* also parallel the ten *sefirot*: *Arikh Anpin* parallels *Keter*, *Abba* parallels *Chokhmah*, *Imma* parallels *Binah*, *Malkhut* parallels *Malkhut*, and *Zer Anpin* is a combination of *Chesed, Gevurah, Tiferet, Netzach, Hod,* and *Yesod.*

The term *sefirah* is related to the word *SaPeiR,* meaning to "express" or "communicate." It is also related to the word *SaPiR,* "brilliance" or "luminary," and to *SePhaR,* "boundary." In essence, these related concepts define the two basic functions of the *sefirot.* On one hand, the *sefirot* are lights, luminaries or energies that serve to reveal and express God's greatness. On

12 For a broader and detailed explanation of these Kabbalistic concepts, the reader is directed to *Innerspace* by Rabbi Aryeh Kaplan (Moznaim Publishers). See also *Anatomy of the Soul* by Chaim Kramer (Breslov Research Institute).

13 See the charts in Appendix A that illustrate the Order of the *Sefirot,* the Structure of the *Sefirot* and the relationship between the *sefirot.* The charts will help the reader to visualize the ideas behind the *sefirot,* the Universes and the Worlds.

the other hand, they are vessels that limit and delineate God's Infinite Light, bringing it into the finite realm of boundaries.

The *sefirot* parallel many other concepts as well, such as the human body, the Patriarchs, and the Worlds of Prayer (see Appendices).

The hierarchy of the *sefirot* is as follows:

***Keter*—Crown.** This is the highest *sefirah* and acts as the interface between the Light of the Infinite and the entire Creation. *Keter* parallels the *Partzuf* of *Arikh Anpin*, sometimes referred to as *Atik*.

***Chokhmah*—Wisdom.** The next level below *Keter* is *Chokhmah*, represented as the mind of a person. *Chokhmah* is the wisdom that a person garners and retains during his lifetime. It is the ability to see objects and clearly know what they are. *Chokhmah* parallels the *Partzuf* of *Abba*.

***Binah*—Understanding.** Following *Chokhmah* is *Binah*. It is the ability to understand the wisdom we have gathered and retained in order to be able to make use of it. For example, let's say a person sees a red streetlight. With *Chokhmah*, a person recognizes the color red, whereas with *Binah*, a person associates the meaning of the red light with the need to stop. *Binah* parallels the *Partzuf* of *Imma*.

There is also a concept of *Daat* (Knowledge), which is both a combination of *Chokhmah* and *Binah* as well as the external manifestion of the hidden *Keter*. Therefore, we can define the "three intellects" as *Keter, Chokhmah* and *Binah*, or we may group them as a combination of *Chokhmah, Binah* and *Daat*.

Keter, Chokhmah and *Binah* are considered the *mochin* (i.e., mentalities or intellects) of the *sefirot*. The seven lower *sefirot* are referred to as the "body" of the array of the *sefirot*.

The following six *sefirot* (i.e., *Chesed, Gevurah, Tiferet, Netzach, Hod* and *Yesod*) parallel *Zer Anpin*. *Arikh Anpin*, referred to as an extended countenance, is the source of blessings that descend to this world. On the other hand, *Zer Anpin,* referred to as the diminished countenance, acts as a receiver of those blessings and transfers those blessings according to Divine Favor.

Chesed—**Lovingkindness.** *Chesed* is the concept of continuous and unrestricted love and giving.

Gevurah—**Strength and Restraint.** *Gevurah* refers to the idea of restraining one's unlimited generosity with the strength necessary to conduct oneself with discipline. It parallels fear and awe.

Tiferet—**Beauty and Justice.** *Tiferet* is a balance of both compassion and righteousness. It is considered beauty because it combines both the unrestricted side of giving and the restraint of holding back and limiting one's giving, tempering with both too much and too little. This is why, at times, *Tiferet* is also known as *Mishpat* (Justice).

Netzach—**Victory.** *Netzach* represents the ability to step forward and conquer the challenges with which we face.

Hod—**Splendor and Empathy.** *Hod* represents the ability to take the necessary step backward and feel sensitivity towards a situation.

Yesod—**Foundation.** *Yesod* represents morality because it is the foundation upon which a person stands. A person with a solid foundation will be able to face life and its complications and stand solid. He can be anywhere, yet not be afraid of complicating his life.

Malkhut—**Kingship.** *Malkhut,* the lowest *sefirah,* translates as authority. It is the *sefirah* which receives all the bounty and blessing from Above and transmits it to the worlds below. *Malkhut* has the power to transfer bounty to those deserving of blessing, while it can also disburse that bounty to the wicked, who will use that authority to bring suffering to people. It also at times acts as an interface between the realm of holiness and the realm of impurity. The *sefirah Malkhut* parallels the *Partzuf* of *Malkhut.*

It is important to realize that the prayers we offer are directly connected to the Divine Persona of *Zer Anpin* and *Malkhut.* As *Yesod* is the lowest *sefirah* of *Zer Anpin,* the bounty and blessings are transmitted through *Yesod* to *Malkhut*

The Yoke of Heaven

As the ARI explains, the forms of *Zer Anpin* and *Malkhut* are completed and perfected by our good deeds, Torah study and prayers. For example, although *Malkhut* refers to the lowest *sefirah,* it also refers to accepting upon oneself the *Ol Malkhut Shamayim* (Yoke of Heaven). A person who accepts upon himself to serve God, is interacting directly with *Malkhut* and can draw the bounty that descends to this world.

But *Malkhut* also parallels faith. A person accepts the yoke of heaven only because he has faith in God. Furthermore, *Malkhut* also parallels prayer, for if one accepts God's reign, then he will pray to Him. In other words, if a person accepts that God is in charge of the world, he will turn to God in prayer, asking Him for his needs.

Several basics Kabbalistic concepts are also necessary to understand the potency of prayer, such as where it reaches, how it can be effective. These concepts will be briefly discussed here.

Unifications

Above (Chapter 1), we mentioned the idea of unity and unifications. The importance of these unifications is that in order for us to benefit from God's bounty and blessing, all the above-mentioned *Partzufim* and *Sefirot* have to be aligned in their proper order and position. This is because it facilitates the flow of bounty to the recipients. Thus, when we perform the *mitzvot,* pray and study Torah, we effect this alignment and unify the spiritual energies to bring blessing to all humanity. Where there is unity among people — jealousy and hatred are eradicated — blessing and bounty are available to all. Therefore, it is customary to recite the *L'Sheim Yichud* prayer prior to performing several *mitzvot.*

Shattering of the Vessels and the Sparks of Holiness

When God created the Universes, He first made the *Sefirot* and then made vessels to contain and filter their light / energy. But He created the vessels with a built-in flaw. The vessels were unable to contain that light, so they shattered. Imagine a glass bulb built to withstand 60 watts of incandescent electricity. But the filament is one of 100 watts. That glass would overheat and shatter into many pieces. So too, the *sefirot* energies were too intense and those vessels shattered.

The purpose of this was that the original Creation was adjacent to God's very intense spirituality. By causing the vessels to shatter, it spread them away from His essence and allowed for a more material creation to emerge, one where humanity would be able to exist without being overwhelmed. This, in turn, became the catalyst for the Sparks of Holiness from these vessels to be scattered all over the world. It is man's mission to elevate these sparks back to their original place by performing *mitzvot.* The ability to accomplish this is because the word *miTzVah* (מצוה) shares the root of the word *TzeVet* (צוות) which translates as "to join." Thus, every mitzvah we perform joins together these fallen sparks and creates a unity, a rebuilt and restored vessel.

There are many teachings about these Shattered Vessels and Fallen Sparks, which would require a separate book to explain. However, one important idea about these sparks is that when a person sins, he shatters these vessels and decreases their size, forcing mankind to further have to seek out these sparks in distant places and remote areas. As we shall see throughout this book, the intent of many prayers is to gather the sparks and aid in restoring the vessels.

The *Kelipot*

Another important teaching is that forces of evil exist, which are called *kelipot*. In Hebrew, a *kelipah* is a shell or covering of the holiness, much as an orange has a shell covering it or an apple has its skin. These are also referred to as the forces of the Other Side. "God made the one as well as the other" (Ecclesiastes 7:14), which means that God created opposing forces to enable a person to have free will to choose between good and evil. If a person sins, he adds power to the forces of the Other Side so that they can cause damage to man and his environs.

The idea is that sanctity is protected so that one who is unworthy shall not enter into it. An additional purpose is that there be a deterrent which makes it difficult to find God and the spirituality that permeates the world. The search for God is what creates the energy to unite the spiritual energies necessary to draw blessing and bounty. Thus, the *kelipot* serve an important function which, when overcome, allows us to ascend the spiritual ladder and realize great spiritual levels.

God's Names

One more thought that we will encounter below is the mention of several names of God. One Name is the Name of

Forty-Two, while a second Name mentioned is the Name of Seventy-Two.

To understand these ideas, the Talmud and Kabbalah speak of the entire Torah being a compilation of God's Holy Names. Every word or phrase is, in one way or another, a variation of a Name of God.

The Name of Forty-Two (in Hebrew, *Mem-Bet*) is alluded to in the *Ana B'Koach* prayer, which has seven verses of six letters and 7x6=42. There are additional times it is referred to in the prayers. What exactly this means is for the great Kabbalists to know and for us to believe in. But the letters, *Mem-Bet* (מב) form the acrostic of *Ma'aseh Bereishit* (the work of Creation; see *Zohar* III, 256b). It is the Name God used when creating the Universes and its implication for us is that by invoking it we arouse our creative abilities and can become more productive in our lives.

The Name of Seventy-Two. In Hebrew, the number 72 is the *gematria* of *CheSeD* (חסד, lovingkindness). It is an unearned gift from God to us to be able to invoke His lovingkindness and thereby invoke His blessings and bounty. The Mishnah in Tractate Sukkah (4:5; see *Tikkuney Zohar*, Introduction p. 8) speaks of this Name and describes where the Name is alluded to in the Torah. It consists of combinations of three letter words, and some will be referred to below in our text.

There are four main Names of God we come across in our prayers:

- *Eil* (אל): This Name represents *Chesed* / Lovingkindness as in (Psalms 52:3), "the *Chesed* of *Eil*, is all day."
- *Elohim* (אלהים): This Name represents judgments. It means "God Who is the Judge and His Will dominates."
- *YHVH* (יהוה), which is never pronounced as written but as *Adonoy*. The Name means "*I exist or I am*," In Hebrew, we

pronounce it as *HaVaYaH,* and translates as *HaYah,* I was; *HoVeH,* I am (now in the present); *YiHiYeH,* I will be. This Name represents *Mishpat,* Justice, a blend of *Chesed,* and Lovingkindness.

- *Adonoy* (אדני): This Name represents strict judgment and translates as *Adon* or Master. See Appendix where this Name is in *Malkhut,* the Authority, to carry out the judgments which have been decreed.

In a general sense, these are the Names we use when praying to God.

Prayer to God is My Life

Rebbe Nachman teaches that the essence of life-force comes from prayer as it is written, "Prayer to God is my life" (Psalms 42:9). When a person prays with all his strength and concentrates his energy on the words making up the prayers, his energy is renewed. As it says, "They are renewed each morning; great is Your *emunah* (faith)" (Lamentations 3:23). And we learn that faith means prayer, as it says, "And his hands were *emunah*" (Exodus 17:2), which *Onkelos* renders, "His hands were spread out in prayer" (LM I, 9:1).

Representing both faith and prayer, *Malkhut* is the connection and interface with the spiritual energies that descend to us from the *Keter.* Since these spiritual energies are flowing down from Above, it behooves us to use our energy as best as we can in order to receive that bounty. The Rebbe taught that we should pray with all our energy so that we can renew our strength.

As Reb Noson said above, prayer is so great that it is able to ascend to the *Keter.* When we pray, we can access the highest levels (i.e., the "Heights of Creation,") accessing our souls which touches our very essence!

CHAPTER 5

Preparation for Prayer

We've learned that prayers are extremely powerful and can ascend to the loftiest of heights. But just like you wouldn't take a bow and arrow and shoot without preparation, you can't expect your prayers to reach the One Above without first putting yourself in the proper environment. It takes a lot of discipline to be able to shoot your projectile so that it hits its target. The same applies to prayer. If you want your prayers to ascend to the proper place for them to be answered, they must be aimed precisely so they will be on target and make a "direct hit."

For that, you need preparation. What does this entail?

Joy

The Talmud teaches, "The Divine Presence does not rest [upon the person if he is] depressed, or if he is lazy, or from joking or mockery…or [if he is engaged in] idle chatter—*just from joy*" (*Shabbos* 30b). Therefore, we learn that joy is a primary preparation for prayer.

Rebbe Nachman explains that the sole reason that people are distant from God and do not draw close to Him is that they lack *yishuv hadaat* (a settled mind). It is hard to compose one's mind if one is depressed. Only by being in a state of *simchah* (joy) can a person direct his mind as he pleases and attain *yishuv hadaat*. Joy is freedom of the soul; through joy a person becomes free and can emerge from his personal suffering and exile (LM II, 10).

It's great to be free—free of worry, free of problems, free of external and even internal pressures. But reality makes this very difficult, if not impossible. Rebbe Nachman suggests that a person try to free himself of some of his burdens, especially during the moments of prayer. After all, we are trying to concentrate on the words, to ask God to help us in whatever endeavor we are involved with. But how can we concentrate if we're filled with worry?

The answer is to strive for happiness and joy. When you're happy, your mind is free from worry. Therefore, you can concentrate on what you're thinking and on what you're saying. When our Sages teach that the Divine Presence will rest upon a person who is joyous, it means, simply, that the person can connect with God during his prayers.

Identifying Positive Aspects in Yourself

In the aforementioned lesson, Rebbe Nachman offers several approaches for attaining joy. The first is: "The way a person achieves joy is by recognizing your positive traits." In *Azamra* ("I Will Sing") (LM I, 282), Rebbe Nachman emphasizes the importance of looking for and finding merits in other people, and then stresses the importance of finding the good in oneself. It's easy to find fault with ourselves; we do it all the time. But if we are down on ourselves, we become depressed. If we are positive and recognize the good we have within, we can—and do—become joyous. This process creates music; when we harp on our positive points, we create melodies that bring joy and happiness.

Cleansing

Another preparation for prayer is cleanliness. Our Sages teach that in order to accept the yoke of Heaven, a person should first cleanse his body of waste matter and make sure to wash his hands. Only then should he don the *tefillin*, recite the *Shema*, and pray (*Berakhot* 15a). Some people immerse in a *mikvah* prior to the prayers, which is reminiscent of the *Kohanim* who were required to immerse before they began the service in the *Beis HaMikdash*.

Torah Study

In *Likutey Moharan*, Rebbe Nachman tells us that our prayers are answered due to Torah study. The Rebbe teaches:

> Know! By means of the Torah, all our prayers and all our requests are accepted. The grace and importance of the Jewish people are thus enhanced and elevated in the estimation of all of whom they may have need, whether in spiritual or physical matters.
>
> As a result of our many sins, the true grace and importance of the Jewish people have fallen… By means of the Torah, however, the Jewish people's grace and importance are enhanced… And through this, all prayers and requests are accepted (LM I, 1).

Rebbe Nachman explains how the Torah brings *chein* (grace) upon those who study it. Words that lack grace, importance or favor are not always accepted. If you want your prayers answered, you have to spice them up with grace. This is accomplished through Torah study. Even a few minutes of engaging in Torah study before praying in the morning will inject a measure of grace into your prayers.

It is interesting to note that the inclusion of the passages of *mishnayot* in "*Eizehu Mekoman*" and "*Beraita d'Rabbi Yishmael*" at the end of the section of the *Korbanot* indicates learning Torah before beginning the prayers of *Pesukey d'Zimrah*. We also recite the Torah portion of *Akeidat Yitzchak* (the Binding of Yitzchak) prior to reciting the passages of the sacrifices. These passages of Torah are specifically placed towards the beginning of the Shacharit prayer in order to give us grace so our prayers will be answered.

Charity and Guarding the Covenant

One should donate to charity before praying.[14] One can give this charity before praying by placing a few coins in a charity box in his home or in the synagogue. Additionally, one must be cautious with the covenant.[15]

Rebbe Nachman discusses the connection between charity, the covenant and prayers (LM I, 2). He explains that prayer is the essential weapon of *Mashiach* and also of each and every Jew. How can we wield that weapon so it reaches its intended target and goal? The answer is by guarding the covenant. The Rebbe explains:

> Now, this weapon must be received by means of the aspect of Yosef—i.e., guarding the covenant (*Yesod*), as in "Gird your sword upon your thigh" (Psalms 45:4).[16] Yosef, who guarded the covenant [by withstanding the test with Potifar's wife; Genesis 39] gained the rights of the firstborn. This corresponds to the Divine service of prayer, which is an aspect of the double portion inherited by the firstborn.[17] Prayer is itself twofold, as it is comprised of both praise of God and requesting one's needs.[18] This corresponds to "a double-edged sword in their hand" (Psalms 149:6)—i.e., two edges, a double portion...for the birthright is dependent upon guarding the covenant.

The Kabbalah expounds on the connection between the *sefirot* of *Yesod* (the covenant) and *Malkhut* (prayer).[19] It is *Yesod* which delivers bounty; however, if the *Yesod* is not in order,

14 *Bava Batra* 10a; *Orach Chaim* 92:10.

15 The *brit* (covenant) refers to the pact God made with Avraham and sealed with the mitzvah of circumcision. Guarding the covenant means keeping oneself morally pure and abstaining from illicit relationships.

16 The thigh alludes to the sexual organ, which corresponds to the *sefirah* of *Yesod*. See Charts, Appendix A.

17 See Deuteronomy 21:17.

18 See *Berakhot* 54b.

19 See Charts, Appendix A; above Chapter 4.

then the bounty that is meant for *Malkhut* goes astray—that is, the prayers cannot be as effective as they should be.

On the other hand, it is impossible to know how to do battle without the attribute of *mishpat* (justice), which corresponds to the *sefirah* of *Tiferet*. *Tiferet* is the center column.[20] In other words, one must strike with his weapon at the precise point, inclining to neither the right nor the left. And the bounty from Above is drawn through the center columns—*Tiferet*, *Yesod* and *Malkhut*.

The Rebbe adds:

> And how does one merit the aspect of *mishpat?* Through charity… For charity is itself a product of *mishpat,* as in "God is judge, He brings down one and lifts up another" (Psalms 75:8)—meaning God impoverishes one and enriches another. When a person gives charity, he "brings down one," because he subtracts from his own money; and he "lifts up another," because he enriches the poor man. Consequently, through charity, man embraces the attribute of *mishpat*. This is the reason it is necessary to donate charity before praying, so that he will balance his words with *mishpat*—he can "strike at a hair and not miss."

Rebbe Nachman adds that the main cause of extraneous thoughts during prayer is the corruption of *mishpat*. Giving charity before praying helps a person concentrate better during the prayers and guard himself from foreign thoughts, which are the corruption of justice.

Attachment to the Tzaddikim

Rebbe Nachman suggests that people attach themselves to true tzaddikim. All people have attachments to others, such as family, friends, groups or gangs. Obviously, an attachment to a gang will bring a person to misery. On the other hand, an attachment to tzaddikim, who are always engaged in good

20 *Tikkuney Zohar,* Introduction, 7a.

deeds, will lead a person on a straight and narrow path, filled with positive deeds and goals.

The act of prayer itself reflects the importance of attaching oneself to tzaddikim. The prayers are in place of the sacrifices which were brought in the *Mishkan* (Tabernacle) and the Beis HaMikdash.[21] Rebbe Nachman explains that in the desert, all the Jews participated in building the *Mishkan*. But when everything was ready, there was no one who was able to place all the various parts in their proper positions — except Moshe.

Similarly, each of our prayers is a figurative brick in building the *Mishkan*. When the prayers are attached to the tzaddikim (who represent Moshe), they can be included in erecting the *Mishkan* and revealing the Kingdom of God.

The custom among Breslover chassidim is to recite a short paragraph prior to praying in which they attach themselves to the tzaddikim. This paragraph begins: "*Hareini mekasher atzmi b'sefilasi l'chol hatzaddikim haamitiyim*..." (Behold, I hereby bind myself through my prayer to all the true tzaddikim).[22]

The Two Types of Prayer

As we prepare for prayer, we should also prepare our hearts for the correct attitude to have when we pray.

Our Sages tell us, "Do not make your prayer *keva* (by rote); make it with compassion and supplication" (*Avot* 2:13).

Rebbe Nachman speaks about two types of prayer. The first and foremost is pleading and supplications for compassion: "I know I don't deserve Your compassion, but I ask for it anyway." The second type of prayer, which one must be careful about reciting, is a demanding approach: "You should give me what

21 *Berakhot* 26b.

22 See Breslov Siddur.

I am asking for, I demand it." The first is called "prayers of *rachamim* and *tachanunim*" (asking for compassion and requests through supplications). The second is called a prayer of *keva*, of *din* (judgment). In Hebrew, the word *keva* (by rote) also translates as "stealing." It's as if you are stealing from God, demanding He do what you want (LM II, 8:2-3).

We should always adopt the first type of prayer, searching for God and seeking His compassion. No matter how we have lived (as a tzaddik or otherwise), God is ready to hear our prayers. But we should not be demanding of God. If God grants your wishes, good; if not, then not.[23]

The following is a short prayer that Reb Noson composed about praying with supplication:

> Arouse Your vast compassion and intense lovingkindness on our behalf. Pour compassion, mercy and graciousness onto us. Help us recite our prayers before You with all our heart and soul, with grace, kindness and compassion, like a son approaching his father. May our conversations, prayers and pleadings be sweet to You. May we arouse Your true compassion toward us. Please view us as an only, precious, beloved child who comes close to his father and does his father's will with love, kindness and compassion, with mercy and grace. May we pour forth our hearts like water before Your countenance, God.
>
> (LT II, 8)

23 LM I, 196; see also ibid. I, 20:5.

PART II

Shacharit – The Morning Prayer

CHAPTER 6

Beginning the Day: Initial Prayers and Actions

Modeh Ani

מוֹדֶה אֲנִי לְפָנֶיךָ מֶלֶךְ חַי וְקַיָּם. שֶׁהֶחֱזַרְתָּ בִּי נִשְׁמָתִי בְּחֶמְלָה. רַבָּה אֱמוּנָתֶךָ:

I give thanks to You, O Living and Eternal King, for restoring my soul to me with mercy; Your faithfulness is very great.

When people deposit things with a custodian, these deposits may sometimes get mixed up. Yet every night when people go to sleep and they deposit their souls with God, He always returns each soul to its rightful owner (*Midrash Tehillim* 25).

This is one of the reasons why when we open our eyes we should immediately recite the *Modeh Ani* prayer: "Thank you, God, for restoring *my* soul to *me* so that I may repair the things that need correction, and for allowing me to continue to better myself and maybe even perfect my life." Some people, when given a guarantee for a loan, might seize the collateral and hold onto it. Have we been perfect? Certainly not! Perhaps God should seize our souls and hold them as collateral for our misdeeds? But no! He returns our souls to us daily, giving us yet another chance to do good. It is only right that we show gratitude by thanking Him for this.

Reishit Chokhmah

רֵאשִׁית חָכְמָה יִרְאַת יְיָ שֵׂכֶל טוֹב לְכָל עוֹשֵׂיהֶם תְּהִלָּתוֹ עוֹמֶדֶת לָעַד:

The first wisdom is fear of God. Good intellect is granted to all who perform them. His praise will endure forever.

Following *Modeh Ani,* we say "*Reishit Chokhmah*". Reb Noson explains that the *sefirah* of *Chokhmah* (Wisdom) is on the highest of levels, but we cannot get there unless we first display fear of God. Fear of God is the first stepping stone to acquire true wisdom (LH, *Sefirah* 1).

The recital of *Reishit Chokhmah* continues with, "*Seichel tov l'chol oseihem*" (Good intellect is granted to all who perform the *mitzvot*). The Talmud (*Berakhot* 17a) teaches that "it is good intellect to those who perform the *mitzvot,* for they will come to understand the greatness of performing the *mitzvot,* but it doesn't make sense to those who just study them but without performing the *mitzvot*."

The *Zohar* states that the first word of the Torah, *Bereishit* (בראשית), contains an allusion to the first and foremost mitzvah, fear of God, as it includes the word *Reishit* (ראשית), referring to *Reishit Chokhmah,* denoting fear of God. This is the beginning of the Torah, and it is the beginning of every day: to awaken and immediately draw fear and awe of God, Who is omnipotent. This is the optimal way to start your day! (*Zohar* I, 11b).

Washing Our Hands

בָּרוּךְ אַתָּה יְיָ אֱלֹהֵינוּ מֶלֶךְ הָעוֹלָם, אֲשֶׁר קִדְּשָׁנוּ בְּמִצְוֹתָיו, וְצִוָּנוּ עַל נְטִילַת יָדָיִם:

Blessed are You, HaShem our God, King of the universe, who set us apart in order to sanctify us with His commandments and instructed us regarding the washing and elevation of the hands.

The first action you should take upon wakening is to wash your hands. You can recite *Modeh Ani* even before you wash your hands because you are not directly mentioning God's name, but you should wash your hands soon after. The reason for the prayers is to recognize God's kingship upon us and thus the Talmud teaches, "Whoever wants to accept God's kingship should cleanse himself, wash his hands, don *tefillin*, recite the *Shema*, and pray" (*Berakhot* 15a). That is, "Cleanliness comes before Godliness," so you should take care of your bodily needs and wash your hands before you accept the yoke of Heaven.

The *Shulchan Arukh* explains that handwashing serves two purposes. First, during sleep, your hands most probably touched various parts of the body that may not have been clean. Second, you are compared to a new creation upon wakening, and it is fitting that you cleanse yourself first before you begin to praise God for your new day.

Reb Noson quotes the verse, "The world will be filled with knowledge of God, as waters cover the sea" (Isaiah 11:9). He explains that "waters" are drawn from *daat* (knowledge and recognition of God). When we wash our hands, we are drawing knowledge of God. We have to wash our hands because "hands" represent faith, as in, "His hands were faith" (Exodus 17:12; LH, *Hashkamat HaBoker* 5:6).

Elsewhere,[24] Reb Noson discusses the concepts of *k'seider* (in order) and *shelo k'seider* (disorderly). *K'seider* parallels the day, when the light allows a person to see around him. Nighttime corresponds to *shelo k'seider*, when darkness obscures our vision and thus conceptually, confusion reigns. Generally, we sleep at night, since when we are tired our *daat* does not function properly. We need to negate ourselves (and rest up) in order

24 LH, *Netillat Yadayim* 3:2.

to receive fresh intellect. When we awaken in the morning, we must wash our hands with water, since water represents *daat.* We wash in order to draw the *k'seider* into our lives.

When we wash our hands, we recite the blessing of "*al netillat yadayim* (regarding the washing and elevation of the hands.) Our Sages teach, "One should be very careful to wash his hands" (*Shabbos* 108b). There is a spirit of death[25] that rests on a person when he is asleep and departs every morning, but only after he washes his hands. Additionally, the initial letters of the words *al netillat yadayim* (על נטילת ידים) spell the acronym *ANi* (עני, meaning poor). To underrate the importance of washing the hands can lead to poverty. Poverty is not only financial. As explained above, water refers to *daat.* One can forget his learning or lose his intellect or his ability to think clearly, all because he did not wash his hands.[26] The worst type of poverty is the lack of *daat.* Then one is apt to commit errors and even sins, God forbid (*Nedarim* 41a).

Getting Dressed

While dressing, one should give primacy to his right side by donning his clothes on the right side first (e.g., socks and shoes). According to Kabbalah, the right side is the side of *Chesed* (Lovingkindness), while the left side represents *Gevurah* (Judgment).[27] The feet parallel *Malkhut* and are very close to the realm of impurity, which is why we wear shoes to keep us separate from that realm of the *kelipot* (forces of evil). By giving primacy to the right side, we infuse our days with *Chesed* in order to be able to counter the negative influences of the *kelipot* (LH, *Hashkamat HaBoker* 4:8).

25 Sleep is one-sixtieth of death (*Berakhot* 57b).

26 See *Orach Chaim* 4:18.

27 See Charts, p. 454.

Tzitzit

בָּרוּךְ אַתָּה יְיָ אֱלֹהֵינוּ מֶלֶךְ הָעוֹלָם, אֲשֶׁר קִדְּשָׁנוּ בְּמִצְוֹתָיו, וְצִוָּנוּ עַל מִצְוַת צִיצִית:

Blessed are You, HaShem our God, King of the universe, who set us apart in order to sanctify us with His commandments and instructed us concerning the commandment of *tzitzit*.

One of the first *mitzvot* we perform in the morning is putting on *tzitzit*, the four-cornered garment with strings. The Torah tells us that we should wear these four-cornered garments and see them, and thus be reminded of all the *mitzvot*. As it says, "That we will not stray after our hearts (atheism) or our eyes (immorality)" (Numbers 15:37-41).

The mitzvah of *tzitzit* is equal to all the *mitzvot* of the Torah. In Hebrew, the word *TzITzIT* (ציצית) has the numerical value of 600.[28] Add to this the eight strings and five knots on each side of the *tzitzit*—totaling 13—and you have 613, the number of *mitzvot* in the Torah! Wearing *tzitzit* therefore reminds us of and helps us keep all the *mitzvot*.[29]

Rebbe Nachman teaches that the *tzitzit* are a *segulah* for becoming attached to the tzaddikim and attaining a guarded covenant (LM I, 7:3-4).

Rebbe Nachman also teaches that one must be very careful to guard his clothing and keep them clean, for this protects them from the *kelipot* that attach to one's clothing and draw him to sin (LM I, 29:3-4). The Prophet Zekhariah (3:3-4) states that the priest, Yehoshua, was clothed in filthy garments and was told to remove them and dress in festival clothes. The filthy garments represent sin.

28 See Charts, p. 461. (*gematria*).

29 *Shavuot* 29a; Rashi on Numbers 15:39.

Clothes tend to become soiled easily. Reb Noson states that *tzitzit* is a remedy for helping us keep our clothes clean.

Reb Noson also points out that, "Clothes make the man." That is, they bring honor and respect to the one who wears them. Therefore *tzitzit,* which are clothing of a mitzvah, are the guardians of one's garments. Wearing *tzitzit* is a means of respect and thus reveals the respect and honor we should show to God. Reb Noson adds that the passage in the Torah which speaks about *tzitzit* (Numbers 15:37-41) is part and parcel of the daily *Shema* prayer, because *tzitzit* are meant to honor God and reveal His kingship (LH, *Tzitzit* 2).

Tallit and *Tefillin*

It is customary to wear *tzitzit* on or under our shirts. Afterwards, we put on the *tallit,* and then we don the *tefillin.*

בָּרוּךְ אַתָּה יְיָ אֱלֹהֵינוּ מֶלֶךְ הָעוֹלָם, אֲשֶׁר קִדְּשָׁנוּ בְּמִצְוֹתָיו, וְצִוָּנוּ לְהִתְעַטֵּף בַּצִּיצִית:

Blessed are You, HaShem our God, King of the universe, Who has set us apart in order to sanctify us with His commandments, and instructed us to envelop ourselves in the *tallit.*

The four *tzitzit* allude to spirit of life, the *ruach* (wind, spirit) that comes from all directions of the earth, the four corners of the earth. *Tzitzit* carry the idea that they are made of wool, similar to hair, which is represented by Esav, evil personified (see Genesis 25:25). When putting on the *tallit* we check the strings of the *tzitzit* to see that they are separated and complete. This is because *tzitzit* have the power to subdue the evil forces. By ensuring that the *tzitzit* are indeed separate, we are ensuring, spiritually, that the forces of evil are separate and not joined in their evil ideas (LM I, 8:8; LH, *Tzitzit* 4).

בָּרוּךְ אַתָּה יְיָ אֱלֹהֵינוּ מֶלֶךְ הָעוֹלָם, אֲשֶׁר קִדְּשָׁנוּ בְּמִצְוֹתָיו, וְצִוָּנוּ לְהָנִיחַ תְּפִלִּין:

Blessed are You, HaShem our God, King of the universe, Who has set us apart in order to sanctify us with His commandments, and instructed us to don *tefillin*.

בָּרוּךְ אַתָּה יְיָ אֱלֹהֵינוּ מֶלֶךְ הָעוֹלָם, אֲשֶׁר קִדְּשָׁנוּ בְּמִצְוֹתָיו, וְצִוָּנוּ עַל מִצְוַת תְּפִלִּין:

Blessed are You, HaShem our God, King of the universe, who has set us apart in order to sanctify us with His commandments, and instructed us regarding the commandment of *tefillin*.

The mitzvah of *tefillin* is mentioned in the *Shema* prayer (Deuteronomy 6:8). Additionally, it is referred to several times in the passage about the Exodus from Egypt (Exodus 13).

Tefillin are placed on the left arm[30] and on the head. By placing the *tefillin* on the arm, we recognize that it is God who actually gets things done rather than our own power, and we respectfully acknowledge His presence in our lives. The head-*tefillin* are positioned on the forehead between the eyes to remind us not to be swayed by our enticements, but rather focus our eyes and minds on God.

"*Tefillin* is compared to the entire Torah" (*Kiddushin* 35a) and is considered one of the three signs of constant devotion to God (the other two are Shabbos and *milah* / circumcision). Rebbe Nachman teaches that *tefillin* represent our attachment to God (LM I, 38:1). All the intentions of the *tefillin*, as explained by the ARI, are readily available for a person to know in order to attach himself to God. The upshot is that *tefillin* are so lofty

30 *Orach Chaim* 27:1.

and have incredible power to bring a person to awareness of God and to great intellects to enhance his spirituality.

Moreover, Rebbe Nachman teaches, *tefillin* are the vehicle that shows the will of God. *Tefillin* are so meaningful, yet we are commanded to make them not from gold which would seem fitting for such a great mitzvah, but rather from leather. Torah passages inscribed on parchment are then inserted into square leather boxes. That is God's will.

Reb Noson explains that *tefillin* are made specifically from the hides of kosher animals because, as the Torah tells us, "The Torah of God shall be in your mouth" (Exodus 13:9). Our Sages explain this to mean "From that which is permitted to your mouth" (*Shabbos* 108a). Reb Noson further writes that there are certain things represented by extremely harsh *kelipot* which are totally evil, while other things represent *nogah*, a *kelipah* which is an admixture of good and evil. Rebbe Nachman explains that *nogah* is a *kelipah* which can be elevated into holiness, simply by guarding one's tongue (i.e., that which is permitted to the mouth). *Tefillin*, too, must be made from what is permitted to the mouth — from holy speech and from elevating the mundane to holiness. With holy speech we can merit the intellects of the *tefillin* (LH, *Tefillin* 1).

Thus, Reb Noson is explaining that one can take skins and hides and turn them into a holy vessel.

The Three-Pronged Attachment

Life changes constantly: Every day new things happen for both the individual and the community, and these changes can even occur at every moment. One has to adjust to change and know how to act, feel and serve God at each moment. This is called "capturing the moment."

Rebbe Nachman teaches that we can experience the moment via a three-pronged attachment made by communication. The first type of communication is speaking to a tzaddik or your teacher every day (i.e., study his writings and capture the teacher's ideas in your heart). The second type of communication is holding a conversation with a friend, capturing his essence of that moment, and binding it on your heart to learn and receive as much as you can from that simple conversation. The third type of communication is between you and your Maker, speaking to God and expressing your innermost feelings of that moment to Him (LM I, 34:8).

Reb Noson explains that the *tefillin* represents this three-pronged attachment. There are the arm-*tefillin* and the head-*tefillin*. But there is also a third part, the knot of the head-*tefillin*, which is placed on the back of the head. The head-*tefillin* corresponds with the conversation with the tzaddik; the arm-*tefillin* represent the conversation with God; and the knot of the head-*tefillin* parallels conversations with a friend.

Since the primary ways of attachment are via a conversation with God and with tzaddikim, the *tefillin* on the arm and on the head have a box with holy words written within them. However, conversing with friends is also essential. It creates the bridge that draws down the lessons one receives from the tzaddik into one's conversation with God. This is represented by the knot on the back of the head.

Reb Noson notes that these ideas parallel the three daily prayers. *Shacharit* and *Maariv*, the two prayers which include the recital of the *Shema*, represent the arm- and head-*tefillin*. *Minchah* represents the bridge between the morning devotions and the evening devotions (LH, *Tefillin* 2:2,4,9).

The verse, "It is the garment for his skin" (Exodus 22:26), refers to a poor person and how we must take care that he has garments to wear. The *Zohar* teaches, "It is the garment for his skin"—this is the leather of the *tefillin* (*Tikkuney Zohar* #69, p. 100b). This refers to donning *tefillin,* which is the "garment" for the Divine Presence in exile. That is, the "poor person" is the *Shekhinah* who, in exile, is impoverished. When we perform *mitzvot*—notably the mitzvah of donning the *tefillin*—we are conceptually "clothing the *Shekhinah.*" While the *Shekhinah* is being enriched, we, too, are enriched and saved from poverty (LM I, 47:3).[31]

Love Your Fellow as Yourself

> הֲרֵינִי מְקַבֵּל עָלַי מִצְוַת עֲשֵׂה שֶׁל וְאָהַבְתָּ לְרֵעֲךָ כָּמוֹךָ אֲנִי יְיָ:
>
> Behold, I accept upon myself the positive command "Love your fellow as yourself; I am HaShem."

The ARI writes that prior to the prayers, a person should accept upon himself to love every Jew as he loves himself.

Reb Noson points out that a person is likely to succeed in this world if he has the correct advice. When there is unity between people, then people can dialogue with each other and look for the right thing to do. All this depends on the love and peace between people. Praying with a minyan, a symbol of love and unity, furthers this idea (LH, *Taanit* 4:13; ibid. *Beis HaKnesset* 1).[32]

Mah Tovu

> מַה טֹּבוּ אֹהָלֶיךָ יַעֲקֹב מִשְׁכְּנֹתֶיךָ יִשְׂרָאֵל:
>
> How wonderful are your tents, O Yaakov, your dwelling places, O Israel.

31 The Breslov Research Institute has produced a book, *Tefillin: A chassidic Discourse,* written by Reb Noson and translated by Avraham Greenbaum. Based on the story of "The Seven Beggars," this book explains the concepts of *tefillin,* the housings, the passages, and the mystical concepts of the *tefillin.*

32 See Breslov Siddur.

We begin the morning prayer with *Mah Tovu*, praising the Jewish nation for its steadfastness in turning to God. The "tents" mentioned in this verse refer to the synagogues and houses of study where Jews assemble for the daily prayers. Thus, it was established that when we enter the synagogue, we recite *Mah Tovu*.

It is extremely important to pray with a *minyan* (prayer quorum) of ten men. The Talmud teaches that an individual's prayer might not be accepted in Heaven. However, a prayer offered with a *minyan* will never be rejected (see *Berakhot* 8a).

Reb Noson explains:

> Rebbe Nachman's story of "The Master of Prayer"[33] illustrates this concept in a most incredible manner. The story revolves around a King whose entourage is comprised of ten people: the King, the Queen, the Princess, the Mighty Warrior, the Child, the Faithful Friend, the Bard, the Wise Man, the Treasurer, and the Master of Prayer. These ten represent the realm of holiness (i.e., the ten *sefirot*).
>
> Those of the realm of holiness represent the *Olam HaTikkun*, the World of Rectification. When one includes himself in a *minyan*, he is joining that realm. Though he might not know the impact of his deed, he nevertheless has contributed his portion to building and maintaining the realm of holiness (LH, *Tefillah* 4:1).

וַאֲנִי בְּרֹב חַסְדְּךָ אָבֹא בֵיתֶךָ אֶשְׁתַּחֲוֶה אֶל הֵיכַל קָדְשְׁךָ בְּיִרְאָתֶךָ:

As for me, it is solely through Your great loving kindness that I am able to enter Your house. I therefore prostrate myself before the sanctuary of Your holiness in awe of You alone.

33 *Rebbe Nachman's Stories* #12.

The *Zohar* (I, 11a) teaches that this verse refers to the three Patriarchs: "Loving kindness" refers to Avraham (the paradigm of *Chesed*); "Your sanctuary" refers to Yaakov (of whom it is written, "He built himself a house" [Genesis 33:17]); and "In awe of You" refers to Yitzchak (who parallels awe and *Gevurah*). The *Zohar* thus states that because the Patriarchs were the ones who established the daily prayers, we should invoke their merit when we enter the synagogue to pray.

Adon Olam

אֲדוֹן עוֹלָם אֲשֶׁר מָלַךְ. בְּטֶרֶם כָּל יְצִיר נִבְרָא:

Eternal Hidden Master of the universe, He reigned as King alone before any being was created.

This prayer is a very special praise to God. The commentaries offer that this prayer is based on the Talmudic teaching "From the day God created the worlds, no one ever called Him *Adon* (Master) until Avraham" (*Berakhot* 7b). Therefore, we begin our prayers by calling God "Master" in order to evoke the merit of Avraham, who established the morning prayer.

CHAPTER 7

The Torah Blessings

Torah Study

בָּרוּךְ אַתָּה יְיָ אֱלֹהֵינוּ מֶלֶךְ הָעוֹלָם, אֲשֶׁר קִדְּשָׁנוּ בְּמִצְוֹתָיו, וְצִוָּנוּ לַעֲסוֹק בְּדִבְרֵי תוֹרָה:

Blessed are You, HaShem our God, King of the universe, who set us apart in order to sanctify us with His commandments and instructed us to occupy ourselves with words of Torah.

Quite a few blessings are included in our daily prayers, but the blessings over the Torah and Torah study stand out in several ways. First, if one rises early in the morning, though it is not yet time to pray, he still can, and should, recite these blessings even before daybreak. Second, the *Shulchan Arukh* states about these blessings: "A person must be very careful to recite the blessings over the Torah" (*Orach Chaim* 47:1).

The Torah blessings are a series of three requests. The first blessing thanks God, who sanctified us with His commandments and instructed us to occupy ourselves with words of Torah. Rebbe Nachman points out that it is impossible for anyone to be attached to Torah study at all times (LM II, 78). Just considering the body's need for sleep, food, and bodily functions alone, won't allow a person to study all the time even if he finds the greatest amount of pleasure in the Torah. How then can we be involved and occupied with Torah all the time?

Notice that the blessing uses the word *laasok* (לעסוק, to occupy), not *lilmod* (ללמוד, to study). This means that even while eating, working and going about our daily chores and activities, we should be occupied in Torah. How?

Rebbe Nachman explains that the Torah is the blueprint of the world (*Bereishit Rabbah* 1:1). Thus, Torah and God (who is united with the Torah) is everywhere, in every part of creation. When one seeks a connection with God and with the Torah through everything he does, he is always occupied with the Torah. Such a person will find that eating, drinking, sleeping and any other material activities are, in reality, occupying oneself with Torah. In other words, this blessing reminds us that everything we do contains Torah, and we should focus on our connection to Torah.

Rebbe Nachman further draws a connection between Torah and life itself. He teaches:

> Know! Life comes primarily from Torah, as the verse states, "For it is your life and the length of your days" (Deuteronomy 30:20). And the *Zohar* says, "Whoever departs from the Torah, it's as if he departed from life" (LM II, 78).

In another lesson, the Rebbe explains these ideas. He states:

> The way to achieve "length of days" is through the study of Torah, because the Torah is the name of God (*Tikkuney Zohar* #10, p. 25b). Just as when we have to summon someone, we summon him by his name, so too, when we have to summon the Life of life (i.e. God, the Source of life), in order to draw from Him life and length of days, we have to summon him by His name. And His name is the Torah. Thus, it is that by studying Torah, we summon length of days.
>
> But when one receives the life force, he must receive it in measure. Without measure and contraction, it is impossible to receive life force from God, lest there be too much light. Just as an

> increase in oil causes a flame to be extinguished, the life force has to be received with measure.
>
> We merit this through Torah study... The Torah is the aspect of a measure, because the Torah has letters, words, verses, chapters and portions, which are measured and precise. These are the aspect of measures within which the life force is contained with measure. Therefore, by means of the Torah (i.e., the name of God), which is the aspect of measures, it is possible to receive the life force (ibid. I, 56:3).

Rebbe Nachman adds that our Torah study must specifically be vocal. This, too, corresponds to calling someone by name, for it is impossible to call someone by name in thought alone. Likewise, calling the Life of life by His Name is only possible verbally, not by thought alone. It develops then that when a person occupies himself with Torah and connects everything in his life to Torah (as mentioned above), he is making a special connection to God, Who gives life. Thus, it is that we pray to be "occupied with Torah."

Make the Words of Torah Sweet

וְהַעֲרֶב נָא יְיָ אֱלֹהֵינוּ אֶת דִּבְרֵי תוֹרָתְךָ בְּפִינוּ וּבְפִיּוֹת עַמְּךָ בֵּית יִשְׂרָאֵל. וְנִהְיֶה אֲנַחְנוּ וְצֶאֱצָאֵינוּ. (וְצֶאֱצָאֵי צֶאֱצָאֵינוּ) וְצֶאֱצָאֵי עַמְּךָ בֵּית יִשְׂרָאֵל. כֻּלָּנוּ יוֹדְעֵי שְׁמֶךָ וְלוֹמְדֵי תוֹרָתֶךָ לִשְׁמָהּ:
בָּרוּךְ אַתָּה יְיָ הַמְלַמֵּד תּוֹרָה לְעַמּוֹ יִשְׂרָאֵל:

And, HaShem our God, please make the words of Your Torah pleasant in our mouths, and in the mouths of Your people, the family of Israel, so that we, our offspring (our descendants' offspring), and the descendants of Your people, the family of Israel—all of us—may be knowers of Your Name and learners of Your Torah for its own sake. Blessed are You, HaShem, Who teaches Torah to His people Israel.

In the second blessing, we ask for the Torah to taste sweet in our mouths so that after we learn something, we should find that sweetness again and again, and always review our studies. For one who is entrenched in his Torah studies will always find something new and sweet in his studies (see *Eruvin* 54a). This includes understanding the mysteries of the Torah.

The reason we mention our offspring and descendants is found in the Talmudic teaching, "Whoever is a scholar, and his son is a scholar, and his son's son is a scholar, the Torah will not cease from his family" (*Bava Metzia* 85a).

When we ask that we become "knowers of His name," we mean that we want to realize Divine providence and see God in all that occurs to us in our lives.

We also ask to become "learners of Your Torah for its own sake." Some people study Torah in order to become a well-known rabbi, receive a salary (such as a pulpit rabbi), or for honor and position. Even worse, some people study Torah just to be contentious in matters of Torah and religion. The Talmud rejects these types of study, which are not for the sake of Torah but rather for the individual's own position and gain. There are varying factors here because there are innocent people who desire Torah but get caught up in honor or financial gain. Referring to these people, our Sages teach, "A person should always occupy himself with Torah even not for its sake, because from *lo lishmah* (not for its sake) one will come to occupy himself *lishmah* (for its sake)."

Reb Noson explains our Sages' statement in an exquisite manner: "A person should always occupy himself with Torah even not for its sake, because from within the thoughts of 'not for its sake' one will find positive thoughts to occupy himself with Torah 'for its sake.'"

Giver of the Torah

בָּרוּךְ אַתָּה יְיָ אֱלֹהֵינוּ מֶלֶךְ הָעוֹלָם, אֲשֶׁר בָּחַר בָּנוּ מִכָּל הָעַמִּים
וְנָתַן לָנוּ אֶת תּוֹרָתוֹ: בָּרוּךְ אַתָּה יְיָ נוֹתֵן הַתּוֹרָה:

Blessed are You, HaShem our God, King of the universe,
who chose us from all the nations and gave us His Torah.
Blessed are You, HaShem, Giver of the Torah.

Reb Noson points out that the third blessing over the Torah concludes with *Notein HaTorah* (נותן התורה), literally, "Who gives the Torah." Each day God gives us the Torah anew, displaying the incredible power of renewal one can receive from the Torah. For this reason, both the second and third blessings are phrased in present tense: "Who *teaches* the Torah," "Who *gives* the Torah" (LH, *Birkhot HaShachar* 5:63).

We find in Jeremiah's prophecy: "Who is the wise man who will understand this?"... Why was the land lost, left as a desert through which no one passes? God said, "Because they have forsaken My Torah which I gave them; they did not listen to My voice, nor have they walked on its path" (Jeremiah 9:11-12).

The Talmud asks, "Why the redundancy? They did not listen to My voice or walk on its path." If they did not listen, then obviously they did not walk on its path! The Talmud answers that God asked the wise men, the angels and the prophets why the land was lost and the Jews were exiled, but they were unable to reply. God told them, "They did not listen to Me (i.e., to observe the Torah), nor have they walked on its path (i.e., they did not recite the blessings over the Torah before studying it)" (*Nedarim* 81a; *Bava Metzia* 85a-b).

Rabbi Yoel Sirkis, author of the *BaCh* on the *Tur* (*Orach Chaim* 47) quotes this Talmud and explains:

> God's intention in giving us the Torah was that we should be able to bind and attach ourselves to Him and His very essence. The Torah provides that means to be able to do it. Then we can actually form a most intimate connection with the *Shekhinah*—but only if we recognize the spirituality of the Torah and accept it as being a Godly tool. If, for whatever reason, we lack the faith or belief that the Torah is the essential tool to bind us with God, then we lose our connection to His essence, to His Divine Presence, which manifests in the land. We no longer can attain His Essence, and for that reason we lose even the physical connection to God (i.e., His land).

The *Mishnah Berurah* (*Orach Chaim* 47:2) adds that at that time, Torah study was not for the sake of God but as a study schedule for higher learning. Though the Jews accepted Torah study as a spiritual guide, the Torah lacked importance in their eyes, and they equated it with expanded and extensive studies, but not as the spiritual guide that God intended.

Therefore, they didn't say the Torah blessings. They didn't attribute importance to Torah study as a goal in itself, but only as a means to achieve knowledge. This resulted in the exile; hence, the importance of the Torah blessings.

We have just seen that because the Jews failed to recite the blessings over the Torah, they were exiled from their land. Reb Noson asks, "Is the failure to recite the Torah blessings really worse than the three capital sins of idolatry, adultery and murder (which were the major sins committed at that time)?! Did we lose the land as a punishment for not reciting the blessings, and not because of the major sins?"

Reb Noson answers that in the blessings we say, "Who chose us from all the nations." Once we attain our Jewish pride and recognize that we are God's chosen nation and His special people, we won't commit those misdeeds. However, if we lose pride in our Jewishness, we lose our focus and fall into vagaries and sin (LH, *Birkhot HaShachar* 5:7). Moreover, when we lose our focus of being a chosen nation, we also lose the chosen land and are exiled from it.

Reb Noson adds another insight into our Sages' teaching about losing the land. The fact that Jeremiah asked the question ("Who is the wise man...") implies that yes, the land was lost—but what can we do to rectify the situation?

God wanted us to realize that although we sinned, we *can* rectify! Despite our ill-advised deeds, God still loves us and wants us. And the Jews also want God. However, their collapse happened because they did not value their small accomplishments in Torah study, and therefore they didn't recite the blessings and rejoice with the Torah. They failed to realize that their small accomplishments meant so much and eventually would have pulled them away from their sins. Without that appreciation and awareness, they steadily declined until they lost everything (LH, *Perikah U'Te'inah* 4:35).

Rebbe Nachman speaks about the greatness of will and desire. A person should yearn for a connection with God while yearning for the *mitzvot* and all spiritual achievements.[34] However, everyone has a different level of desire, and each day an individual has a different degree of yearning. So when a person awakens with his renewed soul, he should renew his desires and inject them with a new will to serve God.

Among the many benefits of desire is that one can draw down Torah and material blessings.

Reb Noson explains that this is why we say *Birkhat Kohanim*[35] immediately after reciting the Torah blessings. The first blessing

34 See *Rebbe Nachman's Wisdom* #51.

35 The verses of the blessings of the *Kohanim*; Numbers 6:24-26.

of the *Kohanim* is "May God bless you and safeguard you." The Midrash states on this verse, "May God bless you with money and guard it for you!" For one of the factors attained through desire is an abundant livelihood.

And this is also why we recite the Mishnah during the morning prayer, "These are the precepts for which no fixed limit is prescribed" (*Pe'ah* 1:1). There is "no fixed limit" because with the *mitzvot* stated in this Mishnah (such as doing deeds of kindness) a person can ascend to great levels of desire without limitations. There are "no fixed limits" because desire is applicable and important for all people at all levels. Those at very low levels need desire to elevate themselves, and those who are at very high levels also need desire to reach even higher levels because there is no end to God's greatness (LH, *Birkhot HaShachar* 5:63-64).

To experience a revelation of Torah, one must first be tested in the "crucible." The main test is immorality. When a person passes this test, he merits Torah. Therefore, everyone, according to his morality, merits the light of Torah. This light is constantly available, but it has to be received in the vessels created by the person. That is, God's light is constantly descending in a pure delivery. But each person receives it according to his vessel (LM I, 36).

Reb Noson explains:

> This is why we must recite the Torah blessings each day. Our recital forms the vessel for us to receive God's light in a beneficial manner. For the Torah contains two potions: one an elixir of life, one a potion of death (see *Yoma* 72b). Therefore, we recite the blessing to occupy ourselves with Torah. The second blessing is that God should make the words of Torah sweet in our mouths so that we, our descendants and all of our offspring become knowledgeable of Your Name and devoted students of Torah. This is because we desire to receive the Torah in a beneficial manner. This is also why the blessings of the *Kohanim* are said right after

the Torah blessings, since the *Kohanim* are better equipped to receive God's light and transmit it to us.

To recite the blessings is to draw the light of God to us in a beneficial manner. But when the Jews did not draw that light, by omitting the Torah blessings, the Torah could not protect them. Therefore, they lost the land. The land represents morality, since it was given to Avraham when he was commanded to perform circumcision, the organ of morality (LH, *Birkhos HaTorah* 1).

An interesting insight into the Torah and by extension the importance of reciting its blessings is found in the Talmud. When Moshe ascended to Heaven to receive the Torah, the angels argued against it being given to human beings. The angels argued, "The Torah is so exalted—how can mere beings of flesh and blood benefit from it?" God told Moshe to reply to them. Moshe asked the angels, "Were you enslaved in Egypt? Are you among idol worshippers? Do you work that you need Shabbos for rest? Do you have parents to honor?" (*Shabbos* 88b).

Reb Noson asks, "What were the angels' thoughts? They knew that there are no Torah commandments that are applicable to them. What was their reasoning?" He answers that the angels knew of the exaltedness of Torah. They were referring to the idea that the Torah contains incredible wisdom, far above the human capacity to attain it. The angels could certainly use this wisdom even if they didn't perform the *mitzvot*. But Moshe replied to them, "Were you enslaved in Egypt? Are you among idol worshippers?" With these questions, Moshe implied that the primary aspect of the Torah is its counsel for people who are living in a materialistic world, attacked by the evil inclination and bad temptations that prevent them from serving God. It is the human being who requires the Torah so he can survive in and navigate this material world. The angels simply don't need it (LH, *Taanit* 4:14).

CHAPTER 8

Blessings upon Rising

בָּרוּךְ אַתָּה יְיָ אֱלֹהֵינוּ מֶלֶךְ הָעוֹלָם, אֲשֶׁר קִדְּשָׁנוּ בְּמִצְוֹתָיו, וְצִוָּנוּ עַל נְטִילַת יָדָיִם:

Blessed are You, HaShem our God, King of the universe, Who set us apart in order to sanctify us with His commandments, and instructed us regarding the washing and elevation of the hands.

בָּרוּךְ אַתָּה יְיָ אֱלֹהֵינוּ מֶלֶךְ הָעוֹלָם, אֲשֶׁר יָצַר אֶת הָאָדָם בְּחָכְמָה וּבָרָא בוֹ נְקָבִים נְקָבִים חֲלוּלִים חֲלוּלִים ...

Blessed are You, HaShem our God, King of the universe, Who formed man with wisdom, and created within him many openings and passageways, and cavities and hollows ...

"Bless God, my soul, and all that is within me bless His holy Name" (Psalms 103:1). This verse teaches us that when a person comes to bless God, he should be cleansed from waste matter. Therefore, upon rising, we wash our hands and expel our waste matter so that our bodies are as clean as could be before God (*Kitzur Shulchan Arukh* 3:7).

When we wash our hands and relieve ourselves upon wakening, we recite two blessings. The first is *Al Netillat Yadayim* (regarding the washing and elevation of the hands). The second is the *Asher Yatzar* blessing, which details the formation of the human body with its many orifices and ability to breathe in fresh air and expel waste matter. A top surgeon in New York City once remarked, "If I had to write about God's wonders, I would start with the *Asher Yatzar* blessing which details the incredible miracle of the human body." (By the way, the *Asher Yatzar* blessing is recited every time a person relieves himself throughout the day.)

The *Asher Yatzar* blessing concludes, "Blessed are You God, Healer of all flesh and Worker of wonders." The "wonders" we refer to here is the fact that both the physical and the spiritual coexist in the human body. Based on a lesson by Rebbe Nachman about the constant battle between the gravitational force and the countervailing force (LM I, 70:1), Reb Noson explains that here is a similar battle between the soul, which seeks its spiritual source, and the body, which is pulled towards the enticements of this world. Body and soul are in complete opposition to each other, but they can be made to work in tandem, similar to the gears of a watch that when they work against each other they make perfect time. One has to learn to nourish his soul at the same time he nourishes his body. Only when both parts work together, the human being can do wonderful things (LH, *Yom Tov* 5:7).

My Soul is Pure

אֱלֹהַי, נְשָׁמָה שֶׁנָּתַתָּ בִּי טְהוֹרָה הִיא:

My God, the soul You have placed within me is pure.

The third morning blessing begins, "God, the soul You have placed within me is pure." Because this blessing does not begin with the words "Blessed are You…" it is better to say it immediately following the *Asher Yatzar* blessing (*Berakhot* 60b).[36]

36 Several blessings begin with "Blessed are You, while others do not. The general law is if the blessing is juxtaposed to a previous blessing that begins with "Blessed are You…" then one does not have to begin this blessing with those words. He can begin praising God without the opening words.

This blessing is based on the verse, "He breathed into his nostrils a living soul" (Genesis 2:7). It speaks of the purity of the soul as God gave it, for He created it, formed it, gave it to man, and will reclaim it at a later date. Moreover, God will return our souls to us at the time of the resurrection of the dead. This blessing concludes with the phrase, "As long as we have our souls, we should praise God." As our Sages teach, "For every breath, we thank God!" (*Bereishit Rabbah* 14:9).

Morning Functions and Blessings: A Deeper Look

It may seem obvious that upon rising a person needs to perform certain bodily functions. So why is such importance placed on the washing and cleansing? The ARI writes, "Upon arising in the morning, a person should wash his hands, cleanse himself, then don the *tzitzit* and *tefillin*."[37] The preparations for prayer imply a deeper preparation for spiritual rectifications, which we will now discuss.

The Kabbalah teaches that there are four spiritual worlds,[38] in ascending order: *Asiyah*, *Yetzirah*, *Beriyah* and *Atzilut*. We begin our day with preparations and prayer, hoping to ascend to the highest level of which we are capable. To ascend and rectify these worlds through prayer, we must use our speech.[39] Since speech is on a higher level than action, we can use it to effect greater rectifications. The four levels of prayer are the *Korbonot* (sacrifices), corresponding to the world of *Asiyah*; *Pesukey d'Zimrah* (praises of God), corresponding to the world of *Yetzirah*; *Shema* and its blessings, paralleling the world of

37 *Shaar HaKavanot, Drushei Tefillat HaShachar* 2-3, p. 79*ff*.

38 See above, p. 24; also Appendix, p. 456.

39 See Appendix, p. 456, (Levels of Existence) that each world parallels action, speech or thought.

Beriyah, and the *Amidah* (*Shemoneh Esrei*), paralleling the world of *Atzilut.*

The ARI explains that cleansing our body and going about morning rituals are meant to take us through *Asiyah* and beyond into the higher worlds.

Asiyah refers to this world, where there are many *kelipot* (extraneous and waste matter). When we cleanse our bodies and wash our hands, we disperse these *kelipot.* In addition, we rectify the world of *Asiyah,* which corresponds to the *nefesh* (lower soul). When we don the *tzitzit,* we rectify the world of *Yetzirah,* which corresponds to the *ruach* (spirit). Putting on the arm-*tefillin* rectifies the world of *Beriyah,* which is a merit for the *neshamah* (upper soul). And laying the head-*tefillin* rectifies the world of *Atzilut,* which is the transcendental level of the soul, known as *Chayah.*[40] Thus, our morning routines have a great impact on our days.

One Hundred Blessings a Day

The Talmud teaches, "A person is obligated to say one hundred blessings every day, as it is written, "Now, Israel, *MaH,* what does HaShem your God ask of you?" (Deuteronomy 10:12; *Menachot* 43b). Rashi explains that the word *MaH* (מה, what) can be read as *Me'AH* (מאה, one hundred), teaching that God desires from us one hundred blessings daily. *Tosafot* adds that

40 The ARI (*Etz Chaim* 42:3) teaches that there are five levels to the soul. There is a *nefesh* (indwelling or lower soul), rooted in one's blood system, the base desires of a person. Then there is the *ruach* (spirit) rooted in the heart, which offers and leads the person's direction in life similar to "as the wind blows." Above that is the *neshamah* (divine soul), rooted in the brain, which has the ultimate control over the person's choices. These three are immanent. The next higher level, is *chayah* (living essence) which is transcendent to the person, indicating his life-force which comes from God. The highest level is *yechidah* (unique essence) which at that point the person is *achid* (joined together) with God. See *Anatomy of the Soul,* Chapter 3, for a fuller explanation.

the verse contains 99 letters. When we add the *aleph* in *Me'AH* it totals 100; hence, the obligation of one hundred blessings.

During King David's life there was a plague in which one hundred people died each day. No one knew the reason until King David discovered, with Divine inspiration, that they were lacking blessing and praising God. Therefore, he established the ritual of saying one hundred blessings per day (*Anaf Yosef*). Others opine that since 98 curses are found in Deuteronomy, these one hundred blessings supersede the curses (*Taamey HaMinhagim* #32).

The Morning Blessings

Our Sages instituted many blessings to say upon wakening, as the Talmud teaches:

> Upon hearing the rooster crow say, "Blessed are You... Who imbues the heart with understanding to distinguish between day and night." Upon opening the eyes say, "Blessed are You... Who gives sight to the blind." When stretching and sitting up say, "Blessed are You... Who releases the bound." When dressing say, "Blessed are You... Who clothes the naked..." (*Berakhot* 60b).

These twelve blessings are found in the section of the morning blessings. Included are an additional three blessings: "...Who has not made me a gentile," "...Who has not made me a slave," and "...Who has not made me a woman." Altogether, eighteen blessings are recited in the morning order (including for washing the hands, *Asher Yatzar* and *Elohi Neshamah*). The number eighteen is intentional. The ARI speaks about the *Chai* (18) blessings of prayer found in all four parts of the prayer. There are eighteen morning blessings, eighteen mentions of God's Name in the *Yehi Kavod* passage of *Pesukey d'Zimrah*, eighteen mentions of God's Name in the *Shema*, and the eighteen (original) benedictions of the *Amidah*. In practical terms, this means that at every level and in every circumstance (i.e., either in the mundane or if we are spiritually inclined) we can always find ways to connect to God and to bless Him. We can experience the *Chai* (18=life) and feel alive.

In addition, the ARI further teaches that the *sefirah* of *Yesod*, the *brit*, corresponds to *Chai HaOlamim*, the Life of the worlds (since *Yesod* collects all the higher energies from the *sefirot* above it and then sends the life-force into all the worlds below it). The objective in our prayers is to draw the blessings from the *Yesod*, from *Chai HaOlamim*, drawing God's life and light onto us.[41]

The morning blessings were established to thank God for the simple things we experience daily, yet rarely pay attention to. A person can use his eyes to see, a person can straighten out and stretch his limbs, he can place his feet on dry land, wear shoes, and so on. Each blessing is based on a verse in the Bible and is intended for us to become aware of all the good God does for us each day.

Let us look at these blessings in more detail.

בָּרוּךְ אַתָּה יְיָ אֱלֹהֵינוּ מֶלֶךְ הָעוֹלָם, הַנּוֹתֵן לַשֶּׂכְוִי בִינָה לְהַבְחִין בֵּין יוֹם וּבֵין לָיְלָה:

Blessed are You, HaShem our God, King of the universe, Who gives the heart understanding to distinguish between day and night.

The first blessing is "…Who gives the *sekhvi* (translated as either a heart or a rooster) understanding to distinguish between day and night." The rooster crows before dawn, waking us and telling us we should be attuned to the coming day and to take advantage of it. According to the translation that *sekhvi*

41 Cf. *Likutey Torah, Tehillim*, #132, p. 350.

is the heart, Reb Noson explains that we are thanking God for the ability to understand the difference between day and night, between light and darkness — which alludes to the ability to differentiate between truth and falsehood. It is practically impossible to clarify and prove the truth of Torah in this world because someone will always try to contradict it. Therefore, it's vitally important to know the truth in one's heart (*Likutey Halakhot Birkhot HaShachar* 3:11).

בָּרוּךְ אַתָּה יְיָ אֱלֹהֵינוּ מֶלֶךְ הָעוֹלָם, שֶׁלֹּא עָשַׂנִי גּוֹי:

Blessed are You, HaShem our God, King of the universe,
Who has not made me a gentile.

בָּרוּךְ אַתָּה יְיָ אֱלֹהֵינוּ מֶלֶךְ הָעוֹלָם, שֶׁלֹּא עָשַׂנִי עָבֶד:

Blessed are You, HaShem our God, King of the universe,
Who has not made me a slave.

איש מברך: בָּרוּךְ אַתָּה יְיָ אֱלֹהֵינוּ מֶלֶךְ הָעוֹלָם, שֶׁלֹּא עָשַׂנִי אִשָּׁה:

Men say: Blessed are You, HaShem our God, King of the universe,
Who has not made me a woman.

אשה מברכת: בָּרוּךְ אַתָּה יְיָ אֱלֹהֵינוּ מֶלֶךְ הָעוֹלָם, שֶׁעָשַׂנִי כִּרְצוֹנוֹ:

Women say: Blessed are You, HaShem our God, King of the universe, Who has made me according to His will.

The Talmud teaches (*Menachot* 43b) that each day a person should recite three blessings: "...Who has not made me a gentile," "...Who has not made me a slave," and "...Who has not made me a woman." The commentaries explain that the ascending order of these blessings is meant to show appreciation for the fact that as a Jew we have the right and ability to perform the *mitzvot*. A slave is considered higher than a gentile, for he is also commanded to perform some *mitzvot*. A woman certainly ranks higher because she born Jewish and is commanded in most *mitzvot*. However, because she is exempt from time-bound *mitzvot* (such as *tzitzit, tefillin, sukkah* and *lulav*), the man says the blessing that as a male, he is grateful to be able to perform *all* of the *mitzvot.*

A woman says the blessing, "...Who has made me according to His will." Some explain that since woman was the last being to be created, God's will was now complete. Others explain that, in a sense, these words are seen as "accepting the judgment," since a woman is considered subservient to her husband and exempt from time-bound *mitzvot.* The Talmud states that one who is commanded is greater than one who is not commanded (*Avodah Zarah* 3a). The subservience began from when Chavah ate from the Tree of Knowledge. Since she was the first person to sin, her status was changed from Adam's equal to lower.

These three blessings are formulated in the negative: "...Who has *not* made me..." This phrasing reflects a years-long debate that took place between Beis Shammai and Beis Hillel. Beis Shammai contended, "It is better for man not to have been created," while Beis Hillel contended, "It is better for man to have been created. They took a vote and decided, "It is better for man not to have been created—but now that he has been created, he should examine himself and his deeds" (*Eruvin* 13b). In essence, we are not thanking God for creating us as a man, a Jew, or a free person, because there is an opinion that it would be better had we not been created at all. Rather, now that we have been created, we thank God that we are at least not a gentile, or a slave.

The ARI questions if saying these blessings daily seems unnecessary. Since we've recited the blessing once, why is there a need to recite it again and again? The answer is a most incredible insight. In Heaven, there exists a "Chambers of Exchanges." In these Chambers, because of man's deeds, some of his qualities are exchanged for others. For example, people who have wealth can have their fortunes reversed for reasons unknown. People in power can lose their positions suddenly, or someone can suddenly find a fortune or win the lottery. This idea is alluded to in Rebbe Nachman's story of "The Exchanged Children."[42] The Prophet Isaiah says, "Woe to those who call evil, "good" and good, "evil." They change darkness into light and light into darkness; they change sour into sweet and sweet into sour" (Isaiah 5:20). Reb Noson explains that evil, darkness and sour remain evil, darkness and sour. And good, light and sweet will always remain good, light and sweet. But in the Chambers of Exchanges, people tend to see things differently and are likely to mix up opposing attributes. Also, many of the challenges and exchanges that a person endures are a result of the reincarnations of the souls, rooted in the Chamber of Exchanges. Likewise, these Chambers are the reason for all the strife and difficulties that the Jewish nation, as a whole, suffers due to the constant flux of exchanges that occur daily (*Likutey Halakhot Birkhot HaShachar* 3:3, 9, 11).[43]

The ARI explains that when a person deposits his soul with God at night when he goes to sleep, he expects his soul to be returned in the morning. The *kelipot* that work the Chambers of Exchanges try to stop this, but God returns the person's soul each day. So that when a person recites the blessing, "You have not made me a gentile, nor a slave," he realizes that it is his own soul that returns to him, and he praises God for saving him from the Chambers of Exchanges.

In line with this idea of the Chambers of Exchanges, we recite the other blessings. A sleeping person is likened to a lifeless

42 See full text of story in Appendix B.

43 There is a detailed explanation in *Zohar*, the ARI and other writings which discuss this "Chambers of Exchanges." Briefly, there is good and evil and when the forces of evil gain the upper hand then they can tip the balance in favor of evil and can force an innocent person to be subjected to their rule. This is the source of the innocent suffering while evil flourishes.

body; it is as if he is blind, naked, bound, bent, and so on. When he awakens, he wishes to emerge from those constrictions; hence, the need to repeat the blessings every morning anew (ibid. 3:13-14). To thank God for our souls not having been exchanged during the night, we say the blessings daily.

In his well-known lesson *Azamra* (LM I, 282), Rebbe Nachman stresses the importance of finding the good in ourselves. Rebbe Nachman urges each and every person to search for every little bit of good that they have, and to remember the good deeds they performed, because that will give them joy, encouragement and belief that they can do better.

When you don't think about your goodness, you become tired and don't believe you can do anything good in the world. When focusing on your good points, you are alert and ready to accomplish more.

Reb Noson says that this concept is hinted at in the morning blessings. The blessing "...Who gives the heart understanding to distinguish between day and night" means God granted us the wisdom to find the allegorical "day" — the good — in ourselves. The blessing "...Who has not made me a gentile" implies that if we don't think about our goodness, we are likely to fall to very low levels, and disregard *mitzvot*, God forbid. The blessings "...Who gives sight to the blind," "...Who releases the bound," and "...Who straightens those who are bent down" represent our thanking God for opening our eyes to let us see our goodness so we can stand erect and be freed from the captivity of the evil inclination, which makes us feel as if there is no hope for ourselves. The blessing "...Who gives strength to the weary" and the final blessing, "...Who removes the bonds of sleep from my eyes" mean that even when we feel completely spent due to our sins, we can awaken from our slumber and live a full life by focusing on the good things we accomplished in life.

Now we are ready to face the day and improve our lives (LH, *Hashkamat HaBoker* 1:11).

בָּרוּךְ אַתָּה יְיָ אֱלֹהֵינוּ מֶלֶךְ הָעוֹלָם, שֶׁעָשָׂה לִי כָּל צָרְכִּי:

Blessed are You, HaShem our God, King of the universe, Who has provided me with all my needs.

This blessing refers to wearing shoes. Why is wearing shoes catalogued as "...Who has provided me with *all* my needs"?

Reb Noson explains that everyone requires clothing to cover their body. Clothing represents the *chashmal,* the protective clothing for the soul, which originates in the highest of levels.[44] But the feet, which are adjacent to the earth, represent the lowest of levels and are the closest organs to the realm of impurity. Therefore, conceptually, the shoes are required to protect the feet from the forces of evil. In Hebrew, a shoe is called *Na'AL* (נעל), which shares the same root as *No'AL* (נועל, to close or lock). The shoes are meant to close off the forces of the Other Side and lock in the person with protection from the *kelipot.*

Chashmal is mentioned in Yechezkel's vision of the Chariot (Ezekiel 1:4). The word *Chashmal* is translated as an "electrum," which represents a range of colors. As the commentaries explain, *chashmal* is an angel of various colors which radiates light, more like the center of a burning fire, a focused type of light. The Kabbalists point out that the word *ChaShMaL* (חשמל) has the same numerical value (378) as *MaLBUSh* (מלבוש, clothing). In Kabbalah, the number 378 has great value in that it contains the 370 Lights of the Countenance of *Arikh Anpin,* one of the highest spiritual illuminations.[45] From that lofty

44 See Charts, Appendix A.

45 The missing "8" from the *gematria* refers to certain eight levels of compassion.

level comes protection for the person, which is why clothing offers protection for the person. This is especially so for the "feet," which need that protection more than everything else. Therefore, the Talmud teaches, "A person should sell even the beams from his house but make sure to buy shoes for his feet!" (*Shabbos* 129a).

Thus, when it says, "all my needs," they are indeed *all* a person's needs — since all of a person's needs are provided from Above and descend from the Light of the Countenance (LH, *Gittin* 4:10).

A very poor man once came to the Maharil[46] and said he would cease to recite this blessing. He complained that he had absolutely nothing, so how could he say, "...Who has provided me with all my needs"? The Maharil replied, "You have to read the blessing in the correct way. God knows you and your needs, yet He is providing you with very, very little. So read the blessing this way: Pause after the words, "provided me", and then continue, because whatever God provides, is "all your needs" according to His judgment!" (*Rabbi Eliyahu Chaim Rosen*).

וְאַל תְּבִיאֵנוּ לֹא לִידֵי חֵטְא, וְלֹא לִידֵי עֲבֵרָה וְעָוֹן, וְלֹא לִידֵי נִסָּיוֹן, וְלֹא לִידֵי בִזָּיוֹן:

Save us from being brought to inadvertent error or intentional transgressions. Save us from being tested or humiliated.

In this concluding blessing from the order of the morning blessings, we ask God to save us from sin — intentional or accidental — and from tests or humiliation. Rebbe Nachman once said, "Either a test, or else humiliation." When one fails a

46 Acronym for Rabbi Yaakov ben Moshe Moelin (1365-1427), Rav of Mainz, Germany.

test, he can suffer immense humiliation (*Rebbe Nachman's Wisdom* #304).

> יְהִי רָצוֹן מִלְּפָנֶיךָ, יְיָ אֱלֹהַי וֵאלֹהֵי אֲבוֹתַי, שֶׁתַּצִּילֵנִי הַיּוֹם וּבְכָל יוֹם ...
>
> May it be in accordance with Your will, HaShem, my God and God of my ancestors, to rescue me, today and every day...

The Talmud details various prayers that the Sages would add after reciting the *Amidah* (*Berakhot* 16b-17a). This paragraph after the blessings is from the prayer of Rabbi Yehudah HaNasi asking God to save us from all sorts of daily problems that arise. For the most part, these problems are due to actions among people we interact with on a daily basis.

CHAPTER 9

The Akeidah: Binding of Yitzchak

The story of the Binding of Yitzchak is discussed in many different tomes. How could God say to Avraham, "Sacrifice your son," when He knew the Jewish nation was due to emerge from Yitzchak? From our viewpoint, it doesn't make sense, yet this passage is said each and every day to "remind" God of His promise to bless Avraham and multiply his descendants. For thousands of years, the Jews have invoked this promise.

The verse states, "I will remember My covenant with Yaakov, and also My covenant with Yitzchak, and also My covenant with Avraham will I remember, and I will remember the Land" (Leviticus 26:42). Rashi asks why the verse doesn't use the word "remembering" when it mentions Yitzchak? He answers that it is because it says, "Yitzchak's ashes appear before Me, gathered up and placed on the altar." Though Yitzchak was not sacrificed, it is as if he were. Therefore, God is reminded of his sacrifice at all times. It is written that reciting the Binding of Yitzchak is a powerful protection for the Jewish nation from illness and disasters (cf. *Zohar* II, 214a).

The Hebrew word *Akeidah* translates as "binding." We begin the prayers each day with this passage of the Binding of Yitzchak (Genesis 22:1-19) to remind ourselves of the ideal to bind and connect our prayers together. Rebbe Nachman teaches that great tzaddikim bind their entire prayer and make it one. As they advance through the pages of the siddur, they don't forget the passages they said earlier. Even when they are at the final word, they are still bound with the first word of prayer.[47]

Yitzchak was offered as a *Korban olah*, literally, a "sacrifice of elevation." Because Yitzchak willingly sacrificed himself for God, he merited to be exalted before God. The same can be true of us. Reciting the *Akeidah* teaches us that by sacrificing ourselves, especially by praying with *kavanah*, we can elevate ourselves to greater levels.

Reb Nachman of Tcherin writes: The main blessings of peace and bounty are found in the Holy Land. Peace is the compound of two opposites, in our case, *Chesed* and *Gevurah*. They are opposite,[48] but when they combine, they bring the greatest blessings. Avraham represents *Chesed*; his attribute was kindness and love. Yitzchak represents *Gevurah*; it took great strength to offer himself as a sacrifice before God. Yitzchak thus represents fear and awe. The Binding of Yitzchak is actually a blend of *Chesed* (Avraham) together with *Gevurah* (Yitzchak). This represents the joining together of opposites, and binding brings peace. Additionally, reciting the Binding of Yitzchak—the willingness to sacrifice for God—leads to the revelation of the sanctity of the Land of Israel and a return of the Jews to their Land. This explains why that after reciting the *Akeidah*, we say many verses about God having compassion on us and returning us to the Land (*Zimrat Ha'aretz* I, 79).

Although we recognize that all our spiritual and material success is from God and praise God for them, we aren't satisfied because we need so much more salvation for our spiritual and

47 LM I, 65:2; LH, *Arvit* 4:16.
48 See Charts, Appendix A.

physical wellbeing. We constantly pray and strive for more.

Reb Noson writes:

> Come see what is written in the passage of the *Akeidah* about Avraham: "On the third day, Avraham looked up and saw the place from afar." What did Avraham see? The Midrash states that Avraham, who was a prophet, saw "the place"—the place of the Beis HaMikdash. He foresaw that his descendants would serve God on that mount, and he saw the greatness to which the Jewish kingdom would ascend. Yet here he was, some one thousand years prior to his vision, taking his only child to that same mount to sacrifice him before God! Yet Avraham did not challenge God. He accepted the command despite his inability to reconcile his vision.
>
> This is how it is for every person in regard to spirituality and material needs. A person is far away from his ultimate perfection, yet he is still standing at a distance.
>
> While it is important to be aware of all the kindness God has given to us until now (in both the material and spiritual realms) and to be thankful, simultaneously, it is important to be aware that we still need much more salvation to reach our goal. This double focus (i.e., on the good we have, plus the long path ahead of us) gives us strength to endure and to be strong until we merit a complete salvation.
>
> On one hand, if we focus solely on our success, we will not strive and pray for more. On the other hand, if we ignore our success and salvation, and focus on how distant we are, we will fall into despair. The combination of both focuses enables us to continue striving and praying, until we will eventually attain the complete salvation (LH, *Shiluach HaKen* 5:2).

We are Your People

אֲבָל אֲנַחְנוּ עַמְּךָ בְּנֵי בְרִיתֶךָ, בְּנֵי אַבְרָהָם ... זֶרַע יִצְחָק ...
עֲדַת יַעֲקֹב ...

But we are Your people, children of Your covenant.
Descendants of Avraham ... descendants of Yitzchak ...
community of Yaakov ...

The next portion of prayer after the *Akeidah* is "But we are Your people." It opens with the words, "A person should always be God fearing." The commentaries explain that fear of Heaven is paramount to serving God. The *Shulkhan Arukh* states that everything a person does should be for the sake of Heaven (*Orach Chaim* 231:1). When we serve God with fear and awe, the service assumes a greater level of devotion toward Him. The passage states that we realize we are not worthy of serving such a great God. What merits do we have to pray and ask for help and salvation? What are we? What is our life worth? What are our values? What makes us different from animals? What value is our service? This passage denigrates us. In a way, it is meant to rid us of arrogance and yet recognize our capabilities.

The passage continues, "But we are Your people," and then speaks of our great worth as the descendants of the Patriarchs. In other words, though as individuals we might not be considered worthy of having our prayers answered, we still have great worth and importance in God's eyes since we are the descendants of Avraham, Yitzchak and Yaakov.

Rebbe Nachman once said that when reciting *psalms,* a person should have in mind that each psalm refers to himself, finding himself in each and every chapter. When asked how one does this, the Rebbe briefly explained that when the text describes how King David entreats God to save him in battle, each person should apply these verses to themselves, referring to their battle against the evil inclination. As for the verses in which King David praises himself—for example, "Guard my soul, for I am devout" (Psalms 86:2)—one should apply the principle of judging himself favorably. He must find in himself some merit and good points, which demonstrate that he is considered devout.

The Rebbe added, "Do we not say at the start of the morning, 'What are we? What is our life?' We belittle ourselves a great deal. Then we say, 'Nevertheless, we are Your people, children of Your covenant.' Afterwards we encourage and boost ourselves and speak of our greatness. We pride ourselves in being His people, children of His covenant, and the descendants of Avraham, Yitzchak and Yaakov. This is how we need to conduct ourselves in the service of God" (LM II, 125).

How Fortunate We Are

אַשְׁרֵינוּ כְּשֶׁאָנוּ מַשְׁכִּימִים וּמַעֲרִיבִים בְּבָתֵּי כְנֵסִיּוֹת וּבְבָתֵּי מִדְרָשׁוֹת ...

How fortunate we are that we rise early in the morning and stay late in the synagogues and study halls in the evening...

The *Zohar* (III, 196a) teaches that until the Jews gather in the synagogues, the Other Side (i.e., the forces of evil or the *kelipot*) wander the earth. However, the prayers stand up against the forces of evil. When the Jews pray, the "windows" of Heaven open, and intense spiritual light rests upon the synagogues, conquering the *kelipot*.

The *Shema* of the Sacrifices

שְׁמַע יִשְׂרָאֵל יְיָ אֱלֹהֵינוּ יְיָ אֶחָד:

Hear O Israel! HaShem is our God. HaShem is One.

The ARI writes that a person should recite the *Shema* four times a day. There is the *Shema* of the sacrifices, the *Shema* during the morning prayer, the *Shema* of the evening prayer, and the *Shema* before retiring at night. Each instance has a very deep Kabbalistic reason regarding the unifications

Above that are generated when we say the *Shema*.

Before fighting Goliath, David took five stones. The midrash says that these stones merged into one stone. Similarly, the *Shema* has six words. The first word, *shema,* means "listen." We are to listen carefully to what we say next. The next few words are "HaShem is our God" and the final word is "One." These five words of the *Shema* gave David victory over Goliath (*Zohar* III, 272a). Thus, reciting the *Shema* brings about closeness to God.

The Torah teaches us how we should behave and guides us how to pull away from the grip of the evil inclination. The problem is that due to sin, our minds don't think straight. Thus, a person can receive counsel from the Torah, expounded on by tzaddikim, and he could nevertheless construe the ideas and misunderstand them. Since his mind is impaired, it distorts the truth, and he understands the concepts improperly. At this point the ideas will harm him more than help him. As the Talmud states, "If one is not deserving, the Torah becomes a potion of death for him" (*Yoma* 72b).

The *Shema* and the sacrifices are the rectification, as they are both about receiving the ideas of Torah in the correct, beneficial way. The *Shema,* which proclaims our faith in God, rectifies the mind, while the sacrifices are the descent of bounty. The Torah ideas from Above in a packaged, protected way can never be ruined or misconstrued. With the combination of these two, we can draw light, blessing and the necessary advice which we need to succeed in life, and merit repentance (LH, *Kriat Shema* 4:14). Furthermore, reciting the *Akeidah* instills in us a sense of self-sacrifice, a willingness to give of ourselves for God. This strengthens our faith in God, which is why the *Shema* is said immediately following the passage of the *Akeidah* (LH, *Hefker V'Nikhsei HaGer* 4:9).

The *Shema* is followed by two paragraphs praising God, which assert the power and majesty of His kingdom. For when we affirm our faith, God's kingdom is revealed. To the degree that we engage in articulating His kingdom, the more widespread it becomes, and the more people return to accepting His rulership. This concept aligns with the recital of the sacrifices because the sacrifices are meant to elevate the sparks of holiness which are found in this world of *Asiyah*. These sparks correspond to the souls who have wandered far from God, and the souls of converts which eventually find their way back to God.

CHAPTER 10

Korbanot: The Sacrifices

צַו אֶת אַהֲרֹן וְאֶת בָּנָיו לֵאמֹר זֹאת תּוֹרַת הָעֹלָה הִוא הָעֹלָה:

Instruct Aharon and his sons saying, "This is the Torah of the burnt-offering."

The Talmud teaches, "'Whoever engages in the Torah study of the offerings, it is as if he brought those sacrifices himself" (*Menachot* 110a).

The different types of sacrifices comprise of offerings from the four levels of physical reality: *domem* (inanimate), the mineral level; *tzomei'ach* (vegetative), the plant kingdom; *chai* (living), the animal kingdom; and *medaber* (speaking), humanity. The idea behind our recital of these offerings is *birur nitzotzot,* the extraction, refinement, elevation and redemption of the sparks of holiness, which are found in all the above levels of reality. This *birur* is what the entire system of Torah and *mitzvot* is about. This is what our prayer, Torah learning, and character refinement and development is all about. In everything we do, our intention is to raise up the sparks of holiness. This job will finally be completed during the era of the Third *Beis HaMikdash.*

As mentioned previously, one should give charity prior to offering his prayers. Rebbe Nachman teaches that charity is akin to a spirit from Above which descends and cools off a person's avarice (LM I, 13:1). Reb Noson writes that the sacrifices brought in the Temple were considered *nidvat lev* (a contribution of the heart), which is akin to charity. Thus, by giving charity, we can rectify our passions for the material and elevate them to a higher level. Therefore, we recite the sacrifices as we begin our prayers (see LH, *Tefillah* 4:19).

Animals as Sacrifices

Why does a person have to bring an animal and slaughter it as a sacrifice? What does this accomplish?

Humans are expected—as well as commanded—to act appropriately. The human brain is capable of knowing what's right and what's wrong, and man is expected to choose the right path. Sin is a subhuman level; only a lower being would act in such a manner. Therefore, when a person errs or sins, he descends from the human level to the animal level. But when he brings a sacrifice, he is admitting to God, "I acted wrongly. I allowed myself to leave my standing and descend to a lower realm. At this point, I regret my wrongful deeds. I offer this animal as a replacement for me and wish to ascend back to my rightful level" (LM I, 25:2).

וְעָרַךְ עָלֶיהָ הָעֹלָה וְהִקְטִיר עָלֶיהָ חֶלְבֵי הַשְּׁלָמִים:

He shall arrange the *olah* upon it, as well as burn the choicest parts of the peace offerings on it.

The most important part of the sacrifices was the fats of the animal that were placed upon the altar. Why the fats? Why on the Altar?

The world is filled with good. This is especially so when we consider the good deeds that we perform. But what happens when one attempts to be good and doesn't succeed? His goals are thwarted. For example, the Roman Empire decreed that the Jews were not permitted to keep Shabbos, nor were they permitted to circumcise their sons (*Me'ilah* 17b). Those *mitzvot*, which were prevented from being done, were captured by the forces of evil and imprisoned under their rule. How can that good be released? Rebbe Nachman explains that the captured good will eventually emerge in future generations. The descendants of the evil people who captured the good will convert and accept the true faith in God. In this way, the captured good will emerge.

The *Zohar* (II, 139a) explains that the altar parallels *Malkhut*. A blemished *Malkhut* represents a blemished altar. A blemished altar occurs when people are not serving God. When converts accept God, they are "repairing the altar," for they are the sparks of holiness that are elevated to God through their acceptance of faith in God (LM I, 17:4-6).

Reb Noson applies this idea to the sacrifices. The fats placed on the altar are called *cheilev*, which also means "choice or good." Thus, the fats represent the "captured good." When the fats are placed on the altar, it represents the elevation of those sparks, the repair and rectification of the captured good which is released from its imprisonment (LH, *Cheilev v'Dam* 3:1-3).

The Laver

וַיְדַבֵּר יְיָ אֶל מֹשֶׁה לֵּאמֹר: וְעָשִׂיתָ כִּיּוֹר נְחֹשֶׁת וְכַנּוֹ נְחֹשֶׁת לְרָחְצָה:

HaShem spoke to Moshe, saying, "Make a copper laver with its own copper base."

We begin the section of the sacrifices mentioning the copper laver from which the *Kohanim* were required to wash their hands and feet before serving in the *Beis*

HaMikdash. The idea behind washing from the laver is to attain purity. This is the reason that many chassidim immerse in the *mikvah* prior to praying. The Baal Shem Tov once remarked, "There is no special mitzvah to immerse in the *mikvah* [aside from the required times specified in Torah] yet immersing in the *mikvah* can bring a person to greater levels than many devotions" (*Rabbi Eliyahu Chaim Rosen*).

Terumat HaDeshen: Removal of the Ashes

וּפָשַׁט אֶת בְּגָדָיו וְלָבַשׁ בְּגָדִים אֲחֵרִים וְהוֹצִיא אֶת הַדֶּשֶׁן
אֶל מִחוּץ לַמַּחֲנֶה אֶל מָקוֹם טָהוֹר:

He shall then remove his garments, don other garments, and remove the ashes to a pure place outside the camp.

Terumat HaDeshen, the removal of the accumulated ashes from the altar prior to beginning the new day's sacrifices, was the first devotion performed in the morning in the *Beis HaMikdash*. This passage also speaks about the fire on the altar, which must be kept burning continually; it must never be extinguished. The fire on the altar parallels the work of the digestive tract, "burning" the ingested food in our stomachs. Removing the ashes of yesterday's offerings from the altar each morning parallels relieving oneself by emptying one's bowels before consuming new food.

Reb Noson points out that the real nourishment we get from food comes from the spiritual life-force within the food. The physical aspect of the food, in contrast, turns into *pesolet* (waste) and must be eliminated from the body. The pure, spiritual aspect of the food corresponds to the Torah, while the physical aspect corresponds to foreign wisdoms. It is imperative that we begin by eliminating the *pesolet*—corresponding to the foreign wisdoms that foster atheism — before we ingest the pure teachings of the Torah, lest the foreign wisdoms latch on to the spiritual aspect in the food (LH, *Hashkamat HaBoker* 4:9).

Olat Tamid: The Daily Sacrifice

וַיְדַבֵּר יְיָ אֶל מֹשֶׁה לֵּאמֹר: צַו אֶת בְּנֵי יִשְׂרָאֵל וְאָמַרְתָּ אֲלֵהֶם, אֶת קָרְבָּנִי... תִּשְׁמְרוּ לְהַקְרִיב לִי בְּמוֹעֲדוֹ:

HaShem spoke to Moshe, saying, "Instruct the children of Israel and tell them: Be careful to present My offering ... at its appointed times."

This is the source for the commandment to bring two sacrifices daily, one in the morning and one in the afternoon. It is called *olat tamid* (a perpetual elevation offering). It is called "My offering" because as opposed to the other sacrifices which are meant to forgive for sins or to spread peace between people, this daily sacrifice represents *Chesed*, God's lovingkindness. In addition, it is meant to invoke God's blessing from Him directly for this world.

> Take with you words and return to God; say to Him, "Forgive all sins and receive us [i.e., our good deeds], and let the offering of our lips replace the oxen" (Hosea 14:3).

The Midrash states that the Jews said to God, "When the *Beis HaMikdash* stood we would bring sacrifices and be forgiven. Today, all we have is our prayers in place of the oxen [sacrifices]" (*Bamidbar Rabbah* 18:21). Thus, our Sages teach that prayers were instituted to replace the sacrifices (see *Berakhot* 26b). When we say the verses of the sacrifices, it is as if we actually bring the sacrifices.

When the *Beis HaMikdash* stood, a daily offering (*tamid*) was brought in the *Beis HaMikdash* twice each day: the morning *tamid* was the first sacrifice brought upon the altar, and the afternoon *tamid* was the final sacrifice of the day. Rashi explains that the morning *tamid* sought forgiveness for nighttime sins, and the afternoon *tamid* sought forgiveness for daytime sins (Rashi on Isaiah 1:21). Rebbe Nachman elaborates that the Jewish people's innate spirituality and their great refinement make it impossible for them to bear the burden of sin for even a single day. Therefore, they needed the *Beis HaMikdash* to atone for them daily. Sadly, with the destruction of the *Beis HaMikdash*, this opportunity was lost.

In place of the daily offerings, the Sages instituted the daily prayers (*Berakhot* 26b). *Shacharit* (the morning prayer) is in place of the morning *tamid*, and *Minchah* (the afternoon prayer) is in place of the afternoon *tamid*. The *Tur* (*Orach Chaim* 237) suggests that the reason we preface *Maariv* (the evening prayer) with the verse "He Who is merciful will forgive sin" (Psalms 78:38) is in case a person has sinned in the interim between late afternoon and nightfall. One begins with this prayer in order to effect forgiveness for any wrongdoing during the interval of time not covered by either of the daily offerings.[49]

In *Shaar HaKavanot*,[50] the ARI writes that one function of the daily offering is to elevate the sparks of holiness which reside in the world of *Asiyah*. He emphasizes that the *Korbanot* purify the dimension of *Asiyah*. It is for this reason that we begin our prayers with the *Korbanot*, specifically in the section of *Shacharit* during which we rectify and elevate the dimension of *Asiyah*. Notwithstanding, the *Zohar* (III, 26b) says, "*Siluka d'Korbana ad Ein Sof*," meaning that the elevation of the *Korbanot* goes all the way up to infinity. That is, the

49 LM II, 7:11, and note 183 there.

50 *Tefillat HaShachar, drush aleph; drush gimel.*

Korbanot elevate not only the world of *Asiyah* but contribute to the elevation of the worlds of *Yetzirah, Beriyah,* and *Atzilut* as well. The *Zohar* adds, "*Ein Sof* is the concept of *ratzon Shebiretzonot, Raava d'Raavin*"—the all-inclusive will of all wills, the desire that includes all desires.

The purpose of the *Korbanot* is the purification and refinement of *Asiyah.* The only way this can be accomplished is by shining the light of the supernal *ratzon* all the way down into *Asiyah,* to the extent that we merit to feel a powerful *ratzon* (desire) to serve God even down here in midst of the thick darkness of *Asiyah.* In this way, *Asiyah* becomes incorporated back into its source in the supernal *ratzon.* Since *Asiyah*—the lowest and most obscure dimension—becomes incorporated in the supernal *ratzon,* all the worlds above it automatically become incorporated in *Raava d'Raavin* as well (LH, *Choshen Mishpat, Arev* 3:24).

The word *OLAT* (עולת, offering) has the same letters as *TOLA* (תולע, worm). The nature of a worm is to consume everything in its path. According to the ARI, each morning the spiritual equivalent of a worm—representing the forces of evil—attempts to devour and destroy everything in the entire world.[51] Therefore, we recite the passage of the *olat tamid,* which has the power to counter this impure "worm." This daily offering represents loving kindness, the exact opposite of evil. In *Likutey Moharan* (I, 28), Rebbe Nachman extends this idea to practicing *Chesed* in our daily lives (especially hosting Torah scholars in our homes), which protects us from the perverted teachings of false and unworthy leaders and acts to strengthen our faith.

51 *Pri Eitz Chaim, Shaar Olam HaAsiyah* 3, pp. 115-116.

Facing North

וְשָׁחַט אֹתוֹ עַל יֶרֶךְ הַמִּזְבֵּחַ צָפֹנָה לִפְנֵי יְיָ:

He shall slaughter it near the base of the Altar, on the north side of the Courtyard, before HaShem.

We say this verse after the daily offering. North in Hebrew is *TzaFON* (צפון). This is a reference to the "ashes of Yitzchak," which are *TzaFUN* (צפון, hidden) before God. Our recital of the daily offering is an additional reminder of the Binding of Yitzchak, which arouses Heavenly compassion upon us.

Furthermore, during prayer man is said to be facing east, from whence the sun rises. Thus, his right side corresponds to the south, his back is to the west and his left side corresponds to the north. According to the Kabbalah, the right side represents *Chesed* / Lovingkindness and the left side represents *Gevurah* / Judgments. When we slaughter the sacrifice while facing north, we are reflecting the idea that we are in control of the judgments and are subduing them to the forces of kindness.

The *Ketoret*: An Incense Offering

אַתָּה הוּא יְיָ אֱלֹהֵינוּ שֶׁהִקְטִירוּ אֲבוֹתֵינוּ לְפָנֶיךָ אֶת קְטֹרֶת הַסַּמִּים בִּזְמַן שֶׁבֵּית הַמִּקְדָּשׁ הָיָה קַיָּם:

You are He, HaShem our God, before whom our ancestors burned the incense compound when the Beis HaMikdash stood.

The *Zohar* speaks of the greatness of the *Ketoret* (the incense offering) and how much it rectifies. Although all the sacrifices are special in God's eyes, the *Ketoret* brings the greatest amount of pleasure to Him (*Zohar* III, 58b). Reciting the passage of the *Ketoret* has the power to ward off death and plagues (ibid. I, 100b). One who makes the effort to recite the *Ketoret* with *kavanah* merits the World to Come (*Zohar Chadash, Shir HaShirim* 83a). Nothing in the world can parallel the power of the *Ketoret* to defeat the Other Side (*Zohar* III, 218b).

Essentially, the *Ketoret* is meant to descend into the realm of the *kelipot* and elevate the sparks of holiness that are trapped there. Furthermore, the smoke that rises from the *Ketoret* "burns" the *kelipot* from the path, so that our prayers have a smooth path to travel toward heaven (see *Zohar* II, 219a).

The *Ketoret* consisted of eleven spices or perfumes. These spices were ground separately and then blended together into a special mixture to be used in the *Mishkan* and, later, the *Beis HaMikdash*. The Talmud states that ten of these spices had pleasant fragrances, while the eleventh spice, *chelbenah* (galbanum), had an unpleasant odor. Why, then, was the galbanum included?

The Talmud teaches that a congregation is not complete unless it includes both righteous people and sinners (*Keritot* 6b). In other words, just as the galbanum is necessary to give the other spices exactly the right pungency, so too, a congregation is not complete without someone who has fallen and who must re-elevate himself through *teshuvah* (repentance). The *Ketoret* teaches us that even the most "evil-smelling" person (or the evil-smelling part of each of us) can be rectified through *teshuvah*.

The word *KeToRet* (קטורת, incense offering) has the same root as *KaTaR* (קטר, bind). The *Zohar* speaks of the *Ketoret* as binding all the worlds together, for it begins with the lowest levels of this world and ascends all the way up to God Himself. The eleven spices of the *Ketoret* correspond to the holy lights (*sefirot*) that are trapped in and give life to the *kelipot*. Our intention in reciting the passage of the *Ketoret* is to extricate these lights from their entrapment and elevate them. The *Zohar* concludes that one who recites the *Ketoret* passage daily will be protected from all evil and suffer no harm (see *Zohar* II, 218b). Were we to know the power of just reciting the *Ketoret*, we would adorn each letter with golden crowns.

Together, the *tamid* (daily offering) and the *Ketoret* play a significant role in elevating the sparks of holiness. The daily offering elevates the sparks from this world of *Asiyah*, but only for those that have not fallen into the realm of impurity. The *Ketoret* descends further into the realm of impurity and extracts the sparks from there.

The ARI comments on the order of the prayers: the passage of the *tamid* precedes that of the *Ketoret*. He explains that it is precisely through the *tamid* that we elevate and redeem the holy life force from the world of *Asiyah*. As a result of this elevation, every level is elevated to the level above it. Then, as each sub-level of *Asiyah* is refined and elevated, each corresponding sub-level of *Yetzirah*, *Beriyah* and *Atzilut* is elevated as well. In other words, the ultimate elevation is activated by *our* work below, and the effect reaches all the way up to the heavens. While still working down in *Asiyah* (i.e., by reciting the *Ketoret*), we elevate sparks of holiness from the depths of the *kelipot*, to have them ascend from the lower levels of *Asiyah*. Following this, all the other worlds become elevated as well.[52]

52 *Shaar HaKavanot, Tefillat HaShachar, Drush Gimel*, p. 87.

CHAPTER 11

The Power of the Ketoret

The Talmud teaches, "The people of Israel were exiled and dispersed among the nations only in order to draw converts" (*Pesachim* 87b). Who are these converts? It is based on the verse, "Not with you alone I am making this covenant... but with those who are standing here with us [physically] today... and with those who are not here with us [physically] today" (Deuteronomy 29:13-14). The Talmud explains that the souls of future converts stood at Mount Sinai to receive the Torah as well (*Shabbos* 146a).

Exile is a punishment for the Jewish people not having fulfilled their mission of being a light unto the nations while living in their Land. But there is a deeper reason for exile. One way or another, Israel must illuminate the world with the light of Torah, to make God's name known throughout the world, and retrieve these kindred souls. Ideally, this light would shine forth from the *Beis HaMikdash*, as it is written, "Torah will go forth from Zion and God's word from Jerusalem" (Isaiah 2:3, Mikhah 4:2). When we failed to illuminate the darkness of the world from the *Beis HaMikdash*, God's light was splintered into millions of tiny sparks — the Jewish people in exile — and dispersed to almost every corner of the world. Now all the fallen sparks that were strewn everywhere throughout the world must be gathered back to their source in holiness. These sparks are the souls of the Jewish people and of the converts. It is the function of the *Ketoret* to gather in these sparks.

The Ascent of the Worlds

The *Ketoret* is meant to infiltrate into the realm of the Other Side and elevate the sparks of holiness found therein. This also initiates the ascent of the *sefirot* to the higher realms and is a process that continues throughout the prayers. To understand this concept, consider the following Kabbalistic insight.

Malkhut ("Authority") is known as the "outpost" of the realm of holiness. As the lowest *sefirah,* it borders on and acts like an interface between the realm of holiness and the realm of evil. Any blemish in *Malkhut* allows the *kelipot* to draw sustenance from it. Since *Malkhut* is the authority when they draw nourishment from it, it empowers the forces of evil to cause damage, both physically and spiritually. On the other hand, because of the proximity of *Malkhut* to the realm of evil, it is the only *sefirah* that can descend into the realm of evil and impurity to gather up the sparks of holiness that fell into those places.

When *Malkhut* ascends from that realm and rises to higher levels, it causes the levels above *Malkhut* to rise to even higher levels. To visualize this, recall that the *sefirot* are in a three-column structure and are best imagined as a human body.[53] *Malkhut* represents the feet, and the next level above it corresponds to the legs. These are alluded to in *Netzach, Hod* and *Yesod* (right and left legs, and genital area). When *Malkhut* ascends, these three *sefirot* also ascend to the next level, which is *Chesed, Gevurah* and *Tiferet* (right and left arms, and torso). When these levels ascend, they rise to the higher levels of *Chokhmah, Binah* and *Daat* (head, brain and intellect), known in Kabbalah by the acrostic *ChaBaD.*

When we reach the top, where do we go from here? As the ARI explains, these ascents all take place in the World of *Asiyah.*

53 See Charts, Appendix A.

Since we've reached the highest level of *Asiyah*, we now enter a new world, the World of *Yetzirah*. What is the bottom level of *Yetzirah*? *Malkhut*. So we begin again. The *ChaBaD* of *Asiyah* ascends into the *Malkhut* of *Yetzirah*. As we progress in our prayers we keep going up, entering the World of *Beriyah* and then the World of *Atzilut*. This is one of the important ideas to remember when praying: there are four parts to the prayers. The *Korbanot* corresponding to *Asiyah*; the *Pesukey d'Zimrah* to *Yetzirah*; the *Shema* to *Beriyah*; and the *Amidah* to *Atzilut*.

The process of ascending all the way to the highest world, the World of *Atzilut*, begins with our reciting the *tamid* and the *Ketoret*.

The Spirit of Generosity

There are other benefits to reciting the *tamid* and *Ketoret*. One of the primary benefits of the *Ketoret* is that it counters avarice. Rebbe Nachman teaches that when people worship money, they forget that their livelihood comes from God. This rouses God's anger. As our Sages say, "As long as there is idol worship in the world, [God's] anger is in the world" (cf. *Sifri* 13:18). The passion for money is comparable to idol worship. Rebbe Nachman teaches that if we abolish this form of idol worship, God's anger will be removed from the world. Then God will lead the world with revealed Divine providence.

How does one overcome this strong passion for money? Rebbe Nachman says the solution is charity. As the *Zohar* (III, 224a) teaches, "A *ruach* (spirit) descends to alleviate the burning of the heart." Rebbe Nachman explains that this *ruach* is the spirit of generosity, which allays and calms the passion for wealth (LM I, 13:1).

The *Ketoret*, too, shatters avarice, because the translation of *Ketoret* is "to bind." The *Ketoret* binds the heart to the spirit of generosity and charity. King Solomon writes, "Incense makes the heart rejoice" (Proverbs 27:9). Rebbe Nachman explains that *Ketoret* binds the heart's burning with its cooling spirit. The Talmud adds that the *Ketoret* brings great wealth to the one who offers it on the Altar (*Yoma* 26a), because true wealth is being satisfied with one's lot. This is the quality of the *Ketoret*: it makes a person happy, since he is content with what he has.

The Mystery of the Eleven Spices of the *Ketoret*

Rebbe Nachman teaches that when a person conducts his business activities honestly, it is compared to bringing the *tamid* (daily offering) and burning the *Ketoret* (LM I, 35:8). For a better understanding, consider the following general overview of the prayers and then a more specific introduction to the *tamid* and *Ketoret*. Though we discussed this concept previously, some ideas are explained here in greater detail.[54]

Shacharit, the morning prayer, consists of four main sections: the *Korbanot* (sacrifices), *Pesukey d'Zimrah* (psalms), *Shema* and its blessings, and the *Amidah*. The Kabbalah teaches that these four sections correspond to the four worlds: *Asiyah, Yetzirah, Beriyah* and *Atzilut,* respectively. We begin the morning prayer at the bottom level of existence, in the lowest world, the World of *Asiyah*. This corresponds to man's basic, animalistic desires. We recite the passages of the sacrifices as an offering to God of our basic desires and as an expression of our desire to ascend above our materialistic yearnings.

After completing the *Korbanot,* we begin reciting the *Pesukey d'Zimrah,* psalms of thanksgiving and praise of God. At this point, we ascend from *Asiyah* (the World of Action), into *Yetzirah* (the World of Formation). *Yetzirah* is the angelic

54 Familiarity with several of the Appendix charts, specifically the Structure of the *Sefirot* and the Levels of Existence, will enhance the reader's understanding of the Kabbalistic teachings relating to this section.

world; just as the angels continually proclaim God's praises, we joyously recite the *Pesukey d'Zimrah* in honor of His glory.

We continue our progression through the spiritual worlds by next reciting the *Shema* in *Beriyah* (the World of Creation), and the *Amidah,* while standing before God, in *Atzilut* (the World of Nearness). The remainder of the morning prayer, and in particular the *Tachanun* prayer, is known as *yeridat hashefa,* guiding the descending bounty which comes from God in response to our prayers.

The *Korbanot* correspond to *Malkhut,* the lowest level of holiness, which must be elevated to the highest level, *Chokhmah,* corresponding to the World of *Atzilut.* In this sense, praying *Shacharit* parallels the act of repentance (i.e., returning a thing to where it has been taken from by returning *Malkhut* to its root in *Chokhmah.*) Then, through the completion of the prayer, new vitality (i.e., a renewal of the soul) is drawn from *Chokhmah* down to *Malkhut.*

The daily offering of an animal in the *Beis HaMikdash* signifies the elevation of man's basic, materialistic desires to the higher level of spiritual yearning for Godliness. Today, our reciting the passage of the *tamid* replaces our forefathers bringing this sacrifice in the *Beis HaMikdash.* Rebbe Nachman teaches that man's intellect parallels the *Beis HaMikdash* (see *Berakhot* 33a). In this sense, the *tamid* is likened to elevating one's aspect of *Malkhut* / faith to *Chokhmah.* But man's faith needs protection from the *kelipot*! This is the mystery of burning the *Ketoret,* which was also part of the service in the *Beis HaMikdash* and is now part of the *Korbanot* section of *Shacharit.*

The Kabbalah states that just as there are ten *sefirot* of holiness, there are ten levels of impurity. However, impurity cannot exist without a spark of Godliness, i.e., holiness, which gives it vitality. Hence the *kelipot* draw nourishment from the devolvement of the *sefirot.* This is represented in the eleven spices of the *Ketoret,* which correspond to the ten levels of impurity and a single spark of holiness. By burning the *Ketoret,* we burn away the power of the *kelipot,* leaving them with only just enough sustenance to exist.

The reason for prolonging the existence of the *kelipot* has to do with God's desire that there be free will in the world. The presence of the *kelipot* ensures that a balance is maintained between good and evil, for a predominance of either would result in man's free will being negated. Only when the world attains a state of perfection, (i.e., when the *Mashiach* comes), will good outweigh evil and free will be deemed unnecessary.

Though all wisdom stems from *Chokhmah,* the more removed it is from true *Chokhmah,* the more likely it is to evolve into extraneous wisdoms. This is why it is important that faith be attached to true *Chokhmah* (choosing to have faith in God rather than in transient beliefs). But when people fall victim to extraneous wisdoms which lead to falsehood, foolishness and sin, they fall into the realm of the *kelipot* and are at the mercy of the forces of evil. Their souls are called "sparks of holiness." They are rooted in *Chokhmah*/holiness, but because they have succumbed to the *kelipot* they have become only sparks of their former selves. Nevertheless, through repentance, they can be rectified and elevated to true wisdom. This is the purpose of the *Ketoret,* to elevate these fallen sparks from the realm of the *kelipot* into *Malkhut,* the lowest level of holiness, so that they too can ascend to *Chokhmah* and renew their souls.

Rebbe Nachman states that when a person engages in honest business practices — business activity being an aspect of knowing and fulfilling monetary law — he is occupied with the Torah according to its plain meaning. This is akin to bringing the daily offering and burning the incense. For by means of the daily offering, *Chokhmah, Binah* and *Daat* (*ChaBaD*) of the World of *Asiyah* ascend into the World of *Yetzirah,* and all the holy sparks within the *kelipot* ascend into the aspect of faith / *Malkhut of Yetzirah.*

At the same time, all the sparks of holiness that are among the nations surrounding Jerusalem also ascend, for the destruction of faith is considered the destruction of Jerusalem. As the Talmud expounds, "Jerusalem was destroyed only once it no longer had any men of faith" (*Shabbos* 119b).[55] But according to the Torah's plain meaning, when Jerusalem (which represents faith) gains strength, then these nations will fall. And all the holy sparks within them will ascend in the mystery of the eleven spices of the *Ketoret.*

The *Ketoret*: Serving God with Joy

Rebbe Nachman stresses the importance of bringing joy into one's life. He teaches that being joyous is the most difficult of devotions.[56] At the same time, he also teaches that lacking joy leads to depression, the worst affliction a person might suffer (cf. LM I, 189). The *Ketoret* offering enables a person to experience joy on a very high level. How does this work?

Rebbe Nachman explains this concept by correlating the *Shekhinah,* the *mitzvot,* and the heart of a Jew. The *Shekhinah* is an aspect of the *mitzvot* and is represented by the heart. When a person is sad, this means the *Shekhinah* / the heart is caught between the *kelipot,* which represent sorrow and sadness. When a person performs *mitzvot* with joy, he frees the *Shekhinah* from the *kelipot,* transforming his sadness to joy.

The *Ketoret* offering raises a person's level of joy because it raises the sparks of holiness — the *Shekhinah* — trapped

55 The Talmud lists several reasons for the destruction of Jerusalem, among them the dishonest business practices of the city's inhabitants. Rebbe Nachman sees the lack of faithful people as synonymous with the decline of *Malkhut* / faith, and so the destruction of faith is the destruction of Jerusalem.

56 *Rebbe Nachman's Wisdom* #23.

by the *kelipot*. Once the *Shekhinah* is freed from the *kelipot*, a person's heart becomes joyous, and then he can ascend to the very highest of levels. Although it is impossible to grasp God because He is so beyond us, nevertheless, by performing *mitzvot* with joy (or by offering the *Ketoret*), one can attain an understanding of God even if he doesn't know anything of the greatness of God (LM I, 24:2).

Rebbe Nachman of Tcherin speaks about the *Shekhinah*/*Malkhut* ascending from the *kelipot*. He writes in his book, the *Parparaot LeChokhmah*:

> We see that this ascent refers to what happens when a Jew performs the *mitzvot* with joy. This joy of the Jewish people is the holiness of the *Shekhinah*, clothed in the mitzvah. By performing the mitzvah with joy, the *Shekhinah* leaves its exile in the realm of the *kelipot*. This is what is meant by, "*Malkhut* of the World of *Asiyah* ascending from the *kelipot*."

Reb Noson adds that since all the *sefirot* and worlds unite and ascend during the prayers, *any Jew* can bring about these elevations in the Supernal Worlds, *at any time*, simply by performing a mitzvah with joy (LH, *Nefilat Apayim* 4:1). In addition, Reb Noson points out that by the onset of Shabbos, the forces of evil have no rule and the worlds are no longer in need of ascending from "exile."[57] Therefore, Shabbos is a time of great joy (LH, ibid. 4:3).

The ARI said that the most exalted level he had attained came as a result of his having performed the *mitzvot* with great joy (see *Mishnah Berurah* 669:11). Reb Noson adds that joy increases one's mental abilities (LH, ibid. 4:2). Therefore, one should make it a daily habit to praise God for all the good that he has. No matter how terrible things are, there must be some good that

57 See *Shaar HaKavanot, Drushey Shabbat*.

each person can be happy about. By doing so, it will lead to joy (LH, *Hodaah* 6:10).

HaShem of hosts is with us

> יְיָ צְבָאוֹת עִמָּנוּ מִשְׂגָּב לָנוּ אֱלֹהֵי יַעֲקֹב סֶלָה:
> יְיָ צְבָאוֹת אַשְׁרֵי אָדָם בּוֹטֵחַ בָּךְ:
> יְיָ הוֹשִׁיעָה הַמֶּלֶךְ יַעֲנֵנוּ בְיוֹם קָרְאֵנוּ:
>
> HaShem of hosts is with us; the God of Yaakov is our assurance and inspiration forever, *selah!*
> HaShem of hosts, happy is the man who trusts only in You!
> HaShem, save us! O King, answer us on the day we call!

The Talmud *Yerushalmi* teaches that one should never abstain from saying these verses (*Berakhot* 5). The ARI writes that after reciting the *Ketoret*, one should say these three verses. These verses speak of God granting us strength to endure any travail we go through. We should never give up and always place our trust in Him. We should always turn to God, for He *will* answer us.

Atah Seiter Li: You Alone are my Secret Hiding Place

> אַתָּה סֵתֶר לִי, מִצַּר תִּצְּרֵנִי רָנֵּי פַלֵּט תְּסוֹבְבֵנִי סֶלָה:
>
> You alone are my secret hiding place. Protect me from affliction. Encompass me with songs of joyous deliverance at all times, *selah!*

Rebbe Nachman teaches the spiritual implications of this prayer:

> Know! There is a Name of God, such that when the Holy One wants to conceal a person from Satan in order to save him from a

death sentence, He covers him with this Name. Then Satan prowls about, looks all around for this person, and seeks a way in under the cover in order to harm him. But the person is concealed, and Satan has no power because of this Name. But know! If, God forbid, he does find a place to enter under the concealment to rule over the person, then the opposite happens. Satan gains extra power from this Name.

Know, too, that the aforementioned Holy Name is *SÆL* (סאל), derives from the initial letters of the verse "*Atah Seiter Li*" (**אתה סתר לי**, you are my secret hiding place) (Psalms 32:7). And the *mem* of [the next word in the verse,] *Mitzar* (מצר, from affliction), is the aspect of the *Samekh-Mem* (ס-מ) [i.e., Satan] who prowls around the concealment in order to overpower a person. If, God forbid, Satan finds a place to rule, then he receives extra strength from this Name. The *mem* will be joined to the Name *SÆL*, the combination forming his [the Satan's] name, *SaMÆL* (סמא-ל) [which one is forbidden to pronounce].

Therefore, it is necessary to pause between the words *Atah seiter li* and *mitzar,* in order not to make the combination of Satan's name, God forbid. For then, when he overpowers the person, God forbid, and receives extra strength from the Name, the Name becomes "*Sof Adam Lamut*" (**סוף אדם למות**; man's destiny is to die) (*Berakhot* 17a), whose initial letters spell a different variation of the Name *SÆL.* But when a person protects himself with the strength of that Name, then the Name is used as a cover, and the aspect of "*Atah seiter li* (you are my shelter)" with "*mitzar tizreini*" (you protect me) guards a person from the Satan.

(LM I, 213)

The Order of the Temple Service

אַבַּיֵּי, הֲוָה מְסַדֵּר סֵדֶר הַמַּעֲרָכָה מִשְּׁמָא דִּגְמָרָא וְאַלִּבָּא דְאַבָּא שָׁאוּל:

Abaye recounted the order of the Temple service on the authority of the oral tradition and according to the view of Abba Shaul.

Serving God has two functions: correcting the sins of the past, and growing spiritually, rising from level to level. The latter is a much more pleasurable and easier service. Who doesn't enjoy the pleasure of success in serving God? The former—fixing the past—is a much more tedious and difficult service, because to fix the past one must first return to the temptations and struggles of the past, and this time pass the tests. God sends a person tests similar to the ones he failed previously, giving a person a second chance to pass them. This corrects the past and raises the sparks of holiness that he lost.

It seems that the correct order would be to first fix the past and then rise to higher levels. But God has compassion on us and lets us do the easier and more pleasurable service first. Because if we will begin with fixing the past by dealing with the evil inclination, we will probably give up before we succeed in our goal to improve our ways.

The sequence of the *Korbanot* and the services of the *Beis HaMikdash* seem to be in an unusual order. It begins with preparing the fire for the courtyard Altar, and before adding the two new logs of wood to this fire, they prepare the fire for the sanctuary Altar. Then they return to add the two logs for the fire of the courtyard Altar.

In addition, the first five lamps of the Menorah are cleaned, then the blood of the morning sacrifice is sprinkled on the Altar, and then a Kohen cleans the final two lamps. Why couldn't the Kohen prepare all seven lamps of the Menorah at once?

Furthermore, it seems that the *Ketoret* (incense offering) should precede the *tamid* (daily offering). The *tamid* raises the holiness that is in the World of *Asiyah*, which consequently elevates all worlds that are above it. The *Ketoret* elevates the sparks of *Asiyah* that have been captured by the *kelipot*.[58]

58 *Shaar HaKavanot, Tefillat HaShachar, Drush Gimel*, p. 87.

Shouldn't the *Ketoret* come first, to bring up all the sparks into *Asiyah*, and only then raise all the holy sparks of *Asiyah* through the *tamid*? It, too, seems out of order.

Reb Noson teaches us that the service of the *Korbanot* seem out of order because that reflects the service of God. To serve God, one must alternate between correcting the past and growing and reaching higher levels. The order is often exchanged so the person will have strength and encouragement to serve God and improve his ways (LH, *Chalukat Shutfim* 5:11).

Ana B'Koach

אָנָּא בְּכֹחַ גְּדֻלַּת יְמִינְךָ תַּתִּיר צְרוּרָה:

We beseech You, with the great power of Your loving right hand, release the bound one!

The *Ana B'Koach* prayer was composed by the Mishnaic sage, Rabbi Nechunyah ben HaKanah. It contains seven verses, each containing six words. The total of forty-two words corresponds to God's Holy Name of Forty-Two Letters. This Name, known as *Mem-Bet* (42 ,מ"ב), stands for *Maaseh Bereishit* (מעשה בראשית, the act of creation), and is the name God used when He created the worlds.

The practical application of *Ana B'Koach* is that it can instill in us the belief that we too can renew ourselves each day. We can recreate ourselves daily, mimicking the act of creation, by invoking the *Mem-Bet*, God's holy name of creation.

CHAPTER 12
Eizehu Mekoman and Kaddish

Eizehu Mekoman

אֵיזֶהוּ מְקוֹמָן שֶׁל זְבָחִים:
What are the locations of the offerings?

Our Sages teach that every day a person should study Torah, Mishnah and Talmud. Therefore, following the recital of the verses of the *tamid* and the *Ketoret* (which are found in the Torah), we recite a passage from the Mishnah (the fifth chapter of the tractate of *Zevachim*), which begins, "What are the locations of the offerings?" Then we recite a passage from the Talmud, Rabbi Yishmael's teaching of the Thirteen Principles of Torah Exegesis by which the Torah is expounded. When we say the verses of the sacrifices, study the Mishnah about the sacrifices, and learn Rabbi Yishmael's principles, we fulfill this precept.[59]

One of the reasons this specific chapter was selected for inclusion in the siddur is that it is the only chapter in the entire Mishnah that does not contain any disagreement among the

59 See also Chapter 5 above about studying Torah before the prayers, which helps our prayers to be accepted.

sages. This teaches us to pursue peace and avoid unnecessary argumentativeness (*Ta'amey HaMinhagim* #46).

One of the great chassidic masters would shed many tears while reciting this passage because it reminded him that the Jewish people were still in exile. He would cry, "What are the locations? Where is the Beis HaMikdash, the place of these sacrifices? Why hasn't it been rebuilt yet?" (*Rabbi Eliyahu Chaim Rosen*).

We can understand the reason for a thanksgiving offering, a peace offering, and a sin or guilt offering, but what purpose does the *olah* (a burnt or elevation offering) serve? The Midrash teaches that an *olah* is brought on account of the heart's intentions, as it atones for forbidden thoughts (*Vayikra Rabbah* 7:3).

Conceptually, a burnt offering represents a person's broken spirit within himself and feeling ashamed before God. He thinks to himself, "How could I have fallen and been cast down from Heaven to earth? I was in such an exalted place. But now I've turned my face away from God." The person's heart breaks, and it causes him to take pity upon himself, for there is nothing more in want of compassion than this. This is the great value of the *olah* (LM I, 108).

The chapter from Tractate *Zevachim* speaks about the locations where the sacrifices were slaughtered. Each sacrifice had a designated place in the *Beis HaMikdash*; some required very specific places, while those of lesser holiness could be slaughtered anywhere within the courtyard.

Reb Noson quotes the *Shulchan Arukh* that a person should designate a specific place (in the synagogue or even in one's home or office) where he will pray (*Orach Chaim* 90:19). Furthermore, he should remain standing in place while he prays (cf. *Berakhot* 26b). Why? Because when one prays, he is attaching himself to the *Makom*, the "Place of the World" (i.e., God.) God is called the Place of the World since He is the creator of every space and place. From each specific place in the *Beis HaMikdash*, one was able to direct and send his prayers to the Holy of Holies, from whence they ascended to the Place of the World, to God. Similarly, when we stand and recite "Where are the locations," we are using our place to focus on the Place of the World (LH, *Shluchin* 4:10).[60]

Reb Noson suggests that identifying specific locations for the sacrifices in the *Beis HaMikdash* hints at the main location in the holy complex—the Foundation Stone— from which the world was drawn (see *Yoma* 54b). From that stone was drawn the light which represents the good to be found in each and every individual in the world, for each person can tap into that source. Similarly, every person can always tap into the Torah, the root of the holiness that can spread out to the world (LH, *Nesiat Kapayim* 5:5).

Reb Noson adds that by establishing specific places for sacrificing the animals, we take a good look at where we are and where the animal is. Meaning, we possess a human spirit, where the sacrifice has an animal spirit. When we recite the sacrifices, it is as if we brought those sacrifices—indicating that we recognize we should act like humans and rise above our animalistic desires. We thereby merit forgiveness for sin

60 The Hebrew word for place is MaKOM (מקום). God's Name, is expanded as such as in the following: *YHVH* (10+5+6+5): 10x10=100; 5x5=25; 6x6=36; 5x5=25. The total is 186, the equivalent of *MaKOM* (*Mem*=40; *Kuf*=100; *Vav*=6; *Mem*=40, total of 186.

and enable our good and human abilities to rise above our base characteristics.[61]

Rabbi Yishmael

רַבִּי יִשְׁמָעֵאל אוֹמֵר. בִּשְׁלֹשׁ עֶשְׂרֵה מִדּוֹת הַתּוֹרָה נִדְרֶשֶׁת בָּהֵן:

Rabbi Yishmael said: These are the thirteen Divinely revealed principles according to which the Torah is expounded.

There are thirteen basic exegetical principles through which the Torah is interpreted. They appear in *Beraita d'Rabbi Yishmael* and are found in the Introduction to *Safra d'bei Rav* (teachings of Rav's Yeshivah, also known as *Torat Kohanim,* which are *Midrashim*) on the Book of Leviticus. Since this opening passage of *Safra* begins the discussions of the sacrifices, it is juxtaposed to the *mishnayot* of *Eizehu Mekoman.*

The *Zohar* (II, 90b) teaches that the Torah itself devolved from the higher worlds down to its present form. This means that the entire Torah is a form of God's Names, though it appears to us in letters and words. Therefore, the words of Torah, whether Biblical, Mishnaic, Talmudic, or Midrashic, are all variations of the different Names of God. The Thirteen Principles also comprise various combinations of God's Holy Names and allude to the various directions and rules with which God will conduct the world (for example, with kindness or judgment.) Depending on our deeds, the principles will be used to either bring down bounty or withhold it.

These Thirteen Principles parallel the Thirteen Attributes of Mercy and therefore correspond to prayer. The same way a person merits to study and clarify the Torah according to these

61 LH, *Birkhot HaShachar* 3:27.

Thirteen Principles, he can attain concentrated and intensive prayer, which arouses Divine compassion (see LM I, 27:4).

The *Kaddish*

יִתְגַּדַּל וְיִתְקַדַּשׁ שְׁמֵיהּ רַבָּא:

May His Great Name be magnified and sanctified.

At this point in the morning service, we conclude the portion of the blessings and the sacrifices—the rectification of the World of *Asiyah*. However, before we ascend to a higher world, *Yetzirah*, with the recitation of the *Pesukey d'Zimrah*, we must make a bridge to connect us from one world to the next. That bridge is *Kaddish*. As the ARI writes, *Kaddish* is said in between every world, whether on ascent or in descent.

We have already discussed that the prayers are divided into four categories representing the four worlds: *Asiyah*, *Yetzirah*, *Beriyah* and *Atzilut*.[62] *Kaddish* is the bridge that connects each world to the next. For this reason, we recite *Kaddish* between the sections of *Korbanot* (associated with the World of *Asiyah*) and *Pesukey d'Zimrah* (associated with the World of *Yetzirah*), and between *Pesukey d'Zimrah* and the blessings of the *Shema* (associated with the World of *Beriyah*). However, the *Amidah* (associated with the World of *Atzilu*t) must be said immediately after the blessings of the *Shema*, without interruption, so *Kaddish* is not said then.

After ascending to *Atzilut* in the *Amidah*, we return and descend through those same worlds all the way back down to *Asiyah*. This explains why *Kaddish* is recited many times at the end of the prayers, for it serves as a bridge from each

62 See above Chapter 2, *The Four Parts of Prayer*.

higher world to the world below it, to bring down blessing and bounty.[63]

Kaddish is a most powerful and amazing praise of God. It is specifically written in Aramaic, a language not understood by the angels. Why? Angels understand Hebrew, the Holy Tongue, because they draw sustenance directly from the "face" or "front" of holiness. But the Other Side, which draws sustenance from the "back" side of holiness, understands Aramaic. When a person attempts to rise to higher levels in holiness, the Other Side tries to stop his ascent. But when he pronounces God's greatness, the Other Side is subdued and cannot block the ascent. Thus, we recite *Kaddish* in Aramaic, to pronounce God's glory and subdue the forces of evil. Only then we can proceed from one level to the next.

The *Kaddish* contains ten different words that praise God. These ten praises parallel the Ten Types of Song found in the Book of Psalms, whose verses we will say when reciting the *Pesukey d'Zimrah* (*Anaf Yosef*).

The word *Kaddish* (קדיש) means "sanctification." Whenever we say the *Kaddish*, we intend to sanctify God's Name in the world, to proclaim our belief in His existence, His oneness, and His providence. As the *Zohar* says:

> *Kaddish* rises up above and it descends below [meaning it reverberates up to the highest level of God's will and descends down all the way into the lowest and darkest corners of creation]. It has the power to break the iron locks of the most evil *kelipot* which act as iron curtains that separate between Israel and our Father in Heaven (*Zohar* II, 129b).

63 See *Pri Etz Chaim, Shaar HaKaddishim*, pp. 126-127.

Rabbi Chaim Vital explains further: When we say this great and holy praise of *Kaddish* in Aramaic—which is precisely the language of the Other Side and the *kelipot*—this effectively breaks their power and elevates God's glory over all dimensions.[64]

One of the phrases in the *Kaddish* is, "*B'olma di bra kiru'sey v'yamlikh Malkhusey*—in the world that He created according to His will, and He will reveal His Kingship." Rebbe Nachman explains: when a person accepts that whatever happens is God's will, then this person is revealing God's Kingship in the world (LM I, 177).

Reb Noson says that one of the reasons *Kaddish* is so powerful is because we ask that God's Name "be magnified and sanctified in the world that He created according to His will." That is, when we accept God's kingship and strive to obey Him, we elevate and bind our will to God's will, which is called *Raava d'Raavin* (the Will of all wills), so that God will then reveal His ultimate will throughout all the worlds (LH, *Kaddish* 1).

יְהֵא שְׁמֵיהּ רַבָּא מְבָרַךְ לְעָלַם וּלְעָלְמֵי עָלְמַיָּא:

May His Great Name be blessed in this world and all worlds forever and for all eternity!

One who responds, "*Amen,* may His Name be great!" with all his might, even if he has in him a bit of idolatry, he will be forgiven.[65]

64 *Shaar HaKavanot, Shaar HaKaddeishim,* p. 126.

65 *Shabbat* 119b; *The Aleph-Bet Book,* Repentance A:88.

Three times a day, Heaven examines those who are suffering in Gehinnom. When we answer "*Yehei Shmei Rabba*" aloud, God is filled with compassion for them. He tells the ministering angel over Gehinnom to begin releasing those trapped in Gehinnom, which gives them an hour and a half of relief (*Zohar* I, 62b). Thus, a total of four and a half hours of relief are provided for those suffering in Gehinnom because of those who answer, "*Yehei Shmei Rabba*."

Reb Noson writes that the praises mentioned in *Kaddish* reflect the Song of the Future, which we will sing when *Mashiach* comes (LH, *Hashkamat HaBoker* 5:7).

Amen

The Talmud gives us several insights into why we answer "*Amen*" in the *Kaddish* and after other blessings.

Whoever answers *Amen* with all his strength, Heaven will open for him the gates of *Gan Eden*" (*Shabbos* 119b).

What is *AMeN* (אמן)? It stands for the acronym, *Eil Melekh Ne'eman* (אל מלך נאמן; God, Faithful King) (ibid.).

By proclaiming *Amen,* in essence we are saying that God is faithful to all His promises, and He will fulfill them. He is King and it is in His hands to be able to disburse the rewards He promises, such as the reward of *Gan Eden*.

The *gematria* (numerical value) of *AMeN* is 91. This number is not random. The *gematria* of God's Holy Names *YHVH* (26=י-ה-ו-ה) and *ADoNoY* (65=אדני) add up to 91. When answering *Amen* to a blessing or a *Kaddish,* we are invoking God's Names and making Him known throughout the world.

The Talmud states, "He who answers *Amen* to a blessing is greater than one who makes the blessing" (*Nazir* 66b). In addition, "From when does a child merit the World to Come? From when he answers *Amen*" (*Sanhedrin* 110b).

When one prays in a synagogue, he gets the extra chance to fulfill many *mitzvot*, because each *Amen* he answers there yields a great reward. Therefore, this is one of the reasons one should pray in a synagogue.

Reb Noson notes that the word *AMeN* implies faithfulness (as above, "God, Faithful King") and is related to the word *EMuNah* (אמונה, faith). While we are declaring our faith *in* God, we are also declaring our faithfulness *to* God (LH, *Umnin* 4:3). Where there is faith, one can truly answer *Amen*. Where there is an *Amen*, one can improve and grow in faith.

The ARI writes that when a person answers *Amen*, he receives an illumination from the Holy Name *EiL* (אל) — twice. One is from *Arikh Anpin* (Extended Countenance), from the verse, "*Mi EiL Kamokha* (Who is a God like You)?" (Mikhah 7:18). The second illumination is from the verse "God! God! *EiL Rachum* (Merciful God)" (Exodus 34:6). However, should a person remain *EiLaM* (אלם, silent or dumb) when he is supposed to answer *Amen*, then about him it is written, "Fill their faces with humiliation" (מלא פניהם קלון) (Psalms 83:17). In Hebrew, the final letters of the words *malEi peneiheM kaloN* (מלא פניהם קלון) spell the acronym of *AMeN* (אמן). Thus, when it comes to *Amen*, one can either draw upon himself great spiritual illumination, or humiliation.[66]

66 *Pri Etz Chaim, Shaar Kavanat Amen* 2, p. 271-272.

CHAPTER 13

Hodu and Pesukey d'Zimrah

Hodu

הודו לַיְיָ קִרְאוּ בִשְׁמוֹ:

Give thanks to HaShem. Call out in His Name.

The verses of *Hodu*[67] were originally composed by King David for the *Leviim* to sing in the *Beis HaMikdash* while the *Kohanim* were offering the *Korban Hatamid* (daily offering).

Specifically, while the *Kohanim* were offering the morning *tamid,* the *Leviim* would sing from "Give thanks to HaShem" to "My prophets you shall not harm", and while the afternoon *tamid* was being offered, they would continue from "Sing to HaShem, all the earth" to "And all the people shall say, *Amen,* praise God!" To this day, we continue to say these verses, in order to prevent the forces of evil from trying to rise up together with the sparks of holiness that have been released as a result of our prayers. This parallels the daily offerings.

Hodu is the opening passage before the *Pesukey d'Zimrah* section. The ARI teaches that *Pesukey d'Zimrah* actually begins with the *Barukh She'amar* prayer. According to Kabbalah, the

67 These verses are from I Chronicles 16:8-36, Psalms 105:1-15, and Psalms 96:1-13, with slight differences.

reason we say *Hodu* beforehand is that after reciting *Korbanot,* we have rectified the World of *Asiyah* and are ascending to the World of *Yetzirah,* the angelic world. At that entrance point, many *kelipot* stand and try to deter our entrance to the higher realm. Though we have risen to a higher level, we are not quite there yet. We first say *Hodu,* since the declaration of God's greatness chases away the forces of evil.[68]

There is a difference of opinions exactly where to insert the *Hodu* passage. In *Nusach Ashkenaz, Hodu* is recited immediately after *Barukh She'amar.* On the other hand, in *Nusach Sephard* (which we are following in this commentary), *Hodu* is said before *Barukh She'amar.* Exactly at which point in time *Hodu* was added to the verses of *Pesukey d'Zimrah* is not known. However, the ARI writes that the few verses beginning with "*El nekamot HaShem*" (O loving God who exacts revenge) were inserted to elevate the sparks found in *Asiyah.* For in the world of *Asiyah,* the *kelipot* are extremely powerful, and only by mentioning the Ten Martyrs[69] who displayed total self-sacrifice are we able to elevate the sparks of holiness trapped by the *kelipot.*[70] However, since the incident of the Ten Martyrs took place only around the destruction of the Second *Beis HaMikdash,* and the order of the prayers was already established several hundred years earlier by the Men of the Great Assembly, we conclude that *Hodu* was inserted into the prayers only later on and was not part of the original *Pesukey d'Zimrah.*

68 See above, p. 118.

69 Rabbi Akiva, Rabbi Yishmael ben Elisha, Rabban Shimon ben Gamliel, etc., who are mentioned during the Yom Kippur *Musaf* prayer, to exact revenge for their deaths.

70 *Shaar HaKavanot, Drush Inyan Tefillat Shacharit* 1, p. 107.

The *Zohar* states:

> Once a person has prepared himself to serve God with *mitzvot* (the *tzitzit*, paralleling *Yetzirah*; the arm-*tefillin*, paralleling *Beriyah*; and the head-*tefillin*, paralleling *Atzilut*), then he should prepare himself to pray with *kavanah* (*Zohar* II, 201b).

The *Zohar* also comments on the advantages of saying the psalms:

> When morning arrives and people are gathered in the synagogue, they should engage in the praises written by King David (the psalms). This arouses great love above and below. When they recite the praises, angels join them (ibid. II, 131b).
>
> It is important to say King David's psalms because they were all written with *ruach hakodesh* (a Divine spirit) (ibid. I, 179a).

Rebbe Nachman teaches that reciting psalms brings a person to repentance (LM II, 73). Reciting *Hodu* in *Pesukey d'Zimrah* can be counted as reciting psalms, which can lead a person to repentance (see *Zohar* II, 202b).

"*Hodu*" means to give thanks. To whom are we speaking? To the angels. We say, "Call out in His Name; make His great deeds known among the nations." "Nations" here refers to the forces of evil, which abound in the realm of *Asiyah*. When the *kelipot* are made aware of God's greatness, it causes them to flee, and they cannot attach themselves to holiness.[71]

Rebbe Nachman expands the ARI's explanation of *Hodu*. He says that it is only possible to subdue the evil forces (i.e., the illusions, evil thoughts, desires, confusions and obstacles to serving God on any level) through the greatness of God (LM I, 25:4). This means speaking about and articulating God's greatness and glory. The Rebbe adds that one can also reveal

71 *Pri Etz Chaim, Shaar HaZemirot* 1, p. 139.

the greatness of God by giving charity to a deserving person in need. This is another reason for giving charity before praying.[72]

> דִּרְשׁוּ יְיָ וְעֻזּוֹ, בַּקְּשׁוּ פָנָיו תָּמִיד:
>
> Seek HaShem and His invincible strength,
> seek His presence continually.

Rebbe Nachman explains this verse as follows: Through which wisdom will you be able to search for God? It is through His strength, which is the Torah, and not through other types of wisdom. By what means can you merit the wisdom of Torah? Through giving charity to the Land of Israel, which is called *tamid* (continual), as it is written, "It is a Land that HaShem your God seeks. The eyes of HaShem, your God, are continually upon it" (Deuteronomy 11:12; LM I, 37:8).

> דָּבָר צִוָּה לְאֶלֶף דּוֹר:
>
> The word He commanded for
> a thousand generations.

Originally the Torah was meant to be given one thousand generations after creation. But God foresaw wickedness and brazenness in many of those generations, so He gave the Torah after only twenty-six generations. What happened to the remaining souls of the 974 generations? Instead of being born in one time frame, they were spread out throughout all generations. These souls are the brazen-faced people in each generation who mock the idea of prayer and disturb those who attempt to pray earnestly (*Chagigah* 13b-14a).

72 See Chapter 5.

בַּשְּׂרוּ מִיּוֹם אֶל יוֹם יְשׁוּעָתוֹ:

Announce His salvation from one day to the next.

Reb Noson teaches: Every day, God sends each person new salvations to save him from the Other Side, which seeks to overpower him each day. Therefore, there is no need to be worried today about what happened previously, because who knows what salvation God will be sending you today (LH, *Basar b'Chalav* 4:14).

סַפְּרוּ בַגּוֹיִם אֶת כְּבוֹדוֹ:

Tell of His glory among the nations.

God's glory cries out from all things, beckoning us to come close to Him. For God, with all His love and mercy, wants us to be close. Sometimes, in the middle of our prayers, we become enflamed, and the words flow from our lips with burning devotion. When this happens, God's own light is inside us, beckoning us to draw near. This arousal is a spark of God's own essence. However, sometimes God withdraws and is far off, but we must still pray to Him. As it is written, "Cast your burden on God" (Psalms 55:23). You must throw your prayers to God from afar (*Rebbe Nachman's Wisdom* #52).

הוֹד וְהָדָר לְפָנָיו, עֹז וְחֶדְוָה בִּמְקוֹמוֹ:

Majesty and splendor are before Him;
strength and joy abound in His place.

When strength and joy abound in its place, then we can merit the majesty and splendor that is before God. Rebbe Nachman explains that this refers to one who is moral and guards his covenant. When that person uses his strength to subdue his base desires, then he merits to bask in the majesty and splendor of God (see LM I, 27:6). The idea is that when one has *oz v'chedvah* (עז וחדוה, strength and beauty)—which means he has a guarded covenant and is morally upright—he merits *hod v'hadar* (הוד והדר, strength and beauty) on his face.

וְהוּא רַחוּם יְכַפֵּר עָוֹן וְלֹא יַשְׁחִית, וְהִרְבָּה לְהָשִׁיב אַפּוֹ וְלֹא יָעִיר כָּל חֲמָתוֹ:

He is compassionate and will forgive our sins instead of destroying us. Time and again He retracts His anger and does not allow the full heat of His judgment to become aroused.

Four types of avenging angels are mentioned in this verse: *Avon* (sins), refers to Satan; *Yashchit* (destroy), refers to the angel of *mashkhit* (an avenging angel seeking to destroy humanity); *Apo* (His anger), refers to an angel of anger; and *Chamato* (His wrath), refers to an angel of wrath. These four avenging angels try to stop our prayers from ascending. Therefore, we pray, "He is compassionate," asking God to help us, so these angels do not interfere with our prayers (*Zohar* I, 23b).

תְּנוּ עֹז לֵאלֹהִים ... אֵל יִשְׂרָאֵל. הוּא נוֹתֵן עֹז וְתַעֲצֻמוֹת לָעָם:

Give strength to God.... The God of Israel, He gives strength and power to the people.

Rebbe Nachman teaches that just as a person who is brazen has no share in the Torah, so too, the person who lacks holy boldness has no share in the Torah. He explains:

> Our Sages teach, "Whoever is brazen-faced, it is certain that the feet of his ancestors did not stand at Mount Sinai" (*Nedarim* 20a). We find therefore that the brazen-faced person has no share in the Torah.

Likewise, a man who is lowly and abject, without any holy boldness, also has no share in the Torah. As our Sages teach, "Why was the Torah given to Israel? Because they are bold" (*Beitzah* 28b). For it is necessary to possesses holy boldness. Our Sages exhort, "Be bold as a leopard" (*Avos* 5:20). Through the holy *AZus* (עזות, boldness) that a person possesses, he receives holy boldness from God in return. This corresponds to "Give *OZ* (עז, strength) to God.... The God of Israel, He gives *oz* (strength) and power to the people."

"Give strength to God" corresponds to an awakening from below. By virtue of our having the holy boldness to oppose all those who rise against us to prevent us from our service, Heaven forbid, we can overpower them. As a result, we give strength and power Above, so to speak. This corresponds to "Give strength to God."

Then the aspect of holy boldness is aroused Above and is bestowed on us, corresponding to "The God of Israel, He gives strength and might to the people." God bestows upon us holy boldness and gives us the strength to oppose the brazenness of the Other Side, and of all the brazen-faced men of the generation. For it is only possible to oppose them through holy boldness; without it, his adversaries will certainly thwart his Torah study and Divine service. Thus, a person has no share in the Torah when he lacks holy boldness. Yet a person must measure his ways, knowing how best to behave with the boldness so that it does not become brazenness, God forbid, which is a very evil trait. He should, nevertheless, possess holy boldness (LM I, 147).

אָנֹכִי יְיָ אֱלֹהֶיךָ הַמַּעַלְךָ מֵאֶרֶץ מִצְרָיִם, הַרְחֶב פִּיךָ וַאֲמַלְאֵהוּ:

"I am HaShem your God who lifts you out of the land of Egypt; open your mouth wide and I will fill it."

Rebbe Nachman teaches[73] that the Torah is God's will, since the letters of the Torah are the embodiment of God's will. Now that the Torah has been given over to our

73 Based on *Yerushalmi, Rosh HaShanah* 1:3.

hands, God's will has also been given over to our hands, so that His will is in accordance with our will. Consequently, when we speak to God in our own words and articulate all our deepest needs, desires and hopes to Him, we can be assured that He will fill our mouths with the right words to say, and He will fulfill our prayers and bless us! (LM I, 34:4).

Mizmor Shir: A Song of Praise for the dedication of the Sanctuary

מִזְמוֹר שִׁיר חֲנֻכַּת הַבַּיִת לְדָוִד:

A *mizmor*, a song for the dedication of the Sanctuary by David.

This psalm is said prior to *Pesukey d'Zimrah* to allude to several important concepts. The word *mizmor* (מזמור) refers to the First *Beis HaMikdash*; *shir* (שיר, song) refers to the *Second Beis HaMikdash*; and the initial letters of the words in the opening verse מִזְמוֹר שִׁיר חֲנֻכַּת הַבַּיִת לְדָוִד spell out *L'MiShChaH* (למשחה, for greatness), referring to the Third *Beis HaMikdash*. Our own houses of prayer are called a "miniature *Beis HaMikdash*" (*Megillah* 29a), and the prayers themselves are compared to the sacrifices. We require the *Beis HaMikdash* in order to bring sacrifices to atone for our sins, to have the Divine Presence manifest, and to reveal God's kingship in the world. So, we say this chapter before the prayers to consecrate our Sanctuary.

Reb Noson comments:

The human mind parallels the Holy Sanctuary (LM I, 13:1). Each day we must rededicate our "sanctuary" to God. Because the evil inclination constantly battles against us, we should learn from King David how to strengthen ourselves. The verses in this psalm, which describe how God continually supports us and saves us, give us strength and encouragement. The chapter ends on a note of joy, for by strengthening ourselves, we merit joy (LH, *Sefer Torah* 4:26).

יְיָ הֶעֱלִיתָ מִן שְׁאוֹל נַפְשִׁי:

HaShem, You lifted my soul out of the grave.

The final verse in *Hodu* ends with the words *ki gamal aley* (כי גמל עלי, for He has established His blessing for me). Those final letters form a Holy Name of God from the groups of the Name of Seventy-Two (*YLY*, ילי). This is the Name that extracts souls from the bottommost pit of Gehinnom, or *She'ol* (שאול). *Mizmor Shir* continues this idea, as it contains ten mentions of God's Holy Name *YHVH* (one mention is written as *Adonoy*). These ten mentions parallel the ten *sefirot* and praise God for extracting the fallen souls in *Asiyah* from their fallen state. The ten mentions of God's Name also parallel the Ten Commandments and the Ten Types of Song.[74]

God reigns forever

יְיָ מֶלֶךְ. יְיָ מָלָךְ. יְיָ יִמְלֹךְ לְעֹלָם וָעֶד:

HaShem reigns, HaShem has always reigned,
HaShem will reign forever and for all eternity.

These stanzas should be recited while standing. The King is being announced; in His honor we rise.

The prophet says, "On that day, God will be One and His Name will be One" (Zekhariah 14:9). The Talmud asks: How can it be written, "On that day, God will be One"? Isn't He One now?

74 See *Pri Etz Chaim, Shaar HaZemirot* 2, p. 141.

The answer is that this world is not like the World to Come. In this world, when hearing good tidings, we say, "Blessed is He Who is good and Who does good," and when receiving bad news we say, "Blessed is the Judge Whose judgment is truth." In the World to Come, however, we will say only one expression: "Blessed is He Who is good and Who does good" (*Pesachim* 50a), because in the future we will recognize that everything is good. By expressing God as one, we wish to already internalize that level of consciousness that will be revealed in the future.

Rebbe Nachman teaches that when we attain *daat* (knowledge and awareness of God) we are able to recite the blessing, "Who is good and Who does good" as well. This is because in the future, *daat* will be totally revealed, and we will see that all was for the good (LM I, 4:3-4). When we declare God's oneness, we ascend beyond the apparent duality of the world, which seems to possess good and bad, and we recognize that oneness—as it will be revealed in the future—even now!

Dedicated to the Master through melodies

לַמְנַצֵּחַ בִּנְגִינוֹת מִזְמוֹר שִׁיר:

Dedicated to the Master through melodies, a *mizmor*, a song.

Reb Noson writes that when a person seeks God and calls out to Him, he causes God to be revealed even in the darkest and most distant places. Therefore, any time we wish to enter into the realm of holiness, the way to begin is by speaking of God's greatness and revealing it—even to the nations. This psalm speaks about seeking God and hoping that all the nations will come to recognize Him. This idea ties in with the concept of *Hodu* being meant to deter the *kelipot* and make God known on earth, so that the holy sparks can be gathered and returned to the realm of holiness. Therefore, we recite this psalm as we are about to begin the *Pesukey d'Zimrah* (LH, *Rosh HaShanah* 6:5).

> לָדַעַת בָּאָרֶץ דַּרְכֶּךָ:
>
> To know your path on the earth.

A somewhat notable chassid came to see Rebbe Nachman. He was an older man and was knowledgeable in the writings of the holy ARI. Wanting to impress the Rebbe, he began to speak in the manner of important chassidim, those very advanced in performing God's service, asking, "Would the Rebbe teach us the path to serve God?" The implication was that he wanted to learn unique paths—beyond the ordinary—befitting those who are extremely righteous and dedicated to God's service.

The Rebbe looked at the chassid with wonder and responded by quoting the verse, "To know Your path on the earth?" The Rebbe was taken aback that someone who was still "on the earth"—meaning, immersed in earthliness—would want to know the path to come close to God before perfecting his path on Earth.

We see from this anecdote that the man spoke in a haughty manner, saying that he was seeking the path to God, as if he had already perfected himself to the extent that he lacked nothing else but to choose the appropriate path and walk up to God. The Rebbe saw through this and encouraged the chassid to speak to him honestly (*Rebbe Nachman's Wisdom* #292).

CHAPTER 14

Thanking, Praising and Glorifying the Creator

The Book of Psalms was authored by King David with Ten Types of Song.[75] These ten types of songs, tunes, and melodies, bring joy and happiness to all. Most importantly, through song (and therefore with psalms) one is able to connect to God. As Reb Noson writes, "We see this happening: Even a person who is very far from God can usually reconnect to God via song."

Our prayers—primarily the *Shema* and the *Amidah*—are meant to bind us with God. We recite *Pesukey d'Zimrah* first because the songs of *Pesukey d'Zimrah* have the potential to bind us to God. We say "*Halleluyah*" (Praise God) ten times during the *Pesukey d'Zimrah* because these songs prepare us for properly and fully uniting with God through the *Shema* and the *Amidah* (LH, *Nesiat Kapayim* 5:6-7).

The Ten Types of Song are rooted in the highest levels of power in creation. The words of the Torah contain, in descending order: cantillations (the sounds of the musical notes); vowels (the dots and dashes); crowns on several of the letters; and, of course, the letters themselves. These four aspects allude to levels of Torah understanding:

Cantillations: not having any grasp of Torah at all

Vowels: having tiny insights

75 Rashi on Psalms 1:1; see *Pesachim* 117a; *Tikkuney Zohar* #13.

Crowns: something we can grasp onto

Letters: insights we can comprehend

Note that the cantillations have no form or shape; the symbols for them can be made into sounds, but these sounds do not have any form. They represent the Ten Types of Song which are at the level of the origin of the creation.[76] Thus, by connecting to these types of song a person can ascend to the highest of levels and effect rectifications for even the worst sins. We can begin to accomplish this by saying the *Pesukey d'Zimrah*.

Praying with a "Full Mouth"

The Talmud teaches, "A person should always thank God for the past and cry out for the future."[77] After reciting *Korbanot*, which deal with our personal lives (i.e., performing *mitzvot* or seeking atonement for sins that require sacrifices,) we are now ready to ascend to the main body of prayer (i.e., praise of God and our requests.) In *Likutey Moharan* (I, 34), Rebbe Nachman gives an overview of prayer to God. Reb Noson expands this concept further in *Likutey Halakhot* (*Nesiat Kapayim* 5).

Rebbe Nachman teaches:

> It is written, "Disgrace has shattered my heart" (Psalms 69:21). That is, although disgrace and humiliation shatter a person's heart, the rectification for this is to bind one's heart to the *nekudah* (point) applicable to one's heart *at that exact moment*. Through this, the disgrace that weighs on one's heart is eliminated.

Reb Noson explains:

> Because a person faces new situations and challenges daily, the point applicable to his heart at any given moment is constantly changing. And since each moment differs from the one that

76 *Etz Chaim, Shaar TNTA* 1.

77 *Berakhot* 54a; *Avodah Zarah* 7b.

preceded it and from the one that will follow, it is essential that a person make use of every moment for spiritual growth and not push off repentance or devotion to God for a later time. Someone who truly wants to serve God can always draw strength from this fact that every moment is unique and affords him the ability to repent for the past and draw closer to God. Thus, the "point" in a person's heart is the emotion of that moment and how the person feels at any given moment. The idea is to turn to God and not to be disgraced by feelings of inadequacies, or sin, even if one has committed one. He must overcome that disgrace or humiliation.

How does one go about "binding his heart to the exact point"? Rebbe Nachman explains:

> The tzaddik has the power to rule, since it is written, "Yosef was the ruler" (Genesis 42:6). Since the tzaddik is the encompassing root of all Jewish souls, the souls are the extensions that receive from him. Now, the essence of this rule is to... awaken people's hearts to serving God. As it is written, "May God hear Yehudah's voice and bring him to his people" (Deuteronomy 33:7). In other words, the tzaddik shines his radiance into the extensions — into the Jewish hearts. This is what is meant by "bring him [i.e., the tzaddik] to his people."

According to the Kabbalah, Yosef is associated with the *sefirah of Yesod,* and the *brit* (the sexual organ). Rebbe Nachman teaches that only when one guards the *brit* is he called a tzaddik.[78] We have just seen mentioned above that a person who merits the level of tzaddik becomes a ruler. Thus Yosef, who spurned the advances of his master's wife (Genesis 39:7-12) merited the accolade of "tzaddik" and became ruler in Egypt. Therefore, the verse states, "Yosef was the ruler over the land; it was he who provided for the people" (ibid. 42:6). Because Yosef (i.e., the tzaddik — indicating righteousness and morality) ruled, he was able to provide their needs as he saw fit.

78 LM I, 23:3. Guarding the *brit* (covenant) entails abstention from forbidden marriages and adultery, immorality, masturbation, homosexuality and other sexual sins.

In Kabbalistic terminology, "Yosef was the ruler" alludes to the role of *Yesod* in its basic bond with *Malkhut* (because Yosef's *sefirah* is *Yesod,* and *Malkhut* represents rule). The *sefirah* of *Yesod* bears the primary responsibility for transferring *the shefa* (bounty) it requires from the upper *sefirot* down to *Malkhut.* However, if there is a break between *Yesod* and *Malkhut,* God forbid, the bounty instead goes to the *kelipot* and is wasted. Thus, when a person reaches the level of tzaddik, he must be careful not to abuse his power. Rather, his power and authority must be a vehicle through which he provides for the people's spiritual and material benefit (*Yekara d'Shabbata* I, 34).

So far, we have seen that each person has a "point" in his heart. That point is meant to be reached by the tzaddik through his teachings and ability to arouse the Jewish soul to God. A person who is willing to receive from the tzaddik can bind his heart to the "point" of the moment. By virtue of the tzaddik, bounty can then be drawn and received by each individual.

Rebbe Nachman discusses a person's ability to pray to God with a "full mouth"—one that represents purity and completeness—to praise God with honesty and integrity. There are ten *sefirot* and nine corresponding vowel-points (the tenth corresponds to *Malkhut,* which has no vowels).[79] Furthermore, each *sefirah* corresponds to God's Holy Name *YHVH* with a different set of vowel-points.[80] The Rebbe specifies one of the vowels of the Hebrew alphabet, the *m'loopum* (וּ), which consists of the letter *vav* (ו) with a dot in the middle of the letter.[81] The form of *YHVH* identified with *Yesod* is vocalized with the *M'LooPUM,* which has the same letters as *M'LO PUM* (מלא פום, a full mouth). This indicates that the mouth of the

79 See Charts, Appendix A.

80 Ibid.

81 This vowel is pronounced "oo," as in the word הוּא (*HU,* he).

tzaddik is "full" of Godliness and that his utterances, without a doubt, are complete and "full."

Rebbe Nachman continues:

This aspect of "Yosef was the ruler" corresponds to the *m'loopum*. As it is written, "The *brit* (corresponding to Yosef) is the vehicle for *Yesod*, the *HaVaYaH* (*YHVH*) which is punctuated with a *m'loopum*. This is because the letters of *M'LooPUM* (מלאפום) spell *M'Lo PUM* (מלא פום, a full mouth), indicating that the vessels of bounty—i.e., the tzaddik's mouth—are filled with Godliness. For on the face of it, it is hard to understand why we have to pray when God knows all our thoughts. However, this is because words are the vessels of bounty, through which we receive the influx of bounty. As it is written, "And bless you as He said to you" (Deuteronomy 1:11)—meaning, the influx of bounty is in accordance with the speech. If the words (i.e., the vessels of bounty) are perfect and complete, then we can receive abundant bounty in them. Now, the words of the tzaddik are certainly spoken with perfection and fullness. Therefore, the tzaddik can draw bounty to the Jewish people. Therefore, the tzaddik is called an aspect of *m'loopum*, "a full mouth," to indicate that his mouth is full and perfect.

Now, each and every Jew possesses an aspect of "a tzaddik rules," corresponding to "a full mouth," as it is written, "Your people, all of them are tzaddikim" (Isaiah 60:21). For in every Jew there is something precious ... which categorizes him as a tzaddik in his special nature.

We see that for prayer to be effective, we must attain the level of a "full mouth." Only then we can draw the blessings with our prayers and supplications. Rebbe Nachman now elaborates on the implications of *m'loopum*.

Chokhmah corresponds to a point—this is the letter *yod* (י), the fountain and source of the blessing and bounty. *Binah* is the brook that extends from the fountain. Therefore, *Binah* is a *vav* (ו).[82]

82 The Kabbalah teaches that the letter *yod* (י), which is shaped like a single point or dot, corresponds to the *sefirah* of *Chokhmah*. Just as the *yod* has the

The *m'loopum* is a point with a *vav*. This is a combination of *Chokhmah* and *Binah*. For the aspect of Yosef (*Yesod*) is drawn from *Chokhmah* and *Binah*, as it is written, "Now that God has made all this known to you, there is none so *understanding* and *wise* as you" (Genesis 41:39), referring to *Chokhmah* (wisdom) and *Binah* (understanding), resulting in "Yosef was the ruler."

Rebbe Nachman next illustrates four ideas which are connected to the *m'loopum*, the vowel which is comprised of a *yod* and a *vav*.

1. **The Torah and the World**
   The Torah is *yod*, because it is called "the beginning of wisdom (i.e., *Chokhmah*)" (Psalms 111:10),[83] and the world is *vav*, because it was created during the Six Days of Creation (the letter *vav* has a numerical value of six).
2. **The Torah and the Tablets**
   The Ten Commandments are a *yod*,[84] and the Tablets are a *vav*, as our Sages taught, "The Tablets were six handbreadths long by six handbreadths wide" (*Bava Batra* 14a).[85]
3. **The Tzaddik and the Jewish People**
   The tzaddik is *yod*, because the tzaddikim are called "the wise men of the congregation," and the Jewish people correspond to the *vav*, because they are "supporters of Torah" and are referred to as "*vavey* (hooks, i.e., supporters) of the pillars" (Exodus 27:10).

numerical value of 10, in *Chokhmah* the ten *sefirot* are still undifferentiated. Therefore, Rebbe Nachman states that *Chokhmah* is the *yod*, the point or dot in the *m'loopum*. Continuing this metaphor, *Binah*, which emerges directly out of *Chokhmah* and in which the other *sefirot* become separated and diversified, is seen as the brook that flows out from the fountain. This brook, the extension of the fountain, is depicted by the leg of the *yod* being drawn-out and extended until it forms a *vav* (ו). This is the *vav* in the *m'loopum*.

83 See above, where the Rebbe explains that *Chokhmah* (Wisdom) is represented by the letter *yod*.

84 The letter *yod* has the numerical value of ten.

85 The letter vav has the numerical value of six.

4. **The Individual**

   Each Jew himself is also an aspect of *m'loopum*. *Yod,* on account of the mouth, as is written, "My mouth will speak wisdom" (Psalms 49:4). *Vav,* on account of the heart, as in, "The meditations of my heart are understanding." This is an aspect of the Tablets, which, as explained, are a *vav*, as it is written, "Bind them around your throat, write them on the tablet of your heart" (Proverbs 3:3).

Rebbe Nachman now ties together the importance of binding one's heart to the point "of the moment" (which can be accomplished by the *m'loopum* / full mouth), with prayer and binding to the tzaddik.

> Now, when the heart, which corresponds to the *vav* / the Tablets, is immersed in evil loves—i.e., disgrace and humiliation—it is then an aspect of the shattered Tablets, corresponding to fallen and shattered love.
>
> And when the heart is immersed in evil loves / disgrace (corresponding to the shattered Tablets, as it says, "Disgrace has shattered my heart") and a person binds the heart / *vav* to the *yod* / point (corresponding to the tzaddik / *m'loopum*) then the disgrace of the heart is eliminated. This is because the tzaddik is the point at which the light of holy love resides, shining into the *vav* / heart and eliminating the disgrace of the heart. Thus, when a person is attached to the tzaddik, his heart becomes whole, and he can truly pray.

The *M'loopum* and the Morning Prayer

Reb Noson explores this lesson in depth and ties the *m'loopum* into the daily prayers. He writes:

> From the lesson it is understood that, in essence, prayer is meant to illumine and bind the point (i.e., "My mouth will speak wisdom") to the heart (i.e., "The meditations of my heart are understanding"). When this is accomplished, then the tzaddik—and by extension, each Jew—attains prayer and can draw bounty and healing, and even alter nature, by virtue of the "full mouth."

Reb Noson now proceeds to connect these ideas with the rectifications achieved through the four sections of the morning prayer.

The Sacrifices: The Torah and the World

The first section of prayer contains the sacrifices and the *Ketoret,* the intent of which is to purify the World of *Asiyah* (elevating the sparks of holiness). This corresponds to the *m'loopum* in the connection between the Torah and the world. Certainly, prior to purifying this world one lacks the strength to bind the world with the Torah. But by reciting the sacrifices, the daily offering and the *Ketoret,* one purifies this world from the *kelipot.* Through this, the world, which was created in six days (the *vav*) can now be attached to the Torah (the *yod,* wisdom). Therefore, we find that in the *Beis HaMikdash* there were groups called *Maamadot* (literally, "positions"—referring to men who stood over the sacrifices and read passages of the Torah), to connect the sacrifices (*vav*) to the Torah (*yod*). In the *Beis HaMikdash,* each of the sacrifices had its specific place where its laws applied. This corresponds to the special "points of the heart," the special moments that have to be bound to the tzaddik, the *m'loopum.*

Pesukey d'Zimrah: The Torah and the Tablets

After the sacrifices, we recite the *Pesukey d'Zimrah,* connecting the idea of *m'loopum* of the Ten Commandments (*yod*) and the Tablets (*vav*).

The Torah is God's wisdom. Just as God is infinite, so is the Torah. It is above and beyond all spiritual conceptions. How then can something so spiritual become so physical whereby the letters of Torah become inscribed onto physical Tablets?! The answer is that God, in His wisdom, constricted that wisdom into forms and shapes that can appear in a physical form in order for the Jews to receive it and become attached to God through them. (This was the reason why, when the Jews served the golden calf, Moshe saw the letters ascending from the Tablets and disappearing [*Tanchuma, Ekev* 11]; and the Tablets became heavy and Moshe cast them to the ground and broke them, since the Tablets were no longer being held together by the spiritual letters.)

Our Sages teach that if the first Tablets would not have been broken, the Torah would not have been forgotten from the Jews (*Eruvin* 54a). Thus, forgetfulness is associated with the broken Tablets, which represents the broken heart. We infer from this that the Torah letters, when not present, represent broken Tablets. When we can recall Torah and study it, these represent the Tablets themselves.

The *Zohar* (II, 19a) says that the essence of melody and musical instruments was brought into the world by Levi, the son of Yaakov. Leah said, "This time my husband *yeLaVeh* (ילוה, will become attached) to me" (Genesis 29:34). We learn from this that when *LeVi* (לוי) was born, the aspect of melody and musical instruments came into the world, because the joining of two things is best accomplished via melody and musical instruments (LM I, 237).

This means that the main way to bring together distant things is through music. The main attachment and binding of the letters to Torah is through song and melodies, and the main attachment of a person from this lowly physical world to God is through music and melodies. We see empirically that even one who is distant from God, or one who wallows in depression and does not want to "wake up" from his slothfulness, could become aroused and instilled with a renewed spirit of vigor to draw closer to God. Hearing music (not the type designed to arouse hatred, anger and depression) will awaken a person to think of where he is in this world and return to God.

This is why King David authored the Book of Psalms, which contains the Ten Types of Song. Song enables us to lift up our heart and bind it to God. We can then repair our broken heart / tablet and inscribe on it the letters of Torah (i.e., God's wisdom.) As the verse says, "Bind them around your neck; write them [the Torah] upon the tablets of your heart." Bind them around your neck—from where the voice of song emerges. Then you can inscribe them on your heart and repair your broken tablets.

We recite the *Pesukey d'Zimrah* prior to saying the *Shema* because we need song and melodies to arouse our hearts to God. This is the connection between the Ten Commandments (*yod*), paralleling the Ten Types of Song and the Tablets (the *vav*). This also explains why we say the word *Halleluyah* ten times during the *Pesukey d'Zimrah* and why we recite the *Shirat HaYam*, the Song of Deliverance, before the *Shema*.

Shema: The Tzaddik and the Jewish People

After the *Pesukey d'Zimra* we enter the third and next higher world, in which we say the *Shema* and its blessings. This corresponds to the *m'loopum* of the tzaddik and the Jewish people. The tzaddik is *yod,* because the tzaddikim are called "the *wise* men of the congregation," and the Jewish people correspond to the *vav,* because they are "supporters of Torah" and are referred to as "*vavey* (hooks, i.e., supporters) of the pillars."

Reciting the *Shema* is accepting the yoke of Heaven. This is the main devotion of a person, to bind himself to God. This refers to the tzaddik, the *yod,* who is completely attached to God and reveals His Godliness to the nation, the Jewish people (the *vav*). Therefore, we find in the blessings of the *Shema* a blessing for the celestial bodies (i.e., sun and moon), for they represent light as does the tzaddik. Similarly, we find a blessing for Torah study (*Ahavas Olam*), which is transmitted by the tzaddik to the nation. The third blessing of the morning *Shema* comes just before the *Amidah* and is called *GaaL Yisrael* (Who has redeemed Israel), for the tzaddik represents the redeemer, *Mashiach*, of Israel.

Amidah: The Individual

The fourth level of the prayers is the *Amidah*, representing the fourth concept of *m'loopum*, that of the individual. The *yod* represents his mouth ("My mouth will speak wisdom") and "The meditations of my heart" parallels the *vav*, as explained above. When a person prays with *kavanah* and hearkens to the words that emerge from his mouth, he connects his heart and mouth, leading to the rectifications that prayer is meant to bring about (LH, *Nesiat Kapayim* 5:5-11).

CHAPTER 15

Pesukey d'Zimrah: Ten Types of Song

The second section of *Shacharit* corresponds to the World of *Yetzirah* (Formation), the world of the angels. Just as the angels sing God's praises, we can ascend to that angelic level and sing God's praises as well. *Pesukey d'Zimrah* (Verses of Song) is comprised of many verses containing praises to God, (mostly from Psalms as well as from several other books of the Bible.) The *Beit Yosef* emphasizes that one should recite these verses unhurriedly, since soon we will articulate our requests before God, and it is not fitting to rush through the praises of the Authority who will shortly be asked to answer our prayers (*Tur, Orach Chaim* 51).

Subduing the *Kelipot*

Pesukey d'Zimrah can also be translated as "Verses of Cutting / Pruning," alluding to the fact that reciting verses of song and praise to God has the power to cut down and clear away the obstacles that seek to prevent our prayers (and us) from rising up. As Rebbe Nachman states:

> It is only possible to subdue the *kelipot*—the illusions, negative thoughts, desires, confusions and obstacles—through recognition of the greatness of the Creator. Because we are now ascending from the World of *Asiyah* (*Korbanot* / Sacrifices) to the World of *Yetzirah*, *Hodu* was instituted at the beginning of the *Pesukey d'Zimrah* in order to subdue the forces of the *kelipot*.

Precisely by proclaiming the greatness of the Creator, the *kelipot* are subdued (LM I, 25:4).

This also explains why *Hodu* contains praise of God for the past, present and future. Precisely by thanking God for all the miracles He has done for us in the past—which shows that the *kelipot* were indeed subdued and His glory revealed—we strengthen our faith that we will merit to experience more of His kindness, now and in the future, and defeat the forces of evil (LH, *Hodaah* 6:72).

Our recital of *Pesukey d'Zimrah* can push away the *kelipot* that seek to prevent our prayers (and us) from rising higher. We could ask: Weren't the forces of evil already subdued by our reciting the passages of *Korbanot*? Why must we subdue them further?

Rebbe Nachman teaches that life is not static; each person has to ascend the spiritual ladder one step at a time. With each step forward, however, a new set of *kelipot* arises to block our advancement to the next level. Therefore, we precede each step forward with praise of God. By honoring Him and exulting in His praise, we cut off and defeat those *kelipot* and are able to advance higher and higher (see LM I, 25:5).

This also answers the question of why we must pray each day, for weren't the *kelipot* defeated when we prayed yesterday? Each day presents new challenges. By recognizing God today and praising Him again, we can face today's challenges and succeed.

Barukh She'amar

בָּרוּךְ שֶׁאָמַר וְהָיָה הָעוֹלָם, בָּרוּךְ הוּא:

Blessed is the One who spoke the world into existence. Blessed is He.

We say *Barukh She'amar* as an initial blessing prior to saying the psalms, and we conclude these psalms with the blessing of *Yishtabach*. Immediately afterwards we say the blessings of the *Shema* and then the *Amidah*. From the time we begin *Barukh She'amar* until the end of the *Amidah*, it is forbidden to speak out. (Imagine holding a conversation with an important person and then stopping in the middle to say hello to someone who's passing by!)

When we begin *Barukh She'amar*, we take the *tzitzit* in our hands and hold them until we conclude the blessing. Then we kiss them and release them. Holding the *tzitzit* at this point alludes to the four levels with which we start the day, which correspond to the Four Worlds: relieving ourselves (*Asiyah*); donning *tzitzit* (*Yetzirah*); laying the arm-*tefillin* (*Beriyah*); and laying the head-*tefillin* (*Atzilut*). Since we are now entering the World of *Yetzirah*, we take hold of the *tzitzit*. Another reason for holding the *tzitzit* at this moment has to do with *Pesukey d'Zimrah* which parallels the melodious song that will be sung in the future. Reb Noson adds that this song is a result of the *Chut shel Chesed* (string of kindness) when God spreads His compassion over the world. Hence, we take the strings of the *tzitzit* in our hands as we begin to recite the songs of *Pesukey d'Zimrah* (LH, *Tzitzit* 5:20).

One should stand while reciting *Barukh She'amar*, as we find in the verse "*Seraphim* (angels) stood above Him" (Isaiah 6:2). Since we have entered the angelic realm, we act like the angels and stand.

Previously, we discussed Rebbe Nachman's story of "The Exchanged Children" and Reb Noson's commentary on it.[86]

86 See Chapter 3. The full text of the story appears in Appendix B.

When speaking of the rectification of the prince, Reb Noson states that he was "chasing the animals," alluding to the section of the sacrifices in the morning prayer. The sacrifices, as explained, refine the human spirit from the animal spirit within a person. Music is also created through a process of refinement. The person who plays an instrument gathers up with his hand the good *ruach* (wind or spirit) from within the *ruach* of depression. He must know how to collect the components of the *ruach* one by one, in order to build the tune, the joy (LM I, 54:7). When the prince was in the home of the Forest Man, he was able to hear the wonderful melody of the animals of the forest and was given a vessel which played that song. This is the function of the *Pesukey d'Zimrah*: to produce wonderful and melodious tunes in order to elevate our spirit to higher and greater levels (LH, *Birkhot HaShachar* 3:28).

Barukh She'amar was established by the Men of the Great Assembly when a note descended from Heaven with the exact wording of this praise inscribed on it. It contains eighty-seven words, the *gematria* of *PaZ* (פז, gold), as alluded to in the verse "[The crown on] His head is of the finest gold" (Song of Songs 5:11).[87] The Men of the Great Assembly understood this to mean that the "head" (beginning) of this section of the prayers should consist of this blessing of exactly eighty-seven words.

In *Barukh She'amar* the word *barukh* (ברוך, blessed) appears thirteen times, paralleling the Thirteen Attributes of Mercy.[88] Reciting this prayer arouses Supernal Compassion upon us.

87 *Tur, Orach Chaim* 51; *Taz,* ibid. 51:1.

88 As detailed in the *Pri Etz Chaim, Shaar HaZemirot* 4, p. 143.

Mizmor L'Todah

מִזְמוֹר לְתוֹדָה, הָרִיעוּ לַיְיָ כָּל הָאָרֶץ:

A Song of Thanksgiving: Let the whole earth call out to HaShem.

When a person recites this chapter of Psalms, it is considered as if he brought a *Korban Todah* (thanksgiving-offering).[89] Our Sages teach that four kinds of people are required to bring this sacrifice (*Berakhot* 54b):

- One who safely passed through the desert
- A seriously ill person who has recovered
- One who was interned in prison and released
- One who safely crossed the seas

According to the ARI, this sacrifice is greater than all others because the other sacrifices are in the realm of *Asiyah,* as they are brought for sins. The *Korban Todah* is meant to say thanks to God, so it is in the realm of *Yetzirah,* like the angels who give praise to God. The Midrash teaches that in the future, all sacrifices will be abolished except for the *Korban Todah* (*Vayikra Rabbah* 9:7).

In the Mishnah of *Eizehu Mekoman,* it states that the time frame for eating the *Korban Todah* was during the day until midnight. Therefore, we do not recite *Mizmor L'Todah* on Erev Yom Kippur, since we must begin fasting that afternoon; nor do we recite it on Erev Pesach, for the sacrifice was accompanied by *chametz* which is forbidden after just a few hours in the day. In these cases, the full time allotted for eating the offering was not applicable and the sacrifice would be left over and rendered inedible.

89 The *Korban Todah* was an animal sacrifice brought together with four different types of bread. Some parts of the animal were burned on the Altar, others were given to the Kohen, and the remainder was eaten by the owner.

Additionally, since the *Korban Todah* was a personal sacrifice and not an obligatory one, we do not recite *Mizmor L'Todah* on Shabbos or the Festivals.

Rebbe Nachman teaches that the four categories for which one gives thanks also allude to misfortunes of the soul, as follows:

- One who safely passed through the desert—this is the soul that wanders about tired, hungry and thirsty in the spiritual wilderness.
- A seriously ill person who has recovered—this is the sickness of the soul that has become so faint that even if given some spiritual food and encouragement to accomplish in life, it cannot tolerate "eating" it.
- One who was interned in prison and released—these are the binds and difficulties that make us feel trapped and unable to overcome.
- One who safely crossed the seas—these are challenges and troubles we encounter throughout our lives.

All four who are obliged to give thanks allude to the misfortunes of the soul in the service of God. The soul has much opposition and many obstacles stand up against it. It may suffer torment, affliction, great wanderings and unnatural misfortunes. However, God continuously rescues us from misfortunes, and for this we are obliged to give thanks, always.[90]

הָרִיעוּ לַיְיָ כָּל הָאָרֶץ:

Let the whole earth call out to HaShem.

The initial letters of the words, **ה**ריעו **ל**ה' **כ**ל **ה**ארץ (Let the whole earth call out to God), spell *HaLaKhaH* (הלכה,

90 LM I, 163; see also Chapter 44.

Jewish law) (LM I, 11:6). King David is exhorting us to get the entire world to accept God's kingship and serve Him. How can we do this? Rebbe Nachman suggests that the way to get the "whole earth" (i.e., all its people) to "call out to God" is by studying and fulfilling the tenets of *Halakhah*, the codes of law (ibid. I, 11:6).

עִבְדוּ אֶת יְיָ בְּשִׂמְחָה:

Serve HaShem with joy.

דְּעוּ כִּי יְיָ הוּא אֱלֹהִים:

Know that HaShem is God.

It is important to know that *Elohim* (God's Name of judgment), is the same God as *YHVH* (God's Name of compassion). The judgments that challenge a person are actually very great levels of compassion meant to cleanse him from sin and help him merit the World to Come. The *Zohar* (III, 5a-b) reads this phrase: "Know! HaShem (*YHVH*) is *Elohim* (the God of judgment is still the God of compassion)!" When praying and serving God, one must do so with a heart filled with joy. Additionally, when one serves God with joy, this will help him *know* that God (*YHVH*, the Name of compassion) is *Elohim* (the Name of judgment), and when these Names are united, then judgments are mitigated.

וְעַד דֹּר וָדֹר אֱמוּנָתוֹ:

His faithfulness endures from generation to generation.

How can we know that God is One and that His faithfulness endures? Because when we marry and have children, we pass on our faith from generation to generation (LH, *Tefillin* 5:31). Although each child will be very different from the next, the fact that we manage to instill faith in each one of them and they maintain their faith in the One God allows faith to endure and spread (LH, *Perikah U'Te'inah* 4:27).

Yehi Kevod

יְהִי כְבוֹד יְיָ לְעוֹלָם, יִשְׂמַח יְיָ בְּמַעֲשָׂיו:

May HaShem's glory be forever;
HaShem shall rejoice in His works.

The Talmud states:

> Rabbi Chanina ben Pappa taught: The ministering angel of the world said this when God commanded the trees to yield fruit after their own kind, the grasses drew an inference with regard to themselves: If the trees—which are large and do not reproduce in close proximity—were commanded by HaShem "after its own kind" (Genesis 1:11), then all the more so we—who are small and do reproduce in close proximity—must bring forth only "after its own kind." The ministering angel of the world spoke up and said, "May God's glory be forever; God shall rejoice in His works" (*Chullin* 60a, cf. Rashi).

This took place on the third day of creation.[91] "Trees" alludes to the tzaddikim—tall in stature and few and far between. "Grasses" implies the ordinary man—lower in stature and much more common. Though the grasses were not commanded to bring forth "after its own kind," they did so anyway. Thus, "HaShem shall rejoice in His works."

This passage of *Yehi Kevod* expresses the glory of God. It has eighteen verses, each of which contains at least one Name of God (*YHVH*). As the ARI explains, this corresponds to the *Chai Olamim* (eighteen worlds), the conduit through which bounty descends to us.[92]

91 Rashi on Genesis 1:12.

92 *Shaar HaKavanot, Inyan Tefillat HaShachar*, p. 111. See also Chapter 8.

רַבּוֹת מַחֲשָׁבוֹת בְּלֶב אִישׁ, וַעֲצַת יְיָ הִיא תָקוּם:

Many are the thoughts in the heart of a man,
but HaShem's counsel endures.

We may be influenced by false motives and be distracted by many outside thoughts when we pray. Such thoughts actually benefit our prayers for tremendous powers are always at work, attempting to denounce proper prayers. But distracting thoughts serve to disguise our prayers so that they are ignored by the forces of evil. Then these forces do not attack the prayers, and the supplications are allowed to enter.

God knows the truth. We may have improper motives or be distracted, but in the depths of our hearts, our sole intent is to pray to God. God knows this. When we pray, our innermost thoughts are always directed towards God. God sees this innermost desire. He sees through the outer thoughts and accepts the prayer in love (*Rebbe Nachman's Wisdom* #72).

כִּי יַעֲקֹב בָּחַר לוֹ יָהּ, יִשְׂרָאֵל לִסְגֻלָּתוֹ:

For God chose Yaakov for Himself, Yisrael as His special one.

Rebbe Nachman reflects on the difference between Yaakov and Yisrael. He explains that when a person studies Torah but is unable to understand it, this corresponds to "Yaakov"—it is an immanent or incomplete knowledge. The name *yAaKoV* (יעקב) contains the letters of *EKeV* (עקב, heel), signifying a low level of knowledge, when subjects aren't completely clear. Even when a person's knowledge is at the level of Yaakov, God loves his studies (but he shouldn't be teaching that Torah to the public!)

"Yisrael," on the other hand, represents the revelation of intellect. This is seen in the letters of *YiSRAeL* (ישראל),

which can be rearranged to spell *LI ROSh* (לי ראש, I have a head), indicating full and complete knowledge. Thus, "*Yisrael l'segulato*" (Yisrael is His special one) can be expounded to the public.

The Rebbe now explains why the word *segulah* is used to refer to Yisrael in this verse:

> We are called "*am segulah*" (a special nation) (Deuteronomy 7:6). A *segulah* is something that isn't rationally understood. Compare it to a *segulah* used for healing. The dictates of nature would not necessitate that this should induce healing; nevertheless, this *segulah* is propitious for curing. It is supernatural, something that the human mind cannot fathom.
>
> Israel, too, is in the category of *segulah*, because it cannot be understood why and how God chose us as "a special nation" from among the other nations. At the splitting of the Red Sea, Judgment accused, "These serve idolatry, and these serve idolatry" (*Shemot Rabbah* 21:7). Even so, God still chose us as His *am segulah*—a choice that the human intellect doesn't comprehend.
>
> Thus, when one studies Torah, he perceives the transcendent intellects that are above nature and human intellect. This means he understands the Torah on the level of *segulah*. Therefore, it is only fitting that this "specialness,"—this special revelation—should be revealed to the nation, the *am segulah*.
>
> (LM I, 21:8-9)

CHAPTER 16

Ashrey and the Halleluyahs

Ashrey

Ashrey is undoubtedly the most important of the psalms and praises that are included in the *Pesukey d'Zimrah*. If someone is late for synagogue and tries to catch up to the congregation who are holding by *Borekhu*, the law dictates that he should recite *Barukh She'amar, Ashrey*, and then skip to *Yishtabakh* (*Kitzur Shulchan Arukh* 14:6-7). Also, as we shall soon see, *Ashrey* contains the prayer for livelihood. Therefore, one must recite this verse with deep concentration. If one fails to do so, he should repeat the verse because of its importance (*Orach Chaim* 51:7).

אַשְׁרֵי יוֹשְׁבֵי בֵיתֶךָ, עוֹד יְהַלְלוּךָ סֶּלָה:

Happy are those who dwell in Your House; they will merit to sing praises and reflect their gratitude back to You forevermore, *selah*.

אַשְׁרֵי הָעָם שֶׁכָּכָה לּוֹ, אַשְׁרֵי הָעָם שֶׁיְיָ אֱלֹהָיו:

Happy is the people for whom this is so; happy is the people whose God is HaShem.

The *Ashrey* prayer is known as *Tehillah L'David* and is from the Book of Psalms (Psalm 145). The two opening verses are psalms added in order to introduce the concept of *Ashrey*. The first verse speaks of "dwelling in God's House" and is somewhat of a reminder to us to approach the prayers with a settled mind. Our Sages teach that a person should enter the house of prayer and pause for a few moments before beginning his prayers (cf. *Berakhot* 8a). The second verse speaks of how fortunate we are to be able to praise God.

Rabbi Yehoshua ben Levi taught:

> Whoever enters the synagogues and study houses in this world will merit to enter synagogues and study houses in the World to Come, as it is written, "Happy are those who dwell in Your House in this world; they will merit to sing praises to You forevermore in the future" (*Devarim Rabbah* 7:1).

The verse says, "Happy is the people for whom this is so; happy..." (Psalms 144:15). Reb Nachman Tulchiner, a close follower of Reb Noson, used to read the words of this verse in this way: "*Ashrey haam* (Fortunate is the person) *shekakha lo* (through whatever happens to him) *ashrey* (is able to remain happy)!"

Three Times a Day

The Talmud teaches, "Whoever recites *Tehillah L'David* three times daily is guaranteed a place in the World to Come" (*Berakhot* 4b). We say *Ashrey* twice in the *Shacharit* prayer — once during *Pesukey d'Zimrah* and once after the *Amidah* just before "*Uva l'Tzion Go'el*." We say it a third time in *Minchah*, before the *Amidah*.

The *Zohar* teaches:

> The first time we say *Ashrey*, in the *Pesukey d'Zimrah*, is to praise God and strengthen *Malkhut*, the source of bounty and blessing, since we say, "You open Your hands and satiate every living being" (Psalms 145:16). The other two times (morning and afternoon), we ask for our livelihoods, just as we eat in the mornings and evenings, as it is written in the verse, "When God provides you with meat in the evening to eat and bread in the morning to satiate" (Exodus 16:8). Twice a day, we ask for our livelihoods and for the sustenance of all living things, rich and poor, human and animals (*Zohar* III, 226a).

Thus, the *Ashrey* said after the *Amidah* is an important prayer for livelihood and should be recited with deep *kavanah*. We say this second *Ashrey* after we have praised and thanked God, since it is not very honorable to ask God for livelihood prior to the actual prayers.

The Talmud explains what makes the prayer of *Ashrey* so unique to warrant saying it three times a day:

> Rabbi Elazar said in the name of Rabbi Avina: Whoever recites *Tehillah L'David* three times daily is guaranteed a place in the World to Come. What is the reason? If it is because it contains the *aleph-bet*, then let him recite Psalm 119, which contains the *aleph-bet* eight times. Or is it because it contains the verse "You open Your hand" [about God providing livelihood for all]? Then let him recite the Great Hallel (Psalm 136), where it is written, "Who gives food to all flesh" (Psalms 136:25). Rather, we recite *Ashrey* because it contains both ideas [it contains the *aleph-bet*, and it reminds us that God provides] (*Berakhot* 4b).

Reb Noson ponders this teaching, "What is it about reciting verses that contain the *aleph-bet* that merit a person the World to Come? Furthermore, the second reason offered by our Sages is even more confounding: Because a person mentions that God provides, he deserves to merit the World to Come? The Talmud's conclusion leaves us with an additional question: If reciting the *aleph-bet* and that God provides is so rewarding, why don't we recite both Psalm 119 and Psalm 136?" Therefore, writes Reb Noson, there must be a compelling reason to specifically say this chapter. It is because both the *aleph-bet* and livelihood are *combined* in the one chapter of *Ashrey*, a person can merit the World to Come. What is the connection between the two concepts?

Reb Noson offers that the two ideas complement one another and can bring a person back to God in complete repentance. Focusing first on the *aleph-bet*, Reb Noson writes that speech is paramount when returning to God, which is why the recital of psalms is so powerful. It contains words of praise to God along with many cries and supplications to return to Him. The *aleph-bet* is comprised of all the letters necessary to compose words of prayer with which to turn to God, as in the verse, "Take with you words and return to God" (Hosea 14:3).

On the other hand, the *aleph-bet* also contains the letter-word combinations of all the sins that the Torah prohibits and warns us against doing. Sin draws the holy letters to the realm of the Other Side, and the rectification is by saying many prayers and supplications, which return the letters to their rectified state. Thus, in *Ashrey* we find the *aleph-bet* which we use for prayers and repentance. With prayer, everyone can rectify his ways and return to God.

However, says Reb Noson, a very powerful obstacle prevents people from taking advantage of this great counsel and returning to God. This obstacle is "earning a livelihood." One is preoccupied and simply doesn't have time to pray. But this doesn't need to be a deterrent, because we believe that livelihood comes from God alone. As we say in *Ashrey*, "You give the exact amount of sustenance... You open Your hands to satisfy the deepest needs of every living being." Says Reb Noson, we must remember at all times that it is God Who sustains humankind and the world. All our efforts cannot truly provide our needs. The person who merits to recognize that God provides livelihood for all—that He inscribes the amount we will receive throughout the year on *Rosh HaShanah* (*Beitzah* 16a)—will not consider earning a living as an obstacle to calling out to God by using the *aleph-bet*. He will find time for prayer. Thus, when one combines the two ideas together—the *aleph-bet*, which represents the essentialness of prayer, and the realization that God provides for and sustains the world—he will certainly find the time and the words necessary to seek God.

Therefore, our Sages say that whoever recites *Ashrey* three times a day will have a place in the World to Come, for *Ashrey* teaches us to use the twenty-two letters to pray to God. We are reminded that we have time for prayer, because our livelihood comes from God. The combination of these lessons will certainly bring us to repentance, and we will merit the World to Come (LH, *Kriat Shema* 5:14).

חַנּוּן וְרַחוּם יְיָ, אֶרֶךְ אַפַּיִם וּגְדָל חָסֶד:

HaShem is gracious and compassionate, exceedingly patient, and His lovingkindness is boundless.

קָרוֹב יְיָ לְכָל קֹרְאָיו, לְכֹל אֲשֶׁר יִקְרָאֻהוּ בֶאֱמֶת:

HaShem is close to all who call upon Him, but He is especially close when they call Him sincerely and truthfully.

The twenty-one verses of *Ashrey* follow the order of the letters of the *aleph-bet*. Almost all of the verses have the letter *vav* in the middle of the verse, which connects the beginning and the end of each verse. The two exceptions are the verses that begin with the letters *chet* (ח) and *kuf* (ק). These verses don't have the connecting *vav*.

The *Zohar* (II, 180 b) explains that the Other Side seeks to draw sustenance from the holy letters of the *aleph-bet* but is prevented from doing so by the *vav*, which represents God. This is because God's name is alluded to in the *vav*.[93] However, the Other Side is closer to the two letters *chet* and *kuf*, so the *vav* is missing in those verses in order to separate them from God's name / the *vav*. One of the reasons offered why specifically these two letters is that the *gematria* of these two letters is 108, the same *gematria* of Gehinnom (גיהנם), and by saying *Ashrey*

93 The *vav* represents *Zer Anpin* and corresponds to the World of *Yetzirah*; see Chapter 4.

we are defeating the Other Side and extricating ourselves from there.

We now look at the meaning of some of the individual verses in the *Ashrey* prayer:

> דּוֹר לְדוֹר יְשַׁבַּח מַעֲשֶׂיךָ, וּגְבוּרֹתֶיךָ יַגִּידוּ:
>
> Generation after generation will increasingly appreciate Your handiwork; they will also relate Your powerful miracles.

After the sin of Adam, the world was thrown into chaos and confusion, and the fallen sparks of holiness were spread throughout the world. The rectification of these sparks cannot be accomplished in one moment. It is man's mission to complete his tasks during his lifetime, which will rectify *his* sparks in *his* generation. The remainder of the sparks will eventually be rectified in future generations (LH, *Shechitah* 4:3).

> טוֹב יְיָ לַכֹּל, וְרַחֲמָיו עַל כָּל מַעֲשָׂיו:
>
> HaShem is good for all, and His mercies are upon all His works.

Rebbe Nachman teaches that the beginning of this verse expresses the aspect of prayer. "HaShem is good for all" means that when a person believes in God, he believes that God is good for all matters and needs—for health, livelihood, and everything a person needs. When one believes this, then the main focus of his efforts to attain his needs will certainly be from God, instead of pursuing all kinds of strategies. For when one doesn't believe in God, he must employ all kinds of strategies. For example, if he is sick, he must work at getting all sorts of medicines. And there are times when the particular medicines he needs are not available, whereas those medicines that are available are useless for his illness. But "HaShem is good for all" illnesses—and God can heal them. God is also always available, as it is written, "Who is… like HaShem our God, whenever we pray to Him!" (Deuteronomy 4:7).

The Rebbe adds that through prayer, a person ultimately merits universal peace. This is expressed by the end of the verse, "His mercies are upon all His works." In other words, God's mercies are drawn upon all created beings. The created beings will have mercy for one another, and there will be peace between them. As it is written, "And the wolf shall dwell with the lamb, and the leopard shall lie down with the kid… they shall not harm or destroy" (Isaiah 11:6, 9). Moreover, our Sages teach, "Whoever has mercy on God's creations, Heaven has mercy upon him, as it is written, 'And He will give you mercy and have mercy upon you" (LM I, 14:11).[94]

סוֹמֵךְ יְיָ לְכָל הַנֹּפְלִים, וְזוֹקֵף לְכָל הַכְּפוּפִים:

HaShem supports all who have fallen;
He raises up all who are bent down.

It is interesting to note that the verses of *Ashrey* follow the order of the *aleph-bet*, with the exception of the letter *nun* (נ). The Talmud explains that the reason the letter *nun* is omitted is because the letter *nun* would have indicated a *nefilah* (נפילה, fall), indicating a fall in status for the Jewish nation. Still, King David made sure to include this concept in the following verse, "God supports all who have fallen" (*Berakhot* 4b).

Rebbe Nachman elaborates on the implications of the two forms of the letter *nun*—the bent *nun* (נ) which appears in the middle of a word and the straight *nun* (ן) which is used at the end of a word. Citing the *Zohar* (III, 27b), he writes:

> The *teiku* (unresolved issue) spoken of in the Talmud is an aspect of a lack of *tikkun* (spiritual rectification)—i.e., the *Nun* of *TIKkUN* (תיקון) is missing, so that it becomes *TeIKU* (תיקו).

94 Deuteronomy 13:18; *Shabb*at 151b.

And know! When this elongated *nun* (ן) is missing from *TIKkUN* so that it becomes *TeIKU* (*unresolved*), then it is made low and is bent over (נ). This creates the aspect of *KINOT* (קינות, lamentations)—*KINOT* has the same letters as *TIKkUN*, except the *nun* is bent over rather than straight. May God redeem us and may the *kinot* be transformed into *tikkun* to rectify the aforementioned *teiku* (LM I, 247).

This is the meaning of the verse "HaShem supports all who have fallen; He raises up all who are bent down." "All who have fallen" refers to the bent-over *nun* (נ). "He raises up all who are bent down" refers to the straight *nun* (ן) (Reb Nachman Burstyn).

עֵינֵי כֹל אֵלֶיךָ יְשַׂבֵּרוּ, וְאַתָּה נוֹתֵן לָהֶם אֶת אָכְלָם בְּעִתּוֹ:

Therefore, all direct their eyes longingly toward You, for You give the exact amount of sustenance allotted to them in its proper time.

פּוֹתֵחַ אֶת יָדֶךָ, וּמַשְׂבִּיעַ לְכָל חַי רָצוֹן:

You open Your hands to satisfy the deepest needs of every living being.

Rebbe Nachman teaches:

God's bounty is always coming down, but it doesn't have a time frame. Sometimes, something the person needs now will come only in two or three years. But when one trusts in God, this creates a vessel for the bounty, and the bounty will come to him when he needs it. This is the explanation of the verse "All direct their eyes longingly to You"; and through this, "You give them their sustenance in the proper time" (see LM I, 76:1).

The verse "You open Your hands" is the verse for requesting livelihood. The *Zohar* (II, 62a) teaches that when we ask God for our livelihoods, we are, in effect, opening the channels of bounty not just for us but for the entire world.

"Opening your hands" can also refer to the mandate for us to give charity to the poor. The Talmud lists several laws related to this practice (*Ketuvot* 67b). One law states that if a pauper was once wealthy and was accustomed to a life of luxury, the communal charity must supply him with his old habits. Once there was a wealthy person who was used to having servants run before him, and he lost all his money. Hillel the Elder provided such a service for the man. When Hillel could not find a person to service the man on one occasion, Hillel ran before him himself.

Rava was the head of the yeshivah in Pumpedita in Babylonia and was accepted as the leading tzaddik and scholar of his generation. Once a poor man came to him and asked for charity (*Maharsha,* loc. cit.) Rava asked him, "What are you used to eating?" The man replied, "A plump chicken and old wine." Rava asked him, "Aren't you asking too much from the community?" The man answered, "I am not eating from their funds, I am eating from God! Does it not say, 'For You give them their sustenance in the proper time'? This means that God provides the sustenance to each person at the proper time!" At that moment, Rava's sister, whom he had not seen in thirteen years, came to visit him. She brought him a gift — a plump chicken and old wine. Convinced, Rava said, "I accept, come eat!"

Even Rava, the leading tzaddik of the generation, was impressed with the simple faith of the man that God provides at the exact moment.

Rebbe Nachman stresses that people's requests and desires can and will be addressed by Heaven. When we turn to God, He will open His hands and bless us. The question we have is: "What type of blessing do you desire?" The Rebbe teaches that a person should seek the blessing of intellect (LM I, 24:5).

"*Potei'ach et Yadekha*—You open Your hands." This verse expresses the essence of our faith that all livelihood comes from God, that He oversees and supervises everything, and that He nourishes and provides for all. All this is alluded to in the *gematria* of the initial letters of the words *Potei'ach Et Yadekha*,[95] (פותח את ידיך) which is also the sum of the two Divine Names *YHVH* and *Adonoy*.[96]

The Names of God, *YHVH* and *Adonoy*, are sometimes seen as the combination of יאהדונהי. Noting that the first letter of *YHVH* is *Yod*, and the last letter of *AdonoY* is *Yod*, the *Zohar* tells us that this is the key to this verse. When saying *Potei'ach et Yadekha* (You open Your hands), we should also intend: *Potei'ach et Yodekha* (You open Your *Yods*). We should envision Divine illumination flowing from the initial *Yod* of *YHVH* (corresponding to the *sefirah* of *Chokhmah*) all the way down to the final *Yod* of *AdonoY* (corresponding to the *sefirah* of *Malkhut*), through the intervening *sefirot* (*Binah, Chesed, Gevurah, Tiferet, Netzach, Hod and Yesod*).[97] Rebbe Nachman adds that the movement from the *Yod* of *YHVH* to the *Yod* of *AdonoY* alludes to the emergence of Creation from "closed" potential to "open" actuality (LH, *Edut* 1).

קָרוֹב יְיָ לְכָל קֹרְאָיו, לְכֹל אֲשֶׁר יִקְרָאֻהוּ בֶאֱמֶת:

HaShem is close to all who call upon Him, when they call Him sincerely and truthfully.

Reb Noson emphasizes the verse's statement, "sincerely and truthfully." When a person truly turns to God, then

95 *Peh* (80) + *aleph* (1) + *yod* (10) = 91.

96 *YHVH* (26) + *ADoNoY* (65) = 91.

97 *Tikkuney Zohar*, Introduction, p. 7b; *Pri Etz Chaim, Shaar HaZemirot* 5.

God most certainly draws closer to that person and manifests Himself to the individual (LH, *Tefillah* 4:7).

> רְצוֹן יְרֵאָיו יַעֲשֶׂה, וְאֶת שַׁוְעָתָם יִשְׁמַע וְיוֹשִׁיעֵם:
>
> He fulfills the desire of those who revere Him;
> He hears their cries and rescues them.

Rebbe Nachman teaches that the yearning and longing that a person has for a holy thing are very precious. Through his yearning and desire to do God's will, souls are created in potential. And by means of speech—through his cries and requests to God, the soul comes forth from potential to actual.

The soul corresponds to the vowel-points for the letters of the Torah, for letters without vowel-points are like a body without a soul. The vowel-points are what give life and movement to the letters. Thus, through "the desire of those who fear Him"—through the yearning and longing that one has to fulfill God's will—the soul is created in potential. And by expressing those yearnings in a loud voice, "He hears their cries and rescues them"—as a result of speech, the soul is completed and moves from potentiality to actuality. Then the letters combine and become a vessel with which to receive the bounty, and his request is fulfilled in action (LM I, 31:6, 15).

> תְּהִלַּת יְיָ יְדַבֶּר פִּי, וִיבָרֵךְ כָּל בָּשָׂר שֵׁם קָדְשׁוֹ לְעוֹלָם וָעֶד:
>
> My mouth will declare God's praise, and all mankind
> will bless His Holy Name forever.

Rebbe Nachman quotes a beautiful comment from Rabbi Alexander Ziskind (1739-1794), author of the *Yesod VeShoresh HaAvodah*:

> He said, "The verse says, '*My* mouth will praise God.' In that case, certainly 'all flesh will bless His Holy Name forever.'" This

tzaddik was very humble and lowly in his own eyes. His point was: If a lowly creature like himself is able to speak the praise of God, then certainly all flesh — all other creatures — have the right to "bless His Holy Name," for they can't be worse than he is (*Tzaddik* #522).

וַאֲנַחְנוּ נְבָרֵךְ יָהּ, מֵעַתָּה וְעַד עוֹלָם, הַלְלוּיָהּ:

We will bless God, from now throughout all eternity, *halleluyah.*

We conclude the *Ashrey* prayer with the verse "We will bless God, from now throughout all eternity, *Halleluyah*." This verse is written elsewhere (Psalms 115:18) and we attach it to the *Ashrey* prayer so we can conclude with the word *Halleluyah,* which connects *Ashrey* to the next five chapters that begin and end with *Halleluyah.* This verse also contains the promise that one who recites *Ashrey* three times a day is promised a place in the World to Come. The words "from now throughout eternity" allude to praising God in this world and in the next world.

The *Halleluyahs*

הַלְלוּיָהּ, הַלְלִי נַפְשִׁי אֶת יְיָ:

Halleluyah! My soul, praise HaShem.

The Talmud states, "Rabbi Yosi said, 'Let my lot be with those who complete Hallel each day!'" (*Shabbos* 118b). This refers to those who say the *Halleluyahs* in *Pesukey d'Zimrah.*

Rabbi Yehoshua ben Levi said, "The Book of Psalms was composed of Ten Types of Song (praises to God). The greatest of them all is *Halleluyah,* because the song (*Hallelu,* praise) and God's Name (*Yah*) are combined in one word" (*Pesachim* 117a).

We follow the passage of *Ashrey* with the five final chapters of psalms. Each chapter begins and ends with the word *Halleluyah*, so that there are ten recitals of *Halleluyah*, corresponding to the ten *sefirot*. According to the ARI, each of the *Halleluyahs* corresponds to a separate ascent of our prayers to higher levels, culminating with the final psalm (#150) which contains thirteen mentions of the word *Halleluhu* (praise Him).[98]

הַלְלוּיָהּ, אֲהַלְלָה יְיָ בְּחַיָּי:

Halleluyah! I will praise HaShem with my life.

When is it possible to praise God with my life? When I am not dependent on other people—not for honor, not for adulation, and not for livelihood. When I am self-sufficient, then I will be able to honestly praise God (LM I, 66:3).

אֲזַמְּרָה לֵאלֹהַי בְּעוֹדִי:

I will sing to my God with my very being.

In one of his most famous lessons known as *Azamra* (LM I, 282), Rebbe Nachman speaks of finding the good points in others and also in oneself. He bases this lesson on this verse "I will sing to God with my very being"—that is, with whatever good a person can find in himself, because when a person concentrates on the positive instead of the negative, he realizes that he actually has lots of good within himself.

יְיָ מַתִּיר אֲסוּרִים, יְיָ פֹּקֵחַ עִוְרִים, יְיָ זוֹקֵף כְּפוּפִים:

HaShem releases the bound; HaShem gives sight to the blind; HaShem straightens up those who are bent down."

98 *Shaar HaKavanot, Inyan Tefillat HaShachar*, p. 114.

Potifar's wife attempted to seduce Yosef. Every day she would wear different clothes and Yosef would not pay her any attention. She said to him, "I will imprison you." His reply was, "HaShem releases the bound." She threatened him, "I will cause you to be bent over, I will blind you." Yosef's reply was, "HaShem provides sight and straightens out those who are bent down" (*Yoma* 35b). Yosef's faith was absolute; he accepted whatever happens comes from God and believed He can rectify any situation.

> בּוֹנֵה יְרוּשָׁלַיִם יְיָ, נִדְחֵי יִשְׂרָאֵל יְכַנֵּס:
>
> HaShem is the Builder of Jerusalem;
> He will gather in the dispersed of Israel.

When will God build Jerusalem? When the dispersed of Israel are gathered (*Berakhot* 49a). As Jews gather and return to the Land of Israel, Jerusalem is being rebuilt even more. Conversely, the more Jerusalem gets rebuilt, the more the Jews will return to their Land.

> הַמְכַסֶּה שָׁמַיִם בְּעָבִים, הַמֵּכִין לָאָרֶץ מָטָר:
>
> He hides the heavens with clouds.
> He prepares rain for the earth.

No bounty or blessing can come to the world except by way of the tzaddik. (The tzaddik parallels the *sefirah* of *Yesod*, which transfers bounty from Above to *Malkhut*). This is because the tzaddik has love and fear, which are the "hands" for receiving all bounty and blessing. But the tzaddik has to conceal his love and fear, lest the accusatory forces realize he has them and steal the bounty from him.

According to the Kabbalah, fear corresponds to fire and love to water. Thus, "He hides the heavens with clouds"—the word *ShaMaYiM* (שמים, heavens) is a construct of the words *eSh* (אש, fire) and *MaYiM* (מים, water) (Rashi on Genesis 1:8). The tzaddik covers his love (water) and fear (fire) with *AVim* (עבים, clouds)—namely, with something that is *AV* (עב, dense) and corporeal. Then he is able to draw all the blessings, which correspond to rain (blessing and bounty) (LM I, 88). The more we attach ourselves to the tzaddik, the greater our ability to receive this bounty.

הַשָּׂם גְּבוּלֵךְ שָׁלוֹם, חֵלֶב חִטִּים יַשְׂבִּיעֵךְ:

He establishes peace in your borders;
He satiates you with the cream of the wheat.

The Talmud learns from this verse that whoever dreams of wheat can expect peace (*Berakhot* 57a). It also cites this verse to support the contention that strife is found in a home mainly because of lack of food (*Bava Metzia* 59a). The implication being, that where there is food and abundance, there is peace. Rebbe Nachman follows the order of the verse more literally: When there is peace, blessings and abundance abound (LM I, 56:6).

If you are satisfied with whatever you have, it is considered as if you are nourished from the cream of the wheat. Conversely, when you experience a hunger—being overcome by the desire for food—this indicates that you have enemies (ibid. I, 39:1).

הַלְלוּיָהּ, הַלְלוּ אֶת יְיָ מִן הַשָּׁמַיִם, הַלְלוּהוּ בַּמְּרוֹמִים:

Halleluyah! Praise HaShem from the highest heavens;
reflect Him in the celestial heights.

When a person says, "Praise HaShem from the highest heavens... Praise Him, all His angelic messengers;

reflect Him, all His hosts," he is calling on all of them and commanding them to praise God. Rebbe Nachman says that when you recite this passage, you should feel inspired to pray with heartfelt concentration for with your prayers, you are calling all the worlds and their inhabitants to praise and extol the Holy One (LM I, 232).

רוּחַ סְעָרָה עֹשָׂה דְבָרוֹ:

A storm wind that executes His word.

Rebbe Nachman compares blemished speech to a destructive storm wind. He explains that the spoken word is an aspect of *Adonoy,* as it is written, "*Adonoy,* open my lips" (Psalms 51:17). When speech/*Adonoy* is blemished, the blemish turns the "*ruach* (רוח, breath) of His mouth" (ibid. 33:6) into a *ruach se'arah* (רוח סערה, storm wind).

The Rebbe expounds on this idea as follows. There are twenty-seven letters in the Hebrew alphabet (twenty-two letters of the *aleph-bet* plus the five final-letter forms). Each letter can be vocalized by ten vowel-points, paralleling the ten *sefirot.*[99] Twenty-seven times ten yields the same numerical value as *RA* (רע, evil). The aspect of speech (i.e., *Adonoy*), is thus turned into the letters *Reish-Ayin,* indicating evil. The word *Se'ARaH* (סערה, storm wind) contains the letters *Samakh-Heh* (סה), which has the same *gematria* as *ADoNoY* (אדני), plus *Reish-Ayin* (רע). The "storm wind that executes His word" means it executes and rectifies the spoken word and elevates it from the aspect of storm wind.

Rebbe Nachman further explains the nature of the damage that imperfect speech can cause. He teaches that this storm wind becomes the person's Great Accuser, condemning him

99 See Charts, Appendix A.

and demanding that he be punished for his sins. It also causes a person's body to become agitated. All the libel and evil spoken about a person come from this storm wind, for it is an aspect of "an end to all flesh" (Genesis 6:13). Likewise, people who judge their fellow men unfavorably and constantly scrutinize other people's shortcomings, are from the aspect of "an end to all flesh." To counteract all this, every person must try to subdue his blemished speech to the spoken word of holiness (LM I, 38:2).

יִשְׂמַח יִשְׂרָאֵל בְּעֹשָׂיו:

Israel rejoices in its Maker.

When God's works are as they should be and in proper order (that is, there are no judgments and punishments in the world, only kindness and compassion), then God is happy with them and delights in them, as is written, "God rejoices in His works" (Psalms 104:31). Like a craftsman who makes a vessel; if the vessel is beautiful, then he delights in it. God's joy is clothed in the *mitzvot*, because they are His Unity. (The *mitzvot* of the Torah are directly from God, they are one with Him.) When a person performs a mitzvah with joy, he enters into the joy of God, who rejoices in His works. This corresponds to "Israel rejoices in its Maker" (LM I, 5:2).

Therefore, the *Zohar* (III, 219b) adds that a person should always include God as a partner in his joy.

רוֹמְמוֹת אֵל בִּגְרוֹנָם, וְחֶרֶב פִּיפִיּוֹת בְּיָדָם:

Lofty praises of God will be in their throats;
the double-edged sword in their hands.

Prayer is compared to a double-edged sword because it contains both praise of God and requests for one's needs.

A person begins his prayers with praising God, for this reminds him of the many times God answered his prayers and those of the Jewish people. This increases his belief in prayer (which is essential for the prayers to be effective) and it encourages him to pray once again for his needs.[100]

הַלְלוּהוּ בְּתֵקַע שׁוֹפָר, הַלְלוּהוּ בְּנֵבֶל וְכִנּוֹר ... כֹּל הַנְּשָׁמָה תְּהַלֵּל יָהּ:

Praise Him with the call of the *Shofar*. Praise Him with lyre and harp.... Let every soul praise God.

King David is expressing that the praise of God is not elevated through musical instruments, but through every soul that lauds Him. This is where God's praise lies (*Zohar Chadash, Bereishit* 15b).

כֹּל הַנְּשָׁמָה תְּהַלֵּל יָהּ, הַלְלוּיָהּ:

Let every soul praise God, *halleluyah!*

This verse, which we say twice, is not only the grand finale of this psalm, but of the entire Book of Psalms. It embodies the essence of the Book of Psalms, as our Sages said, "It is written, 'Let every *NeShaMaH* (נשמה, soul) praise God.' This means we must praise God for each and every *NeShiMaH* (נשימה, breath) we take".[101] Reb Noson adds, "The main thing is to know that each and every breath is from God and praise Him constantly for this. Therefore, we repeat the final verse twice. First, we praise God, and then we praise Him for the privilege of praising Him! (LH, *Kriat Shema* 5:13).

100 LM I, 2:2; LH, *Nachalot* 4:3.

101 *Bereishit Rabbah* 14:9; *Devarim Rabbah* 2:36.

The final verse of this psalm is repeated. We will also see that at the end of *Az Yashir* (the Song of Deliverance), the verse "God will rule ..." is also repeated. Repeating the verses shows that we are reluctant to end our prayers. Therefore, the Satan should not have an opportunity to criticize the Jews for leaving the prayers.

בָּרוּךְ יְיָ לְעוֹלָם, אָמֵן וְאָמֵן׃

May HaShem be blessed forever, Amen and Amen.

בָּרוּךְ יְיָ מִצִּיּוֹן שֹׁכֵן יְרוּשָׁלָיִם, הַלְלוּיָהּ׃

May HaShem be blessed from Zion, the One who dwells in Jerusalem, *halleluyah!*

בָּרוּךְ יְיָ אֱלֹהִים אֱלֹהֵי יִשְׂרָאֵל, עֹשֵׂה נִפְלָאוֹת לְבַדּוֹ׃

May HaShem, God, the God of Israel, Who alone does wonders, be blessed.

וּבָרוּךְ שֵׁם כְּבוֹדוֹ לְעוֹלָם, וְיִמָּלֵא כְבוֹדוֹ אֶת כָּל הָאָרֶץ, אָמֵן וְאָמֵן׃

May His glorious Name be blessed forevermore, and may the entire earth be filled with His radiant glory. Amen and Amen.

These four verses were placed at this point in the prayers because they are the final verses of several of the Books of Psalms. As we have just completed the verses of psalms of the *Pesukey d'Zimrah*, it is fitting to say these verses here. *Tehillim* (Psalms) is comprised of five books. The verse "May HaShem be blessed forever" appears at the end of Book Three; May HaShem be blessed from Zion" is found at the end of Psalm 135 in Book Five; and "May HaShem, God, the God of Israel, Who alone does wonders, be blessed" and "May His glorious Name be blessed" appear at the end of Book Two.

CHAPTER 17

Vayevarekh David and Az Yashir

The many praises to God that we recite in the blessing *Yishtabach* are culled from *Vayevarekh David* and *Az Yashir*. These praises glorify God and honor Him and His kingship.

Vayevarekh David

וַיְבָרֶךְ דָּוִיד אֶת יְיָ:

David blessed HaShem.

King David said these verses (I Chronicles 29:10-13) praising God after he completed the preparations for building the *Beis HaMikdash*. Rashi explains, "David said: Yitro was one convert among 600,000 Jews, and he said, 'Blessed is God' (Exodus 18:10). It is embarrassing that we Jews did not say 'Blessed is God.' Therefore, I will bless God even more than Yitro did." Thus, "David blessed HaShem…Blessed are You, HaShem, God of Israel, our Father, from eternity to eternity" (Rashi on I Chronicles 29:10).

The initial letters of the words *Vayevarekh David Et YHVH* (ויברך דויד את יי) spell the acronym *VaDAY* (ודאי), which has the same *gematria* as God's Holy Name *EHYeH* (א-ה-י-ה). The Name *EHYeH* corresponds to the *Keter* in the array of the *sefirot*,[102] and as this represents the highest *sefirah*, it is

102 See Charts, Appendix A.

customary and honorable to stand when we recite *Vayevarekh David*. A few sentences further on we say, "*Atah Hu YHVH HaElohim* (**א**תה **ה**וא **י**י **ה**אלהים, You alone are God), whose initial letters also spell *EHYeH*. Some stand at least until the passage which begins "You alone are God," while others remain standing until after we say *Borekhu*.[103]

וְאַתָּה מוֹשֵׁל בַּכֹּל:

You rule over all.

As understood from the ARI, each day contains its own measure of *gevurot* (judgments, constrictions) and *tzedek* (strict justice). These judgments come about due to sin, which gives power and glory to unworthy leaders and the forces of the Other Side. Giving *tzedakah* (charity) mitigates these judgments through compassion. Therefore, when citing the words, "You rule over all," we should give *tzedakah* (by placing it in the charity box or setting aside a few coins to give away later). In this way, Rebbe Nachman explains, we free God's sovereignty and glory from the rule of the Other Side and unworthy leaders and extend His rule over the entire world. We also automatically extricate God's glory from the hands of the brazenfaced and return it to deserving leaders (see LM I, 67:7, note 92).

וְעַתָּה אֱלֹהֵינוּ מוֹדִים אֲנַחְנוּ לָךְ:

Now, therefore, we give thanks to You, our God.

The word *MODIM* (מודים, give thanks) has the *gematria* of 100. King David concluded his praises with "thanks" to establish the idea of making one hundred blessings each day.[104]

103 See *Shaar HaKavanot, Inyan Tefillat HaShachar*, p. 114.
104 See above, Chapter 8.

More Praises

The praises of God's glory now shift from King David and the First *Beis HaMikdash* to the Book of Ezra / Nehemiah and the time of the rededication of the Second B*eis HaMikdash* (Nehemiah 9:5-11). As Rashi explains, these praises are very exalted, above all kinds of praise the mouth can offer (Rashi on Nehemiah 9:5).

וּצְבָא הַשָּׁמַיִם לְךָ מִשְׁתַּחֲוִים:

Therefore, the heavenly hosts bow down before You.

When saying this verse, you may add (in your thoughts) any personal requests that you may have—especially for healing. Explaining the connection, Rebbe Nachman teaches that plants receive their medicinal properties from God via the angelic hosts and the celestial forces (i.e., the constellations) that are under their charge. When God sends a cure, He does so through the celestial forces, which are then ordered to unite and come together to form the healing compound, each transmitting a particular energy to a particular plant. When we say in the prayers, "Therefore the heavenly hosts bow down before You," that is precisely the time when the celestial forces come before God to bow to and praise Him. Therefore, as one says these words, it is recommended that one pray that God should command the celestial powers to infuse the energies that are needed for his cure into the food that he will be eating. Then he will be healed through his meals. *Amen,* may it be His will![105]

אַתָּה הוּא יְיָ הָאֱלֹהִים, אֲשֶׁר בָּחַרְתָּ בְּאַבְרָם ... וְכָרוֹת עִמּוֹ הַבְּרִית ...

You are He, HaShem, the One and Only God, Who chose Avram ... You established the covenant with him ...

105 LM I, 231; see also ibid. II, 1:11-13.

Avraham was the first to truly recognize God and praise Him. His entire generation worshipped the celestial bodies and other idolatries, but Avraham rejected this and believed that "the heavenly hosts bow down before You." Therefore, after repeating Avraham's legacy, we state in our prayers that the exalted God chose Avraham to serve Him.

Because of Avraham's devotion, God made a covenant with him—the covenant of circumcision—and by inference, of morality. And because of that covenant, God granted us the Land of Israel. But the Land was to be given to the Jews only after 400 years (Genesis 15:13). They first had to descend to Egypt and endure brutal servitude. This explains the order of our prayers in this section of the siddur, from "the heavenly hosts bow down before You" until *Az Yashir*, the Song of Deliverance.

The reason for their descent and servitude in Egypt was to rectify the sparks and souls of holiness that were blemished from the time of Adam, when he spilled his seed. The Talmud relates that after Adam ate from the Tree of Knowledge, he separated from Chavah for 130 years and fasted as a means of repentance (*Eruvin* 18b). During this period, demons came to him daily and aroused him, which caused him to spill his seed every day. Seed contains many, many drops of semen, each one a potential soul. Although these souls from Adam's wasted seed were scattered all over the globe, they were mainly banished to the area of Egypt at that time, hence the necessity to descend there. The sacrifices and the *Pesukey d'Zimrah* are meant to help elevate those sparks, which is what happened during the Jews' exile in Egypt. Therefore, after reciting *Pesukey d'Zimrah*, we mention the slavery in Egypt.

Interestingly, had the Egyptians enslaved the Jews because God said they should be slaves, then the Egyptians would not have been punished for their brutality. But the Egyptians enslaved the Jews for their personal pleasure. Therefore, they suffered and were destroyed in the Sea. This is the connection between the prayers of "You established the covenant" and *Az Yashir*.

Reb Noson ties together the ideas of Avraham, the Land and the covenant. God promised Avraham, "I will make your name great" (Genesis 12:2). The main place where a name becomes great is in the Land of Israel, for that is where Avraham was able to truly find God and build an altar to honor Him. In that same Land, the *Beis HaMikdash* was later constructed, and it became the place from where God's Name was revealed to the entire world (LH, *Seudah* 4:6).

But the Land is given over to the Jews only in the presence of morality and a guarded covenant. Therefore, the verse states, "You established the covenant with him [Avraham] to give the land of… the Hittites… And You kept Your word…", for the sign of the covenant is the circumcision, in which the foreskin is removed. The foreskin represents the nations which had to be removed and overcome prior to the Jews inheriting the Land (LH, *Milah* 3:5; see also ibid. 4:11).

וַיַּאֲמִינוּ בַּיְיָ וּבְמֹשֶׁה עַבְדּוֹ:

They believed in HaShem and in Moshe, His servant.

This verse teaches us the importance of faith in the true tzaddikim. As our Sages state, "If they believed in Moshe, then certainly they believed in God?! But this teaches us that whoever believes in the true tzaddik, it is as if he believes in God!" (*Mekhilta, Beshalach* 6). The tzaddikim are the ones we can trust and rely on for the best advice and guidance in our efforts to come close to God.

Rebbe Nachman teaches that the height of knowledge is to know and recognize God in each thing—in its *gestalt* and form, in the details of its parts, structure, and so on — and serve Him through this, until he arrives at that thing's ultimate purpose. But this kind of knowledge is hidden from individuals of lesser stature, such as we are nowadays. Our stature can be compared to the concept of "feet," the lowest part of the human body. We need to cry and long, beg and plead with God, "When will we merit having this awareness so that we can know and recognize the Blessed Creator from the minutest details of all the things of this word, until we can attain the ultimate purpose?"

The true tzaddik can help. Moshe is the exemplar of a truly great tzaddik whose exceptional loftiness enabled him to illuminate even the least of the least. He could illuminate even those who correspond to the "feet," so that although they are far from the mind, they could nonetheless attain and know the ultimate purpose through God's creations. The *Mekhilta* (*Beshalach*) teaches: "A maidservant saw at the Splitting of the Sea what even the Prophet Yechezkiel could not see." We should plead with God to send us such a leader who with the power of Moshe can teach us to find the Godliness hidden in the creation (LM II, 39:1).

Az Yashir

אָז יָשִׁיר מֹשֶׁה וּבְנֵי יִשְׂרָאֵל אֶת הַשִּׁירָה הַזֹּאת לַיְיָ:

Then Moshe and the children of Israel sang this song to HaShem.

"Whoever recites this song with joy will have all his sins forgiven" (*Mishnah Berurah* 51:17). Our job is to visualize in our minds that we are the ones passing through the Red Sea and learn to feel the joy of salvation and redemption. The *Zohar* teaches:

> Whoever is worthy of singing this song in this world and concentrates on its meaning will merit to sing it prophetically

in the World to Come. He will also be worthy of singing it [i.e., attaining the same exalted level of prophecy that was attained at the Red Sea] when the Redeemer comes. He will participate in the joy of perceiving the awesome Oneness of the *Shekhinah* and the Holy One, Blessed is He. This is why the verse says, "'They said, saying." This means that Israel sang then, after crossing the Red Sea, what they would sing in the future when they would dwell in the Holy Land; what they would sing when they were exiled from their Land; what they will sing when they are finally redeemed; and what they will sing in the eternal World to Come (*Zohar* II, 54b).

The Talmud asks, "Where in the Torah does it allude to the Resurrection of the Dead?" Rabbi Meir states: It is written, '*Az yashir Moshe u'Bnei Yisrael*' (Then Moshe and the children of Israel will sing.) It does not say they *sang*, but they *will sing*, in the future (*Sanhedrin* 91b).

There's also a hint here to the specialness of song. *Az yashir* has the ability to resurrect those distant from God, for song connects people to God, even those who are very far from Him. As Reb Noson writes, "Even someone who is very far from God—at the lowest level—usually reconnects to God through song" (LH, *Nesiat Kapayim* 5:6-7).

Az Yashir contains eighteen mentions of God's Name. This parallels the eighteen times God's Name is mentioned in the *Yehi Kavod* prayer, and also parallels the *Chai Olamim* (the life-force of these worlds).[106] As mentioned above, God's Name is mentioned eighteen times in the four sections of the prayers: the sacrifices, *Pesukey d'Zimrah*, the *Shema* and the *Shemonah Esrei*.[107]

106 *Shaar HaKavanot, Inyan Tefillat HaShachar*, p. 116. The word *Chai* (חי, life) has the numerical value of 18.

107 See above, Chapter 8.

The Talmud teaches, "Man's livelihood is as difficult to attain as it is to split the sea" (*Pesachim* 118a). Why is it so difficult to earn a livelihood? God created the entire world *ex nihilo*. He controls the entire world; He directs the entire world. How hard is it for Him to sustain the world and provide livelihood for all?

The answer is that it's not hard at all! But empirically, we see and experience all kinds of hardships in earning a living. Why? It's because we aren't attuned to the Divine Providence of God directing the world. We aren't aware that our livelihood comes from Him and not from our own efforts. This results in the hardships in earning a living that we encounter.

Reb Noson explains that after the Splitting of the Sea, the hand of Divine Providence was revealed, teaching the Jews that God provides at all times. Therefore, they merited immense wealth. As our Sages say, "The loot of the sea was greater than the loot taken out from Egypt" (*Shemot Rabbah* 13:19). Thus, the more we rely on God, the less we will struggle daily for a livelihood (LH, *Tefillah* 4:21).

How was the Sea split? Moshe extended his staff and the sea split (*Tikkuney Zohar* #21, p. 43a).

During the first redemption from Egypt, the Splitting of the Sea took place as Moshe extended his staff over it, splitting the physical sea. In the future redemption, when the *Mashiach* comes, the sea will again split—but that sea will be the Sea of Wisdom. And the staff will be the pen that will write and reveal the mysteries of Torah so that all will be able to partake of them (see *Tikkuney Zohar* #21, p. 43b).

When we recite the Song of Deliverance each day, we should bear in mind that we are actually crossing the sea. Then we can merit to see Divine Providence and learn about the mysteries of Torah. But we must make sure to "cross the sea" with joy and faith. Then we, too, will witness the miracles that occur to us daily!

Every piece of wisdom has its melody, and the melodies are the origins of faith. There is also a melody that is the origin of the highest point in creation: the world of silence, where there are only divine thoughts and no words. All songs and melodies are drawn from that song. This song is the Song of the Future, of the World to Come (LH, *Netilat Yadayim l'Shacharit,* 2:16).

Some people have questions on faith and they can't find an answer. Some are so troubled by those questions that they become heretics and non-believers. This is because their questions descend from the world of thought, where there aren't any words. Therefore, they can't find words to answer their questions. But as we explained, that high world of silence also contains a song, which is its origin. When these non-believers will hear that song, all their questions will be automatically answered.

The only one who merits to the melody of this exalted faith is the tzaddik of the generation, who is conceptually compared to Moshe. He is on this level of faith, which corresponds to silence, as is found in Talmud (*Menachot* 29b) that God told Moshe: "Be silent! Thus, has it arisen in thought."

The verse says, "Then Moshe will sing." The song that he sang at the Sea is the origin of all songs, the song of the future world, and the song which is the root of the world of silence. Our Sages said: It does not say "sang" but "will sing." This is a Biblical source for resurrection of the dead (*Sanhedrin* 91b) because this is the Song of the Future. Rashi comments: "*Yashir* (will sing): the *yod* connotes thought"—i.e., the aforementioned aspect of "Thus has it arisen in thought," the aspect of Moshe (silence).

Therefore, by means of the tzaddik's melody (who is the

aspect of Moshe), all the souls that succumbed to heresy begin to ascend and emerge. This is because his melody is in the summit of faith—i.e., the most exalted faith of all—directly with the Infinite. Therefore, through this melody and faith, all heresy is nullified, and all the sparks of holiness are rectified and elevated (LM I, 64:5).

God desires to bestow kindness on the Jewish nation and He bestows His kindness with His speech. He decrees salvations for the individual and / or for the community, and His decrees go into effect. But due to our sins, God's speech is also in exile. How can we rectify this?

Rebbe Nachman teaches:

"Every person must say, 'The world was created for my sake' (*Sanhedrin* 37a)—and he is obliged to improve it. What is its rectification? One must see to raise up all the sparks of holiness in all things. These sparks are letters. When one raises up letters and the letters become words, then through God's speech bounty is provided to the Jewish people.

Yet how can a person raise up the sparks to God? The advised course of action is as follows: When a person observes some object, he must immediately believe with complete faith that this object contains letters and sparks. From this faith the letter *zayin* is made, as the verse states, "All His acts are done with faith" (Psalms 33:4). The "doing" is the six days of the week, and faith is the seventh.[108]

Afterwards, he should combine faith with wisdom, as it is written, "Know the God of your father" (I Chronicles 28:9). We have faith in God, that He is the God of our fathers. "Know" refers to wisdom and intellect. Wisdom corresponds to the letter *yod,* as Rashi explains, "'Then Moshe will sing.' It does not say *shar* (שר, sang) but *Yashir* (ישיר, will sing)—the *Yod* refers to thought" (Rashi on Exodus 15:1). Thus, *yod* represents wisdom. And from

108 Faith parallels *Malkhut*, which is the seventh *sefirah* when joined with *Zer Anpin*; see Appendix A.

the aforementioned *yod* (10=י) and *zayin* (7=ז), an *ayin* (70=ע) is made. This is because in Hebrew letter numerology, *zayin* (7) multiplied by *yod* (10) is *ayin* (70). The *AYiN* indicates wisdom, for the wise of the community are called "*EINei* (עיני, the eyes of the community)" (Numbers 15:24).

Furthermore, *Ayin* means eye. When one looks at the world with faith and with wisdom, acknowledging that everything was created by God, this elevates the holy sparks and the holy letters from their exile. The letters become words, and with them God bestows His goodness on the Jewish nation. Thus, speaking words of holiness draws bounty and blessing.

(LM I, 94:2)

יְיָ מַלְכוּתֵהּ קָאֵם לְעָלַם וּלְעָלְמֵי עָלְמַיָּא:

HaShem's hidden sovereignty is established in this world and in all worlds forever.

This is the concluding verse of the *Az Yashir*. It's interesting to note that this verse is said twice and then we say the *targum* (Aramaic translation) of the verse. Rebbe Nachman teaches that the Holy Tongue is pure; the world was created with it. Still, we live in a material world and face temptations and challenges to keep our tongues holy. We can attain such a level only if we learn to sanctify even our mundane activities. The mundane is referred to as the *targum* (translation).

To explain this further, there are basically three levels: The pure and holy which stands opposite the impure and the evil, and in between are our mundane activities — eating, sleeping, business, daily activities, etc. When we sanctify our everyday activities, we connect our "*targum*" to holiness, elevating our simple, daily activities into the realm of holiness. Rebbe Nachman explains that one cannot truly reach the level of holiness, of the Holy Tongue, unless he brings with him the mundane (LM I, 19:3-4).

Although we have recited *Pesukey d'Zimrah* (songs of praise to God) by engaging the Holy Tongue, in order to actually elevate our words, we need to elevate the mundane to God.

וְעָלוּ מוֹשִׁיעִים בְּהַר צִיּוֹן לִשְׁפֹּט אֶת הַר עֵשָׂו:

Anointed deliverers ascend Mount Zion to judge Mount Esav.

From the blessings of Yitzchak, Esav chose for his portion this (temporary) world, while Yaakov chose the eternal World to Come. When the *Mashiach* comes, this temporary world as we know it will cease. Then Yaakov will inherit the blessings of both above and below, while Esav's portion will be entirely lost (*Zohar* I, 143b) and God will be recognized as King of the entire world.

This verse is appended to *Az Yashir* for the main intent of all of these songs, and the entire *Pesukey d'Zimrah* is to glorify God and seek to reveal His Kingship over the entire world.

The *Chazan*

At this point in the prayer service, it is customary for the *chazan* to go to the lectern at *Yishtabach* (*Orach Chaim* 53:1). The *chazan* is the person who can find and bring out the good qualities to be found in each person. These good qualities parallel the songs and melodies that each person can "compose" about himself. The one who can find and gather these good qualities in others is eligible to be the *chazan*, since he can collect all the songs together and "lead" the congregation in prayer (LM I, 282).

Reb Noson writes that this is why the *chazan* ascends to the lectern at *Yishtabach*. The morning prayers begin with the congregation saying the sacrifices in order to elevate the lost sparks, which means finding the good points mixed in with the bad. This creates melodies, which is the reason we say next the songs of *Pesukey d'Zimrah*. The *chazan* then ascends to the *amud* (lecturn) at *Yishtabach*, because now he can collect these melodies and good points of the community and pray with them before God (LH, *Chakhirut v'Kablanut* 1:5).

The word *TziBuR* (ציבור, congregation) is an acronym for *Tzaddikim* (**צ**דיקים, righteous people), *Beinonim* (**ב**ינונים, average people) and *Reshaim* (**ר**שעים, wicked people) (LM I, 55:4). A congregation contains all sorts of people. The goal of the *chazan* is to find the good in *all* of them. Then he can claim the title of a *shaliach tzibur*, a messenger sent by the people, since he is the messenger of all the people (ibid. I, 282:3).

Additionally, we find that the *chazan* is called *yored lifnei hateivah* (יורד לפני התיבה, one who descends before the lectern.)[109] The word *teivah* can also be translated as "word." Rebbe Nachman teaches that the words of the prayers can be compared to beautiful flowers and blossoms. One who begins the prayers is compared to one who enters a garden and begins to pick lovely flowers one at a time. As he utters each word of the prayers, he is collecting and joining together the letters and words to make a beautiful bouquet of them and keep them together. That is, he should recognize the beauty of each word and not forget it as he advances on to the next word. Thus, the *chazan* is one who is *yored lifnei hateivah* — he goes down before the word, and is able to bear it in mind and not leave it behind as he advances to the next word (LH, *Din HaShatz*).

Yishtabach

יִשְׁתַּבַּח שִׁמְךָ לָעַד מַלְכֵּנוּ:

May Your Name be increasingly praised forever, our King.

109 *Rosh HaShanah* 34b.

The blessing of *Yishtabach* is the conclusion of the *Pesukey d'Zimrah.* Normally a blessing begins with the words "Blessed are You, God." Since *Barukh She'amar,* the opening blessing of *Pesukey d'Zimrah,* didn't begin with the words "Blessed are You, God", then *Yishtabach,* the concluding blessing doesn't need to as well.

שִׁיר וּשְׁבָחָה הַלֵּל וְזִמְרָה עֹז וּמֶמְשָׁלָה נֶצַח גְּדֻלָּה וּגְבוּרָה
תְּהִלָּה וְתִפְאֶרֶת קְדֻשָּׁה וּמַלְכוּת:

Inspired song and appreciation, thankful praise and soaring melody, strength and dominion, mastery, loving greatness and power, radiance and splendor, holy transcendence and immanent sovereignty.

The Midrash tells that when the Egyptians were pursuing the Jews at the Sea, they asked Moshe what to do. Moshe replied, "Sing to God." When God rescued them, they sang the Song of Deliverance. Thus, we sing songs to God in the *Pesukey d'Zimrah*, then say *Az Yashir*, and immediately afterwards say *Yishtabach*.

Just as in *Barukh She'amar* we find a reference to the Thirteen Attributes of Mercy, so too, we find in *Yishtabach* thirteen praises to God that correspond to, and arouse, the Thirteen Attributes. A person should be careful not to interrupt these thirteen praises. Some opinions are to say them in one breath; others are more lenient and allow one to pause between the words, but never to interrupt the recital of these thirteen praises (*Zohar* II, 132b).

The *Siddur Otzar HaTefillos* mentions that the introductory part of *Yishtabach* was written in honor of King Solomon. Thus, we find that the initial letters of the words *Shimkha Laad*

Malkeinu HaEl (**ש**מך **ל**עד **מ**לכינו **ה**אל, Your Name forever, our King, the only God) spell *ShLoMoH* (שלמה, Solomon). The blessing itself was composed by the patriarch Avraham. An acrostic of his name is formed by the five concluding phrases of this blessing:

- *Adon haniflaos* (**א**דון הנפלאות, Lord of wonders)
- *Borey kol haneshamos* (**ב**ורא כל הנשמות, Creator of all souls)
- *Ribon kol hamaasim* (**ר**בון כל המעשים, Director of all events)
- *Habocher b'shirey zimrah* (**ה**בוחר בשירי זמרה, Who delights in songs)
- *Melekh yachid chey ha'olamim* (**מ**לך יחיד חי העולמים, Singular King, Life of the worlds)

From the Depths I have called You

שִׁיר הַמַּעֲלוֹת, מִמַּעֲמַקִּים קְרָאתִיךָ יְיָ:

A Song of Ascents: From the depths
I have called out to You, HaShem.

During the Ten Days of Repentance (from *Rosh HaShanah* to Yom Kippur), it is customary to say Psalm 130 after saying *Yishtabach* and before saying the *Kaddish*. The *Zohar* (II, 63b) teaches that one who cries out to God should always do so from the depths of his heart.

Reb Noson writes: I was once standing before the Rebbe as he lay in his bed. Suddenly these words flew out of his holy mouth: "*Der iker iz: Mi-beten she'ol shivati*! (The main thing is, 'From the belly of hell I cried out!')" (*Rebbe Nachman's Wisdom* #302).

The main thing, Rebbe Nachman always taught, is to call out to God, especially from the depths — from the midst of our most frustrating trials and challenging moments.

CHAPTER 18

The World of Beriyah

With the recital of *Az Yashir* and *Yishtabach*, we have concluded the *Pesukey d'Zimrah* which parallels the World of *Yetzirah*, the angelic world. We are now ready to advance to the next world, which is called *Beriyah* (Creation), also known as the World of the Throne. Another name for this world is the realm of the souls, as our Sages teach that the souls of the Jewish people are hewn from the Throne of Glory (*Zohar* 1, 113a).

This realm is greater than that of the angels. Rebbe Nachman teaches, "The Jew is created to have dominion over the angels" (LM II, 1:1). Because our souls originate in a higher place, they have the power to literally rule over and control angels. Rabbi Eliyahu Chaim Rosen (1899-1984), a leading Breslover, used to say, "You have that power. It's awesome. However, first start with control over your evil inclination (which is also an angel!)"

יִתְגַּדַּל וְיִתְקַדַּשׁ שְׁמֵיהּ רַבָּא:

May His Great Name be magnified and sanctified.

Since we are leaving one world and entering another, we need to bridge between them. This is accomplished with the *Kaddish*.[110] Thus, right after *Yishtabach*, we say a *Kaddish* so we can cross over to the next level.

Following *Kaddish*, we recite *Borekhu*, blessing God. Reb Noson explains that all blessing comes from the place of *Chesed*

110 See above, p. 117.

(Kindness). When we recite the *Pesukey d'Zimrah,* we elevate awe of God (for saying His praises brings about awe of the One we are praising.) Elevating awe brings us to *Chesed* and thus we are able to bless and draw blessing (LH, *Kaddish* 1).

We begin the *Kaddish* with *Yitgadal v'yitkadash Shmei Rabba* (May His Great Name be magnified and sanctified). Reb Noson says that God's name is sanctified once we become aware that even when God acts according to His Attribute of Judgment, it is ultimately His Kindness (LH, *Kila'ey HaKerem* 2:9).

We mentioned earlier that *kelipot* stand between the worlds and try to stop the prayers from ascending, as well as try to disturb the person who is attempting to pray.[111] For that reason, between the World of *Asiyah* (the sacrifices) and the World of *Yetzirah* (the psalms) we say the *Hodu* prayer, forcing the *kelipot* to flee (see LM I, 25:4). Similarly, between the World of *Yetzirah* and the World of *Beriyah* we say *Kaddish* (which extols God), and with the subsequent blessing over the celestial bodies, we are chasing away the *kelipot.* This way we can say the *Shema* and the *Amidah* with concentration and the *kelipot* won't be present to disturb us.

It is forbidden to speak out between the *Pesukey d'Zimrah* and the blessings of the *Shema.* "Whoever speaks out between *Yishtabach* and *Yotzer Or* has committed a sin and must return from the battlefront" (*Sefer HaManhig, Dinei Tefillah*).[112] Why? With

111 See above, p. 123.

112 See Deuteronomy 20. The reference is that when Jews went out to war they were told if a person has a sin he should return from the battlefield and not cause his sin to prosecute him during the battle. The Talmud teaches that even speaking between *Yishtabach* and *Yotzer Or* is sin enough to cause him to return.

the songs of the *Pesukey d'Zimrah* we elevate the good sparks of the world from the bad sparks that held them captive, and when they depart, the bad becomes null and void. Then we read the *Shema* and announce that everything is under God's dominion and that everything is good. If we speak out between the song and the declaration of faith, we defeat our purpose of elevating everything to God. Therefore, we must not speak out; otherwise, we must "return from the battlefield" (i.e., we cannot be victorious) (LH, *Sekhirat Po'alim* 1:6).

Shema and its Blessings

At this point, we begin the third section of the morning prayer. Since this section of the prayers corresponds to the World of *Beriyah* (also known as the World of the Throne), we recite this section while seated. Additionally, since *Beriyah* translates as "Creation," accessing this world enhances our creative abilities, but we need true faith that we are able to access them.

Recall that the *Shacharit* prayer begins in the World of *Asiyah* (corresponding to *Malkhut*) with the morning blessings and the sacrifices. In the *Pesukey d'Zimrah*, we rise up to the World of *Yetzirah* (corresponding to *Tiferet* or *Zer Anpin*); in the Shema and its blessings, we rise up to the World of *Beriyah* (corresponding to *Binah*); and in the *Amidah*, we rise up to the World of *Atzilut* (corresponding to *Chokhmah*).

According to the *Zohar* (I, 132b), we sit when we say the *Shema* and stand when we pray the *Amidah*. The difference between the *Shema* (*Binah*) and the *Amidah* (*Chokhmah*) is the difference between sitting and standing. The *Shema* and its blessings are associated with the World of the Throne. Therefore, we sit in the presence of this level of manifestation of Godliness. In the same way that a king sits on his throne to interact with his subjects, God's "sitting" implies a lowering of His Essence in order to be involved with His creation. For us, sitting is the position most conducive to contemplating something and exerting mental effort to understand its implications (cf. *Megillah* 21a). On the other hand, standing face to face with someone implies direct experience and knowledge of that person.

The difference between understanding something and actually experiencing it can be summed up with another analogy. The World of *Beriyah* corresponds to the *sefirah* of *Binah*. The word *BiNah* (בינה, understanding) is connected to the words *BiNyan* (בנין, building) and *BeiN* (בין, between). When bricks are piled one atop the other to construct a wall of a building, the method is specific: namely, putting two bricks below and one brick above and between them. This way a building can maintain its structural integrity.

Conceptually, we can view each of the two lower bricks as premises, with the third brick being the logical conclusion that results from them. Similarly, *Binah*-consciousness involves understanding relationships and drawing conclusions. This is exactly how the Talmud understands the word *Binah*—as the capacity to understand and logically deduce one thing from another or one conclusion from many premises.[113]

By saying *Shema,* we attain this state of *Binah*-consciousness vis-à-vis our relationship with God. In other words, when we say "*Shema Yisrael YHVH Eloheinu YHVH Echad,*" we are admitting that we sense God's presence in our lives, but we still haven't penetrated the "curtain" in a world that reveals God up to a certain point. Beyond that point, it blocks us from directly experiencing Him. In the *Shema,* we intuit and logically deduce that God is there behind the latticework of creation. It's as if

113 *Sanhedrin* 93b. See above, p. 30, which speaks about the true prince who attains the level of understanding one thing from another. See Appendix.

we are saying, "God, I know that You are there. Please help me move aside the "curtain" so I can experience You!"

In the *Amidah*, we move beyond *Binah*-consciousness to *Chokhmah*-consciousness. *Chokhmah* (wisdom) does not involve a logical conclusion based on a set of premises or facts. It is not a derivative or implied knowledge, rather direct and unmitigated knowledge. Standing face to face with God, as it were, we aren't fooled by a world that implies God's existence even as it hides it. When we say the *Amidah*, we are completely aware of God's existence at all times. After finishing our prayer, we can return to the world and know that whatever duality we see, it is all one, only God.

Yotzer Or

בָּרוּךְ אַתָּה יְיָ אֱלֹהֵינוּ מֶלֶךְ הָעוֹלָם, יוֹצֵר אוֹר וּבוֹרֵא חֹשֶׁךְ,
עֹשֶׂה שָׁלוֹם וּבוֹרֵא אֶת הַכֹּל:

Blessed are You, HaShem our God, King of the universe, Who forms light and creates darkness; Who makes peace and continually recreates everything.

King David says, "Seven times a day I praise You" (Psalms 119:164). Rashi explains that this refers to the seven blessings of the *Shema*. In *Shacharit* we recite two blessings before we say the *Shema*, and one blessing afterwards. In *Maariv* we say two blessings before the *Shema* and two blessings afterwards. These are the seven times a day we bless God. Interestingly, the Talmud teaches that King David praised God for the seven *mitzvot* that He gave us. They are: (1) *tefillin* upon the head, (2) *tefillin* upon the arm, (3-6) four *tzitzit* surrounding us, and (7) a *mezuzah* on our door. With these seven *mitzvot* we can be protected from sin (*Menachot* 43b). Since we wear *tallit* and *tefillin* while reciting the *Shema* (and presumably while praying in a synagogue or a room that has a *mezuzah*), these seven *mitzvot* also accompany us as we say the blessings of the *Shema*.

The first blessing said prior to the *Shema* is *Yotzer Or* (Who forms light). This blessing speaks about the creation of the world and the forces of nature—the sun, moon and the other constellations. It goes on to praise God for his creations and speaks of the angels who praise God. The second blessing, *Ahavas Olam* (Eternal Love), speaks of God's love for us as the chosen nation, and about His gifts to us, the Torah and *mitzvot*. It also mentions our longing for God and to merit returning to our Holy Land. The blessing said after the *Shema* is known as *Emet v'Yatziv* (It is true) and speaks about the Exodus from Egypt.

The Talmud states that we are meant to include the concept of the day (light) during the nighttime prayers and conversely, we include the concept of night (darkness) during the daytime prayers (*Berakhot* 11b). This is to teach us that the One who created light also created darkness, and the One who created darkness also created light. This teaches us that there is One Creator, as opposed to separate powers that created the many different things in the world. Thus, in the morning prayers we say, "Who forms light and creates darkness," and in the first of the evening blessings of the *Shema* we say, "Who causes light to recede before darkness, and darkness to recede before light" (*Etz Yosef*).

Rebbe Nachman teaches that the idea of diverse phenomena stemming from oneness, from God's unity, runs counter to human reasoning. To explain: there is an essential difference between the diverse phenomena that man creates and the original matter that God created during the Six Days of Creation. Whereas God created the universe out of nothing (*creatio ex nihilo*), all phenomena of human formation are created from pre-existing matter (*creatio ex material*). The Kabbalah teaches that the spiritual essence of that original matter is nothing other than the Infinite Light of God. Therefore, all that exists is *creatio ex Deo*, created out of God, so to speak. Furthermore, God is the source of all the diversity in existence. While this is true, it is also incomprehensible. How is it possible for God to be One, without form, structure or plurality, and at the same time be the origin of the many?

Reb Noson points out that the tzaddikim are the only ones who can comprehend how the undifferentiated oneness of pre-Creation is indivisibly linked with the multiplicity of post-Creation, yet even they are incapable of retaining this awareness permanently. As for the rest of us, the paradox of God's Simple Unity giving rise to and being inherent in all duality remains incomprehensible. Only the faith we derive from attaching ourselves to the tzaddikim enables us to "know" that it is so (LH, *Nefillat Apayim* 4:16).[114] Ultimately, we must rely upon faith—the declaration of the *Shema*. This is why we speak about differing forces and creations within the *Shema* blessings.

The Codifiers[115] speak about the connection between the creation of light and darkness and the forces of nature with the blessings of the *Shema*. The Talmud teaches, "Why was Jerusalem destroyed? Because its residents did not recite the *Shema* in the morning or in the evening, as it is written, 'Woe to those who rise in the morning to strong drink and continue until the night with wine...but they did not look at the works of God and they did not see His creation'" (Isaiah 5:11-12; *Shabbos* 119b). That is, they did not see the greatness of the creation

114 LM II, 2:6 and note 107 there.

115 *Tur* and *Orach Chaim* #59.

because they did not say the *Shema*. They couldn't see His wonders!

Reb Noson explains that the *Shema* is our declaration of faith and the manifestation of God's will and His power. When we say the *Shema*, we acknowledge that God rules over the four corners of the world as well as above and below. We declare that God created the entire world and the forces of nature *ex nihilo*. Therefore, each day when we make this declaration, we are saying that God created everything, which reveals that there actually is no power or force that exists besides Him. Our faith declares that all of nature is completely subjugated to God and His will—the sun, moon and all natural forces—so we say this blessing daily together with the *Shema*. Thus, we begin the blessings of the *Shema* with praise of God for creating light and darkness and all of nature, reinforcing our faith that He created all and everything is subject to His will (LH, *Birkhos HaShachar* 5:28). To emphasize this, the prophet states, "*Se'u Marom Aineichem* (שאו מרום עיניכם, Raise your eyes upward) and see Who created these" (Isaiah 40:26). In Hebrew, the initial letters of the opening words spell *SheMA* (שמע) (*Tikkuney Zohar* #49, p. 85b).

There are four elements: Fire (heat), air, water (fluids), and earth. Everything in this world is composed of these four varying—actually, opposing—forces. An example is the human body: it was formed of earth, it contains fluids, it breathes air, and its power of consumption is the fire or heat of the body. Any changing of the balance between these four elements causes illness or different types of discomforts and problems.

Thus, God created the world of differing, opposing forces. Under normal circumstances, each element seeks domination and would overpower another element, causing disasters in the world. So just as God created the varying forces, He also created peace, allowing differences to exist and yet remain united. In this manner, God created everything in the world.

The *Yotzer Or* blessing was taken from Isaiah but was slightly changed in the process. In Isaiah (45:7) we read, "I form light and create darkness; I make peace and create evil; I am God, Who does all these." Besides shifting the original into third person, the Sages who composed the prayers changed only one other word. Instead of *borey ra* (בורא רע, creates evil), they substituted *borey es hakol* (בורא את הכל, creates everything). Indeed, even this change is justified in view of the final clause: "I am God, Who does all these," where the prophetic *kol eleh* (כל אלה, all these) is clearly the source for the rabbinical *hakol* (הכל, everything). The key to this verse is its three verbs, *borey* (בורא, create), *yotzer* (יוצר, form), and *oseh* (עושה, make). *Beriyah* (creation) refers to creating something from nothing; next is *yetzirah* (forming something from something); and finally, is *asiyah* (making, bringing to completion).

Rabbi Aryeh Kaplan explains the profundity of Isaiah's statement:

> Darkness (Constriction) allows for the existence of a finite world where God's Presence is absolutely undetectable and both good and evil can operate freely. This in turn sets the stage for a creature far removed and opposite from God who can resemble Him by freely choosing "light" over "darkness," "good" over "evil." The very existence of evil, in fact, is solely in order to be transformed by man in the act of choosing good. Through his struggle man attains peace and unifies himself and the creation with God.[116]

מְחַדֵּשׁ בְּכָל יוֹם תָּמִיד מַעֲשֵׂה בְרֵאשִׁית:

He renews, each day, continuously, the Act of Creation.

116 Rabbi Aryeh Kaplan, *Innerspace* (Moznaim Publishers, 1991), p. 27.

A master architect never designs the same building twice. This is even truer of the Master Architect of the world. God not only breathes newness and freshness into each day, but literally recreates the world from nothing at every moment (LH, *Birkhot HaShachar* 5:28).

Rebbe Nachman teaches that prayer corresponds to miracles—the supernatural—for prayer transcends nature. The natural course dictates a certain existence, but prayer changes nature's course. This is a miracle. And for this, one needs faith. A person has to believe that there is a *Mechadesh* (Originator) with the power to originate as He sees fit (LM I, 7:1).

The *Zohar* teaches that whoever gives testimony each day that God created all, is guaranteed a place in the World to Come (*Zohar Chadash, Bereishit* 16b).

Mah Rabu

מָה רַבּוּ מַעֲשֶׂיךָ יְיָ, כֻּלָּם בְּחָכְמָה עָשִׂיתָ:

How manifold are Your works, HaShem;
You made them all with wisdom.

Everything that God made contains wisdom that man can learn from—even the grasses and the fauna! (*Zohar* II, 15b).

Rebbe Nachman teaches:

> Actually, this is a very amazing and awesome matter—that God created the entire creation in which there are any number of very many amazing and awesome things. 'How many are the works of God!' Even in this world alone, God's wonders are countless. He created inanimate objects and vegetation, and so on. Who can fathom the greatness of God contained in the creations of this world, all the more so the other worlds?! And every single thing was created solely for the sake of the Jewish people (LM II, 39:1).

Rebbe Nachman similarly teaches:

> A Jew must always focus on the *seichel* (inner intelligence) of every matter and bind himself to the wisdom and inner intelligence that is to be found in each object. He should do this so that the intelligence, inherent in each object may enlighten him, and so he may draw closer to God through that object. For inner intelligence is a great light that reflects off a person, as it is written, "A person's wisdom causes his countenance to shine" (Ecclesiastes 8:1; LM I, 1:2).

Eil Barukh

אֵל בָּרוּךְ גְּדוֹל דֵּעָה ...

God, intrinsically blessed, Omniscient One ...

The *Eil Barukh* prayer praises God, using the twenty-two letters of the Hebrew alphabet. Since all speech uses the letters of the *aleph-bet,* the earlier poets and composers of the prayers used the method of alphabetical acrostics to form our prayers (*Iyun Tefillah*).[117] The *Etz Yosef* adds that the whole world was created for the sake of the Torah, which contains these twenty-two letters. Many of the *piyutim* (poems and hymns) that we recite on Festivals and Tisha b'Av were composed by Rabbi Elazar HaKalir, a Mishnaic-era sage. It is told of Rabbi Elazar that when he wanted to begin composing *piyutim* he ascended to Heaven and asked the archangel Michael how the angels compose their praises. The reply was, "By using the *aleph-bet*!"

This prayer is said daily, except for Shabbos which has a longer passage that begins "*El Adon al kol hamaasim* (God is Master over all creation)." The difference between them is that the *Eil Barukh* prayer contains the twenty-two letters of the *aleph-bet* with no spaces between the words, whereas the *Eil*

117 It also helps us to remember the prayers!

Adon prayer contains spaces between the letters of the *aleph-bet*, as each letter is placed at the beginning of a string of words. The reason for this is that on Shabbos, the letters represent a rectification of *Binah*, whose illumination can extend very far. During the weekdays, however, the letters are residing in *Malkhut*, which represents a more closed effect of illumination and rectification. Hence, during the weekdays, the letters of the *aleph-bet* follow one another very closely (*Zohar* II, 205b).

Tisbarakh Tzureinu

תִּתְבָּרֵךְ לָנֶצַח צוּרֵנוּ ...

May You be blessed forever, our Rock...

Until this point in the prayers, the blessing praised God for giving us the Heavenly luminaries to light our paths and allow us to see what we are doing and where we are going. Starting with these words, we begin to praise God for creating the angels who do His bidding and praise Him.

יוֹצֵר מְשָׁרְתִים וַאֲשֶׁר מְשָׁרְתָיו. כֻּלָּם עוֹמְדִים בְּרוּם עוֹלָם:

Who forms the ministering angels, and Whose ministering angels all stand at the height of the universe.

The prayer is specifically written in present tense (יוצר משרתים, Who forms the ministering angels), implying that even up to the present, God is continuously creating angels to serve Him. As the Talmud teaches, each day angels are created that praise God and then they are nullified (*Chagigah* 14a).[118] *Vaasher meshartav* (ואשר משרתיו, and Whose ministering

118 Some angels are created for a specific purpose or time and are then nullified. Others, such as Michael or Gavriel, were created for long term purposes.

angels) refers to the well-known angels created from the time of Creation, such as Michael and Gavriel. These angels are considered His long-standing servants and stand at the height of the universe to praise God.

> כֻּלָּם אֲהוּבִים. כֻּלָּם בְּרוּרִים. כֻּלָּם גִּבּוֹרִים.
> כֻּלָּם קְדוֹשִׁים ... וְכֻלָּם פּוֹתְחִים אֶת פִּיהֶם ...
>
> All of them are beloved, all of them are pure, all are powerful, all are holy ... All open their mouths ...

Each angel has its individual mission and purpose, yet all turn to God as one to praise Him in purity, with awe and reverence. Similarly, we too should know our strengths and perform our missions, yet we must set aside any individuality to join others for a higher goal.

There is a folk saying about the Jews when they are together in the synagogue: "All are beloved ... all are pure ... all are powerful ... all are holy ..." But the evil inclination's job is to get people to talk during the prayers. Thus, it is written, "And all open their mouths"! Apparently, this malaise goes back many centuries. The *Tosafos Yom Tov*[119] composed a special *Mi Shebeirakh* to say for those who remain silent during the prayers. Shortly after the Chmelnitzki massacres of 1648-1649, Rabbi Yonasan Eibeschitz was asked, "How can we avoid these terrible massacres and pogroms?" He answered: When the Egyptians threatened the Jews at the Red Sea, it is written, "God will fight for you, and you will remain silent" (Exodus 14:14). He explained, "God will fight for you and protect you. But you have to remain silent during the prayers!"

119 Commentary on the entire six orders of the Mishnah by Rabbi Yom Tov Lipman Heller (c. 1579-1654).

Kadosh! Kadosh! Kadosh!

קָדוֹשׁ קָדוֹשׁ קָדוֹשׁ יְיָ צְבָאוֹת, מְלֹא כָל הָאָרֶץ כְּבוֹדוֹ:

Holy! Holy! Holy! is HaShem of hosts.
The whole world is filled with His glory.

This verse is from Isaiah's prophecy when he saw how the angels in Heaven gathered to praise God. They said, "Holy! Holy! Holy! is HaShem of hosts. The whole world is filled with His glory!" (Isaiah 6:3). The Talmud teaches:

> The Jews are more precious than the angels. The angels praise God once a day. A Jew can praise God an entire day. The Jews can say God's Name after two words,[120] the angels must first recite three words.[121] Additionally, the angels are held back from saying God's praise until after the Jews praise God" (*Chullin* 91b).

Why does the verse repeat "Holy" three times? Rabbi Eliyahu, the Gaon of Vilna (1720-1797), explains that this is to emphasize that God is above everything. When comparing two items, one can say that one is higher than the other. But when comparing three or more, one has to be the highest.

Rebbe Nachman teaches that there are two kinds of people: those who "dwell above" and those who "dwell below." Those who dwell above are mindful of Heaven even in the midst of the mundane, constantly striving for closeness to God. Those who "dwell below" are engulfed by the mundane, pursuing materialistic lifestyles. The tzaddik must reach both types of people.

The tzaddik must show the ones who dwell above that they haven't yet begun to apprehend God and His glory. He teaches

120 That is, "*Shema Yisrael YHVH* (שמע ישראל יי, Hear, Israel, God)."
121 That is, "*Kadosh Kadosh Kadosh YHVH* (קדוש קדוש קדוש יי, Holy, holy, holy, is God)."

them to ask, "*Ayeh mekom kevodo* (איה מקום כבודו, Where is the place of His glory?)." God's greatness is endless and they should feel that they haven't begun to even touch the surface. Conversely, the tzaddik has to show the ones who dwell below that "The whole world [or earth] is filled with His glory." For there are those who dwell in the earth: they are sunk in the lowest levels, where it seems they are very far from God. The tzaddik's job is to reveal to them that God is with them and that they are capable of becoming close to God because "the whole world is filled with His glory."

Ultimately, these two levels are interrelated. No matter how distant you feel from God, never give up hope, for He is always close to you. Yet no matter how close you feel, you must never stop seeking God on a higher plane. By maintaining both perspectives, one merits bounty and livelihood (LM II, 7:7, 10).

וְהָאוֹפַנִּים וְחַיּוֹת הַקֹּדֶשׁ בְּרַעַשׁ גָּדוֹל מִתְנַשְּׂאִים לְעֻמַּת שְׂרָפִים.

Now, the holy *ofanim* and *chayot* raise themselves up toward the *serafim*.

Ofanim, *chayos* and *serafim* refer to various angels and are understood from the Chariot of God that was seen by the prophet Yechezkel (Ezekiel 1). *Ofanim* are described on the Chariot as the "wheels," referring to a lower angel. *Chayos* are those angels represented by the "animal faces" on the Chariot. *Serafim* are the fiery angels, the highest of these angels.

בָּרוּךְ כְּבוֹד יְיָ מִמְּקוֹמוֹ:

May the glory of HaShem be blessed from its place.

"From its place" refers to the fact that absolutely no one knows God's place.

Rebbe Nachman explains this verse as follows: "Blessed" corresponds to the hands (similar to the priestly blessings which were given with the hands extended). "The glory of God" is synonymous with faith. "From its place" is the concept of *Keter.* One receives the blessing in his hands. In order to receive that blessing, he has to have faith. *Malkhut* (God's kingship) corresponds to faith as well as glory, as in "The King of glory" (Psalms 24:10). When we praise God and recognize through our faith that He alone rules the entire world, we can draw blessing from the highest of places, the source of everything: the *Keter* (LM I, 24:6).

L'Eil Barukh

לָאֵל בָּרוּךְ נְעִימוֹת יִתֵּנוּ ...

They offer these sweet words to God ...

Our Sages say that the conclusion of a blessing should repeat what was written at its beginning. At the beginning of this blessing, we praise God for creation, particularly the creation of the luminaries. In this theme, the blessing concludes by describing the power of God as well as His work in creating the luminaries that bring benefit to His world.

עוֹשֶׂה חֲדָשׁוֹת. בַּעַל מִלְחָמוֹת:

He creates new circumstances;
He is the mastermind of wars.

When a person embarks on a new path of life or a brand-new business, his family is often worried, and rightfully so. They are familiar with their old lifestyle (for better or worse) and they don't know what challenges the new lifestyle will bring. Sometimes a new path in life can lead to severe financial problems or new enemies among one's competitors. But changes in lifestyle are at times necessary. Sometimes it can be the best thing for a person and his family. Therefore, when choosing a new path in life, one must be very cautious, and he should pray that God helps him choose wisely.

זוֹרֵעַ צְדָקוֹת:

He sows righteousness.

"What profit is there for a man from all his labors under the sun?" (Ecclesiastes 1:3). King Solomon questions all of man's efforts and labors in this world. Man will eventually pass away, and then what remains from all his labor? The Talmud states, "Below the sun he does not have [profit]. Above the sun he does have" (*Shabbat* 30b). That is, any work a man achieves in this world will cease and become naught; there is no profit or gain. But whatever a person labors for above the sun — meaning Torah study and fulfillment of *mitzvot* which bring him reward in the World to Come — he retains. The *Zohar* (II, 59a) teaches that when a person gives to charity, he "sows *tzedakah*." This mean that his good deed is fruitful, for it rises "above the sun" and creates an angel. That angel accompanies the person's soul and directs it to ascend to its resting place in Heaven and to be bound up in the bond of life with God!

בּוֹרֵא רְפוּאוֹת, נוֹרָא תְהִלּוֹת, אֲדוֹן הַנִּפְלָאוֹת:

He creates miraculous cures. Awesome beyond all praises, Master of the supernatural.

Rebbe Nachman opposed going to doctors (medicine was very primitive in his day; the stethoscope wasn't even invented until some 25 years after his passing!). In his words, "You might as well hand over the patient to the Angel of Death." The Rebbe teaches: "Look at our prayers: "He creates miraculous cures. Awesome beyond all praises, Master of the supernatural." But what do we do? First, we go to a doctor for cures. Then, when all seems lost, we turn to God, the Master of the supernatural, Who can change nature and heal even the worst sickness. So why not go straight to God and beseech Him right away, if eventually we're going to turn to Him anyway? (*Rebbe Nachman's Wisdom* #50).

אוֹר חָדָשׁ עַל צִיּוֹן תָּאִיר וְנִזְכֶּה כֻלָּנוּ בִּמְהֵרָה לְאוֹרוֹ:
בָּרוּךְ אַתָּה יְיָ, יוֹצֵר הַמְּאוֹרוֹת:

Shine a renewed light on Zion and may we all soon be worthy of its glow. Blessed are You, God, Who forms the luminaries.

The verse states, "Your sun shall not set, nor your moon be gathered in, but God will be your light" (Isaiah 60:20). Despite the great luminaries that illumine our world, we pray that God shines His light upon us so that we can experience Him directly and not through His intermediaries.

The blessing concludes, "*Yotzer HaMeorot* (יוצר המאורות, Who forms the luminaries)." "Luminaries" is in plural, as it refers to the light of this world and the light of the future, the Messianic era. The word, "forms" is in present tense, because each day the world is created anew. And each day we strengthen our hope for a better and brighter future!

CHAPTER 19
Eternal Love

The second blessing of the *Shema* is called *Ahavas Olam* (Eternal Love). The *Zohar* comments that when we say, "Your love for us is an eternal love," we are arousing God's eternal love for us and bringing it to a greater degree of love (*Zohar* II, 202b). This explains the reason that we say, "You should love your God" in the *Shema* (verse 2). Love should be a two-way street; we arouse God's love for us, and at the same time we should enflame our hearts with love and longing for God.

There are several opinions about how to phrase the beginning of the blessing of *Ahavas Olam*. The Talmud debates whether one should use the phrase *Ahavas Olam* (אהבת עולם, Eternal Love) or *Ahavah Rabbah* (אהבה רבה, Great Love) (*Berakhot* 11b). *Nusach Sephard* of the Breslov Siddur uses *Ahavas Olam*, while *Nusach Ashkenaz* uses *Ahavah Rabbah*. *Tosafot* (s.v. *v'Rabbanan*) points out that we should say *Ahavah Rabbah* in the morning and *Ahavas Olam* in the second blessing of the evening *Shema*. However, the *Zohar* (II, 202b) accepts the phrase *Ahavas Olam*. The ARI explains that since *Ahavas Olam* belongs in the World of *Beriyah*, it should be said in the morning blessings of the *Shema*.[122]

This blessing discusses Torah study and about binding ourselves to God; it also asks God to redeem us from exile and bring us to our Holy Land. It follows the blessing about the

122 *Pri Etz Chaim, Shaar Kriat Shema* 3, p. 161.

luminaries, since the light of Torah is far greater than the light of the sun and moon. King David also employed this order in Psalm 19. He begins with, "The heavens declare the glory of God ... Day to day ... the sun goes forth." He then continues with, "The Torah of God is perfect, restoring the soul ... the testimony of God ... The statutes are right, rejoicing the heart."

These pleas are so powerful that some Sages are of the opinion that if a person forgets to say the blessings over the Torah in the morning, he can now fulfill his obligation when reciting the *Ahavas Olam* blessing.

Ahavas Olam is a very heartfelt blessing, with much pleading and cajoling of God to draw us closer to Him. One Breslover chassid, Reb Shabsai, would place much effort into this prayer. When asked why, he replied, "If Reb Nachman Tulchiner (a close follower of Reb Noson) would shed rivers of tears when saying this blessing, certainly, I should put effort into it!"

וְתֵן בְּלִבֵּנוּ בִּינָה לְהָבִין וּלְהַשְׂכִּיל, לִשְׁמֹעַ, לִלְמֹד וּלְלַמֵּד, לִשְׁמֹר וְלַעֲשׂוֹת וּלְקַיֵּם אֶת כָּל דִּבְרֵי תַלְמוּד תּוֹרָתֶךָ בְּאַהֲבָה:

Imbue our hearts with understanding in order to comprehend, discern, pay attention, learn and teach, safeguard and practice, and fulfill the teachings of Your Torah with love.

After praying for understanding (*Binah*), this verse lists eight aspirations for the study and fulfillment of Torah. Reb Noson explains that all true advice and ideas must be drawn from *Binah*, which is the eighth *sefirah* that transcends the seven *sefirot* below it. By articulating each word in this verse and recognizing that each is a special prayer for us to attain understanding, we can internalize the transcendent light of the Torah and fulfill its commandments (LH, *Hefker v'Nikhsey HaGer* 4:18).

מַהֵר וְהָבֵא עָלֵינוּ בְּרָכָה וְשָׁלוֹם מְהֵרָה מֵאַרְבַּע כַּנְפוֹת כָּל הָאָרֶץ ... וְתוֹלִיכֵנוּ מְהֵרָה קוֹמְמִיּוּת לְאַרְצֵנוּ:

Quickly bring us blessing and peace and bring us home soon from all four corners of the earth ... Lead us speedily to our Land with our heads held high.

In the end of the previous blessing we said, "Shine a renewed light on Zion," which refers to the Holy Land and Jerusalem. We asked that the luminaries shine forth the light of God, until the Jewish nation becomes "a light to the nations."[123] In our prayers, we have already asked God to return us to Zion, to our Land. Now, in this blessing, we add to that prayer, asking that we be gathered from among the nations and returned to the Holy Land. King David states, "He gave them the lands of nations ... so they should observe His statutes and preserve His Torah" (Psalms 105:44-45). There is an integral connection between the Land and the Torah. Therefore, after praying for the Torah in the first part of this blessing, we pray that we merit to return to our Land.

The ARI teaches that the reason for the exile was Adam's sin, the wasting of seed. This caused many souls and sparks of holiness to be spread out across the globe—all "four corners" of it. Therefore, the Jewish people are also spread out all over the world and wherever they go, when they perform a mitzvah, they elevate those sparks. This also explains why certain people end up in faraway places—because their soul has a connection to that specific spark that causes them to travel or even be born in a distant place. Our Sages teach that the Jews were destined to be exiled among all the nations. And when a single Jew ends up in a faraway place, it is considered as if all the Jews were

123 Isaiah 42:6, 49:6, 60:3.

exiled there (since all Jews have a common bond).

Thus, the ARI explains that when we pray to gather the souls together and to be returned to our Land, we are asking that we become rectified from the sin of wasted seed which caused the sparks to be scattered in the first place. This will connect later on with the third blessing of the *Shema*, which speaks about the Exodus from Egypt. When the Children of Israel descended to Egypt they began the rectification of Adam's sin, for this is the place that the sparks were first refined and rectified.[124]

Rebbe Nachman teaches that the mitzvah of *tzitzit* helps a person guard his covenant and protects him from immorality and wasted seed (LM I, 7:4). Therefore, it is customary to gather the four *tzitzit* of the *tallit* and hold them in your left hand and near your heart when you say, "Blessing and peace from all four corners of the earth." Even though the earth is round and has no corners, this refers to the four directions of the earth: east, south, west and north, wherever Jews are found. We ask God to gather us from all over the globe and return us to the Land of Israel. The Ingathering of the Exiles is a prelude to God being pronounced King of the entire world, as we say in the *Shema*.

וּבָנוּ בָחַרְתָּ מִכָּל עַם וְלָשׁוֹן, וְקֵרַבְתָּנוּ מַלְכֵּנוּ לְשִׁמְךָ הַגָּדוֹל סֶלָה בֶּאֱמֶת בְּאַהֲבָה, לְהוֹדוֹת לְךָ וּלְיַחֶדְךָ בְּאַהֲבָה וּלְאַהֲבָה אֶת שְׁמֶךָ:

You chose us from among all nations and tongues; You drew us close to Your great name forever, in truth, with love; to thank You and to proclaim Your oneness with love; and to love Your name.

At the end of the prayers, we find that the Kabbalists suggest saying Six Remembrances, in order to merit a portion in the World to Come.

124 *Pri Etz Chaim, Shaar Kriat Shema,* 3, pp. 162-165.

The ARI notes that four of these remembrances are alluded to in this blessing:

- Remember the Revelation at Sinai
- Remember what Amalek did to us
- Remember the slander spoken by Miriam against her brother, Moshe
- Remember the Exodus from Egypt

These four are positive *mitzvot* that we are instructed to remember every day. Therefore, the ARI says that when we say the words "You chose us from among all the nations and tongues," we should think of the Revelation at Sinai when we were chosen to be God's nation. When we say, "You drew us close to Your Great Name," we should bear in mind the mitzvah to eradicate Amalek, for God's Name cannot be complete until Amalek is eradicated from the world (Exodus 17:16; see Rashi). When we say, "To thank You," we should think of Miriam and learn to use our tongue to thank God and not slander or speak evil speech. And the fourth remembrance, that of the Exodus, we will recite as the last passage of the *Shema*.[125]

125 *Shaar HaKavanot, Inyan Kavanat Yotzer*, p. 119.

CHAPTER 20
Faith and Prayer

Rebbe Nachman describes at length the process by which we can increase our faith, how this affects the world, and how this eventually leads us to an even higher level of faith. Reb Noson shows how this process is represented by the daily prayers. The following is a brief synopsis of these ideas as we approach the *Shema*.

Strengthening Faith

Rebbe Nachman stresses, "First and foremost, every person must check and make sure that his faith is complete, and he must constantly try to increase and strengthen his faith in God." He outlines the process as follows (LM II, 5): One strengthens his faith by crying out to God from the depths of his heart—a prayer without words. In this way, a person draws from his heart the proper advice he needs in life, as it is written, "Like deep waters is the counsel in the heart of man; an intelligent person will draw it out" (Proverbs 20:5). The counsel that he attains strengthens his faith.

False beliefs (such as beliefs of idol worshippers and non-Jews) get their strength, nourishment, and existence when people's faith isn't complete. When one improves his faith, these false beliefs lose their nourishment and appeal, and the non-Jews abandon their beliefs. Some remain non-believing non-Jews, while some become converts and join the Jewish nation.

However, these converts bring with them their negative characteristics. This blemish is temporary, because the converts themselves are eventually completely rectified. However, in the interim, these negative characteristics—especially pride and arrogance—enter into the Jewish nation. These attributes go to the false and unworthy leaders of the Jewish nation, who use their arrogance to govern over people unjustly and to punish those who don't accept their leadership.

The arrogance of the false leaders brings lust, passion and immoral desire to the Jewish people. This results in wasted seed, as it is written, "Issue that seals the flesh" Leviticus (15:3). *Tefillin*, on the other hand, is called a "seal of holiness," as in, "Place me as a seal upon your heart, as a seal upon your arm" (Song of Songs 8:6). (The hand *tefillin* are placed on the arm, near the heart.) When the immoral desires are rectified, they turn into *tefillin*, which means a greater awareness of God.

To summarize: the process begins with increasing one's faith (by shouting out to God from the depths of one's heart and attaining good counsel). The improved faith results in new converts. The converts bring arrogance to the false leaders, which results in bad temptations for the Jewish nation. When the bad temptations are rectified, they become *tefillin*—or, in other words, an even higher awareness of faith. So we begin with faith, and we end with faith increasing even more.

What's left for us to describe is the process by which one rectifies the bad temptations, turning them into *tefillin*. Rebbe Nachman teaches:

> There are righteous people in our nation who struggle with their thoughts. Temptations for immorality constantly come to their minds, and they banish those thoughts by thinking holy thoughts. Their battle enables all Jews to battle with their lustful thoughts, and to turn them into holy thoughts. This becomes like *tefillin*, and the "issue that seals the flesh" becomes "a seal of holiness" (cf. LM II, 5:5).

Reb Noson elaborates:

> When one has many bad thoughts, and he fights, escapes and breaks them, he is making a great rectification. He is elevating

> the holiness that was in the *kelipah* and drawing the holiness of *tefillin*, which is to know and reveal God in the world. The greater the struggle, the greater will be the rectification of *tefillin* that he is creating. This is the sole reason these bad thoughts were sent to him: so he can create the rectification of *tefillin*.
>
> (*Kitzur Likutey Moharan* II, 5:7)

Increasing Faith through Prayer

Reb Noson proceeds to show that this process happens each morning with the deeds we perform and through the prayers we say (LH, *Hefker v'Nikhsey HaGer* 4).

He explains that the process begins when a person awakens for the *Chatzot* prayer,[126] and he cries out from the depths of his heart. These shouts bring forth the true, good counsels, from where faith grows. It is also customary to study Torah at night after the *Chatzot* prayer because the Torah contains all the true counsels. When the sun rises, it represents the fact that faith has become stronger and clearer, as it is written, "New every morning, great is your faith" (Lamentations 3:23).

This improved faith attracts converts, and they bring arrogance to the false leaders, which results in bad passions for the Jewish nation. We don the *tzitzit* in order to rectify these matters. Converts are associated with *tzitzit*, as it states, "In those days [in the Messianic era], ten people from all of the [non-Jewish] nations will grab hold of the corners of a Jew's garment [the *tzitzit*], saying, 'We will go with you, because we have heard that God is with you'" (Zekhariah 8:23). The *tzitzit* is also an article of clothing associated with pride — the pride that should be God's but was taken by the false leaders. The *tzitzit* also remove bad temptations. We then don the *tefillin*, which is

126 The Midnight Lament over the destruction of the *Beit HaMikdash*. For full text, see the Breslov Weekday Siddur. See also "*The Sweetest Hour*," from Breslov Research Institute.

a "seal of holiness" to counter immorality, bringing our faith to even higher levels.

Then we recite the morning blessings, which also demonstrates the process of faith emerging, and the rectifications that we must perform until faith is perfected. One of the morning blessings is "Who stretches out the dry land above the water." The dry land — the earth — parallels faith, as it is written, "Dwell in the land and pasture in faith" (Psalms 37:3). The waters parallel the counsel which must be drawn forth as in (Isaiah 11:9), "The earth will be filled with the knowledge of God as waters cover the sea." The next blessing is "Who prepares and guides man's steps." This refers to counsel, as in, "You and all the people who are at your feet" (Exodus 11:8). As Rashi (loc. cit.) explains, this refers to "the ones who follow your advice." The next blessing, "Who has provided me with all my needs," is said about wearing shoes which protect the feet; in our case, it refers to guarding our paths and protecting us from bad advice.

After the morning blessings, we recite the *Akeidah*, the binding of Yitzchak. This represents the self-sacrifice that one must perform in order to cry out from the depths. We then say the morning *Shema*, for if we merit to put in effort to cry out to God, we have elevated faith.

Following the morning *Shema*, we say the passages of the sacrifices, because when faith is elevated, it leads to converts. The sacrifices represent converts, for their purpose is to rectify the sparks of holiness and elevate the converts!

After saying the sacrifices, we recite the *Pesukey d'Zimrah*. We mentioned earlier that when converts join the nation they are accompanied by their negative characteristics, through which false leaders seize control of the nation and introduce immorality. They must be countered by revealing God's greatness. The *Az Yashir* passage speaks of God's pride and His greatness, which counters the fallen pride and arrogance of these leaders.

Following the *Pesukey d'Zimrah,* we recite the first blessing of the *Shema,* which speaks of the fiery angels and their fear of God. Their fiery fear rectifies the fiery passions and bad temptations that have developed in the Jewish nation.

Then we read the *Shema,* for at this point faith is perfect and complete. Although we said the *Shema* at the beginning of the prayers, at that point the faith wasn't yet perfect, since there was still the influence of arrogance and immoral temptations. But after everything has been rectified—through the *tallit* and *tefillin,* and through the prayers that we said—we can now read the *Shema* with perfect belief in God.

Reb Noson further explains the rectifications brought about by the blessing following the *Shema,* which we will discuss after studying the *Shema* itself.

CHAPTER 21

The Shema: David and Goliath

שְׁמַע יִשְׂרָאֵל יְיָ אֱלֹהֵינוּ יְיָ אֶחָד׃

Hear O Israel! HaShem is our God, HaShem is One.

One of the 613 *mitzvot* is to recite the *Shema* twice daily.[127] The *Shema* is our declaration that we believe in God. He is our God; he created us; and he created the entire world *ex nihilo.* We are the fortunate nation to accept His kingship and be considered His Chosen Nation. Rashi explains this verse as follows:

> HaShem, Who is presently our God and not [accepted as God] by the nations, will in the future be the One God [of everyone], as it is written, "For then I will turn the nations to a pure language, that they may all call out in the Name of God" (Zephaniah 3:9), and it is written, "On that day, HaShem will be One and His Name will be One" (ibid. 14:9; Rashi on Deuteronomy 6:4).

The idea of the *Shema* is to exclaim our belief publicly, which is why it is usually said aloud. We proclaim God's greatness and His Unity, and we accept that all that happens is the revelation of His will. This can be illustrated by the well-known story of King David and his opponent, the giant Goliath (I Samuel 17):

> The Philistines sent their army out to battle with King Saul and the Jewish nation. The Philistinian forces stood on one mountain, while the Jewish army stood on the mountain opposite it, with a

127 *Rambam, Mishnah Torah, Mitzvah #76.*

valley between them. A giant Philistine warrior named Goliath clad himself in heavy copper armor and wielded a weighted spear. Every day he would come to the edge of the Philistine camp and blaspheme God. He would challenge the Jews, saying, "Why should our armies battle each other? Choose a warrior to represent your nation, and I will represent the Philistines. If he vanquishes me, then we will be your slaves. If I win and vanquish him, then you will be our slaves." When the Jews saw this giant approaching, they all fled in fear. For forty days Goliath would go out in the morning and evening and torment the Jewish nation with his blasphemy.

Three of David's brothers had joined King Saul's army, however David was the shepherd of his father's flocks and was not present on the battlefield. One day his father asked him to bring provisions to his brothers, and he arrived at the camp just when Goliath was blaspheming God. When David heard Goliath's words he exclaimed, "Who is this uncircumcised Philistine who dares taunt the armies of a living God?"

David was brought to King Saul and said he was willing to battle the giant. When asked what qualifications he had to fight the Philistine warrior, David replied, "I was a shepherd to my father's flock. Both a lion and a bear came and took a lamb from the flock. I went after them and defeated the animals. When they arose to battle me, I grabbed hold of their *zaken* (beard or facial hair) and killed them. This uncircumcised Philistine shall be like them, because he blasphemed our living God. God, Who saved me from the lion and the bear, will save me from this Philistine!"

King Saul agreed for David to enter into battle with Goliath. David donned the king's armor, but it was not his size, so he elected to do battle without armor. David then took his shepherd's staff and sling and chose five smooth stones from the brook. He placed them in his pouch and approached Goliath. The giant looked at who was approaching him to do battle—a young, unarmored soldier in regular clothes with a staff and a sling. Goliath said disdainfully, "Am I a dog that you dare come against me with sticks?!" Goliath then cursed David with his god's name. He said to David, "Come to me, I will place your flesh as fodder for the birds and the domestic animals." Hearing that, David thought,

"Domestic animals don't feed on human flesh," which meant that Goliath had lost his mind.

Encouraged, David replied, "You come against me with your sword, spear and javelin. I am coming towards you in the Name of HaShem, the God of Hosts, the God of the army of Israel whom you blasphemed. Today, God will put you in my hands and I will slay you and remove your head. I will place the Philistine camp as fodder for the birds of the sky and the wild animals of the field. The entire world will know that there is a God in Israel! Everybody who is gathered here will know that it is not by sword and spear that one is victorious; battle belongs to God, and He will place you in our hands."

As Goliath approached, David ran toward him. He removed a stone from his pouch and slung it toward Goliath. It hit the Philistine squarely on the forehead and the stone entered his skull. He fell forward and died. David ran towards Goliath, took Goliath's sword and beheaded him. Seeing their leader slain, the Philistines fled.

According to our Sages, what was this battle all about?

David had full faith in God; he believed that everything happens by His decree. Goliath was an atheist; he denied God's providence and declared that everything is subjugated to the forces of nature. He had no qualms about blaspheming God, none whatsoever.

Our Sages teach that his name implies his brazenness. *GaLYat* (גלית, Goliath) implies *GiLuY panim* (גילוי פנים, open-faced brazenness) against God. Goliath tormented the Jews for forty days; his intention being to deny the Torah that was given in a forty-day period (*Sotah* 42b). Furthermore, he went out to taunt the Jews each morning and evening, intending to prevent them from saying the *Shema* (ibid.). Thus, Goliath's whole purpose was to deny God and destroy the Torah.

David was a true believer. He knew that his victory over the lion and the bear was a sign from Heaven and that he would need that encouragement at a future time. When he saw Goliath and heard his blasphemy, he knew that with God's help, he could defeat him. When David tried on King Saul's armor and it did not fit him, he was prepared to go to battle without protection and without powerful weapons. He went with pure faith alone.

David took five smooth stones from the brook, and slung one stone into Goliath's forehead, defeating him. The five stones represent the five words "*Shema Yisrael YHVH Eloheinu YHVH*" (שמע ישראל יי אלהינו יי)—the first five words of the verse of *Shema*. These five stones merged into one stone, the word *Echad* (אחד, One) (*Tikkuney Zohar* #21, p. 62a). David's belief was more powerful than Goliath's atheism. By declaring the *Shema* (God's greatness and unity), David was able to subdue the enemies of faith.

David's main weapon was his belief that God leads the world in accordance with His will. This is alluded to in the verse, "A perfect stone is His will" (Proverbs 11:1). David took five stones, meaning he took a declaration of faith to stand up to the leading atheist. These "stones" transformed into a "perfect stone," defeating Goliath. Not only was Goliath defeated, but he was beheaded by his own sword, his own weapon that he used to spread atheism.

The *Zohar* (III, 129a) teaches that God's will is represented by the *metzach* (מצח, forehead). It is called the *metzach haratzon* (מצח הרצון, the forehead of will). Opposite the *metzach haratzon* exists the *metzach hanachash* (מצח הנחש, forehead of the Serpent), referring to the Primordial Serpent that caused man to rebel against God. Goliath didn't believe that God leads the world according to His will. He followed the view represented by the *metzach hanachash*, the belief that everything happens by chance. Goliath wore copper armor all over his body. The word *NeChoShet* (נחשת, copper) is similar to *NaChaSh* (נחש, serpent), which implies that Goliath represents the Serpent, the forces of evil, the belief that the world is run by natural causes.

Rebbe Nachman expands on this story (LM II, 4:11). Miracles happen in the world, and these miracles proclaim the faith that God runs the world according to His will. But there are atheists who roar and rage and cause deafening noises, until we don't hear the call of faith. These atheists are the *metzach hanachash*, and they are referred to as wild beasts (e.g., the lion and the bear). David grabbed the wild beasts by their beards and defeated them, which means he defeated the atheists. He drew from those battles encouragement that he would also be able to defeat Goliath's "forehead of atheism." And indeed, David's stone—which represents the *Shema*—fell into the "forehead of atheism." Belief in God triumphed over atheism.

As we begin our discussions about the *Shema*, it's very important to know that the *Shema* is not just our declaration of faith; it is a major weapon with which each and every one of us can defeat the forces of evil. Every enemy, every opposition, or every challenge we face is a giant Goliath unto itself. Each and every Jew is a David who, with faith in God, has the power to defeat these gigantic enemies.

CHAPTER 22

The Shema: A Declaration of Faith

The Talmud states, "Whoever says the [bedtime] *Shema*, it is as if he is holding a double-edged sword in his hand" (*Berakhot* 5a). The *Zohar* adds that though the bedtime *Shema* is powerful enough to be compared to "holding a double-edged sword," it is only to ward off the forces of evil. However, the morning *Shema* is far more powerful; it can actually eradicate those evil forces (*Tikkuney Zohar*, Introduction, p. 8b).

We recite the *Shema* four times each day—twice in the morning and twice at night. In the morning, it is recited first prior to the sacrifices, and then among the blessings prior to the *Amidah*. At night we say the *Shema* first during *Maariv*, and then again before going to sleep. The ARI explains that though we say the same words each time, they have different Kabbalistic meanings and different implications in the rectifications that we effect with our prayers. By far, the most important of the four times is the *Shema* said during the morning blessings prior to the *Amidah*.[128] The ARI adds that though the accomplishments of the supernal unifications of the *Shema* are different, the intentions of the *Shema* are universal and equal.[129]

128 *Shaar HaKavanot, Inyan Kavanot Kriat Shema, Drush* 2, p. 124.

129 Ibid. *Drush* 4, p. 132.

שְׁמַע יִשְׂרָאֵל יְיָ אֱלֹהֵינוּ יְיָ אֶחָד:

Hear O Israel! HaShem is our God, HaShem is One.

Shema Yisrael! YHVH Eloheinu, YHVH Echad (Deuteronomy 6:4). Reciting the *Shema* means that a person is declaring that he accepts HaShem as his God. In Talmud and *Shulchan Arukh*, this is described as accepting the yoke of Heaven upon oneself. The word *SheMA* (שמע) is a backward acronym for *Ol Malkhut Shamayim* (עול מלכות שמים, the yoke of the Kingdom of Heaven). One who accepts upon himself the yoke of Heaven can see wonders all the time. As we have mentioned above that the initial letters of the phrase "*Se'u Marom Aineikhem* (שאו מרום עיניכם, Raise your eyes upward)" (Isaiah 40:26) are an acronym for *SheMA* (שמע) as well.[130] One who recites the *Shema* and displays his faith will merit to pray fervently before God and have his prayers answered. *SheMA* (שמע) is also an acronym for *Shacharit, Minchah, Arvit* (*Maariv*) (שחרית, מנחה, ערבית), the three daily prayers.[131]

The commentaries offer further insights to instill in us the profundity of faith and what can be accomplished by a man of faith. We present here several ideas learned from the *Shema* and insights that can help us throughout life.

Shema (Listen!)

The Talmud explains that the word *Shema* refers not only to hearing, but also to instilling those messages deep into our hearts (*Berakhot* 15a). Therefore, we begin this declaration of faith by saying, "*Shema* (Listen)!" as if we are going to announce

130 See above, p. 195.

131 *Tikkuney Zohar* #50, p. 56a.

something very profound and we want everyone—ourselves included—to pay close attention.

Reb Noson elaborates:

> The Jewish nation is very firm in their faith of God. It is their inheritance from their forefathers, and they don't have any doubts about it. Nevertheless, we must proclaim the *Shema*—our belief in God—every day, because God's greatness is endless, and each day one can perceive God in a new way, as he never had before.

The *Shema* begins with "Hear O Israel." Reb Noson notes that these words seem superfluous. Wouldn't it be enough if we only proclaimed, "God is One"?

When someone wants to tell a friend something that's new and wondrous, he will say, "Listen to this wonderful new concept!" So, too, we tell people (ourselves included) to listen and to pay close attention to our words because we are about to say something new and wonderful, for today we perceive God in a new way (LH, *Kriat Shema* 5:2).

The Talmud offers another explanation for the *Shema*: "Say it in whatever language you understand" (*Berakhot* 15a). There are seventy languages; the *Shema* can be said in any of those languages.

Reb Noson says that both commentaries in the Talmud are really one. Because when we make sure to hear what we are saying and internalize the profound truth that HaShem is the One God, then even if a person is at a very low level and struggling with bad thoughts he will believe that he can connect himself to God. This is because God is One and God is everywhere (LH, *Kriat Shema* 5:5).

Testimony and Joy

In a Torah scroll, the letter *Ayin* of *ShemA* (שמע) and the letter *Dalet* of *echaD* (אחד) are written larger than the other letters of the verse. These two letters form the word *EiD* (עד, witness or testimony). Whenever we articulate our belief in God, we are actually giving testimony to God's unity and that He created the world. Similarly, when a person declares his faith daily, God Himself gives beneficial testimony for this person as well. The remaining letters, *ShM* (שמ) of *SheMA* and *ECh* (אח) of *EChad* form the word *ESMaCh* (אשמח, I will rejoice). When one recites the *Shema*, Heaven bestows joy upon that person (*Zohar* III, 258a).

The *Zohar* adds that Heaven testifies to the morality of that person. If one blemishes the covenant, then the upper right-hand tip of the *Dalet* (ד) is erased and the letter turns into a *Reish* (ר). The final word in the *Shema* then becomes *acheR* (אחר, other), implying idolatry, the opposite of the *Shema* (*Tikkuney Zohar* #69, p. 99a).

Covering One's Eyes

It is customary to recite the *Shema* in a louder voice than usual in order to arouse one's *kavanah* (*Orach Chaim* 61:4). Also, you should cover your eyes with your right hand when reciting the *Shema* in order to avoid seeing anything that might divert your concentration (ibid. 61:5). (The left hand is still holding the *tzitzit* since the blessing of *Ahavas Olam*.[132])

The *Zohar* (II, 95a) provides the following riddle:

There is a beautiful maiden who has no eyes.
Her body is concealed and revealed.
She comes out in the morning and is covered during the day.
She adorns herself in ornaments that were not.

132 See above, p. 209.

The beautiful maiden with no eyes

The commentaries on the *Zohar* explain that this "beautiful maiden" is *Malkhut* (i.e., the *Shekhinah*) which according to Kabbalah associates with Rachel.[133] The Torah relates that while Leah's eyes were weak, Rachel was very beautiful (Genesis 29:17). Nothing, however, is said of Rachel's eyes, and so she is referred to as "the beautiful maiden who has no eyes." This aligns with the teaching that *Malkhut* has no light of its own but radiates the light it receives from the *sefirot* above it (*Zohar* I, 249b). Others explain that "the beautiful maiden" is the *Shema* prayer, which we recite with our eyes closed (*Nitzutzei Orot, Zohar,* loc. cit. #1).

Rebbe Nachman connects "the beautiful maiden who has no eyes" with faith. "Who has no eyes" refers to the questions that at present we cannot understand the answers to them.

Her body is concealed and revealed

Unlike the 'concrete' knowledge of the intellect, faith has no tangible 'body' by which to grasp it. Faith is not something one can logically explain to anyone else or even to oneself. Yet it is revealed because to the true believer, believing is seeing.

Reb Noson adds: When we are confronted by something we cannot understand and can't rely on our intellect, we strengthen our faith—as though we were actually seeing and understanding the thing with our mind's eye (*Torat Natan* I, 62:5). Reb Noson teaches: Looking to God with our eyes of faith—trusting in Him and believing that life and livelihood are only from Him—engenders a reciprocal look from God. With the 'sight' of Divine Providence focused upon us, we do, in fact, see that which we trust and believe in (ibid. I, 62:6).

133 See Charts, Appendix A.

She comes out in the morning and is covered during the day

Once again, this is referring to faith, which becomes stronger and renewed each morning. Then it becomes concealed during the day due to the many burdens of daily existence.

She adorns herself in ornaments that were not

The main adornment of faith is when those who were not close to her are brought closer (LM I, 62:5).

Thus, faith is called "a beautiful maiden who has no eyes." This might explain why we cover our eyes when we say *Shema*: it is because faith doesn't have eyes. The custom of covering our eyes when saying the *Shema* may actually be an ingenious way of strengthening our faith!

Rebbe Nachman teaches that the eyes represent physical desires and temptations, encompassing the evil traits of the seventy nations of the world.[134] By covering our eyes when reciting the first verse of the *Shema* and accepting the yoke of Heaven, one escapes from the influences of the temptations of the seventy nations (LM I, 36:3).

Echad

The word *EChaD* (אחד, One) is composed of three letters, *aleph, chet* and *dalet*. It is customary that when we say the word *Echad*, we bear in mind that God is the *aleph* (the One God) Who rules over the seven heavens and the earth (which together add up to eight, the numerical value of *chet*). He also

134 The word *ayin* (עין, eye) is also the name of the letter *ayin* (ע), which has the numerical value of 70.

rules over the entire globe (the four corners of the earth, the numerical value of *dalet*). Rabbi Yisrael Salanter would say, "It is appropriate that when thinking of God as ruler over the heavens and earth, we also bear in mind that He rules over us, too" (*Rabbi Eliyahu Chaim Rosen*).

Cities of Refuge

When the Jewish nation entered the Land of Israel, they were commanded to set aside six cities of refuge. If a person killed someone unintentionally, he could flee to one of these cities. An additional forty-two cities were given over to the *Leviim*, and they also became cities of refuge (Numbers 35). Being exiled there atones for the murder, and it protects the murderer from the vengeance and wrath of the murdered person's relatives.

Reb Noson writes that these forty-eight cities of refuge correspond to the forty-eight words in the *Shema*. The six cities of refuge correspond to the six initial words of *Shema*. The forty-two cities of the *Leviim* correspond to the forty-two words in *V'ahavta*, the first paragraph of the *Shema*.

Shema is our proclamation of faith, and when one has faith, he is attached to life—to true living. When one doesn't have faith, although he is alive physically, spiritually he is like the dead.

One who murders someone unintentionally has attached himself to the realm of death. He is also at risk of being killed by the victim's relatives. He can find refuge and life in the forty-eight cities. Similarly, when one doesn't have faith and has fallen to the point of committing the worst types of sins, he is spiritually dead. But he can find refuge and life within the *Shema*, with faith in God. The *Shema*, with its forty-eight words, are his place of refuge (LH, *Eruvey Techumin* 5:37).

The Battle Cry

The Torah states, "When you go out to battle with the enemy...do not fear them, for God is with you" (Deuteronomy 20:1). The battle leader would then say, "*Shema Yisrael*—Hear O Israel" (ibid. 20:3) and would speak to the warriors, encouraging them on how to battle. Why, the Talmud asks, does the leader say, "*Shema Yisrael*?" This teaches us that even if we only have the merit of saying the *Shema* morning and evening, we are considered worthy of God protecting us and doing battle for us (*Sotah* 42a).

CHAPTER 23
Barukh Shem

The *Zohar* teaches that one who says the *Shema* and *Barukh Shem* with *kavanah* is considered an elevated and dignified person who will, in the future world, be counted with the righteous before God (*Tikkuney Zohar* #66, p. 97b). When we finish saying the six words of the *Shema* aloud, we then say *Barukh Shem K'vod Malkhuto L'olam Va'ed*—May the Name of the glory of His Kingdom be blessed for all eternity. However, the accepted practice is that the words *Barukh Shem* should be said quietly, in a whisper.

The verse of *Shema Yisrael* comes from the Torah (Deuteronomy 6:4). *Barukh Shem,* however, is not mentioned in the Torah. Why were these two verses put together?

The Talmud relates:

> On his deathbed, our patriarch Yaakov (also known as Yisrael), called his twelve sons together in order to bless them (Genesis 49:1). He was also going to reveal to them the length of the exile and when the final redemption would come. But as they stood before Yaakov, the *Shekhinah* left him, and Yaakov could not foresee when the exile would end. He was worried and thought, "Maybe one of my descendants is unfit, just as Avraham had Yishmael and Yitzchak had Esav?" His sons, all of them tzaddikim, immediately declared, "*Shema Yisrael*—Hear Yisrael, our God is the One God! Just as there is only One God in your heart, there is only One God in our hearts." At that moment Yaakov exclaimed, "*Barukh Shem K'vod Malkhuto L'olam Va'ed*—May the Name of the glory of His Kingdom be blessed for all eternity" (*Pesachim* 56a).

Our Sages faced a dilemma. Naturally, we should say the *Shema,* since Moshe said it and it is written in the Torah. But what about *Barukh Shem*? On the one hand, Yaakov said it, so perhaps we should say it too. On the other hand, Moshe did not say it, so maybe we shouldn't say it. The Sages were not sure what to do so they compromised: they ruled that we should say it in a whisper.[135]

The Talmud explains this reasoning with a parable. A royal princess smells a pudding called *Tzikey Kederah,* a savory pudding made by the lower classes.[136] If she asks for it, she is disgraced—after all, she is royalty. But if she does not ask for it, then she is discomforted. Therefore, she commands her servants to bring it to her quietly (*Pesachim* 56a). Thus, *Barukh Shem* is to be said quietly, not to detract from the words of the Torah.

Reb Noson examines the story of Yaakov and his children, the idea of the *Tzikey Kederah* (savory pudding), and what our role is in drawing people closer to God (LH, *Birkhos HaShachar* 5:27).

Yaakov saw that his children were very solid in their faith, so he thought he could reveal to them when the *Mashiach* would come. However, when the *Shekhinah* departed from him, he suspected that perhaps they had sinned and weren't worthy of hearing about the final date of the redemption. When they replied, "*Shema Yisrael*—As you believe in the One God, so do we," Yaakov was mollified, and he understood that there must be another reason that the *Shekhinah* had left him. The reason was that there were too many sparks of holiness that still had to be rectified, even—or especially—those trapped in the deepest depths of impurity. Therefore, Yaakov said, "*Barukh Shem*," meaning that God's kingship had to be revealed all over

135 Moshe's verse is said aloud while Yaakov's verse is said quietly. See *Tikkuney Zohar* #69, p. 101a.

136 *Tzikey Kederah* is a pudding made of leftover minced meat cooked with wine and spices.

the world, even for those who are at very low levels. Yaakov realized that it was still an inopportune time to reveal the date of the final redemption.

For this reason, Moshe did not mention "*Barukh Shem*" in the Torah itself. Of course, Moshe was aware of the rectifications made when we recite *Barukh Shem*. But considering that this is one of the deepest mysteries in the world—how we can spread knowledge of God all over the globe—it is too deep to be revealed. Therefore, the Sages compared it to a savory pudding, something that only the "lower classes" (i.e., those who are very distant from God) can partake of. Yet these "sparks" (i.e., those who are very distant from God, who are in the process of conversion or otherwise drawing closer to God) must be brought to the princess (i.e., to their rectification). However, it is a secret and a mystery and must be kept hidden as their rectification unfolds.

The upshot is that when we declare our faith with the *Shema*, we are actually spreading that faith all across the globe. But many people are too distant to even hear that exclamation. Therefore, we quietly and unobtrusively spread faith through declaring God's glory as spreading throughout the world. This quiet message will ultimately reach the farthest corners of the earth and make its way into the hearts of those who are distant, to arouse them and awaken their hearts to God (LH, *Hefker v'Nikhsei HaGer* 4:21).

The Fourteen Letters

The *Shema* contains the holy names of God, *YHVH Eloheinu YHVH* (יי אלהינו יי). The initial letters of these names form an acrostic for the three patriarchs: Avraham (אברהם), Yitzchak (יצחק), and Yaakov (יעקב). The Patriarchs represent faith, since they were the ones to discover and establish the faith in

God. Furthermore, these names contain fourteen letters, the *gematria* of the word *YaD* (יד, hand). An oath is taken with the hand. The idea of the hand covering the eyes implies faith and honesty (LH, *Chezkat Metaltelin* 5:3).

The Twenty-Five Letters

The first verse of the *Shema* contains twenty-five letters. In Hebrew, the numerical value of twenty-five equals the word *KoH* (כה). These twenty-five letters invoke the blessing of the *Kohanim* which begins, "*Koh* (This) is how you must bless the Jewish people," (Numbers 6:23). This brings *Chesed* and kindness to those who recite the *Shema* (*Tikkuney Zohar*, Addendum, p. 140a).

The Twenty-Four Letters

The *Shema* is followed by the verse *Barukh Shem K'vod Malkhuto L'olam Va'ed*—May the Name of the glory of His Kingdom be blessed for all eternity. In this verse we find twenty-four letters, corresponding to the twenty-four books of the Bible (*Tikkuney Zohar*, Introduction, p. 14a).

The Forty-Nine Letters

The Talmud teaches, "Fifty gates of *Binah* (wisdom) were created in the world, and all were given to Moshe except one," (*Rosh HaShanah* 21b). The forty-nine letters of the *Shema* and *Barukh Shem* together correspond to these forty-nine gates of *Binah*, which, by our saying them, open the gates of wisdom to us (*Tikkuney Zohar*, Introduction, p. 7b). Furthermore, the forty-nine letters of *Shema* and *Barukh Shem* parallel the forty-nine days between the Exodus and the revelation at Sinai, when we received the Torah. Thus, by reciting the *Shema*, we open up for ourselves the paths of purity to receive the Torah (*Tikkuney Zohar* #19, p. 39a).

The 245 Words

The three paragraphs of the *Shema* contain 245 words. In the synagogue, the *chazan* will repeat the final three words, *YHVH Eloheikhem Emet* (HaShem your God is the ultimate reality) to bring the total to 248 words, corresponding to the number of limbs in the human body. Each limb absorbs the words of the *Shema* to bring healing.[137] A person who prays alone recites three words before beginning the *Shema*, *Eil Melekh Ne'eman* (God, Faithful King) in order to complete the total of 248 words. Note that the initial letters of *Eil Melekh Ne'eman* (אל מלך נעמן) spell *AMeN* (אמן) — testimony to God being faithful to His flock just as we declare our faithfulness to God (*Tikkun Tefillah*).

Note that the Hebrew word *RoMaCh* (spear) has the *gematria* of 248 as well. One who recites the *Shema* creates a metaphysical spear to fight his spiritual battles.

The Ten Commandments

The Talmud teaches that the Ten Commandments are found within the *Shema* (*Yerushalmi, Berakhot* 1:5). See a chart of the parallels:

Ten Commandments	Shema
"*Anokhi* — I am HaShem your God"	"HaShem is our God"
"Do not have any other gods before Me"	"God is One"
"Do not take the Name of HaShem your God in vain"	"*V'ahavta* — Love HaShem your God"

137 *Orach Chaim* 61:3; *Zohar Chadash, Ruth*, p. 95a.

"Remember the Shabbos day"	"Remember and fulfill all My *mitzvot*" (since Shabbos is equal to all the *mitzvot*)
"Honor your father and mother, so that your days will be lengthened"	"Your days and your children's days will be prolonged"
"Do not murder"	"You will quickly vanish"
"Do not commit adultery"	"Stop going astray after your hearts and after your eyes"
"Do not steal"	"You may then gather in your grain" (and not the grain of others)
"Do not bear false witness"	"I am HaShem your God—the true, ultimate reality"
"Do not desire your friend's house"	"Write them on your doorposts" (on a *mezuzah*; and not on your friend's house)

Thus, the *Shema* parallels the Ten Commandments, which comprise the entire Torah. It also parallels the Creation, for the Ten Commandments correspond to the Ten Sayings with which the world was created (*Avos* 5:1). It also corresponds to the Ten Types of Song, which carry a powerful rectification as mentioned in Chapter 15 about *Pesukey d'Zimra*.

CHAPTER 24

The Diversity of the Shema

One of the most interesting ideas behind the *Shema* is its declaration of unity, despite the diversity of the people who say it.

Earlier (see Chapter 18), we mentioned Rebbe Nachman's teaching about "the diverse phenomena that stem from God's Simple Unity." It is wondrous that so many diverse creations all came from the One God, especially human beings who have different ideas and opinions.

Reb Noson elaborates: The soul is very cognizant of God's Unity, as all souls are connected to God. But the souls are sent down to this physical world into separate bodies—diverse phenomena—each with different composite makeups and different ideas. Yet when each body nullifies itself before its soul and says, "*Shema Yisrael*," they are all included in God's Unity once again.

However, those who cannot, or do not, recite the *Shema* live a life which is very distant from God's Unity. They become immersed in the diversities of this world and when they have to face daily challenges, they serve to divert their focus towards the material and obscure the spiritual. This is the future miracle of the *Shema* as Rashi explains: "Our God of now will at that time be the One God of the entire world." The beauty is that notwithstanding the diversity of humankind—there are over seven billion people in the world today—all will approach God and say, "*Shema Yisrael*—God is One!" (LH, *Perikah u'Te'inah* 4:24).

Seventy Jewish Souls

The *Likutey Moharan* (1:36) discusses the *Shema* and some of its benefits:

> Every Jewish soul is rooted in the seventy souls of Yaakov's family (listed in Genesis 46), and the seventy souls of Yaakov's family are rooted in the seventy "faces" (or facets) of the Torah (because the Torah can be understood in seventy ways). Opposing them are the seventy nations of the world, each with their own bad attribute. These bad attributes are negative temptations or bad character traits, such as anger, jealousy, immorality and arrogance. These seventy nations and their seventy bad attributes are the exact opposites of the seventy souls of Yaakov's family and the seventy faces of the Torah.

The *Likutey Moharan* writes:

> The principle is that every Jewish soul is rooted in the seventy souls of the House of Yaakov, and the seventy souls of the House of Yaakov are rooted in the seventy faces of the Torah. But "God made one to contrast the other" (Ecclesiastes 7:14), so that in contrast to the seventy souls of the House of Yaakov there are seventy nationalities. Each and every one has its own evil trait, specific to that nation causing them to be distant from the seventy faces of the Torah.

Additionally, all nations share a particular bad attribute, which is the root and origin of all their other bad attributes. That is the colossal drive for immorality (in its negative form).

The *Likutey Moharan* writes:

> And know, encompassing all the seventy nations and their bad traits is the desire for immorality. Thus, anyone who breaks this desire can then easily break all the desires.

To summarize these ideas, imagine the soul of a Jew at the middle point of a chart, surrounded by two rings circling it. The first ring represents the seventy souls of Yaakov's family (because the origin of every Jewish soul is from there), and the next ring represents the seventy faces of the Torah (because the seventy souls of Yaakov come from the seventy faces of the

Torah). On the opposite side stand the seventy nations and the seventy bad attributes. These are like shells, covering over the seventy faces of the Torah, preventing people from attaining them. When a Jew experiences a bad attribute of the seventy nations, he must break the shell, overcome the bad temptation or character trait, and then the portion of Torah that it was covering will become revealed, as if emerging anew.

Rebbe Nachman teaches that the way to rescue oneself from the seventy bad traits of the nations is to shout to God. These cries are compared to a birthing mother who cries out seventy times from the bitter anguish of her birth pangs. The mother's seventy cries correspond to the seventy words contained in the psalm, "May God answer you in time of trouble" (Psalms 20:2; see *Zohar* III, 249), for without these cries, it is impossible for her to deliver. Similarly, a person experiences a revelation in Torah and Divine service by crying out "seventy times," until God has compassion on him, and he merits to prevail and overcome the physical enticements.

To clarify these matters further, the *Kitzur Likutey Moharan* (I, #36) says:

> Before every Jewish soul experiences a revelation in Torah and Divine service, it is tested and refined in the exile of the seventy nations — that is, in their physical desires.
>
> To explain: Each one of the seventy nations has some negative character trait of its own, which is not dominant in any other nation. As a result, these nations are distant from the seventy "faces" (or "facets") of the Torah. Just as "the shell covers the fruit," and a person who wishes to eat the fruit must first break through this shell, before receiving a revelation of understanding in Torah, the soul is forced to go into exile — that is, into the exile of the character traits and physical desires of the seventy nations — in order to break those traits and desires and subsequently come to a revelation in Torah and Divine service.
>
> Know that the primary test and refining process that a person must undergo involves his sexual desire. This desire encompasses

> all the evil desires and negative character traits of the seventy nations. A person who breaks this sexual desire can then break all his other desires with ease. Therefore, when a person is tested in the exile of this desire, each person in his own particular way, he must then cry out to God seventy times.
>
> The more a person has affected this general rectification of morality, and the farther he is removed from the craving for sex, the closer he is to a revelation in the Torah. The opposite is true as well; the more a person harbors such cravings, the more distant he is from this revelation, God forbid. When a person stands up to the test and breaks this craving, he merits to attain the *sefirot* (i.e., *Chokhmah* and *Binah*), and the secrets of the Torah are revealed to him.

The *Likutey Moharan* connects this concept with *Shema.*

> When a person accepts upon himself the yoke of the Kingdom of Heaven [when he says the Shema] his soul is attached to, and included in, the Twelve Tribes of Israel. This is because reciting the twelve words of the first two verses of the *Shema* and *Barukh Shem*, correspond to the twelve tribes. In addition, these two verses contain forty-nine letters, which parallel the forty-nine letters of the twelve tribes.
>
> All this, however, applies only to a person who occasionally experiences an immoral thought. In that case, it is sufficient for him to control his desire by reciting these two verses of the *Shema.* But if a person habitually thinks immoral thoughts and is unable to separate himself from them, he must actually shed tears as he accepts upon himself the yoke of the Kingdom of Heaven. This is because tears come from an excess of black bile (i.e., melancholy), and the black bile is connected to the spleen, which is identified with the Kingdom of Evil, (i.e., *Lilit*). Accordingly, when such a person sheds tears, this excess matter — namely, the sexual drive that derives from impurities in the blood, resulting from excess bile in the spleen — is expelled and leaves the body, and his soul is included within the Kingdom of Heaven.

Once a person rescues himself from the seventy bad attributes of the seventy nations, he is now able to study Torah and understand it correctly. But as long as his attributes remain blemished, his mind will also be warped, distorting and misunderstanding the Torah that he studies.

When a person blemishes his sexual purity, his mind becomes tainted to the point that he cannot grasp or comprehend the words of the tzaddik and of the Torah at all. Consequently, such a person is liable to stumble in the words of the tzaddik and the Torah if he goes ahead and follows the crookedness of his own heart and heeds the inane doubts and questions that enter his mind. "The pathways of God are straight; the righteous will walk in them, and sinners will stumble in them" (Hosea 14:10). In other words, each person receives and interprets the Torah teachings of the tzaddik according to his own understanding, which is determined by the quality of his own vessel — namely, his own mind. Thus, when a person has properly rectified his sexual purity, his mental faculties are then intact and unblemished.

The *Zohar* (II, 110a) says, "*Yesod* ascends up to *Abba* and *Imma*." *Abba* and *Imma* correspond to the letters *Yod* and *Hey* (of God's Name, YHVH), which relate to the two sides of the brain, one's mental faculties. Accordingly, when *Yesod* — corresponding to the reproductive organ and to morality — is rectified, then a person can understand the words of the tzaddik and he obtains a new soul through the tzaddik's revelations of Torah. On the other hand, a person who is not rectified in this area, God forbid, is in the category of "sinners will stumble in them," since one's comprehension and understanding accords with the degree to which he has rectified his sexual purity.

It is a fundamental principle that "From the Mouth of the Supernal One, good and evil do not emanate" (Lamentations 3:38) — but rather, only undifferentiated Divine light. This light then takes its form in accordance with the vessel that receives it. But if the vessel is not whole, God forbid, then a person receives this light as a curse. This is the reason why Bilaam advised Balak to entice the Jewish people with sexual transgression (*Sanhedrin* 106a), in order to ruin their vessels for receiving Divine light. The craving for sex blemishes the mental faculties and a person can become literally insane, God forbid.

God is always revealing to us thoughts of goodness and repentance. What do we do with these thoughts? What do we focus upon? The Rebbe's answer is our own deeds. God sends us pure thoughts, which are closed and clenched with purity. But how are we receiving them? It is up to us to open our hearts and minds in order to accept these thoughts in a positive mode. This determines whether we receive God's blessing as a blessing or as a curse. We have the ability to choose.

Thus, reciting the *Shema* has the power to help us become aware of God and Godliness and to form God's blessings for us in a positive manner.

The Time for Saying the *Shema*

The *Shulchan Arukh* teaches that one must recite the *Shema* during the first quarter of the day. For example, if the day begins at 6:00 a.m. and ends at 6:00 p.m., a quarter of the day would be at 9:00 a.m., and the *Shema* must be said prior to that time (*Orach Chaim* 58:1). One who does not say the *Shema* within the correct timeframe can get a reward for studying Torah but has lost out on the mitzvah of the *Shema* in the proper time (ibid. 58:6). Reading the *Shema* specifically within its *halakhic* timeframe draws blessing and bounty (*Tikkuney Zohar* #21, p. 60a).

Reb Noson discusses the importance of the *Shema* being said at the right time (LH, *Kriat Shema* 4:2, 7-9). He begins by recounting the story of Bilaam, who wanted to curse the Jewish nation. He had a plan: Bilaam knew that he would receive a prophecy of blessings from God. However, since the prophecy would be received in his blemished mind, the blessing would become warped and become a curse. This could happen because the blessings that God sends down are accepted and formed according to the vessel—the mind—that they enter. So what did God do? He completed the form of the blessings *before* it reached Bilaam's mind. Then Bilaam received it as a blessing and it could not be ruined by his mind.

The same occurs with Torah study. If a person doesn't have a pure mind, then when the Torah enters into his mind, it can become formed as a curse. What's the solution? Reb Noson writes that a person should believe in God because then the blessing will be formed as a blessing *before* it reaches his mind. In Reb Noson's words:

> With his faith, he becomes inclusive in God, and in the tzaddikim in whom he believes, and in their Torah. They will form the light for him as a blessing, and they will draw it down to him as a perfected light, in the form of a blessing... His blemished vessel won't ruin the light to form it in a bad way because the light was already formed as a blessing.

Thus, when we say the *Shema*, we focus on our faith. This results in God forming the light as a blessing, and it won't be ruined by our blemished, intellect vessels.

The timeframe for reciting the *Shema* is as follows: The evening *Shema* can be recited the entire night, while the daytime *Shema* can be recited only until the first quarter of the day. Why the difference?

When we begin the blessings of the *Shema*, we say, "Who forms light and creates darkness." "Forms light (*YoTzeR or*, יוצר אור) connotes *YeTziRah* (יצירה), a lower level. "Creates darkness (ובורא חשך, *u'VoRei choshekh*)" connotes *BeRyiah* (בריאה), a higher level. It is dark at night because the light (the spiritual light) is concealed from us. It is beyond us and it hasn't yet reached our world. Therefore, we have the entire night to form the light as a blessing and we can recite the evening *Shema* all night. On the other hand, the light is being formed in the early hours of the daytime. One can recite the *Shema* then and form the light that is coming down as a blessing, before it is totally formed down below. But after it has been formed, which is after the time of *Shema*, it is too late.

Thus, reciting the *Shema* at the appropriate time forms the light in a positive manner for the person to receive the proper dosage of light from God.

One may ask, "Why the three-hour deadline?" Reb Noson answers that in general we find that the mentalities of a person are three: *Chokhmah, Binah* and *Daat*. When we say, "*Kadosh! Kadosh! Kadosh!* (Holy! Holy! Holy!)" we prepare ourselves for sanctity, we prepare ourselves for purity, and we guard the covenant in order to be sanctified. Thus, the three mentalities manifest to us in a three-hour period at the beginning of the day.

We can also relate this three-hour timeframe to the Talmudic teaching, "God studies Torah the first three hours of the day" (*Avodah Zarah* 4a). This is a wonder! The entire Torah is from God; what does it mean that He studies and is involved in Torah? It is due to God's great compassion on the Jews that He gets involved in Torah for the first three hours of the day, helping the Jews form the light from Above into a beneficial blessing.

CHAPTER 25

The Shema: A Comprehensive Look at the Prayer

The *Shema* prayer consists of the initial sentences of *Shema* and *Barukh Shem* plus three Biblical paragraphs. The first paragraph (Deuteronomy 6:5-9), contains forty-two letters corresponding the forty-two letters of the Holy Name (מב, MB), the name used by God to create the world (see above *Ana B'Koach*, Chapter 12). This paragraph discusses our call to accept upon us the yoke of Heaven. It is written in the singular because each person must feel an obligation individually. Doing so invokes our creative abilities with which we can create a life for ourselves.

The second paragraph (Deuteronomy 11:13-21) contains seventy-two words from the first word *v'ahavta* until *v'samtem* (v. 18). This parallels the Holy Name of God of Seventy-Two letters (עב), which equals *Chesed* (חסד), drawing lovingkindness upon ourselves. The remaining fifty words parallel the Fifty Gates of Understanding, to draw knowledge of God. It is the Torah's call to accept the yoke of heaven as a nation. Therefore, it is written in the plural (*Shaar HaKavanot, Inyan Kavvanot Kriat Shema*, p. 140).

The third paragraph (Numbers 15:37-41) speaks of the *tzitzit* and contains seventy-two words, including the three words at the end that the *chazan* repeats. This corresponds to the Holy Name of Seventy-Two letters (עב). (Alternatively, if one does not pray with a *chazan*, then prior to the Shema he says the three words, *Eil Melekh Neeman*, instead.) In total, the entire prayer adds up to 248 words, which parallels the 248 limbs of a human being. This teaches us that we are obligated to accept God's Kingship over each and every limb of our bodies.

When we recite the Shema and *Barukh Shem* we are accepting upon ourselves the yoke of Heaven (i.e., that God is our God and that we are His servants). When we recite the next paragraph, *V'ahavta,* we should accept upon ourselves the positive commandments and intend to perform them. When reciting the second paragraph, *V'hayah im shamoa,* we should accept upon ourselves to abstain from the prohibitive *mitzvot* so that we do not have to endure any punishment for transgressions. Finally, when we recite the third paragraph about the *tzitzit,* we remember the Exodus and declare that God is with us at all times.

Additionally, the first passage is written in singular, indicating the individual's acceptance of the yoke of the *mitzvot.* The second paragraph is written in plural, indicating the community's responsibility to accept the *mitzvot.* The third passage states the commandment not to stray after one's heart or eyes and to focus on the "straight and narrow" path of serving God.

V'Ahavta

"You should love your God with all your heart, with all your soul and with all your possessions." The first word, "*v'ahavta*" is the mitzvah to love God. In addition to loving God, our Sages teach, "One should ensure that God is beloved through your actions" (*Yoma* 86a). If you are a religious Jew, and especially if you are a Torah scholar, people are watching how you act. If you speak kindly with people and conduct business honestly, people will view you as a role model and love God. Anyone who conducts his business affairs faithfully thereby fulfills the positive commandment, "You shall love God your Lord" (Deuteronomy 6:5). This mitzvah is the root of all the positive commandments, as it is written, "Then prepare a tasty dish for me, the way I love it" (Genesis 27:4). "Love it" refers to the positive commandments (*Tikkuney Zohar* #21, p. 51a, 52a). As Rebbe Nachman teaches, "When doing business honestly, we fulfill the mitzvah of *v'ahavta*" (LM I, 93).

With all your heart: You should love God with both your inclinations: the good and the evil. That is, you should perform the positive *mitzvot* (i.e., good inclination) and avoid the prohibitive commandments (i.e., evil inclination).

With all your soul: You should love God, even if you have to sacrifice your life for Him.

With all your possessions: You should love God, even if He takes away your possessions.

I command you today: You should accept the commandments as if they are fresh and you just received them today! This concept ties in with what we mentioned earlier (Chapter 17) that each day has its own rectifications which are not connected to the previous day or to the following day. Therefore, when we say, "Today!" we merit to fulfill the obligations of "today" (LH, *Shecitah* 4:3).

You shall teach your children: A person is obligated to teach his children to be well versed in their Torah studies. When asked a question in Torah, they should be able to reply immediately and eloquently, without stammering.

In your house...on the road: Your actions should be consistent, whether by yourself, in your home, or if you are traveling to foreign places. You should be faithful to God whether you are by yourself or with other people. If you can perform the *mitzvot* when you're alone before God with the same caution and perfection as when you are among others, then you are serving Him in truth (LM I, 251).

***Tefillin* (called *totaphot*):** Why use the word *totaphot*? Rashi explains that *Tat* in the Coptic language means two. *Pot* in the African language means two (*Menachot* 34b). Therefore, the head *tefillin* (*totaphot*) is comprised of four separate housings for the four passages, as opposed to the hand *tefillin* which has only one housing for all four passages. But why would the Torah use foreign languages to teach us about the housings of the *tefillin*? Rebbe Nachman explains: Our Sages wanted us to understand that all corporeal things have God's life-force in them. Using the foreign word *totaphot* teaches us that Godliness is found everywhere. A person can always find God, even in foreign lands, languages and environments (LM I, 33:2).

It is customary to touch the *tefillin* when saying the verses related to *tefillin*. The reason is that one should not divert his thoughts from the *tefillin* while he is wearing them (*Orach Chaim* 61:25; cf. ibid. 38:4). Some place an edge of the *tallit* on the arm *tefillin* and then they kiss the *tallit* and kiss the head *tefillin*. Some use the straps of the *tefillin* to kiss them and others use their hands.

You shall write upon your *mezuzot*: The *Zohar* (III, 263b) writes that there are certain *kelipot* which remain at the entrance to a person's home. When a person leaves, these *kelipot* try to attack him in order to make him sin now that he's left the security of his home. Therefore, we are commanded to place *mezuzot* on our doors to fight against these forces of evil. Therefore, we find that the word *MeZUZoT* (מזוזת) forms the words *ZaZ MaVeT* (זז מות, death is removed).

Rebbe Nachman explains 'death' as the burning desire of avarice. It consumes a person's life not letting him live and breathe. A *mezuzah* is a powerful counter force to protect a person from greed. With the *mezuzah*, one is able to be happy with his lot. Money is called *ZuZim* (זוזים, coins). The *MeZuZah* (מזוזה) protects from this burning desire for *Zuzim* (LM I, 23).

V'Haya im shamoa

The second paragraph begins by stating that if you listen [to what you already practice] you will hear new teachings (Rashi, loc. cit.) The recipe for spiritual growth is in the person's ability to listen to and accept what he learns with honesty and faith. If a person accepts the Torah as it has been taught for these past thousands of years, he is now capable of receiving a new infusion of spirituality. This helps the person grow, spiritually, emotionally, financially and physically.

Take heed and guard yourselves from being enticed: We are commanded to accept the Torah anew each day. Why? The evil inclination finds new ways each day to entice a person away from God. In every generation, it presents new opportunities for a person to fall into these traps. A person must be aware of the opportunities for growth, as well as the enticements that present themselves daily.

Do not veer from God's service: The Baal Shem Tov explains that the minute a person veers from serving God, that moment becomes for him a moment of serving idolatry (LM II, 62). After all, if he strays from God, he is now facing another deity. As a result, God blocks our bounty and blessing, for wherever there is idolatry, there is divine anger (*Sifri*).

Your days and the days of your descendants shall be increased upon the land: The Talmud (*Berakhot* 8a) tells us that Rabbi Yochanan was surprised when he heard that there are elderly people living in Babylon. He asked, "Doesn't the verse state, 'Your days…shall be increased upon the land?' This implies that longevity is solely in the Land of Israel, and not in the diaspora." But then he heard that the people of Babylon are meticulous about going to synagogue. They arrive early and leave late. Therefore, Reb Yochanan concluded that was the reason they lived a long life in Babylon.

Still, the question begs an answer. The verse seems to imply that longevity is solely in the Land of Israel and nowhere else. However, the Talmud teaches (*Megillah* 29a) that in the future, all synagogues will be transported to the Holy Land. Therefore, the synagogues of the Diaspora have the sanctity of the Holy Land. Thus, attending the synagogues of the Diaspora is like living in the Holy Land. This is how the elders of Babylon merited a long life (*Kli Yakar* on Deuteronomy 11:21).

Upon the land: "Do not say that the pit and the grave will be your refuge (*Avos* 4:21). In this world you have many worries, including the burden of livelihood. You might not even be aware of minor annoyances. For example, a mosquito can bite you and you may not even feel it. But in the grave, you have no other distractions (*Rebbe Nachman's Wisdom* #84). Rabbi Elchonon Spector (d. 1984) would say, "This is why the Torah states, 'Upon the Land.' One should not be in a rush to look for an escape or refuge. Make the most of your life!"

The passage of *Tzitzit*

Although we have discussed the mitzvah of *tzitzit* previously (see Chapter 6), here we present some ideas about reciting the *tzitzit* during the *Shema*. We already gathered the *tzitzit* prior to saying the *Shema* during the blessing of Eternal Love. As we gather the *tzitzit*, it is as if we are, "gathering in the exiles." The ARI writes that when we reach the passage of *tzitzit*, we should take hold of the strings of the *tzitzit* in our right hand and place the knots of the *tzitzit* near our heart in our left hand. While reciting the passage one should hold and look at the *tzitzit*, especially when reciting the verse, "And you shall see them." Then one should look at the *tzitzit* and kiss them. It is also customary to kiss the *tzitzit* when saying the word "*tzitzit*" during the *Shema*. If a person is careful with the mitzvah of *tzitzit*, he will overcome his urge and be protected if confronted with sin by recalling the verse, "And you shall see them."

In Hebrew, the word *tzitz* translates as "to look." Rebbe Nachman teaches that when one "looks" at the teachings of the tzaddikim and accepts their advice, he merits to have a guarded covenant, truth and faith (LM I, 7:4). Wearing *tzitzit* helps a person attain the "look."

***Tzitzit* and Anger**: The ARI writes further that *tzitzit* is a protection against anger. There are four *tzitzit*, placed on the four corners (*kanaf*, כנף) of the garment. The numerical value of anger (*KA'aS*, כעס) is the same as the numerical value of *kanaf* (כנף), 150. In addition, four times *KaNaF* (4x150) equals 600, the numerical value of *tzitzit* (ציצית). Thus, *tzitzit* is a protection against anger.

I am your God who took you out of Egypt: By saying this verse, we can fulfill the mitzvah of recalling the Exodus, which is one of the 248 positive *mitzvot* of the Torah.

I am your God: The Shema concludes with the words, "I am your God" and we add the word "Truth," as in the verse "God is the Lord of truth" (Jeremiah 10:10). The Midrash teaches that God's seal is truth as the word *EMeT* forms an acronym with the final letters of the story of Creation. The verse reads (Genesis 1:31), "ברא אלוהים לעשות / *BarÆ ElohiM La'asoT.*" The final letters form the acronym *EMeT*, which means that God sealed creation with truth.

Also, the word *EMeT* (אמת) contains the first, middle and final letters of the Hebrew alphabet. This indicates that something is absolute when it begins, fills with, and concludes with truth. It also teaches us that God is First, Last, and Always (Isaiah 44:6).

CHAPTER 26

Emet v'Yatziv

The third blessing of the Shema begins with *Emet v'Yatziv* (truth and stability). The blessing speaks of faith in God, that He is trustworthy and will deliver on His word and promises. It also includes praise to God for the Exodus, for taking us out of Egyptian bondage.

In this paragraph, we recite fifteen words which mean "truth." The Mishnah teaches that one should not pause between the words *"Emet"* and *"v'Yatziv"* so that the ideas of truth remain joined together (*Berakhot* 2:2).

The fifteen words, each beginning with the letter *vav,* express various forms of truth. One reason for the repetitive wording is that fifteen times *vav* (numerically equal to six) is 90. And with the unit itself, it adds up to 91.

Ninety-one is the *gematria* of *AMeN* (אמן), but even more so, it stands for *Æil Melekh Ne'eman*" (God, Faithful King) (*Shabbos* 119b). As mentioned earlier, the *Shema* has 245 words and when the *chazan* repeats the last three words, "*YHVH Eloheikhem Emet,* this adds up to 248 words, paralleling the 248 limbs of a person's body. If a person is not with a *minyan,* then he can add the three extra words at the beginning of the *Shema, "Æil Melekh Ne'eman,"* to obtain the total of 248 words. At the very least, a person can have in mind that the fifteen "*vavs*" of *v'Yatziv* replace the extra three words of the *Shema*.

Emet v'Yatziv

אֱמֶת וְיַצִּיב וְנָכוֹן וְקַיָּם וְיָשָׁר ...

True and certain and well-established and enduring...

This blessing is said after the *Shema,* immediately following the passage about *tzitzit.* The first two passages in the *Shema* speak about how to strengthen our faith in God, and the passage of *tzitzit* represents the morality necessary to attain Godliness and faith. The passage of *tzitzit,* where it mentions the Exodus, is specifically attached to the Shema because both the Shema and the story of the Exodus are meant to strengthen our faith in God.

When the Jewish nation first believed in God, other nations were attracted to believe in God as well, which is why at the time of the Exodus the *Eiruv Rav* (Mixed Multitude) converted to Judaism and joined the Jewish nation. We see that when true faith is revealed, it spreads even to those distant from God, and they, too, wish to attach themselves to the true faith. In other words, the ascent of true faith draws converts, for when true faith is spread there are others who wish to be part of it.

Furthermore, when true faith and morality (a guarded covenant) become attainable, this creates "pure words" (i.e., comforting and consoling words) which reach out and draw those distant from God to Him.

This is the purpose of the blessing, "*Emet v'Yatziv.*" It is comprised of pure words (i.e., words of truth) which accentuate the true faith revealed in the *Shema.* This is the reason we repeat the word "truth" in many forms, for they are sweet words of the faithfulness of God. In addition, immediately following these words of truth, we say, "His words are living and enduring, trustworthy and desirable forever, and for all eternity." These words of truth and faith will endure, console all those weakened souls, and rebuild their faith.

Eight times *Emet* (truth)

We find a reference to truth eight times in this blessing:

1. The word *Emet* right at the end of the *Shema.*
2. It is true: The eternal God is our King.
3. This declaration has forever remained good and enduring, true and confirmed.
4. It is true: You are our God.
5. It is true: Happy is the man.
6. It is true: You have been the Master.
7. It is true: You are in the beginning and You are in the end.
8. It is true: You redeemed us from Egypt.

Reb Noson explains that tzaddikim, who are guardians of the covenant, use consoling words to help raise up fallen faith. Due to their purity, they become the masters of advice who can bring forth the knowledge and counsel necessary to attain perfected faith. These tzaddikim are able to access the "deep waters" (i.e., impart good advice) in order to help a person elevate his faith and proceed on a proper path of success in life. They are able to do this because they know the truth and can thereby counsel truth to others.

Reb Noson ties together the idea of truth, tzaddikim, counsel and faith. "Deep waters are the counsels in the heart of man; an understanding man will draw them forth" (Proverbs 20:5). Good advice is rare because it must be absolutely true. If it is not true, then of what value is that advice? True advice is drawn from the level of *Binah,* a level beyond the parameters of this world. *Binah* translates as understanding, while *Malkhut* represents *emunah* (faith). Thus, a tzaddik and moral person (i.e., an understanding man) is on the level where he can draw advice from the highest levels. The Kabbalah teaches that *Binah* is the third level and extends down to *Malkhut,* the tenth *sefirah* or the lowest level. There are eight levels between *Binah* and *Malkhut,* between the source of advice and faith. When we draw true advice we elevate faith—but only if the advice is true, through and through. Thus, if we search for truth, it must be drawn from *Binah* through the eight levels down to become true and absolute faith.

Reb Noson continues to elaborate: There are many types of advice; they all have some truth to them, otherwise they wouldn't even be considered. However, if there are flaws in that counsel, even minor ones, there exists the possibility of error which can eventually mislead a person. For example, a person might choose to become a rabbi solely because he sees this as a way to earn a living. All his study is *shelo lishmoh* (not for the sake of God), but for the sake of a livelihood. Others are too involved in the pursuit of earning a living, until they don't have any time left for serving God. They have good intentions — they have families to support! But they are not taking into consideration their duty to themselves, their obligation to God, and their eternal reward. Doesn't that come into play? Reb Noson explains why the word *Emet* appears eight times in these blessings. We already said the *Shema* and articulated our faith. However, if we want true faith, it only comes with true advice (LH, *Hefker v'Nikhsei HaGer* 4:17).

Fifteen times *vav*

After the *Shema,* we say fifteen words that begin with the letter *vav,* all referring to "truth." These sweet and pure words are the advice that is alluded to in the verse, "*Shiv'ah meshivei ta'am*" (Seven paths of reason; Proverbs 26:16). A *vav* in Hebrew is a "hook," referring to the *vavey ha'Amudim* (hooks of the pillars; Exodus 27:10) because they represent pillars upon which we can stand. Thus, the pure words are the "seven paths of reason" and together with the eight levels of truth add up to fifteen. Hence, we say fifteen words beginning with *vav* to draw true counsel into our faith (LH, *Hefker v'Nikhseiy HaGer* 4:18).

Ezras Avoseinu

עֶזְרַת אֲבוֹתֵינוּ
You have been our ancestors' assistance

Similar to the conclusion of *Pesukey d'Zimra* which ends with *Az Yashir* (Song of Deliverance) and speaks of the Exodus, so too, we end the *Shema* blessings with a prayer about the Exodus. In this paragraph, we recall the miracles of the Exodus: the slaying of the Egyptian firstborn, the redemption of the Jewish firstborn, the Splitting of the Sea, and so on. One of the reasons we recite the Exodus repeatedly in prayer is to emphasize the significance of God's salvation. The Midrash teaches that the Egyptians were very cruel to the Jews; never in its history had a slave escaped from Egypt. Therefore, it was miraculous that several million people left Egyptian slavery in one fell swoop, in front of the eyes of their captors, and were not restrained in any way (*Mekhilta, Shemot*).

Recalling these miracles strengthens our faith that we, too, will one day merit God's miracles and we ask that He end the exile and redeem His people. This is very important to bear in mind as we are about to begin the *Amidah* (*Shemoneh Esrei*) and are about to pray for the things we feel we need. If we believe and have faith that God listens to our prayers, we will recite them with stronger conviction.

Ozer Dalim

עוֹזֵר דַּלִּים
He Who assists the poor

When saying, "He Who assists the poor," a person should consider himself as a poor person and identify himself with the Divine Presence, who while in exile, is considered poor. As the Divine Presence ascends into *Atzilut*, we hope to ascend together with the *Shekhinah*, the Divine Presence (*Matok Midvash*). The *Zohar* teaches (III, 195b) that though we have said the *Shema* and have willingly intended to make self-sacrifices for God, we should not feel we are elevated people; rather we should consider ourselves poor, and as we pray to God, we should appear as needy people before Him.

Tehilot l'Eil Elyon

תְּהִלּוֹת לְאֵל עֶלְיוֹן

Praises to the Supreme God…

Whatever praise you offer God it is really insufficient when considering His greatness. Still, whatever praise you can think of should be offered to God for He is deserving of all praises.

At this point in the prayers it is mandatory to stand up, since we are concluding the World of *Beriyah* (the Throne) and are going to enter the World of *Atzilut* (standing with God.)

Mi Khamokha

מִי כָמֹכָה...

Who is like You

There are twelve words in this verse from the Song of Deliverance, corresponding to the twelve tribes for whom the sea was split into twelve sections.

Shirah Chadashah

שִׁירָה חֲדָשָׁה
With a new song

This was one of the great miracles at the sea. Imagine! All 600,000 Jews broke out into song to thank God for His deliverance and everyone sang the exact same words! It was a blessing of Divine Spirit which descended upon them because of their unity.

Tzur Yisrael

צוּר יִשְׂרָאֵל
Rock of Israel

The name *Yisrael* (Israel) appears five times in this paragraph corresponding to the redemption from the four exiles, as well as the redemption of our souls from the *kelipot*. Additionally, it also corresponds to the verse (Numbers 8:19) in which the "Children of Israel" are mentioned five times. Rashi explains this is to show the love and favor that the Jews have in the eyes of God.

Ga'al Yisrael

גָּאַל יִשְׂרָאֵל
Who has redeemed Israel

This blessing is in the past tense for it speaks of the Exodus and redemption from Egypt. Nevertheless, it certainly refers to God Who is constantly redeeming us.

The juxtaposition of *Ga'al Yisrael* to the *Amidah* parallels the juxtaposition between *Yesod* and *Malkhut*. *Yesod* is called the *Go'el,* the redeemer, while *Malkhut* is considered prayer. One must illumine *Yesod* (redemption) so that *Malkhut* (prayer) can be redeemed. Therefore, one is forbidden to pause between the words *Ga'al Yisrael* and the *Amidah.* They should be said without interruption, not even to answer *Amen* after the blessing.

Rebbe Nachman explains that the connection between *Go'el* (*Yesod*) and prayer (*Malkhut*) is the story of Boaz and Ruth. About Boaz it is written, "I am a *go'el*" (Ruth 3:12). The name Ruth (רות) shares the same root as *riva* (ריוה), to sate, and Ruth's descendent was King David who sated God with songs and praises (*Berakhot* 7b). Thus, Ruth alludes to prayer. On the other hand, Boaz alludes to morality since Boaz connotes *BO AZ* (in him is strength), the strength of morality and a guarded covenant. One who is moral and guards his *Yesod / Brit* can pray and even bring forth salvation, as did Boaz and Ruth who brought forth the soul of King David and *Mashiach* (LM II, 102).

A further insight into the juxtaposition of *Goel Yisrael* and the *Amidah* is as follows: The Talmud teaches (*Berakhot* 6b), that there are things that stand at the greatest heights of the world, yet people make light of and are flippant about them. Rashi explains that prayer is so great, yet people are irreverent about it. Therefore, Rebbe Nachman explains that prayer must be viewed as if it is in exile. Our mission is to redeem the prayer (LM II, 1:8). Thus, immediately after saying *Goel Yisrael* we begin the *Shemoneh Esrei,* as if to say we are going to pray with concentration and redeem our prayers.

CHAPTER 27

The Amidah: Background

The next section of the *davening* is referred to in the Talmud and *Shulchan Arukh* as the *Amidah* (meaning, standing) as in the verse, *Va'Yaamod Pinchus va'yefallel*—Pinchus stood, and he prayed (Psalms 106:30; *Berakhot* 6b). It is also known as the *Shemoneh Esrei* which translates as "The Eighteen" since it originally consisted of eighteen blessings.

The Members of the Great Assembly composed these eighteen blessings upon their return to the Land of Israel from Babylon, while under the rule of the Persian kingdom. Among the members of that assembly were several prophets (such as Chagai, Zekhariah, and Malakhi) and elders (such as Shimon HaTzadik) who composed the prayers specifically to address the needs of the Jewish people. Among these blessings are concepts and ideas that apply to all facets of life. Originally, the blessings were established as individual prayers to be said in whatever order a person desired. However, in the days of Rabban Gamliel (circa 35 CE), the *Shemoneh Esrei* was codified in the order that we follow today. We will discuss below (Chapters 30 and 31) the reason Rabban Gamliel chose this specific order (*Megillah* 17b; see *Tikkun Tefillah*).

At first there were eighteen benedictions. However, due to the pervasion of the Greek and Roman empires, an additional blessing was added. The Roman presence in the Holy Land gradually increased their influence to control much of Jewish life. At the time, Rabban Gamliel, who lived during the tumultuous times prior to the destruction of the Second Temple, was the president of the *Sanhedrin* (Jewish High Court). Under the tutelage of Rabban Gamliel, Rabbi Shimon HaPekuli established the order of the prayers as we know it today.

Shortly after Rabbi Shimon HaPekuli made the order, the idolatrous Roman influence increased and many people became *apikorsim* (atheists and idolaters). Some even began working with the Roman authorities by handing over information about their neighbors and harming Jewish life in order to curry favor in the eyes of the Roman authorities. Unfortunately, they caused much damage to the communities. The Elders then gathered and asked, "Who can author a blessing against these *apikorsim*?" Shmuel HaKatan, about whom the Talmud says was worthy of having the Divine Presence rest upon him, agreed to author the blessing "*v'LaMalshinim,*" asking God to protect the Jews from those who would slander them to the Romans. Therefore, this blessing was added to the *Shemoneh Esrei* as the nineteenth blessing.

Rebbe Nachman teaches about nature and prayer:

> Know! The philosophers call nature *Em Kol Chai* (mother of all living objects). With our prayers, we nullify nature, for through prayer the course of nature can be changed. This is the aspect of the *Shemoneh Esrei* (not counting the extra blessing for overcoming atheists). For with the *Chai* blessings (numerical value of eighteen), we nullify nature (i.e., *Em Kol Chai*), subjugating and nullifying the atheists and heretics (the nineteenth blessing).

Reb Noson expands: There are seven planets and twelve constellations which guide the forces of nature on our planet. Together, seven planets and twelve constellations add up to nineteen forces of nature which guide our lives. Therefore, through the nineteen blessings of the *Amidah*, we can overcome nature and cause Divine Providence to manifest. In turn, this changes the course and forces of nature (LH, *Nesiat Kapayim* 3:3).

The Blessings—A General Introduction

As mentioned earlier, these blessings cover concepts and ideas that apply in all facets of life. The *Arugat HaBosem* displays the parallels between each blessing and its historical connection:

Historical event	Blessing
Avraham was saved from the fire at Ur Kasdim.	Blessed ... the Shield of Avraham.
Yitzchak was spared at the Binding of Yitzchak.	Blessed ... Who restores the dead to life.
Yaakov came upon the Place of Sanctity where he lay down.	Blessed ... The Holy God.
The angel Gavriel taught Yosef the seventy languages.	Blessed ... Bestower of consciousness.
Reuven repented over his blemish with Bilhah.	Blessed ... He Who desires repentance.
Yehudah repented over his deed with Tamar.	Blessed ... He Who forgives abundantly.
God told the Jews in Egypt He will redeem them.	Blessed ... Redeemer of Israel.
Avraham was healed after his circumcision.	Blessed ... Healer of the sick.
Yitzchak sowed the fields in the Philistine's land during a famine.	Blessed ... He Who blesses the years.
Yaakov, Yosef and the brothers were united in Egypt.	Blessed ... Gatherer of His People.

Moshe revealed civil law.	Blessed ... King Who loves charity and justice.
The Egyptians drowned in the Red Sea.	Blessed ... Breaker and Humbler of the wicked.
God told Yaakov that Yosef will continue his legacy.	Blessed ... You Support and Trust the Righteous.
King Solomon built the Temple.	Blessed ... Builder of Jerusalem.
The Jews passed through the Red Sea and sang to God.	Blessed ... Who makes salvation spring forth.
The Jews sighed and cried out to God in Egypt.	Blessed ... Hearer of prayers.
The *Shekhinah* rested upon the Sanctuary in the desert.	Blessed ... He Who restores His presence to Zion.
King Solomon brought the Holy Ark into the Temple.	Blessed ... Good is Your Name and to You thanksgiving is due.
The Jews entered the Holy Land and peace reigned.	Blessed ... He Who blesses His people with peace.

The idea behind the above Midrash is that these are the basic challenges, frustrations, difficulties, and general problems that we face on a regular basis. Therefore, the Members of the Great Assembly established the *Shemoneh Esrei* with these specific topics in mind. It teaches us that just as God was there for the earlier generations, He will be here for us too and answer our prayers.

Rabbi Yaakov ben Asher (1269-1343), author of the *Tur Shulchan Arukh,* discusses each of these nineteen blessings in detail. He counts the words of each blessing and speaks of its intentions.[138] He says that each blessing was not randomly composed; rather it was composed with *Ruach haKodesh* (Divine Spirit). Furthermore, each word was weighed and considered prior to its being placed into the blessings.

The *Tur* writes (#113):

> The chassidim of Ashkenaz (i.e., Germany and France) would count each word of *Shemoneh Esrei* and weigh its importance. For example, there are 107 words in the first three blessings. These correspond to the 91 words found in Psalm 29 and to the 16 words found in Isaiah (29:23), "They shall sanctify the holy ones of Yaakov and the God of Israel they will venerate." Psalm 29 contains various praises of God which are found in the first and second blessings, while the third blessing speaks of sanctity.
>
> Our Sages teach (*Berakhot* 32b), "A person should first make order of his praises to God, and only afterwards should he make his requests." The *Zohar* asks (I, 243b), "What if a person is frustrated and challenged and cannot concentrate?" Even so, he should do whatever he can to concentrate on praising God.

138 *Tur Orach Chaim* from Chapter 113 until Chapter 122.

CHAPTER 28

The Amidah: Posture and Movements

With the *Amidah,* a person ascends from the World of *Beriyah* into the World of *Atzilut. Beriyah* is the World of the Throne, while *Atzilut* translates as adjacent (i.e., next to God), as in a person is standing next to and adjacent to God in His palace.[139] Imagine standing right next to royalty or a very important person. We would stand in awe and respect, taking care of our every movement. So too, in *Atzilut,* we should be aware of before Whom we are standing and wish that our prayers be accepted and answered. The ARI writes that when we enter *Atzilut* we should stand in awe of God, which is why the *Amidah* is said while standing (*Pri Etz Chaim, Shaar Kriat Shema,* Chapter 29).

As a person prepares for the *Amidah,* he should consider his soul as joined together with all those who pray with a full heart. This way his prayer can ascend amongst those other prayers. Furthermore, through the *Amidah* prayer, a person merits to rectify his body and soul and becomes complete before God (*Zohar* II, 215b).

139 Why does it say "in His palace"? God is everywhere — in all places, in all worlds, in all universes. When we speak of the Four Worlds, to us it is an understanding of the different levels in which we experience God and Godliness. Thus, we are close to God in *Asiyah,* in *Yetzirah* and in *Beriyah* as well. But when we recite the *Amidah* we should think of ourselves as actually standing right next to God, in His Palace.

Through prayer, a person draws the blessings from the Treasury of Unearned Gifts (see Chapter 31 below). This is the reason that it is important to give charity before praying because by doing kindness to others, we draw kindness from Above and open up the gates of blessing (LH, *Tefillah* 3:6).

Before commencing the *Amidah,* it is customary to take three steps back (as if leaving the place we are standing upon) and then take three steps forward (as if entering the next world). One reason why we take these steps is offered by the commentaries: When King Chezkiyahu was healed, the sun moved back several movements to add more hours of daylight (Isaiah 38:8). The king in Babylon (Merodakh Biladan; Isaiah 39:1) was amazed that such a miracle occurred and wrote a letter to Jerusalem, honoring King Chezkiyahu, God and the city of Jerusalem. Nevuchadnezzar was a scribe at the time in the Babylonian king's court and took three steps to recall the messenger with that letter, saying to the king, "It is proper to first honor God, and only then, Chezkiyahu." As a result, the king had the letter rewritten to honor first God, then the king. Because Nevuchadnezzar took three steps to honor God, he was rewarded by allowing his family to rule the entire world for three generations! The *Mishnah Berurah* comments (123:1) that if a non-Jew took three steps to honor God and was rewarded with kingship for three generations, how much more is the reward that awaits a Jew who takes three steps to honor God in his prayers.

During the *Amidah* a person should stand with their legs together as if to say, "We are weak and barely able to stand before You. But we do have requests and we are asking that You fulfill them." Another reason we stand with our legs together is that we are considered as bound to our places; we can go nowhere without God. Others opine that we stand with our legs together to appear as angels who legs are said to be one. As it is written, "Their legs are as one straight leg" (Ezekiel 1:7).

There are four times when we bow before God during the *Amidah*:

1. In the beginning of the very first blessing.
2. At the end of that blessing, "The Shield of Avraham."
3. At the beginning of the blessing "*Modim.*"
4. At the conclusion of that blessing, "Your Name is good..."

We bow by first bending our knees and lowering ourselves forward (a bit); then we bend our heads forward; and before we mention God's Name, we straighten our bodies and lift our heads. Only when we are standing straight again should we mention God's Name.

Our Sages taught: "One should not make personal requests in the first three blessings or in the final three blessings." The first three blessings are praises of God during which one should focus upon God alone. He can, and should, make his requests during the middle blessings. During the final three blessings we are thanking God, so we should not make personal requests as well. It is similar to a servant first praising his king, then making his requests, and finally thanking his king for acceding to his requests.

A person should make sure to keep his eyes in the siddur (or at least closed) and not look around during the *Amidah*. The simple reason is it interferes with his concentration. The *Zohar* says that one whose eyes are opened during the *Amidah* will see the Angel of Death at the time of his passing (who is made of eyes) and not merit to see the *Shekhinah* (Divine Presence) (*Zohar* III, 260b; *Mishnah Berurah* 95:5).

Additionally, the *Amidah* should be said in a whisper. A person should never raise his voice during the *Amidah* for this gives strength to the forces of the Other Side. We learn from Chanah that the *Amidah* is meant to be said silently. As it says, "Chanah spoke from her heart but her voice was not heard" (1 Samuel 1:13). The commentaries teach that this means the person should not say the words aloud—even to the point that he himself does not hear the words he is saying. When the prayer is said aloud, the Other Side receives that prayer and it does not ascend to its intended place (*Zohar* I, 209b*ff*).

The first three blessings are praises of God and are to be considered as one unit. That is, if a mistake is made in any of those blessings, one must return to the beginning of the first blessing and repeat them all. After all, if you are speaking directly to the King and praising Him, how would it look if you err and say the wrong thing? So, we begin again. For example, consider the third blessing: *Ha'Eil HaKadosh*. During the year, we conclude the blessing with *Ha'Eil HaKadosh*. However, during the Ten Days of Repentance we conclude the blessing with *HaMelekh HaKadosh*. Though this is the conclusion of the third blessing, if during the ten days of repentance one says *Ha'Eil* instead of *HaMelekh* by mistake, he must return to the beginning of the first blessing.

One must never pause between the blessing of Redeemer of Israel and the *Amidah*. Nevertheless, we begin the *Shemoneh Esrei* with the verse, "*Adonoy s'fasaiy tiftach*... (God open my lips ...)" (Psalms 51:17). Though at face value it seems to be a break between the blessing of *Go'al Yisrael* and the *Amidah*, our Sages placed this verse at the beginning of the *Amidah* because we are asking God to open not just our lips, but also our hearts and to say His praises with concentration. The Talmud refers to the addition of this verse as "an extended prayer" (*Berakhot* 4b). The ARI explains that at this point in our prayers, we are now ascending from *Beriyah* to *Atzilut.* Therefore, the verse acts as the bridge between the two universes, elevating everything from below (*Shaar HaKavanot, Inyan Kavanat Ha'amidah*, pp. 182-183). Only then can we enter the World of *Atzilut* and begin the *Amidah.*

CHAPTER 29

The Opening Blessings

A person must try to concentrate on the blessings of the *Amidah.* If he cannot concentrate on all of them, the minimum concentration should be on the first blessing, *Magen Avraham* (i.e., the "Patriarchs"). The *halakhah* used to be that if a person failed to say this blessing with *kavanah,* he must repeat the blessing. The *Rema* writes that this *halakhah* was subsequently changed because today we lack the ability of total concentration and it is likely that even if a person repeats the *Amidah,* he will once again fail to have the necessary concentration (*Orach Chaim* 101:1).

The *Mishnah Berurah* explains that this blessing is the beginning of the praises of God and when praising God, a person's mind should be focused on the words he is saying. Others opine that since the *Avot* (Patriarchs) established the prayers, without the Patriarchs there would be no prayer. Hence, we should learn to concentrate on our prayers, especially in the first blessing that mentions the *Avot.*

בָּרוּךְ... מָגֵן אַבְרָהָם

Blessed ... the Shield of Avraham

This blessing refers to the verse, "I will make you a great nation, I will bless you, and I will make your name well-known ... and you will be a blessing" (Genesis 12:2). Rashi (loc. cit.) explains: "I will make you a great nation," refers to the God of Avraham; "I will bless you," refers to the God of Yitzchak; and "I will make your name well-known" refers to the God of Yaakov.

But since "you will be a blessing" refers only to Avraham, the blessing is referred to as "the Shield of Avraham."

בָּרוּךְ... מְחַיֵּה הַמֵּתִים
Blessed ... who restores the dead to life

The second blessing is called *Gevurot* (strengths). It contains references to the Talmudic teaching that there are "four keys" which God retains: the key to rain, the key to livelihood, the key of the resurrection and the key to children (*Taanit* 2a,b). With this blessing, we acknowledge that God's strength, might and power extends even to areas upon which we have no control, similar to the resurrection which is considered a miracle. We conclude the blessing with "You will faithfully fulfill Your promise to revive the dead...Who restores the dead to life." This strengthens our faith in God that He will ultimately fulfill His promises to all Israel. (The laws of *Mashiv HaRuach* and *Morid HaTal* are in the Siddur.)

The expression, "Restores the dead to life," appears five times in this blessing. Reb Noson comments that the words "revival and resurrection" refer to the mind—whether it goes beyond its boundaries to seek understanding of matters above its capabilities, or conversely, if it is not exploited to attain knowledge of God. Therefore, these five mentions are geared to revive the five senses that are rooted in the mind in order to awaken them to awareness of God (LH, *Hefker VeNikhsey HaGer* 4:28).

בָּרוּךְ... הָאֵל הַקָּדוֹשׁ
Blessed ... Holy is God

The Third Blessing is called *Kedushot* (Sanctification or Holiness). It concludes with *Ha'Eil HaKadosh* in which we declare God's sanctity. As the *Tur* writes (#114), the fourteen words in this blessing parallel the fourteen words in the verse, "Holy, Holy, Holy is God" (Isaiah 6:3).

Since the Patriarchs established the prayers (*Berakhot* 26b), the Sages teach us that we must include the traits of the Patriarchs into our prayers. Avraham represents kindness which implies love, desire and attachment to God. This is manifest in a person's faith in God and prayer to Him. Yitzchak was willing to sacrifice himself to God (at the Binding of Yitzchak) thus showing us the importance of placing our whole being into our prayers. This way we can merit to reveal Godliness.

But these efforts were insufficient to completely conquer the forces of evil that reigned in those days. Yishmael and Esav, offspring of Avraham and Yitzchak, represent the *kelipot*, which always try to conceal Godliness. When a person prays with effort and *kavanah* he is compared to Yitzchak's self-sacrifice and can destroy the *kelipot* of Esav and Yishmael. Still, it wasn't until Yaakov's day, when he begat the twelve tribes, that the idea of Godliness was able to be passed on from generation to generation (LH, *Tefillah* 5:2).

The Patriarchs referred to the place where the temple would eventually stand in three different ways. Avraham called the place a "mountain," as in the verse, "the mount where God revealed Himself" (Genesis 22:14)." Yitzchak called the place "a field" as in "Yitzchak went out to the field" (Genesis 24:63). Yaakov called the place "a house" as in "This is the house of God" (Genesis 28:17).

Rebbe Nachman explains that the term each Patriarch chose reflected the extent his prayer had on people. For example, a mountain is used by very few people; a field has greater use; and a house is a necessity for everyone. Avraham was the first to introduce prayer, but during his life it had limited reach and offered little importance to people. When Yitzchak came along, he established the idea of prayer to the extent that many more people were able to understand and benefit by prayer to God. But it was Yaakov who revealed the necessity of prayer for all people, in all situations (LM I, 10:3).

Kedushah

The Sages instituted the custom of the repetition of the *Shemoneh Esrei*. The reason was that although everybody must pray, not everyone was literate. Therefore, they instituted the repetition of the *Shemoneh Esrei* so someone who could not read was able to listen to the *chazan*. By following what the *chazan* repeated, the person fulfilled the mitzvah of praying. The ARI writes that while we pray, certain Divine Unions occur, while in the repeated *Shemoneh Esrei* additional unifications occur.

When the *Amidah* is repeated and we reach the Blessing of *Ha'Eil HaKadosh* (the Transcendental King), we recite the *Kedushah* prayer. The ARI writes that at this point of the prayers a person should focus upon this opportunity to sanctify God's Name as in the verse, "And I will be sanctified amongst the Children of Israel" (Leviticus 22:32). So that when we say "God is Holy" we should try to draw sanctity to the Jewish People (*Shaar HaKavanot, Inyan Kavanat Chazarat Haamidah* 3, p. 258).

This sanctity occurs when we say the words, "The whole world is filled with His radiant glory." Rebbe Nachman teaches that God is always shining His light and His bounty upon us, but our physicality creates a shadow which prevents the light and the bounty to reach us. However, when we humble ourselves into nothing, we can experience God's light and we can receive God's bounty (LM I, 172).

When the ARI said, "Holy! Holy! Holy!" he would raise his voice. And each time he said the words "Holy!" he would raise his heels as if he were dancing (*Shaar Hakavanot,* ibid.)

Note that the angels (who dwell in Heaven and are with God at all times) are the ones who ask "*AYEH?*" (Where is the place of His glory?) We on earth say, "The whole world is filled with His glory" because no matter where a person is, no matter the depths of his descent, we believe that God is always near us. However, there are those who think they have attained a measure of God's greatness and think they are nearer to God than others. To this the verse states, "*AYEH*?" Even angels cannot fathom God's greatness, let alone mortal man.

The Order of the Eighteen Blessings

Relying upon verses from the Bible, R. Shimon HaPekuli made a set order. The eighteen blessings parallel the eighteen times God's Name appears in Psalm 29. Some opine that the eighteen blessings correspond to the eighteen times God's Name is mentioned in the *Shema*, while still others offer that they correspond to the eighteen ribs in a person's body (*Berakhot* 28b). The Talmud teaches us that each blessing has a foundation from a verse in the Torah:

#	Blessing	The Biblical Connection
1.	The Shield of Avraham (*Avos*)	It is written (Psalms 29:1), "Ascribe to God you mighty" (referring to the Patriarchs).
2.	Restores the dead to life (*Gevorot*)	It is written (Psalms 29:1) "Give to God honor and strength."
3.	Holy is God (*Kedushah*)	It is written, "Give to God honor due to His name; bow down to God with the splendor of His holiness."

4.	Understanding (*Atah Chonen*)	It is written (Isaiah 29:23-24), "They will sanctify God ... and they that erred should come to understanding."
5.	Repentance (*Teshuvah*)	It is written (Isaiah 6:10), "With his heart he will understand; he will return and be healed.
6.	Forgiveness (*Selach lanu*)	It is written (Psalms 103:3-4), "He Who forgives, He Who heals, He Who Redeems."
7.	Redemption (*Re'ei na b'anyeinu*)	The seventh blessing is Geulah (redemption) since the Talmud teaches that the Final Redemption will come in the Seventh year of *Shmittah* (a Sabbatical Year).
8.	Healing (*Refaeinu*)	The eighth blessing is healing since a circumcision should be performed on the eighth day and it requires healing.
9.	Livelihood (*Bareikh Aleinu*) The laws of *V'Tein Berakha* and *Tal U'Matar* are in the Siddur	The ninth blessing refers to the profiteers who take advantage of the markets which adversely affects the poor. King David prayed for us to be protected from them and his prayer is found in the ninth psalm.
10.	Ingathering of the Exiles (*Teka b'shofar gadol*)	It is written (Ezekiel 36:8), "And you, the mountains of Israel shall sprout forth your leaves and produce your fruit for my nation since they are gathering to come close."

11.	Justice (*Hashiva Shoftainu*)	Once the Jews are reestablished in their land, judgment can be passed upon the wicked as it states (Isaiah 1:25-26), "I will avenge my enemies... I will return your judges as in the beginning."
12.	Against slanderers and the atheists (*v'lamalshinim*)	This blessing was added later on, when the *apikorsim* (atheists) began to spread their antagonism against God. Once judgment is enacted against the wicked, atheists will cease to be as in (Isaiah 1:28), "The destruction of the wicked and sinners will be complete."
13.	For the righteous (*al haTzaddikim*)	Once the wicked cease to exist, the dignity and honor of the righteous becomes clear for all to see. As in the verse (Psalms 76:11), "For the honor of the wicked I will cut off, the honor of the tzaddikim I will raise."
14.	Jerusalem (*v'liYerushalayim irkha*)	The greatness of the tzaddikim can be apparent in Jerusalem. Jerusalem is a city of peace, as in (Psalms 122:6), "Ask for the peace of Jerusalem, those who love you shall prosper."
15.	The lineage of King David (*Et tzemach David*)	Once Jerusalem is rebuilt, King David will return. As Hoshea prophesied (Hosea 3:5), "Afterwards the children of Israel will return and seek God and their King, David."

16.	Hear our voices (*Shema Koleinu*)	When King David returns he will bring with him prayer so our voices will be heard. As in the verse (Isaiah 56:7), "I will bring them to My holy mountain, and get them to rejoice in My house of prayer."
17.	Desire of God (*Retzei*)	When prayer is restored then the service in the Temple will be restored, as it is written (Isaiah 56:7), "Their burnt offerings and their sacrifices will be accepted on My altar."
18.	Bow to God (*Modim*)	Once the Temple service is restored, praise to God will become widely-known and be on everyone's lips, and we all will praise and bow to God, as in (Psalms 50:23), "Offering a thanksgiving sacrifice will honor and praise Me."
19.	Place peace (*Sim Shalom*)	At this point in the repeated *Shemoneh Esrei* the Priestly Blessings are said. The Torah teaches (Leviticus 9:22), "After offering the sacrifices, Aharon raised his hands towards the people and blessed them." As it says (Numbers 6:26-27), "They will place My name upon the Children of Israel, and I will bless them [with peace]."

Speaking of the praises that we offer to God, Rebbe Nachman explains that these praises and depictions are products of our imagination. (Because what words can suffice to praise a God we know nothing about?!) But these praises are actually a sign of God's lovingkindness to us because were it not for His lovingkindness, it would be inappropriate to call out and make reference to God with imagery and praises, with words and letters (LM I, 15:5; LM II, 8:14). This is the power of prayer since it expresses God's love for us.

CHAPTER 30

The Intermediate Blessings

Prior to saying the blessings, it is important to focus on one's actual needs. If we are unclear about what we want, how can we express our needs before God? Rebbe Nachman speaks about the Talmudic scholar, Rabba bar bar Chana, who focused solely on his spiritual needs during prayer, even for the blessings which are intended for the physical body. Rabba was of the opinion that where a rectification takes place in the spiritual realm, the physical is automatically rectified (LM I, 14:9).

Obviously, this is an extreme devotion; not many people can attain this level. But the message is clear: There is a temporal life which consists of material needs, and there is the afterlife, a spiritual eternal life. Therefore, it's important to focus on what we really need to get through this temporary life and to focus on how our physical existence can bring us to a higher plane and spiritual growth for eternity.

Our Sages teach that the Torah is the blueprint of the world; therefore, each aspect of creation has its roots in the Torah (*Bereishit Rabbah* 1:1). Logically speaking, if everything in existence is from the Torah, we should all attach ourselves to it day and night in order to draw sustenance and life from it. But a human being has physical needs as well to attend to and cannot possibly be attached to Torah at all times. So how can a person draw sustenance if he is not attached to the Torah? And what about those who have no connection to Torah at all? From where is their nourishment?

Rebbe Nachman teaches that there is a Treasury of Unearned Gifts that belongs to God and that He can portion gifts from this treasury to whomever He wants. After all, he explains, the world was created before the Torah was given. It took 2448 years for the Torah to descend to this world. What sustained the world until then? It was the free gifts from this treasury. These gifts are called, "*Matnat Chinom*" (LM II, 78).

Reb Noson explains that these free gifts are basically the gift of prayer and the ability to express ourselves before God. The Mishnah states (Avos 2:13), "Do not make your prayer a set prayer; rather it should be offered with pleas and supplications." (Supplication is translated from the word *tachanunim*, referring to the words *Matnat Chinom.*) Furthermore, even though the tzaddikim have many righteous deeds, they do not ask God to reply in their merits; rather they always ask for God to reply to them with a *Matnat Chinom* (free gift) (Rashi on Deuteronomy 3:23).

This is the reason we begin the prayers with mention of the Patriarchs, who established the prayers themselves. They lived prior to the Giving of the Torah, and they developed the power of prayer, the power of the *Matnat Chinom* that God grants to all (LH, *Tefillah* 3:2-5).

As mentioned above, the first three blessings which parallel the Patriarchs are praises to God. At this point in the prayers, we begin to focus upon our own needs, which, no doubt, are many. Each person has his unique "*pekele*" (baggage) which he feels he should unload before God, asking for salvation from his troubles and requesting things that are beyond his reach.

These requests reflect the current situation of a person's status and change from time to time, and even from day to day. When the Members of the Great Assembly established the prayers, they took into account all the needs that could arise in a person's life. For example, we ask for wisdom, for forgiveness of wrongdoings, for health and livelihood, for advice and salvation and more.

The Twelve Tribes

There are twelve intermediate blessings (actually thirteen including the added blessing against the atheists) which correspond to the twelve tribes of Israel. Just as each tribe was different from his brothers, so too, our needs vary from person to person and from day to day. Since our life situation changes on a daily basis, we fluctuate between different emphases for our requests. One day we may pray for a health issue; another day livelihood may be a predominant problem; and another time we may need advice or just to get our act together.

Reb Noson explains the connection between each tribe and the corresponding blessing in order to help us extract the most from our prayers (LH, *Tefillah* 5:3).

אַתָּה חוֹנֵן
Conscious awareness

The intermediate blessings start with a request for *daat* (conscious awareness). After mentioning that God is Holy and thus transcends all levels of holiness and awareness, He grants human beings the intellect with which to function. We need that *daat* to connect to higher levels in order to attain greater levels of sanctity and intellect, and develop a greater understanding of God, of the world around us, and of ourselves. With this growth, we can even attain *ruach haKodesh* (Divine Spirit) (Rashi on Exodus 31:3). In addition, we ask for wisdom and understanding, which are the tools to bring us to *daat.*

This is the only blessing of the intermediate ones which begins by praising God. Following the first three blessings which are solely His praises, we continue that flow and begin the blessing with praise: *Atah Chonen Daat* (You grant to man conscious awareness).

This blessing corresponds to Reuven, the first of the twelve tribes. Reuven was named because of sight—*REu VeN* (See [my] son). *Daat* is called sight as well, as it is written, "Their eyes were opened" (Genesis 3:7). Rashi explains that this "eye-opener" means understanding, *daat*.

הֲשִׁיבֵנוּ אָבִינוּ

Return us, Father

The prophet Isaiah says (6:10), "With his heart he will understand, and he will repent and be healed." Since the previous blessing asked for understanding, now we are able to ask God for the ability to repent and return to Him. The blessing begins with, "*Hashiveinu Avinu*" (Return us our Father). We mention the word "Father" in this blessing because a father has an obligation to teach his child the proper path to walk upon. We request that God return us to the Torah, for our Sages teach that when the person is gestating during the nine months in his mother's womb, he is taught the entire Torah. In the embryonic stage of life, we were pure and innocent. Therefore, we ask God to return to us that innocence and purity.

This blessing corresponds to Shimon. Leah called him ShiMOn, from the root word *ShMA*, "to hear." Leah said, "God heard me that I am hated" (Genesis 29:33). One who gets trapped in a sinful life filled with misdeeds feels hated by God and even by himself. When we ask of God to return us to Him, we are asking to rise above that ill feeling of hatred and return to Him in love.

סְלַח לָנוּ אָבִינוּ
Forgive us, Father

The next blessing asks for forgiveness from God for all the wrongdoings we have committed. We refer to God as our Father because it is proper for a parent to forgive His child's misdeeds. As the verse states, "As a father has compassion on his son" (Psalms 103:13). Rabbi Pinchus of Koretz explains why we say the phrase, "For *we* have sinned," in plural. We can speak for ourselves, but why mention others? Rabbi Pinchus answers that the plurality mentioned includes God. It is our argument in our defense when asking for forgiveness. We are implying that God is our partner in sin. We argue, "If You had not given us the *yetzer hara* (the evil inclination) and the ability and the freedom to sin, we couldn't have sinned. So, I didn't sin by myself. 'We have sinned'—God and I, together" (*Tzaddik* #610).

The blessing concludes with חנון המרבה לסלוח (He Who is compassionate and increasingly forgives). The numerical value of these letters adds up to 500, which is the same numerical value of נתן (Noson). When he was passing away, Reb Noson was heard to be repeating these words many times. His chassidim remarked that this was because often in his writings, Reb Noson made God's forgiveness a central theme. God's compassion is never-ending, and one can always turn to Him and ask forgiveness, no matter what the person did! It is important to know that God is Infinite and that therefore His Compassion is Infinite.

This blessing parallels Levi, from whom came the *Kohanim* and *Levi'im* who served in the Temple where sacrifices were brought to effect forgiveness.

רְאֵה נָא בְעָנְיֵנוּ
Consider our affliction

When we were sent into exile, God made the nations take an oath that they would not burden the Jewish people with excessive suffering. Yet, we continue to suffer in exile from the heavy burden of unwarranted taxations and the untoward hatred from the host nations. It is written (Zechariah 1:15), "I released My anger a little bit [against the Jews] but they [the host nations] added to their suffering." That is, the nations of the world gleefully added much suffering and heavy taxations against the Jews over and above what they were charged to do. Therefore, we ask God to look into our suffering and relieve us of the exile. The blessing follows that of forgiveness for when one repents, he is deserving of redemption.

Unlike the conclusion of the blessing prior to the *Amidah* which ends with *Ga'al Yisrael* ("He has redeemed Israel," past tense), this blessing ends with *Go'eil Yisrael* ("He redeems Israel," present tense). We mention the redemption in the present tense because each day contains its individual redemptions and salvations. This blessing corresponds to Yehudah from whom the *Mashiach* will come to redeem Israel.

רְפָאֵנוּ

Heal us and we will be healed

Why the redundant language? The *Zohar* teaches that God heals everyone. Sometimes He heals a person directly; other times the healing may come through His messengers (such as a medicinal herb or a doctor.) The difference is that when there is a go between, the illness may recur. However, when God Himself, heals a person directly, then the healing is complete and perfect. Hence we pray, "Heal us and [then for sure] we will be healed."

This blessing parallels the tribe of Yissachar who were steeped in Torah study (*Yoma* 26a). And the Torah in known to bring healing as it is written, "It [the Torah] shall be healing for the body" (Proverbs 3:8).

בָּרֵךְ עָלֵינוּ
Bless upon us this year

The verse states, "He Who makes peace in your borders, He Who fills you with the finest of wheat (i.e., crops)" (Psalms 147:14). The Talmud asks, "When will your borders be in peace? When there is plentiful to eat" (*Bava Metzia* 59a). So, we pray that there should be abundant crops and income for all. Additionally, this means that a person will feel sated from the food he eats as it enters his body. That is, there will be blessing in the food itself so that one need not overeat (Rashi on Deuteronomy 11:15).

This blessing corresponds to the tribe of Zevulun who were merchants and traveled the seas to bring livelihood.

תְּקַע בְּשׁוֹפָר גָּדוֹל
Blow the big Shofar

This blessing is based on the verse, "For on that day [of the redemption] there will sound a big Shofar to call together all the exiles" (Isaiah 27:13). There are two blessings that mention the redemption: this one and the blessing to redeem Israel. The first redemption refers to our physical salvation from the suffering of exile, while this blessing focuses upon our spiritual redemption from the material attractions that divert us from God.

We ask God that "He gather us together from the four corners of the earth." The ARI explains that this refers to the sparks of holiness that are spread out all over the globe due to the sin of Adam, especially that of wasted seed (*Pri Etz*

Chaim, Shaar HaAmidah, #19, p. 244). The widespread problem of concentration and focus is due largely to the sin of wasted seed, which forces a person to be "spread out" in many directions and leave his thoughts unfocused. This is because the sin of wasted seed causes a Shattering of the Vessels and spreads out the sparks of holiness in many directions. The rectification of this sin will happen when we "get our act together" and gather in those lost sparks.

This blessing parallels Dan. The tribe of Dan traveled at the end of the encampment as the Israelites traveled in the desert. Their mission was to gather up any objects lost from the other tribes (Numbers 10:25). This idea is found in this blessing "to gather up" the exiles.

הָשִׁיבָה שׁוֹפְטֵינוּ
Restore our righteous judges

Isaiah prophesies, "I will return your judges as of old times, and your advisors as in the beginning" (Isaiah 1:26). After the Jews are returned to their rightful land, God will bring back justice. In this blessing, we pray for good and honest judges and for proper advisors. As the above verse continues (ibid. 27), "Zion will be redeemed with justice."

The blessing continues, והסר ממנו יגון ואנחה (Remove from us sorrow and anguish). Just as we often combine the words *sasson v'simchah* (joy and happiness), we also combine the words *yagon v'anachah* (sorrow and anguish). In Yiddish, the word for *yagon* (sorrow) translates as "hurry up." We find that when people are in a rush, it usually leads to anguish. One should measure "his steps" in order to avoid the stress and pressure of "hurrying up" (*Rabbi Eliyahu Chaim Rosen*).

This blessing corresponds to Naftali as is written, "Naftali is as a swift deer; he offers words of beauty" (Genesis 49:21).

"Words of beauty" are words of truth, justice and good advice. This blessing mentions God as a King as in, "A King Who loves righteousness and justice." This is because the perfection of a kingdom is when justice prevails. Thus, at this point, *Malkhut*, God's Kingship, begins its ascent to a higher level.

וְלַמַּלְשִׁינִים
For the slanderers let there be no hope

This blessing follows the one about judges and justice, because when justice is honestly adjudicated, the slanderers and heretics will find no place for themselves. The blessing is directed against those whose faith is misplaced and they misdirect others with their interpretations of Torah. If they choose to mislead themselves, it is bad enough; but to mislead communities with false and erroneous ideas is devastating. Therefore, this blessing implies a major boost for those who keep the faith and seek the truth.

This blessing does not parallel any of the tribes. Reb Noson explains that the idea behind this blessing is to eradicate the kingdom of impurity and cause the Kingdom of holiness to ascend. The kingdom of impurity also refers to arrogance and haughtiness which lead to atheism and other evils. The ARI adds that this blessing against the atheists relates to rectification of *Malkhut*.[140]

עַל הַצַּדִּיקִים
For the Righteous and the devout

Once the wicked and slanderers have been eradicated, one gets the opportunity to see the clear difference between

140 *Shaar HaKavanot, Inyan Kavanat HaAmidah Drush* 6, p. 230-232.

the righteous and the evildoers. We take this opportunity to pray also for the righteous converts and include those Jews who have sinned and have repented, for they, too, were distant from God and have now drawn close. We ask that we all draw close to God and to the true tzaddikim who teach us the spiritual paths toward success.

The ARI questions why it is necessary to say, "May our portion be with them (i.e., the tzaddikim)." He explains: If a person is a tzaddik, of course his portion is with them; on the other hand, if a person is wicked, then clearly, he is not with them. So, isn't it a wasted prayer? The ARI answers that people do good deeds and sins. Sometimes the sins are so powerful that the reward for doing *mitzvot* is taken from the person. In the interim, these rewards are passed on to tzaddikim. Yet, there are very righteous tzaddikim who are not interested in another's reward. These tzaddikim will return that reward to the real owner, when he repents. Therefore, we pray to be attached to those true tzaddikim so that even if we aren't worthy, we will receive our reward which we had lost (*Pri Etz Chaim, Shaar HaAmidah* 19, p. 245).

This blessing parallels Yosef who is called "tzaddik" since he guarded his covenant and did not sin with Potifar's wife.

וְלִירוּשָׁלַיִם עִירְךָ
Return to Jerusalem, Your city

The place where the tzaddikim are most recognized is in Jerusalem, the city of God, where the Temple will be rebuilt and God's Presence will be manifest for all. We ask that God dwell in it even now, as our Sages teach, "The Divine Presence never left the Western Wall" (*Yalkut Shimoni* #986).

The blessing continues, "Re-establish the throne of David, Your servant." The Throne of God is as yet incomplete until the seed of Amalek is wiped off the face of the earth (Rashi on Exodus 17:16). Thus, we pray for the restoration of King David's throne. This symbolizes God's *Malkhut* where His Throne will be perfected and complete (*Pri Etz Chaim, Shaar HaAmidah* 19, p. 246).

This blessing corresponds to Binyamin, for a large part of Jerusalem (and certainly the Temple Mount) was in his portion in the Holy Land.

אֶת צֶמַח דָּוִד
Make the shoot of David

Having prepared King David's throne, we now ask that King David himself make his appearance and lead us as he did so long ago. The blessing continues, "We yearn throughout the day for Your salvation." The Talmud teaches (*Shabbos* 31a), that there are six questions posed to a person when he appears before the Heavenly Tribunal after he passes away. One of the questions is, "Did you hope for salvation?" The ARI teaches that if a person recites, "We yearn throughout the day for Your salvation," he is considered amongst those who yearn for God's salvation (*Pri Etz Chaim, Shaar HaAmidah* 19, p. 246).

Reb Nachman Tulchiner, a very close follower of Reb Noson, printed the first volume of the *Likutey Halakhot* in Iasi, Romania. When he was near the Russian-Romanian border he heard that the authorities were searching for non-nationals near the border. As a result, he fled from the area due to the wicked authorities. When he told this to Reb Noson, the latter replied, "We must wait and yearn for God's salvation [even at the border], not only for the redemption of all Israel, but even for our personal redemption!"

This blessing parallels Gad because Eliyahu the Prophet will come from the Tribe of Gad and bring with him the tidings of the final salvation.

אָב הָרַחֲמָן שְׁמַע קוֹלֵנוּ
Compassionate Father, hear our call

King David is the Master of Prayer; therefore, when he arrives, prayer will be commonplace for all. After asking that King David return, we recite a blessing that is a general theme of prayer: "God! Even if I do not or cannot focus properly upon my prayers, please, compassionate God, accept my pleas and calls to You."

This blessing parallels Asher whose name is rooted in *Ashrey* (fortunate is he). This teaches us that when God hears the prayers and supplications of the Jews, the entire world will witness how fortunate we truly are.

This final blessing of the intermediate group of the *Amidah*, *Shema Koleinu*, is considered a comprehensive blessing and a person can include all requests and pleas while reciting the blessing. Originally it was permitted to add additional pleas during any blessing, in any familiar language. For example, during *Refa'einu*, one can ask God to heal a sick relative, or during *Bareikh Aleinu* one may ask for a better livelihood. However, the Codifiers suggest that a person should wait until *Shema Koleinu* (or even better, the end of the *Shemoneh Esrei*) to ask whatever he wants to his heart's content.

Just as the Patriarchs are part of our prayers, the Twelve Tribes are embedded in our prayers as well. If we feel an affinity to a specific need or have a special request, we can rely on the merits of the Twelve Tribes and evoke their qualities for our benefit. The qualities of the Tribes can be discerned from the blessings they received from Moshe (Deuternomy 33) and Yaakov (Genesis 49).

CHAPTER 31

The Concluding Blessings

There are three blessings with which we conclude the *Amidah*. The first blessing, *Retzei*, asks God to restore the service in the Temple. Right after we say *Retzei* we add the *Ya'aleh v'Yavo* prayer when it is relevant (*Rosh Chodesh* or *Chol HaMoed*), for it also speaks of our service in the Temple and asks that we be redeemed to perform that service.

The second blessing, *Modim*, offers thanks to God for all the good we receive and for all the daily miracles that occur. Right after *Modim* (in which we thank God for His miracles), we add the *v'Al HaNissim* passage on Chanukah and Purim to thank God for the miracles He wrought during those times.

The third blessing is our request for peace. As Rashi explains, "Peace has the value of all the rest of the blessings" (Leviticus 26:6). In the *chazan's* repeated *Shemoneh Esrei*, right before reciting the final blessing, the *Kohanim* bless the congregation. The Priestly Blessings conclude with a blessing for peace, which is why it is juxtaposed to the final blessing.

רְצֵה

Take pleasure God in Your people Israel

Since we have concluded the intermediate blessings with a comprehensive prayer that includes all our personal needs, we can now ask for national needs. We request to restore the service in the Temple. Isaiah prophesies, "I will bring them to My holy mountain and have them rejoice in My House of Prayer, their burnt and other sacrifices will be accepted upon

My altar, for My House will be a prayer House for all the nations" (Isaiah 56:7). Once the potency of prayer is revealed, the Temple will be restored and the sacrifices can once again be offered.

In this blessing we say, "Accept Israel's fire-offerings and sacrifices... May the service of Your people Israel always find favor in Your eyes." The Midrash speaks of the Angel Michael who stands by the Heavenly Altar and sacrifices the souls of the Tzaddikim [as an act of forgiveness] (*Tosafot* on *Menachos* 110a).

יַעֲלֶה וְיָבוֹא

May there rise up, enter in, arrive, be seen, accepted, heard, considered and remembered

We add the prayer of *Ya'aleh v'Yavo* on *Rosh Chodesh* and *Chol HaMoed*. There are eight mentions of ascensions before God, paralleling the ascent of the prayers to the seven Heavens and above before God. There are also five requests for remembrance: of ourselves, our Patriarchs, the *Mashiach*, Jerusalem and the entire Jewish Nation. These correspond to the five mentions of remembrance found in the Torah in which God promised to redeem us.[141]

The blessing concludes with, "Let us behold Your return to Zion with compassion." As in the verse, "Eye to eye they will see God's return to Zion" (Isaiah 52:8).

מוֹדִים אֲנַחְנוּ לָךְ

We gratefully acknowledge

The Hebrew word *Modim* is numerically equal to one hundred, recalling the one-hundred blessings we should say every day (see above, Chapter 8). We thank God for choosing us as His nation and not exchanging us for another.

141 Exodus 6:5; Leviticus 26:42 [3x]; ibid. 26:45.

It is customary to bow our heads while saying the blessing of *Modim.* This is one of four instances during the *Amidah* that we bow. The first two are during the blessing of *Avos*, and the final bow is at the end of the *Modim* Blessing.

The blessing continues, "We will thank You and relate Your praises...for Your constant, miraculous providence which we experience daily." Reb Noson repeated this verse again and again. He worked hard to make us aware of God's goodness and graciousness toward us at all times.

וְעַל הַנִּסִּים

And for the miracles

During the holidays of Chanukah and Purim we add the *v'Al HaNissim* passage in which we thank God for the miracles. We also thank God for those times when He raised us above the veil of natural law. The word *nissim*, comes from *nes*, which means both "miracle" and "banner." This is because miracles lift us up like a banner above the laws of nature. We thank God for redeeming us from our enemies, intervening in the natural course of history, and rescuing us from annihilation. When we thank God for having saved us, we usually refer to having been rescued from some threat of danger (as in the case of Chanukah and Purim, from imminent annihilation); performed supernatural wonders (that which is hidden and beyond our comprehension); and comforted us when we thought all was lost. We especially thank God for all the miracles He performed for our ancestors throughout history as if they took place today.

שִׂים שָׁלוֹם

Grant peace, goodness, blessing, life, grace, lovingkindness, and compassion for us and for all Your people Israel

This final blessing of the *Amidah* is an all-inclusive one—*shalom* (peace). As Rashi explains, "If one has food and drink [i.e., blessings] but does not have *shalom*, he has nothing" (Rashi on Leviticus 26:6).

Rebbe Nachman teaches that there are two types of peace: inner peace and universal peace. Initially, a person must strive for inner peace, which can be attained through fear of God, as it is written, "Those who fear Him suffer no lack" (Psalms 34:10). The *Zohar* comments, "Where there is fear, there is *sheleimut* (wholeness)" (*Zohar* I, 79a). Once in possession of inner peace, a person can then spread peace to the world (see LM I, 14:8).

The blessing continues, "Our Father, bless all of us as one (together) with the light of Your countenance." The verse states, "In the light of the King's countenance is life" (Proverbs 16:15). This alludes to a life of joy and contentment. By asking God to bless us with His countenance, we are asking Him to grant us a life of happiness and contentment, a life of fulfillment in our endeavors. Rebbe Nachman adds that when we live morally, we can attain this "life" and its accompanying blessings (LM I, 23:1-3).

We conclude the final blessing with, "Blessed are You, God, Who blesses His people Israel *b'shalom* (with peace)." The ARI writes that *B'ShaLOM* (בשלום) has the same letters as *MaLBUSh* (מלבוש, cloak). Therefore, we draw upon ourselves a cloak that will protect us from the *kelipot*, since we will now begin descending into the lower worlds.[142]

Elohei! Netzor
My God, guard my tongue

It was acceptable for Talmudic rabbis to add their own prayers after concluding the *Shemoneh Esrei* (*Berakhot* 17a).

142 *Pri Etz Chaim, Shaar HaAmidah* 20, p. 252.

Mar, the son of Ravina, composed the passage of *Elohei! Netzor*. This has become the standard conclusion of the *Amidah*. The prayer is far reaching and covers most of the areas that a person should spend — or not spend — his life with. For example:

לשוני מרע (Guard my tongue)

Speech corresponds to the *ruach*, the spirit of life. The tongue is the major means of communication (e.g., prayer and conversation). When used positively and encouragingly it can build people and even worlds. On the other hand, if, God forbid, it is used negatively, then it has the power to destroy. As King Solomon teaches us, "Death and life are in the tongue" (Proverbs 18:21).

ושפתי מדבר מרמה (My lips from uttering deceit)

When a person utters a falsehood, whom is he deceiving — another person or himself? Once a person deceives himself, then his whole life is one big falsehood." Rebbe Nachman once said, "The world deceives you. Take it from me, do not let yourselves be fooled!" (*Rebbe Nachman's Wisdom* #51). One cannot live life to the fullest if he allows himself to be misled.

ולמקללי נפשי תדום (May my soul be silent in the face of those who curse me)

The essence of repentance is that when a person hears himself being insulted, he remains quiet and silent in the face of adversity (LM I, 6:2). Rebbe Nachman explains how the process of humiliation causes a person's blood to rush to his face, which turns red from blood and then turns white. This process is very cleansing.

ונפשי כעפר לכל תהיה (Make my soul like dust [earth] before all)

Rebbe Nachman taught (LM I, 277:1):

> Know! When a person encounters opposition, he should not take a stand against his enemy, saying, "Whatever he does to me I will repay in kind." For this causes his enemy to achieve his goal;

> it enables his enemy to see what will happen to him, God forbid, precisely that what the enemy wanted to see happen to him. On the contrary, it is right that he judge them favorably and do for them every good. This is the aspect of "Let my soul be like earth to everyone"— everyone treads on it, yet it provides them with every good: food, drink, gold, silver and precious stones; it all comes from the earth. Similarly, even though they oppose him and seek his harm, he should nevertheless do for them every good, like the earth.

This is analogous to the case of a person who is digging in the direction of his neighbor's house. If his neighbor positions himself so that he likewise starts digging in his direction, then the person who began the digging will certainly reach his goal with ease. However, if one person digs and his neighbor pours earth into the hole and creates a mound in his way, then he overturns the other's plan. In that case, the enemy is then unable to accomplish his goal. Similarly, one should not take a stand against one's enemies by working against them, for this makes it easier for them to reach their goal. However, he should overturn his enemies' plans as it says, "Let my soul be like earth." Then, "He who digs a pit will fall into it" (Proverbs 26:27). He falls and remains in the pit that he dug for his neighbor as a result of the earth that was poured on it, for his neighbor stands there pouring earth in his way."

Rabban Gamliel saw Rabbi Akiva's ship sink in the sea, with all hands lost. Yet the next day, Rabban Gamliel saw Rabbi Akiva approach him in person! "How did you survive?" he asked. Rabbi Akiva replied, "I clung to a plank of wood from the ship, and for every wave that passed over me I bowed my head until I arrived at the shore" (*Yevamot* 121a). The moral is that wood does not speak; hence, to survive the "churning seas of life," the best way is to grab hold of the attribute of silence. For every wave, challenge, and frustration that overwhelms us, we should just bow our head. Then we can slowly proceed to shore (*Rabbi Eliyahu Chaim Rosen*).

The essence of the *Elohei! Netzor* is to remain focused and to survive the vicissitudes of life. The prayer concludes, "Save me from jealousy, from anger, and open my heart to Torah and prayer." These ideas are like *hitbodedut,* asking for the things that are important to you at the moment. The *Mishnah Berurah* (122:8) quotes the *Chayey Adam* who says that during *Elohei! Netzor,* a person should add his own prayer to be a God-fearing person, have good children, and whatever else he requires in life.

עשה למען שמך (Act for the sake of Your Name)

Whoever says these four "acts," — for the sake of Your Name, Your loving right hand, Your Torah and Your Holiness — will merit to see the Divine Presence (*Tur Orach Chaim* 122:3)

יהיו לרצון אמרי פי (May the words of my mouth)

The verse, *yihiyu l'ratzon,* which is the closing words of the Amidah, holds special meaning. The verse begins with the letter *yod* and ends with the letter *yod.* It has *yod* (ten) words and we find ten times the letter *yod* within the verse. In addition, there are a total of forty-two letters in the verse (corresponding to the Holy Name of Forty-Two). These hint to great secrets, and therefore one must say the verse with extra *kavanah.* Saying the verse with concentration is a very sure means to have one's prayers answered (*Mishnah Berurah* 122:8).

At the conclusion of *Shemoneh Esrei,* we take three steps backwards and then ask for peace, the Holy Temple to be rebuilt, and that our portion shall be with the Torah. Furthermore, we pray to God that we may serve Him in awe as in the olden days.

The three steps backwards are, in essence, our exit from the World of *Atzilut* back into the lower worlds. We take three steps because we are returning from the World of *Atzilut* into the World of *Beriyah,* then the World of *Yetzirah,* and finally the World of *Asiyah* (*Pri Etz Chaim, Shaar HaAmidah* 20, p. 252).

We ask that our steps take us into a world of peace. We take these steps to honor God similar to when we went forward at the beginning of the *Amidah* (see Chapter 29) because we cannot remain forever in a spiritual mode—we must return to our daily lives. And if we are not worthy of having the Temple rebuilt, then at least God should place us in a realm of Torah, for whoever studies the laws of the sacrifices, it is as if he brought the sacrifices in the Temple himself (*Menachot* 110a).

CHAPTER 32

Birkhat Kohanim: *The Priestly Blessings*

יְבָרֶכְךָ ה' וְיִשְׁמְרֶךָ...

God should bless you and guard you. May God shine His countenance upon you and grant you grace. May God shine His face upon you and give you peace.

Aharon, the High Priest, offered sacrifices the day the Sanctuary was consecrated in the desert. Having performed his devotions, he then blessed the people. The verse says, "And Aharon lifted his hands and blessed the nation and stepped down from offering the sacrifices" (Leviticus 9:22). This is the reason *Birkhat Kohanim* is said right after we say the prayers about the sacrifices (i.e., *Retzei* and *Modim*).

Birkhat Kohanim is found in Numbers (6:22-27). God spoke to Moshe and told him to tell Aharon and his sons how they should bless the Children of Israel. He said, "And they [the *Kohanim*] shall put My Name upon the Children of Israel and I will bless them." The blessing ends with "peace." Therefore, immediately following *Birkhat Kohanim* we say the blessing of *Sim Shalom* (Peace upon us) (*Megillah* 18a).

Our Sages discuss the words, "I will bless them." Who does "them" refer to? Rabbi Yishmael explains that the priests bless the Jewish nation. But what about the priests themselves? They also need blessings. Therefore, God says, "I will bless them" referring to the *Kohanim*. Rabbi Akiva says "How do we know that God, too, blesses the Jewish nation? From the words, "I will bless them" (*Chullin* 49a). Our Sages add, "How are we to know if the specific priest who is performing the blessing is not a sinner himself?" God says, "But who is the one who is truly blessing you? Me!" as is written, "I will bless them" (*Yeshushalmi, Gittin,* 5:5).

The custom in the Ashkenazi communities outside of Israel is to conduct *Birkhat Kohanim* only on the Festivals. The *Rema* explains that we can only receive blessings when we are happy, and we are happiest on the holidays (*Orach Chaim* 128:44). As it says, "One with a good heart, he will bless" (cf. Proverbs 22:9). However, Ashkenazim in the Land of Israel, as well as all Sephardic communities throughout the world conduct *Birkhat Kohanim* daily. The *Mishnah Berurah* writes (128:164), "The Codifiers very much praised this custom" which is why in Israel the blessing is said daily. The Talmud comments (*Sotah* 38a), "From where do we know that God desires *Birkhat Kohanim*? From the verse, "And they [the *Kohanim*] shall put My Name upon the Children of Israel and I will bless them."

Birkhat Kohanim is said with the *Kohanim* standing opposite the congregation with their hands outstretched. The reason the *Kohanim* were empowered to bless others is that they have more stringent laws and a greater status of purity (Leviticus 23). Furthermore, since they represent the concept of *Chesed* (Lovingkindness), they are able to draw kindness and blessing. Their outstretched hands represent their ability to transfer those blessings to others. Because of the Priestly status of purity, not only are they on a higher plane of morality than the rest of the nation, but they are also positively affected by pure language and clean speech (LH, *Nesiat Kapayim* 1).

The importance of these blessings cannot be understated (*BaMidbar Rabbah* Chapter 11).

"God should bless you"—with sons and daughters and possessions.

"May He guard you"—from an evil eye and protect you from any damages.

"May God shine His countenance upon you"—so that any anger will be mitigated and that you encounter only compassion in your life.

"And May He grant you grace"—even if you are unworthy, He will be graceful towards you and grant you grace in the eyes of others.

"May God shine His face upon you"—by granting you favor and giving you peace. As the verse says, "Peace is *the* vessel which holds blessing" (*Uktzin* 3:12).

God should bless you and guard you

God promises that with the blessings comes automatic protection. For example, one may come into a financial windfall, but thieves can come and take it away. So, with the blessing we need protection. In addition, God promises to guard us from the evil inclination that comes with extended blessings so that it doesn't distract us from our true goals in life.

May God shine His countenance upon you and grant you grace

God promises to shine upon us from the light of Divine Presence. "Shine" means that God will illumine our face with the light of Torah, and "Grace" means that God will grant us to know how to act with grace toward others and that they will act gracefully to us. In addition, we pray to merit to receive from God's Treasury of Unearned Gifts.

May God shine His face upon you

God promises to shine upon us directly so that we know it is truly from God. And He will give us peace, peace when we enter our home and peace when we leave. Peace — with everyone.

CHAPTER 33

Tachanun: Confession and Supplication

After the *Amidah* we say *Tachanun*. In this prayer, we plead with God to invoke His compassion and have mercy upon us by mentioning His Thirteen Attributes of Mercy (Exodus 34:6-7). Afterward, we recite the *Viduy* (confession of our sins).[143] We then perform *Nefilat Apayim* by sitting down and placing our face on our arms and pleading with God for our sins and asking His forgiveness. Once we return to an upright position, we continue asking God to have compassion upon His people. Finally, we stand up to complete the *Tachanun* prayer.

Twice a week, on Mondays and Thursdays, we add an extended *Tachanun* prayer, consisting of pleas and supplication known as *V'Hu Rachum* (He is Merciful). Mondays and Thursdays are called "Days of Favor" as well as "Days of Judgment." In Talmudic times, Mondays and Thursdays were set aside for the courts to convene, which is why they are called, "Days of Judgment." When Moshe went to plea the Jews' case before God after their having made the golden calf, he ascended Mount Sinai on a Thursday and descended on a Monday, having transformed God's anger into compassion. Therefore, they are also called "Days of Favor." This is the reason additional prayers and supplications are added specifically on Mondays and Thursdays (*Kitzur Shulchan Arukh* 22:9).

143 It is one of the 613 *mitzvot* of the Torah to confess and become aware of one's sins.

There are some days during the year that we are exempt from saying *Tachanun*. Most siddurim provide a list of when we say *Tachanun* and when we are exempt (such as the month of Nissan, *Rosh Chodesh,* and *Chol HaMoed.*) Those special days have an increased level of sanctity; thus, due to the extra sanctity of the day, *Tachanun* does not need to be said.

The *Zohar* states that just as a person praises and thanks God for all the good He has done for him, so, too, a person should confess his sins before God (*Zohar* II, 41a). Why? There is a prosecutor (Satan) who stands before God, pointing out all the sins a person committed and demanding justice and punishment for those sins. If a person precedes the Satan in confessing his sins, he stymies the prosecutor from presenting his case and mitigates the demand for judgments. (The *Zohar* clarifies that the judgments are mitigated only if and when the person repents. If not, then the judgments will be raised before the Heavenly Court again.) Thus, we learn the importance of saying the *Tachanun* every day.

תָּבוֹא לְפָנֶיךָ תְּפִלָּתֵנוּ ... שֶׁאֵין אָנוּ עַזֵּי פָנִים וּקְשֵׁי עֹרֶף...

May our prayers come before You ... For we are not brazen faced people to say ... we are tzaddikim and we have not sinned. Rather, we and our ancestors have sinned.

Reb Noson (LH *Nefilat Apayim* 6:5) suggests that the prayer could be condensed. We could have said, "May our prayers come before You ... for we have sinned." Why do we add "For we are not brazen faced" to claim that we didn't sin? Furthermore, after sinning, we obviously can't say that we are tzaddikim!

Reb Noson explains that sin causes people to question God and disbelieve in the severity of sin. In *Tachanun* we say, "We are not like the brazen-faced people who after sinning deny that they have sinned. So, in the merit that I regret my sins, I request that God forgive me."

Reb Noson continues to explain that Godliness is everywhere—even within sin. By regretting our sins and seeking to improve, we release the spark of Godliness—a very high level of spirituality—that was concealed by the sin. Therefore, the descent to sin becomes our elevation, and in this merit, we request forgiveness.

אָשַׁמְנוּ, בָּגַדְנוּ

We are guilty, we are disloyal

We then recite the *Ashamnu* prayer—the prayer of confession comprised of words according to the *aleph-bet*—recognizing that we have blemished all the letters of the Torah and wish to repent for what we have done. We conclude that paragraph with "*Ta'inu, titanu*" (We have strayed and misled others.) Reb Noson writes that due to sin, we have strayed and fallen to very low places. However, one can find holiness even in low places for God's presence fills the entire world. And since we are striving to improve our ways, our descent becomes an ascent, as we reveal the sanctity that is there (LH, *Nefilat Apayim* 6:5).

ה' ה' אֵל רַחוּם וְחַנּוּן

God, God, Compassionate Deity

After the confession of *Ashamnu*, we say the Thirteen Attributes of Mercy to arouse God's compassion so He will forgive our sins. The Thirteen Attributes of Mercy are rooted in the very first word of Creation, *Bereishit*, which the Talmud refers to as a "Hidden Saying" (*Rosh HaShanah* 32a; *Shabbos* 104a). It is also the root of all spirituality even when concealed in the lowest places of the world (such as under the veil of sin.) Therefore, when one seeks atonement for his sins, he attains the spirituality that was concealed there, and he reveals the Thirteen Attributes of Mercy, for they both come from the same origin (LH, ibid. 6:6).

Then we perform *Nefilat Apayim* (Fall down upon our face) by placing our head upon our arms and saying the passage of repentance. What is the meaning of "falling down on our face?" The ARI explains that during the *Shemoneh Esrei* we have entered the highest World of *Atzilut,* and now that we have left, we return to lower levels. However, we have to bring the illumination from the highest of realms down so that we can illumine and extract the sparks of holiness even from the realms of the *kelipot.* The act of falling down on our faces parallels the act of *mesirat nefesh* (self-sacrifice) where a person sacrifices what he has and works on behalf of those unfortunate souls who are trapped in the realm of evil. Once a person has illumination from the highest realm, he can sacrifice himself and enter those dangerous realms to help elevate the sparks trapped there.[144]

This process is described as, "A fall in order to rise." That is, there are times in a person's life when he falls and it appears detrimental. However, the fall is a step back in order for the person to advance further. Thus, when we find ourselves "falling down on our faces," we have to learn to strengthen ourselves and hang in there, as we grasp and grope to elevate ourselves out of the quagmire. With our ascent from the realm of the *kelipot* by performing *Nefilat Apayim,* we merit to illumine the path and help to extricate others trapped by the *kelipot* in realms of the Other Side (LH, *Nefilat Apayim* 6:2-3).

144 *Pri Etz Chaim, Shaar Nefilat Apayim* 2, pp. 294-297.

Rebbe Nachman teaches that a person's yearning creates souls (LM I, 31:15). For example, if one yearns for evil (such as sin or forbidden temptations), he will create evil souls. On the other hand, if one yearns for God and to return to Him in repentance, he will create good souls. These souls roam from person to person. At times, a soul that was created by a tzaddik will go to an evil person and rouse him to repent. And conversely, a soul created by an evil person will go to a tzaddik and convince the tzaddik to pursue bad temptations. If the tzaddik remains steadfast in his devotions to God, he will eventually succeed in elevating the wicked soul. But if the tzaddik slackens in his devotions, he is in danger of succumbing to the evil of the wicked soul and is likely to sin.

Rebbe Nachman concludes, "This is the inner meaning of *Nefilat Apayim*." By the time we reach the *Tachanun* prayer, a person yearns for God, and this creates good souls that will, in turn, elevate many other souls.

וַאֲנַחְנוּ לֹא נֵדַע

We do not know what to do

VaAnachnu lo neida — On our own, we do not know what to do...

Although we performed such a great devotion by elevating souls, we still must understand that these ideas are very lofty and beyond our ability to conceive. Therefore, we conclude the *Tachanun* prayer with humility by saying, "We do not know what to do."

אָבִינוּ מַלְכֵּנוּ

Our Father Our King

The *Avinu Malkeinu* prayer was composed by Rabbi Akiva as a result of the suffering the Jews endured at the hands of the Romans. It comprises many pleas and supplications for the benefit of the Jewish nation. This prayer is said on days when we need extra prayers, such as on Fast Days and during the Ten Days of Repentance between Rosh HaShanah and Yom Kippur. In addition, it parallels the requests that we pray for in the eighteen blessings of the *Shemoneh Esrei*.

CHAPTER 34

The Torah Reading

The original custom was to read a portion of the Torah every Shabbos. Our Sages teach that "water" refers to Torah, as in the verse, "All that thirst go to the waters" (Isaiah 55:1). Just like a person can't go three days without water, the Jewish nation should not go three days without Torah. Therefore, Moshe established the accepted practice to read the Torah also on Mondays and Thursdays (*Bava Kama* 82a).

In the desert, the Jews went three days without water and then found bitter water (Exodus 15:22), arousing complaints and murmurings against Moshe. Moshe prayed and God provided water. The *Maharsha* (*Bava Kama,* loc. cit.) explains that when one keeps a regular schedule of Torah study, the "waters of Torah" remain sweet. On the other hand, when a person leaves his days empty of Torah, the "waters" turn bitter. Thus, the custom developed of not letting three days pass without reading the Torah.

One should honor the Torah by not talking when it is removed from the Ark and by listening quietly while it is being read. When the Torah is taken from Ark, we say the verse, "When the Ark went forward, Moshe said, 'Rise up God, and let Your enemies scatter'" (Numbers 10:35). We then recite, בריך שמיה (*Brikh Shmei*), a passage from the *Zohar* (II, 206a). The *Zohar* states that when the Torah is removed from the Ark to be read in public, the gates of Heaven and Mercy open, arousing great compassion and love from Above. Therefore, people should make sure to recite *Brikh Shmei,* which contains many heartfelt prayers to God.

The law stipulates that when the Torah is read during the week (i.e., Mondays and Thursdays) there should be three *aliyot* (people called up to the Torah). The three *aliyot* correspond to the *Kohen*, the *Levi* and the *Yisrael*. We specifically call three people to the Torah because there are generally two opposing sides of every issue, and we add a third dimension. The third side acts as a bridge and a peace maker. And when there is peace, the power of Torah can influence the person's life for good (LH, *Kriat HaTorah* 1).

In addition, each *aliyah* should be no less than three verses, but a total of not less than ten verses should be read. This is because prayer parallels *Malkhut, and Malkhut* is the tenth *sefirah*. We read from the Torah during prayers in order to draw life force into our prayers.

Malkhut represents authority, as well as prayer and faith, as we have mentioned previously. Furthermore, *Malkhut* is the lowest of the Ten *Sefirot*, which indicates "smallness" or "shortness." Indeed, most souls of previous generations lived a short life, since their souls were from *Malkhut*. Rebbe Nachman teaches that every person contains the attribute of *Malkhut* (LM I, 56:1). In order to overcome this "smallness" and to bring the life-force into *Malkhut*, we must draw "Length of Days" into *Malkhut* so that *Malkhut* can extend the duration of its life. The Rebbe explains that just like the Torah is comprised of various combinations of God's Name, reading the Torah draws God (i.e., the Length of Days) into *Malkhut*. This concept is displayed in the verse which commands a king to write his personal Torah scroll, as it says, "He shall read therein all the days of his life" (Deuteronomy 17:19). That is, the king (i.e., authority, *Malkhut*) shall read the Torah (i.e., Length of Days) in order to draw life into his kingdom.

Reb Noson explains that we read the Torah to draw God and Godliness into our lives. We read the Torah on Days of Favor (such as Monday, Thursday, Shabbos, and Festivals) for that's when the bounty of life comes down to us.

Reb Noson offers another insight into why the Torah is read during the prayers. The *ToRaH* is so called because it is a *MoReH derekh*, a pathfinder or guide to life, as is written, "Teach them the laws so as to guide them about what they shall do" (Exodus 18:20). Thus, reading the Torah helps us direct our prayers individually along the path of life as we seek personal guidance from God (cf. LH, *Kriat HaTorah* 3).

CHAPTER 35

U'va l'Tzion: Kedushah d'Sidra

The final section of the prayers (after the *Amidah* and *Tachanun*) is known as *Horadat HaShefa* (drawing down the bounty). We invoke the Heavenly blessings through prayer as we ascend through the worlds — from *Asiyah* to *Yetzirah* to *Beriyah* until *Atzilut.* When we reach the *Amidah,* we open the gates of bounty, drawing blessing into our day. The ARI explains that when we say *Ashrey* and *U'Va L'Tzion,* we draw bounty down to *Beriyah*; and with the remaining parts of the prayers (*Tefillah l'Dovid, Shir shel Yom* and *Ein k'Eiloheinu*), we draw the bounty down to *Yetzirah* and *Asiyah.*[145]

Our Sages teach, "Whoever recites *Tehilah L'David* (i.e., *Ashrey*) three times daily is guaranteed a place in the World to Come" (*Berakhot* 4b). During Shacharit we say it twice: once in *Pesukey d'Zimra,* the second time after the *Amidah.* The third time we say *Ashrey* is during *Minchah* (the afternoon prayer), before the *Amidah.* We have already discussed the significance of the *Ashrey* prayer (see Chapter 16). We recite it here to distinguish between the earlier *Ashrey* (recited before the *Amidah*) and the *Ashrey* right after the *Amidah* in *U'Va L'Tzion,* which is also referred to as *Kedushah d'Sidra* (order of sanctity).

145 *Pri Etz Chaim, Shaar HaTefillah* 5, p. 12; see also *Shaar HaKavanot, Inyan Mizmor Ya'ankha* 1, p. 319-320.

The *Zohar* (III, 226a) teaches that one must recite *Ashrey* with sincere concentration. The *Zohar* discusses the importance of saying *Ashrey* three times: The first time we say *Ashrey* in *Pesukey d'Zimra* is to praise God and strengthen *Malkhut* (i.e., the source of bounty and blessing). As the verse says, "Open Your hands and satiate people" (Psalms 145:16). The other two times (morning and afternoon) we have in mind to pray for our livelihoods, just as we eat in the mornings and evenings, as in the verse, "When God provides you with meat in the evening and bread in the morning" (Exodus 16:8). We learn from this that it is not very honorable to begin asking God for livelihood prior to first praising Him for His generosity and thanking him for opening His hand and feeding all people and living creatures.

LaMenatzeach Mizmor l'David

Following *Ashrey* we say the Psalm *LaMenatzeach Mizmor l'David* (Psalms 20). This chapter discusses times of trouble and our wish to be saved from suffering. The words "*B'yom tzarah*" (day of suffering) in this passage allude to the days prior to the coming of the *Mashiach*. This is the reason why this chapter precedes *U'Va L'Tzion Goel* (A Redeemer will come to Zion). Our Sages teach that there are eighteen chapters in Psalms which precede this one. Therefore, we say this chapter after reciting the eighteen blessings of the *Amidah*. (Although *LaMenatzeach* is chapter 20, the first two chapters in Psalms are considered as one chapter; *Berakhot* 9b).

King David recited this chapter when he sent his general, Yoav, and his army into battle. The verse begins "May God answer you on a day of trouble and may the God of Yaakov defend you." Yaakov is singled out because he said, "The God Who answers me on my day of troubles" (Genesis 35:3). Therefore, we invoke the merit of Yaakov to protect and shield us from trouble.

LaMenatzeach contains nine verses (excluding the introductory verse), corresponding to the nine months of pregnancy. It also contains seventy words, paralleling the "seventy cries" that a birthing mother cries out in childbirth. Therefore, it is appropriate to say this chapter during pregnancy and childbirth.[146] In addition, this chapter contains 310 letters, corresponding to the 310 worlds that a tzaddik will inherit in the World to Come (*Uktzin* 3:12).

The Psalm continues, "May He send your help from His holy Sanctuary" (ישלח עזרך מקדש). The final letters of **ישלח עזרך מקדש** spell the word **חשך** (i.e., darkness or troubles and suffering). From this we learn that salvation sprouts forth *from* the darkness. Situations that as first glance seem bad, turn around and become the root of the salvation (cf. LM I, 19:8).

U'Va L'Tzion Goel

After we pray for redemption in *LaMenatzeach,* we ask in *U'Va L'Tzion* for that Redemption to come. As the verse says, "Let there come to Zion the Redeemer and those returnees from sin of Yaakov, says God" (Isaiah 59:20). There are two groups who need healing and redemption: There is the general Jewish community who, spread around the world, need to be redeemed to Zion; and then there are individuals who have sinned who require spiritual healing. Regarding the sinners, we say "*u'leshavei pesha*" (for those who repent). They are promised

146 *Pri Etz Chaim, Shaar Kriat HaTorah* 4, pp. 307-308.

redemption, for the verse states, "*ne'um Adonoy*" (says God). That is, they will attain a spirit of purity (i.e., healing) as they return to God.

U'Va L'Tzion is also known as *Kedushah d'Sidra* (order of sanctity) since it contains the words of *Kedushah*. This is because at a certain point in history, enemies of the Jews forbade them to say the *Kedushah* (both the *Kedushah* before the *Shema* and during the *chazan's* repetition of the *Amidah*.) These enemies would attend the services in order to uphold their evil decrees and afterwards they would leave. Therefore, it was established to recite the *Kedushah* within *U'Va L'Tzion*, when the enemies would not be in attendance. For the same reason, before reciting *U'Va L'Tzion*, we ask God to protect us and save us from these enemies and hasten Redemption. In *U'va L'Tzion*, we say the verse "*Va'Ani zot Briti*" (This is My covenant) (Isaiah 59:21). Since these enemies tried to nullify the Torah, we affirm our faith in the Torah.

The Talmud teaches, "From the day the Holy Temple was destroyed, each day comes with a greater curse! If so, what sustains the world? [The answer is] It stands upon the *Kedushah d'Sidra*" (*Sotah* 49a). The *Yaavetz* explains: The Talmud says, "From the day of the destruction of the Temple, the gates of prayer are sealed" (*Berakhot* 32b). Therefore, our prayers are not accepted. The solution is the repentance of the sinners, as it says, "Great is repentance for it reaches to the Throne of Glory" (*Yoma* 86a). Therefore, we learn that when one repents, his prayers are answered together with his repentance. His prayers pass through all the locked gates until it reaches God's Throne of Glory. Thus, we approach God asking to bond with Torah and to send the Redeemer so that we merit to repent. In order to show that we are sincere in our repentance, we then say the *Kedushah d'Sidra* ("*Kadosh, Kadosh, Kadosh*" as well as its Aramaic translation) so that we are saying words of Torah and causing people to draw close to God.

Reb Noson explains that the reason we say the *Kedushah d'Sidra* is literally to be able to draw upon ourselves additional sanctity. It is said in Hebrew and then in its *Aramaic Targum,* which indicates that we can become sanctified not only through devotions but even through the mundane (LH, *Nefilat Apayim U'Kedusha d'Sidra* 1).

The *U'Va L'Tzion* prayer begins with the verse, *U'Va L'Tzion Goel Ulishavei Fesha B'Yaakov Neum YHVH. Vaani.* The Talmud teaches, "*Mashiach* will not come until all the souls in '*guf*' are terminated" (*Niddah* 13b). Rashi explains that *guf* is the term for "a special place" where all the souls which were created reside until they are born.

The initial letters (גואל ולשבי פשע ביעקב נאם יהוה ואני) form the words *GUF* (גוף, body) and *BaNaYV* (בניו, children). The ARI writes that if, God forbid, a man spills his seed, then his children who are already born will be forced under the realm of the Other Side. When he repents, he returns his children to the realm of holiness. By sinning, the person's seed ejects the soul from the place called *guf,* and when he returns, the soul returns to the *guf.* Thus, the acrostic of *guf* and *banayv,* for a person's children must first be returned to the *guf* before Redemption can occur.

Until a person repents, the length of the exile is extended. When he repents, then he will receive redemption.[147] We discussed this concept previously (Chapter 31) referring to the blessing "Blow the Shofar" (תקע בשופר גדול). The ARI explains

147 *Pri Etz Chaim, Shaar Kriat HaTorah* 5, p. 308.

that the wasted seed refers to the sparks of holiness that are spread out all over the globe due to the sin of Adam (*Pri Etz Chaim, Shaar HaAmidah,* #19, p. 244). In addition, the widespread problem of concentration and focus is due largely to the sin of wasted seed, which forces a person to be "spread out" in many directions at once.

Therefore, the severity of this sin of wasted seed is that souls are created from the seed but have no body. It is like creating a demon who has a soul but not a body. (This may be why some people seem to have demonic behavior.) Rebbe Nachman said that the rectification of a bodiless soul is one of the most difficult challenges facing the tzaddikim who work with these souls. They lack a tangible connection to be able to get a hold of things. Thus, these tzaddikim try hard to find something physical to attach to these souls, making the work extremely difficult. These tzaddikim are searching and seeking a "*guf*" which will be the bridge for the soul's rectification. The rectification of this sin will happen when we "get our act together" and gather in those lost sparks. Only then the *Mashiach* will come.

Ata Kadosh Yosheiv

The verse says, "You are Holy, enthroned upon the praises of Israel." The word "*yosheiv*" implies "waiting" (Rashi in Deuteronomy 1:46). That is, God waits for the prayers of the Jews to ascend before He accepts the praises and prayers of the angels. Additionally, God waits for all the Jewish communities to complete their prayers so that the prayers can come collectively at one time before God. Rebbe Nachman explains, "When there are praises to God, His Sanctity always increases!" Each and every prayer causes God's honor and glory to be revealed in the world (LM I, 20:4).

Kadosh! Kadosh! Kadosh!

At this point we come to the actual *Kedushah,* citing the verse from Isaiah (6:3) which describes the angels praising God. We sanctify God by saying, "*Kadosh, Kadosh, Kadosh*" (Holy! Holy! Holy!) and repeating it in its Aramaic translation of *Targum Yonatan.* Then we continue to articulate about God's Kingdom and how He should reign over the entire world. The fact that the angels are calling to each other shows that they are asking permission from each other as a way of honoring the other. Breslover chassidim point out that the *Targum* uses the word "receive," as in, "They receive from one another." This teaches us that one should not impose his will upon another; instead, one should be willing to receive the opinion of others and to hear another view.

Shamra Zot L'Olam

U'Va L'Tzion continues by asking God to open our hearts and proclaim that we love and fear Him. Only after we repent and sanctify God can we ask that these prayers remain in our minds and hearts.

V'Hivdilanu min HaToim

Having thanked God for creating us with the *daat* to serve Him, we ask that we not go astray. The prayer uses the word "*to'im*" in the plural. Reb Noson describes three types of people who go astray. First there are people who are completely distant from God and miss out on any kind of relationship with God. Second, there are those who aren't fully committed; they benefit from some kind of awareness of God, but do not forge a real closeness and connection with Him. Then there is the third group who think they are close with God, but they are just fooling themselves because they are not as close as they think.

A person must pray to be "set apart" from these different kinds of errors.

We conclude *U'Va L'Tzion* with a request, "May it be Your will...that we do not labor in vain or bring forth in confusion." When we say these words, we should pray that our children merit to grow in their devotions to God so that their lives are "not in vain." Furthermore, we pray that their lives are fruitful and bear fruit so that they shall not grow up in confusion and doubt.

Kaddish Titkabel

As noted earlier (Chapter 13), *Kaddish* is the bridge between the worlds. Just as we recited *Kaddish* several times, ascending from *Asiyah* (the sacrifices) to *Yetzirah* (*Pesukey d'Zimra*), and from Yetzirah to *Beriyah* (*Shema* and its blessings) until we reach the World of *Atzilut* (the *Amidah*); so too, we say *Kaddish* to bridge our descent from *Atzilut* back to *Asiyah*. Therefore, after the *Amidah* (and *Tachanun*) we recite a *Kaddish*, and following *U'Va L'Tzion* we say *Kaddish Titkabel*, in which we ask that all our prayers be accepted. There are several additional times we say the *Kaddish*, such as after the Song of the Day, after *Ein K'Elohenu* and after *Aleinu*. On *Rosh Chodesh* we say *Kaddish* after *Borkhi Nafshi* (Psalm 104), and during the months of Elul and Tishrei, we say *Kaddish* after we recite *L'Dovid HaShem Ori v'yish'i* (Psalm 27).

Our sages say that one who prays with a minyan can be called a tzaddik (צדיק). This is because every day he merits to answer *Amen* ninety times (צ), *Kedushah* four times (ד), *Kaddish* ten times (י) and say one hundred (ק) blessings.

CHAPTER 36

The Conclusion of Shacharit

תְּפִילָה לְדָוִד
Prayer for David

Following *UV'a L'Tzion* we recite *Tefillah L'Dovid* (Psalm 86). According to the ARI, *Tefillah L'Dovid* belongs in the World of *Yetzirah,* the next step down in our descent from *Beriyah* (*Uv'a L'Tzion*). There are eighteen verses in this chapter, including the opening verse of the next paragraph, "*Beis Yaakov*: let us go and walk in the light of God." The number eighteen is noted several times during prayer: there are eighteen mentions of God in the morning blessings, eighteen mentions of God's Name in *Yehi Kavod* (during *Pesukey d'Zimra*), eighteen mentions of God's name during the *Shema* and eighteen blessings of the *Amidah.*

There are 186 words in this passage until the words, "*Shir HaMaalot*." One hundred eighty-six is equivalent to the Hebrew word, *MaKOM* (מקום), a reference to God.[148] One of the Holy Names of God, *YHVH* (when expanded) equals 186. The passage of *Shir HaMaalot* (Psalms 124) contains fifty-seven words. This parallels the Holy Names of God, *YHVH* (יהוה) and *EiL* (אל), which together add up to fifty-seven. Therefore,

148 *YHVH* (10+5+6+5) is expanded as such: 10x10=100; 5x5=25; 6x6=36; 5x5=25. The total is 186, the equivalent of *MaKOM* (*Mem*=40; *Kuf*=100; *Vav*=6; *Mem*=40, total of 186. See also above, Chapter 12.

we learn that the passage *Tefillah L'Dovid* alludes to a deep connection to God.

The *Zohar* (III, 195a) teaches that there are three types of prayer mentioned in Psalms: *Tefillah l'Dovid* (David's prayer; Chapter 86), *Tefillah L'Moshe* (Moshe's prayer; Chapter 90), and *Tefillah L'Ani* (a poor person's prayer; Chapter 102). Notwithstanding the greatness of Moshe and King David, the most effective prayer is that of the poor person and it is the first to be accepted. The *Zohar* explains: a poor person comes before God and cries from his heart; therefore, they are readily accepted. Reb Noson adds that when a person cries before God over his lack of spirituality, his prayers are certainly accepted before God as well (LH, *Tefillin* 5:43).

The prayer continues, "God teach me Your ways so that I may walk in Your truth." Reb Noson explains that it is of utmost importance for a person to walk in "God's truth." A person may mislead himself or rationalize his deeds. Because it is his understanding of the situation, it may be the right course of action. But is it God's truth? Is this *really* what he should be doing? By imploring God to teach us the real truth, we will end up always doing the right thing.

שִׁיר שֶׁל יוֹם
Song of the Day

During the Temple service, the Levites would play musical instruments and sing a psalm that reflected the specific energy of each day. The Levites' song was meant to arouse abundant blessing so that we may draw that energy into the week (*Pri Etz Chaim, Shaar Kriat HaTorah* 5, p. 310).

Each day, the Song of the Day is prefaced with "Today is the first (or whichever) day of the Shabbos week." Why do we mention Shabbos each day? The ARI explains that all blessing is rooted in Shabbos. Due to the abundant blessings drawn on Shabbos, we are able to continue drawing these blessings during the week. Thus, each day is connected to Shabbos: the first three weekdays are connected to the previous Shabbos, while the latter three days are connected to the following Shabbos. Furthermore, by mentioning Shabbos each day, we are fulfilling the mitzvah of the Torah to "Remember the Shabbos and sanctify it" (Exodus 20:8).

The Talmud elaborates on the connection between the Song of the Day and the specific day of the week during Creation.[149]

Day	Psalm	Verse	Connection to Creation
Sunday	24	"To God alone belongs the earth and all it contains."	The first day of Creation was on a Sunday. God was the sole Creator and whatever He created was for those who will eventually dwell in it.
Monday	48	"God is great everywhere, but His radiance shines exceedingly in the city of our God."	On the second day of Creation, God separated the waters to divide between those Above and those below. It also refers to God having ascended to sit Above, which indicates that He is great and praiseworthy.

149 *Rosh HaShanah* 31a; see also *Ta'amei HaMinhagim* #145.

Tuesday	82	"God stands in every tribunal of Heaven; He also sits in the midst of the judges to render judgment."	On the third day of Creation, God created the earth which stands upon truth and justice. Thus, God created an earth with His wisdom in order to prepare it for humanity.
Wednesday	94	"O loving God who executes justice, HaShem… reveal Yourself."	On the fourth day, God created the solar system: the sun, moon, constellations and planets. These were created to serve man, not that man should err and serve the heavenly bodies, which is a form of idolatry. Thus, God will exact vengeance from those who distort the reason and purpose of Creation.
Thursday	81	"Sing joyously to God, our innermost strength."	On the fifth day of Creation, God created birds and fish—a cause for praise and joyful singing to God for the varying species on earth.
Friday	93	"The time will come when God's sovereignty will finally be revealed."	On the sixth day, God created all kinds of animals and then He created the human being. Since He concluded the work of Creation and He now reigns over it, we praise Him that He is king, and He rules.

Shabbos	92	"A song in honor of the Shabbos day."	This is a song for the Ultimate Future, for a day that is completely Shabbos and the fulfillment of Creation, the World to Come.

בָּרְכִי נַפְשִׁי
My soul, bless God

On *Rosh Chodesh*, it is customary to recite *Borkhi Nafshi* immediately following the Song of the Day. The prayer begins with, "My soul, bless God" (Psalm 104). The *Zohar* teaches that on *Rosh Chodesh*, God illumines a renewal of light and arousal to the souls, as well as to all of creation (*Zohar* I, 97b). Thus the psalm praises God for His illuminating our souls. Furthermore, the *Musaf* sacrifice brought on *Rosh Chodesh* is meant to affect forgiveness, as the psalm concludes, "Let sins cease to exist."

לְדָוִד ה' אוֹרִי וְיִשְׁעִי
God is my Light and Salvation

From the second day of *Rosh Chodesh* Elul until *Shemini Atzeret* (a period of fifty-one days) it is customary to recite *LeDavid HaShem* (Psalm 27). The psalm speaks about these days of repentance, asking God to draw us close to Him and protect us. The Midrash explains that the words, "God is my Light" refers to *Rosh HaShanah*; the words, "My Salvation" refers to *Yom Kippur*; and the words, "He will hide me in His Sukkah" refers to *Sukkot* (*Shochar Tov* #27). The psalm contains thirteen mentions of God's Holy Name, *YHVH*, which correspond to the Thirteen Attributes of Mercy. These thirteen attributes are available during the month of Elul to allow anyone—no matter who or what they've done—to return to God.

אֵין כֵּאלֹהֵינוּ
There is none like our God

The poem *Ein K'Eloheinu* is extremely profound. On a simple level, the initials of the first three stanzas (*Ein, Mi, Nodeh*; *aleph, mem, nun*) spell *AMeN*, while the fourth and fifth stanzas begin *Barukh* (blessed) and *Atah* (are You). This hints to the essence of a blessing, *"Barukh Atah… Amen."* In addition, the *gematria* of *Amen* (91) is the numerical equivalent of the combination of *YHVH* (26) and *Adonoy* (65) (*Rokeach*, Chapter 319).

Ein K'Eloheinu states that even in our lowly physical world, not only is there none like God, but there is nothing but God. On a deeper level, the prayer summarizes the overall lesson of the Morning Prayer: *Ein K'Eloheinu* corresponds to *Asiyah*; *Mi K'Eloheinu* corresponds to *Yetzirah*; *Nodeh L'Eloheinu* corresponds to *Beriyah; Barukh Eloheinu* corresponds to *Atzilut;* and *Atah Hu Eloheinu* corresponds to the Infinite One who encompasses and transcends all these dimensions, yet whose presence fills and permeates all existence.

There was a period of time when members of the Catholic Church in Spain decreed against the Jewish form of prayer and insisted on certain reforms that would include their god for which we did not comply. The bishops and priests would attend services to witness that the Jews complied, if not, they would inflict severe punishment. The *Ein K'Eloheinu* prayer enabled the Jews to worship God while under the watchful eyes of the church without them realizing, for the poem contained the words *Barukh, Atah* and *Amen* which their enemies did not understand.

Seeing how *Ein K'Eloheinu* strengthened the nation's faith in God even as they were oppressed by those who attempted to crush our religion, we precede this passage with the verse, "Take strength and be courageous of heart, and direct your hope to God" (Psalm 27:14).

The Talmud teaches, "There are four things which require strengthening and renewal: Torah, good deeds, prayer and *derekh eretz* (business or work)." Now that we are approaching the end of the prayers, we can ask ourselves, "Did I pray correctly? Are my prayers going to be answered?" But how can we really know?! Therefore, the Talmud teaches, "Strengthen yourself. Pray. And if your prayer was not answered, then pray again" (*Berakhot* 32b).

Ein K'Eloheinu continues, "There is none holy like God, for there is none like You; there is no Creator like You" (1 Samuel 2:2). This verse was said by Chanah, who was barren, yet she prayed to God and eventually begat Shmuel the Prophet. Chanah was consistent in her prayers, continuously praying, and she didn't stop until her prayers were answered. Thus, the *Ein K'Eloheinu* teaches us to strengthen ourselves with faith that God does hear our prayers.

פִּטּוּם הַקְּטֹרֶת
Blending of the *Ketoret*

One of the reasons *Ein K'Eloheinu* and the *Ketoret* was placed at the end of the prayers was because of the *kelipot* that pursue the person who chooses to serve God. These *kelipot* will prosecute a person before God saying he is not worthy of having his prayers accepted. Therefore, we recite the *Ketoret* to subdue these *kelipot* (*Taamei HaMinhagim* #146). Additionally, the *Ketoret* actually helps to protect us so that the *kelipot* do not take away the bounty which descends after the prayers (*Pri Etz Chaim, Shaar HaTefillah* 5, p. 13). As a result, in the merit of the *Ketoret,* the prosecuting angels are silenced.

Our Sages teach that the *Ketoret* brings wealth. In order that a person shouldn't mistakenly believe that it is his own efforts which bring success and wealth, we say the *Ketoret* after *Ein K'Eloheinu,* to remind us that it is God Who provides for us after all.

תָּנָא דְבֵי אֵלִיָּהוּ
The lesson of *Eliyahu HaNavi*

Following *Ein K'Eloheinu,* we say *Tana D'Bei Eliyahu* (the House of Study of Eliyahu the Prophet). Whoever reviews the Torah's laws daily will be certain that he belongs in the eternal future world. Rebbe Nachman constantly stressed the importance of studying the codes of religious law. He emphasized this more than any other study, explaining that studying the Codes is a great spiritual remedy. Sin causes good and evil to become mixed up. A legal opinion provides a clear separation between the valid and invalid, the permitted and the forbidden, the pure and the impure. When a person studies religious law, he reaches and understands a clear opinion as to the correct course of action, causing good to once again be separated from evil. This is the connection between *halikhot* (paths) and *Halakhot* (Codes). Studying the Codes helps a person choose a valid path to walk upon during his life.

Rebbe Nachman said that everyone must study the Codes each day without fail... at least one law every day of your life (*Rebbe Nachman's Wisdom* #29).

אַל תִּקְרֵי "בָּנָיִךְ" אֶלָּא "בּוֹנָיִךְ"

Don't read "your children", but rather "your builders"

The Talmud teaches: Do not read just *banayikh* (your children), but rather *bonayikh* (your builders). That is, do not read "Your children will merit great peace," but rather "Your children will be peace-builders." Combining both homilies (i.e., *halikhot* / *Halakhot* and *banayikh* / *bonayikh*) yields: Your children will become true builders of a better world—only when they learn the Torah of God, the Eternal One who guides and directs all the hidden ways of His world toward eternal perfection.

CHAPTER 37

Aleinu

עָלֵינוּ לְשַׁבֵּחַ

It is our responsibility to praise the Lord

After forty years of wandering in the desert with only his Jewish brethren as companions—and all of them serving the One God—Yehoshua led the nation into the Holy Land. He was struck by the inhabitants who served all types of idolatries. As a result, Yehoshua spread his hands heavenward, bowed on his knees and prayed out loud, "It is our responsibility to praise the Supreme Master of all." He thanked God for having the belief in the One God.

Yehoshua praised God, Who is the Creator of everything. Being spared from the idolatries of the nations, he then gave praise that we are not like them and that God did not place us among foolish idolatries. Rather he said, "We bow down to God, the King of kings, the Blessed Holy One, Who stretched the Heavens and founded the Earth...He is our God, there is none other." In simple terms, Yehoshua composed the prayer of *Aleinu*, praising God for Who He is and declaring that He is the One God.

The first paragraph of *Aleinu* expresses our faith in God, that He chose us as a special nation and separated us from idol worshippers and false faiths. The second paragraph expresses the wish that the entire world will accept God as the One God, and all will turn to Him. In a sense, this powerful prayer compares to the *Shema* as it declares our faith. Yet our faith isn't perfect. We are still in the midst of the long and wearying spiritual battle (like Yehoshua) to win the war of faith. However, we still give thanks to God for how far we've come and look forward to winning the war in the future.

One should pray *Aleinu* with fear and awe because the hosts of Heaven listen to this prayer and say, "Fortunate are the people that say this praise." Even God Himself joins in. On *Rosh HaShanah*, we recite the *Aleinu* prayer in *Musaf* in the section of *Malkhiyot*. Just as Yehoshua bowed down on his knees to God and prayed, it was established that it would be proper to bow down before God on a daily basis when we say the words, "We bow down before the King" (and also on Rosh HaShanah and Yom Kippur).

The first paragraph of *Aleinu* begins with an *Ayin* (עלינו) and ends with a *Dalet* (אחד). Similarly, the second paragraph, also begins with an *Ayin* (על כן) and ends with a *Dalet* (אחד). These two letters make up the word *AiD* (עד) (witness). This teaches us that through *Aleinu* we are giving testimony to the Oneness of God.

Know that God is the Lord

The prayer states, "Know today and reflect upon it in your heart that God is the Lord" (Deuteronomy 4:39). Some philosophers use this verse to prove that one must know God philosophically and intellectually. However, Rebbe Nachman said that this is absolutely false. He claims that the only way to know God is through faith. A king's subjects need to know that they have a lord and master, not to philosophize about it. The same is true of the kingdom of heaven. We are told, "Know that God is the Lord!" Yet we must be reminded of this many times because the world is full of temptations and distractions to make us forget

God. Many people hardly ever think about God. Therefore, the Torah reminds us, "Know that God is the Lord; Know the God of your father." By binding your mind to your heart, you will know in your heart that "God is the Lord" (*Rebbe Nachman's Wisdom* #217).

Therefore, we direct our hope to You

Having just declared God's praise and that He is Omnipotent, we now declare our faith in Him and His ability to manifest His majesty and authority over all of creation. We pray that all idolatry should cease to exist and that the world should come to its rectification under God's rule.

The world will be rectified under the Sovereignty of *Shadai* and all humanity will call in Your Name

The world will be rectified when people will repent because the Holy Name *Shadai* represents repentance. *ShaDai* connotes *Sheyeish Dai* (There is enough of My Godliness) for all of creation. This means that everyone will be satisfied with God and have no need whatsoever for idolatry or other blemishes of faith.

All the wicked will turn to You

The wicked alludes to non-believers who convert (i.e., those who until now had blemished faith and now accept the true faith.) They will recognize the greatness of God, which implies they will all attain a perfected knowledge of God (LM I, 17:6).

On that day, God and His Name will be One

The Talmud (*Pesachim* 50a) asks, "Is He not already One?" The answer is that today we judge God's actions to be good and bad. We say the blessing for good tidings, "God Who does good and extends that good to others," while if, God forbid, tragedy strikes, then we say the blessing, "God Who is a true judge." But at the time of *Mashiach*, we will view all of God's actions as good so will only use the blessing, "God Who does good and extends that good to others." Rebbe Nachman teaches that whoever recognizes that everything from God is for the best will merit to value the understanding and knowledge of the World to Come (LM I, 4:1).

Just as we began *Pesukey d'Zimra* with praise to God (*Hodu*), we also conclude the morning prayers with abundant praise of God. As we mentioned previously (see Chapter 14), saying praises of God is a powerful repellant of the *kelipot*. Thus, just as we try to vanquish the forces of evil prior to the prayers, we similarly chase away the *kelipot* afterwards so that they cannot drain any energy from our prayers. Furthermore, we want the bounty and blessing invoked by our supplications to descend and remain with us.

We end the *Aleinu* passage by quoting three verses which teach us that we should never give up hope. When Haman's decree was publicized, Mordechai met three schoolchildren and asked them to recite any verse they had just studied. The children answered, "Do not be afraid of an immediate disaster" (Proverbs 3:25), "Let them scheme against us, it will not succeed" (Isaiah 8:10), and "For God is with us" (Isaiah 46:4). When Mordechai heard these prophecies, he smiled, knowing that everything will come out right (*Esther Rabbah* 7:13; *Bava Batra* 12b).

The verse, "An immediate disaster," teaches us that disaster strikes when we are not expecting it, yet if we strengthen our faith, we can find solace and even hope for a reversal of fate. The verse, "Let them scheme," describes what our enemies have been doing for centuries; yet it is us who survived, not the nations. Lastly, the verse, "For God is with us, even when we grow old...God will sustain us," refers to the length of the exile, which seems to continue on endlessly, yet God always stands by our side.

Six Remembrances

There are six instances in Jewish history we are commanded to remember daily in order to strengthen our recall of the realm of holiness, even in the midst of our daily activities (LH, *Melamdim* 3:5). The commentaries explain that these six items are fundamental to our faith. By recalling these six ideas, we keep our focus and are guaranteed a place in the World to Come. They are:

1. The Exodus: The Jewish people's salvation from slavery in Egypt is mentioned numerous times in the Torah, indicating it is a central theme to the nation of Israel.
2. The Revelation at Sinai: Accepting the Torah, which is our guiding light, was a pivotal experience for the Jewish people.
3. The evil of Amalek: This nation represents the comprehensive spiritual defilement of the entire world, which must be eradicated. Thus, until the coming of *Mashiach,* it is an eternal battle.
4. The sin of the golden calf: We should remember the idolatrous leanings of our nation from which we have not yet been purified of its effects (Rashi on Exodus 32:34). We received the Torah, yet shortly afterwards we committed the sin of idolatry. Similarly, often we do good, but then give into errors and sins. Therefore, we are commanded to be on guard for a mistaken path.
5. Miriam's punishment: We are commanded to recall the terrible sin of *lashon hara* (slander) which is worse than idolatry, adultery and murder combined (*Erkhin* 15b). Furthermore, when a person speaks *lashon hara,* it is as if

the person has gone against God (*Erkhin* 15b). Miriam's act also connotes a blemishing faith in the tzaddikim. Though Miriam herself was a righteous woman, she should have maintained faith in Moshe, a tzaddik, and not slandered him.

6. The Shabbos: We must remember the core of our faith in God.

PART III

Berakhot – The Blessings

Minchah and *Maariv* (The Afternoon and Evening Prayers)

CHAPTER 38

Torah Study

The Talmud comments, "Whoever goes from the *Beis Knesset* to the *Beis Midrash* merits to see the *Shekhinah*" (Divine Presence).[150] Therefore, we learn that upon leaving the *Beis Knesset* (synagogue) one should go to the *Beis Midrash* (house of study). A person should establish time to study Torah and that time should be sacred, even if he stands to lose a large profit. There is a very intimate connection between Torah and prayer. According to the Kabbalah, the Torah represents *Zer Anpin,* while prayer parallels *Malkhut.* Forging the connection between these two forms a unity between these *Partzufim* and the *sefirot,* which is our goal.

The time for prayer begins at daybreak. It is forbidden to engage in any activity (such as eating, greeting others, business, travel, and even Torah study) prior to saying the morning prayers (*Orach Chaim* #89). Therefore, a person should pray as soon as he is allowed. Some people arise before daybreak in order to "study the *daf*"[151] so that they are able to study Torah before prayer at the allotted time. Either way is acceptable. Other people arise to say the *Tikkun Chatzot* prayer, study Torah until daybreak, and only then engage in prayer.

150 *Berakhot* 64a; *Moed Katan* 29a.

151 A reference to the "*daf hayomi*" a commitment to study each day a page of *Talmud,* so that one completes the entire Talmud in a cycle of seven and one-half years. Rabbi Meir Shapiro of Lublin established the *daf hayomi* in 1923 to keep the Jewish nation on "the same page" and it has become a very popular plan of study accepted in many communities worldwide.

The recommended daily regimen of Torah study should include *TaNaCh* (i.e., Torah, *Navi* [Prophets] and / or *Ketuvim* (Hagiographa]) and the Codes (i.e., *Mishnah, Talmud* and *Shulchan Arukh*). Of these studies, the Codes are the most important, since without knowledge of the law one cannot fulfill his religious obligations.[152] With a balanced program one can learn incredible amounts and thus be able to see the wonders of God through the lens of the Torah.

Rebbe Nachman once said, "What does a person have to do in this world? All that is needed is to pray, study and pray" (*Rebbe Nachman's Wisdom* #287). The Rebbe described the connection between Torah study and prayer: through Torah study, one empowers his prayers to ascend to their rightful place where they are accepted by Heaven. This supports the idea that it is preferable to study prior to praying. Furthermore, Rebbe Nachman teaches that with one's Torah study, each letter represents *nitzotzot* (sparks of holiness) which are joined together during one's prayers as they reach their rectification (LM I, 2:6).

Rebbe Nachman continues to explain: Each person has a portion of *Malkhut* within himself. This *Malkhut* enables him to influence others to go in God's way. Through Torah study he is able to exercise that authority properly. How? The Torah is quite vast, yet it is broken down into weekly portions. Then these weekly portions are divided into separate verses. Each verse is separated by words, and all words are made up of letters. This enables a person to receive his life source from the Torah in small measures without being overwhelmed. The Torah is

152 *Mishnah Berurah* 155:3; *Shakh* on *Yoreh Deah*, 246:4.

made up of God's varying Names, thus with Torah we are able to call out to God with each word we articulate (LM I, 56:3).

Reb Noson elaborates: The main life-force a person receives is through the Torah. The fact that the Torah consists of individual letters and words implies that we are taking the "raw material" and forming from them vessels with which we can receive the wisdom and vitality of the Torah. Through these vessels we are able to connect with God and call out to Him with each word we study!

Reb Noson extends the idea to eating, since one is allowed to eat between praying and studying (*Orach Chaim* 155:1). When we pray, taste something, and then study Torah, we fulfill the verse, "Your Torah is in my innards" (Psalms 40:9). Reb Noson explains that food brings sustenance to those who eat. When we recite a blessing over the food we eat, we are calling God, the life-force behind everything, and bringing Him into our lives, our bodies. By praying and blessing God, even over the food we eat, we are internalizing God into our lives (LH, *Hekhsher Keilim* 3:1).

In summary, we draw God's life-force into us first through blessing God and calling out to Him in prayer, then by blessing the food we eat, and certainly by studying Torah. Thus, it is very valuable to set aside time for Torah study after praying.

CHAPTER 39

Blessings over Food

Eating plays a vital part in refining and purifying all aspects of creation. The food we eat is elevated when it is transformed into the beautiful words that we speak: the blessings we make over the food itself; the prayers we offer; our words of Torah; the kind and encouraging words we offer to others; and all the other devotions we are able to perform as a result of the nourishment we derive from the food. It is important to keep this in mind as we eat. Our food becomes "incense," as it were (see above Chapters 10-12), which brings us to true joy (LM II, 16).

There are many laws that are connected to food, such as washing our hands prior to eating and reciting blessings before and after the meal. In addition, there are blessings called *Birkhos Pratiyos*, which are specific blessings for sight, sound, smell, and natural phenomenon. The idea behind all these laws is that we wish to rectify and elevate to God the sparks of holiness that are found in everyday occurrences.

Rectifying the Sparks

Reb Noson explains that the act of eating has the phenomenal power to rectify the sparks of holiness since eating represents a purification process. For example, consider the series of steps involved in eating a piece of bread. First one has to plow the field and plant the seeds. Then the wheat must be harvested and the kernels separated from the chaff. Afterward, the kernels are ground into flour and the coarse bran removed. Only then can one combine the flour with water and begin kneading the dough necessary to bake the bread.

But what happens next? A person takes a bite of the bread, and the purification process begins anew. The teeth grind the food so it can be sent to the stomach, where gastric juices break down the pieces into manageable portions. The good and healthy parts are absorbed into the body, while the bad and unhealthy parts are rejected and expelled (LH, *Betziat HaPat* 5:3).

As the food goes through various purification stages until the most refined parts of the food become absorbed in the person's body, another purification process takes place on the spiritual realm. Everything we eat—be it bread, meat, fruit, drinks, or chocolate—contains sparks of holiness. When we recite the blessings over our food and eat with the intention of serving God, we set the purification process into motion and can rectify those sparks.

In his vision of the Third Temple, the prophet Yechezkel speaks of a special Altar in the Sanctuary, referring to it as a table. The verse says, "The Altar was of wood, three cubits high and two cubits long, including its corners. Its rim and its walls were also made of wood. The angel said to me, 'This is the table that is set before God'" (Ezekiel 41:22). The Talmud learns from this that the Altar affects forgiveness. Similarly, a person can affect forgiveness by inviting guests to his table (*Berakhot* 55a).

There are four levels of creation: mineral, vegetable, animal and human. The Altar received all four levels of creation: water (mineral), oil and wine (vegetable), sacrifice (animal), and the work (performed by humans). Therefore, just as the altar affected forgiveness, a person can effect forgiveness as well when he sits at his table and eats from the different levels of creation. The *Ahavas Eitan*[153] explains according to the ARI that, due to Adam's eating from the Tree of Knowledge, sparks of holiness fell into all four levels of creation. When a person eats with holy intentions—that is, to have strength to serve God—he elevates all these sparks found in his food. By reciting the blessings over food, he praises God for each specific creation, and each blessing thereby acts as the vehicle to rectify and elevate those sparks.

Eating in Holiness

A person's attitude toward eating could earn him the World to Come as well as a livelihood in this world. For if a person conducts his meal properly, he will be recorded for good in the uppermost worlds and is also rewarded with increased power and strength when he needs it (*Zohar* II, 154a; *The Aleph-Bet Book*, Eating A:3).

Rebbe Nachman advised us not to consume our food in a hurry like a glutton, because this is behavior befitting to Esav. Esav said, "Let me swallow some of this red, red stuff" (Genesis 25:30). We should get into the habit of eating without haste, calmly, and with manners. We should always eat with the same dignity we would display as if someone important were sitting at the table, even when we eat alone (*Tzaddik* #515).

If a person eats like a glutton, he will be overwhelmed by foolishness. However, if the food a person eats is pure in accordance with the dietary laws and he eats it with dignity, without swallowing it hurriedly, the powers of his mind will be restored and his foolishness will be subdued (LM I, 17:3).

A person who succeeds in breaking his greedy impulses will find peace. Peace will also reign in the realms above, causing

153 *Ein Yaakov, Berakhot,* loc. cit.

a profound and wonderful contentment to reveal itself in the world (LM I, 39). Furthermore, when a person manages to break his desire for food, God will work miracles through him (LM I, 47:1).

It is an especially suitable time to working on ourselves to develop the fear of heaven while eating. We should be careful to take advantage of the moment and cultivate this fear in our hearts (LM II, 77).

Rebbe Nachman strongly advised against eating unripe fruits. When a fruit isn't ripe, it seeks to draw its nourishment from the tree. When one eats a fruit before it is ripened, the sparks of the fruit are still seeking their rectification and complete growth. Therefore, they will draw their sustenance from the person who eats them, and this may cause the person to lose his soul. Saying the blessing over the fruit with *kavanah* will protect a person from harm, even if the fruit wasn't fully ripe (LM II, 88).

Washing one's hands before eating bread

The Talmud emphasizes the importance of washing one's hands for bread. Rav Chisda said, "I washed my hands with sufficient amounts of water and Heaven filled my hands with blessing" (*Shabbos* 62b). Conversely, one who disregards the laws of washing one's hands for bread is worthy of excommunication, will encounter poverty and will even be uprooted from the world.[154] The words of the blessing are, *"Al Netilat Yadayim,"* (על נטילת ידים) forming the acrostic *"ANiY"* (עני) which means a poor person. Thus, we learn the importance of washing and reciting the blessing.

154 Ibid.; see also *Sotah* 4b; *Orach Chaim* 158:9.

Rebbe Nachman once said that the time will come when a simple person who washes his hands for bread will be considered as great a phenomenon as the Baal Shem Tov (*Sichot VeSipurim*, p. 76).

Water represents *daat* (knowledge) as in the verse, "The world will be filled the *daat* of God, as waters cover the sea" (Isaiah 11:9). When a person wants to eat, he must wash his hands in order to use his knowledge to eat properly and elevate himself, rather than fall into foolish gluttony. After washing your hands, it is customary to raise your hands up to be level with your head in order to draw *daat* (LH, *Netilat Yadayim Li'Seudah* 1:2). Furthermore, by elevating our hands, we spread our faith from our hearts to our hands (LM I, 91).

Mizmor L'Dovid

Many people have the custom to recite *Mizmor L'Dovid* (Psalm 23) prior to eating since the psalm speaks of God's provenance and of His sustaining us. Some people recite the chapter before they wash their hands; others between washing and eating the bread; yet others after saying the blessing of *Motzi* and eating some bread. The *Zohar* teaches that even if the table is set and the food is ready, one should still pray for his sustenance (*Mishnah Berurah* 166:3). The ARI writes that one should say this psalm as it contains fifty-seven words, which is the *gematria* of the Hebrew word *ZaN* (זן, nourish or sustain), implying that God gives sustenance to all living things.

The *Motzi*

Our Sages debate whether the blessing on bread should be "*Motzi lechem min haaretz*" (who has brought forth bread from the earth; past tense), or "*HaMotzi lechem min haaretz*" (who brings forth bread from the earth; present tense) (*Berakhot* 38a). In keeping with the opinion that we say *Motzi* (past tense), it is referring to the actual bread God brought forth for Adam and Chavah prior to their eating from the Tree of Knowledge. On the other hand, in keeping with the opinion that we say *HaMotzi* (present tense), it is because God is continuously providing sustenance and He has promised that loaves of bread will grow on the trees in the Land of Israel in the future (*Shabbos* 30b). In conclusion, the preferred and accepted custom is to say *HaMotzi* (present tense).

On a deeper level, the *Etz Yosef* on *Ein Yaakov* states clearly that the word *lechem* cannot be referring to bread alone. God does not bring forth bread from the earth; rather, He brings forth wheat, from which we make bread. Therefore, *lechem* corresponds to a more general term, like "sustenance" or "nourishment." The *Yefeh Einayim*, on the other hand, states that the word *lechem* in this blessing is used in its specific sense, referring to the bread of *Gan Eden.*

The ARI explains the Kabbalistic or spiritual reason behind this blessing: The *gematria* of the word *lechem* (לחם, bread) is 78, which is also the *gematria* of the Divine Name YHVH (26) multiplied by three (of the letters of God's Holy Name, the letter "*Hey*" can be expanded three ways: *Hay* (הא) with an *aleph*; *Hey* with a *HeH* (הה), or *HeY* with a *Yod* (הי); hence times three). As alluded to in the verse spoken metaphorically by the Torah, "Come and partake of My bread" (Proverbs 9:5), *LeCheM* alludes to *LaChMa shel* Torah (bread of Torah) — i.e., direct spiritual sustenance and illumination from God.[155] Furthermore, the ARI tells us that the prefix letter *Heh* of *HaMotzi* refers to both *Hehs* in the Divine Name *YHVH.* This corresponds, respectively, to the *sefirot* of *Binah* (which is

155 *Yalkut Shimoni* 1:406 on Exodus 34:28; *Baal HaTurim* on Leviticus 6:1.

called *haaretz ha'elyonah,* the supernal earth) and *Malkhut* (which is called *haaretz hatachtonah,* the lower earth). Via these two *sefirot,* spiritual sustenance and illumination flow down to us when we say this blessing with proper intent. For this reason, says the ARI, we should emphasize the *Heh* of *HaMotzi* as if it were two *Hehs,* one large and one small (*Shaar HaMitzvot, Eikev,* pp. 95-96).

Clearly, the Sages formulated the words of this blessing (like all others) with exact precision, in such a way that it would contain various levels of meaning at the same time.

There are ten words in the *Motzi* blessing. Therefore, a person should hold the bread with all ten fingers when he recites the blessing. In addition, there are also ten *mitzvot* concerning the making of the bread. They are divided into three categories:

How to treat plants and field animals

1. Don't plow the land with two different animals (e.g., an ox and a mule).
2. Don't plant a mixture of seeds (e.g., wheat and barley).
3. Don't muzzle an ox when it is plowing the field.

Gifts to the poor when harvesting the field

4. Allow the poor to take some of the harvest.
5. Don't return to collect sheaves if you forgot some.
6. Don't take the last fruits off the trees.

Tithes

7. *Terumah,* a portion is given to the *Kohen.*
8. *Maaser,* one tenth is given to the Levi.
9. *Maaser Sheini,* second tithes are eaten in Jerusalem or in certain years given to the poor.

10. *Challah*, a portion of the dough is given to the *Kohen* (*Orach Chaim* 167:4).

Birkhat HaMazon

We are commanded to bless God after eating, as it is written in the Torah, "You will eat and be satisfied, and bless your God for the good land He has given you" (Deuteronomy 8:10). From this commandment, the Talmud learns that we should also bless God before we eat. The reasoning is that if, when we are sated, we should bless God, how much more should we bless Him when we are hungry? (*Berakhot* 35a).

Birkhat HaMazon contains four blessings, corresponding to the four letters of the Divine Name, *YHVH*. The first blessing (*Birkhat HaZan*) was established by Moshe when the Jews received the manna in the desert. The second blessing (*Birkhat HaAretz*) was established by Yehoshua when he brought the children of Israel into the land of their ancestors. The third blessing (*Birkhat Yerushalayim*) was composed by David and Shlomo. King David wrote, "On Israel Your people, and on Jerusalem Your city," while King Shlomo composed, "On the great and holy Temple that bears witness to Your Name." The fourth blessing (*Birkhat HaTov V'Hameitiv*) was composed by Rabban Gamliel and his high court when, after many years, the Jews were finally able to bury the tens of thousands who died at the hands of the Romans in Beitar (*Berakhot* 48b, *Taanit* 31a).

Rebbe Nachman teaches that God is made known in the world through *Birkhat HaMazon*.[156] The source for this statement is the Midrash that speaks of Avraham's hospitality and how he took in all kinds of wayfarers. When they would

156 *The Aleph-Bet Book*, Eating B:3.

thank him before they left, Avraham would direct them to thank God, the creator, from whose beneficence they had partaken (*Bereishit Rabbah* 43:7). God said, "I wasn't recognized in the world until you, Avraham, made My Name known."

By reciting the *Birkhat HaMazon*, we also draw down Divine favor. When the angels saw God showing Divine favor for the Jewish nation, they challenged Him, "Master of the world, it states in Your Bible 'God does not show favor' (Deuteronomy 10:17), and yet behold, You show your favor to the Jewish nation, as it states, 'May God turn His countenance to you and establish peace for you'" (Numbers 6:26). God replied, "How can I not favor the Jewish people? I commanded them, 'You will eat and be satisfied and bless God for the good land He has given you' (Deuteronomy 8:10), yet they are stringent with themselves to bless Me even on a piece of bread the size of an olive" (*Berakhot* 20b). God was proving to the angels that not only do the Jews bless Him when they're supposed to, they also bless God even when they are not yet satiated!

Rebbe Nachman deduces from this Talmudic passage that by eating in holiness (which includes eating kosher foods, reciting the appropriate blessings, and avoiding gluttonous behavior), we can elicit Divine favor, and that the recital of the *Birkhat HaMazon* draws down this Divine favor. Therefore, the verse states, "He [the angel] said to me, 'This is the table that is set before God'" (Ezekiel 41:22). One's countenance shines on account of one's table — i.e., eating in holiness (LM I, 67:2).

Birkhat HaMazon should be recited with fervor and concentration. The story is told that when Rebbe Nachman moved to Uman, his chassidim were gathered around him in his room at a meal, while their wives and daughters sat in an adjacent room. When the meal was finished and it seemed like a long time had passed, the women said, "The men must have *bentched* (recited the *Birkhat HaMazon*) already." Adil, Rebbe Nachman's daughter, said, "With my father's followers, you will hear the *bentching*!" Shortly afterward, they heard the sounds of the men reciting the *bentching* from the next room (*Aveneha Barzel*, p. 34, #47).

Additional Blessings

There are additional blessings we are commanded to say on fragrances and various natural phenomena (such as rainbows, thunder, and comets), as well as the *Shehecheyanu* blessing on new possessions (such as clothes, furniture, or a car.) Why are there so many blessings?

To answer this question, consider the following two verses that appear contradictory. One verse states, "The earth and all that it contains is God's" (Psalms 24:1). Another verse states, "He gave the earth to the children of man" (Psalms 115:16). So, who is the owner of the world, with everything that's in it? Is it God or man?

The Talmud (*Berakhot* 35a-b) reconciles the contradiction by stating that it all depends on whether one said a blessing or not. Before one recites a blessing, "The earth and all it contains is God's." At this time, it is forbidden to take anything from the world because everything belongs to God. However, after one says a blessing, "He gave the earth to the children of man." Now a person may derive pleasure from the world.

Rav Yehudah said in the name of Shmuel, "Whoever receives benefit or pleasure in this world without blessing God for it, it is as if he benefited from things sanctified for heaven." Rabbi Chaninah bar Papa says: "It is as if he has stolen from God!" (ibid.)

This is because before reciting a blessing, everything belongs to God and not to man. But after saying a blessing, God gives the world with everything that's in it to mankind. Only then may a person benefit and derive pleasure from the world.

Rebbe Nachman teaches that we should always bear in mind the eternal World to Come, and not get confused that this corporeal world is our primary existence.[157] That is, when engaging in material life, we should remember the higher calling of life: eternal life. Still, we must take care of our physical needs (such as eating, drinking, and sleeping). These pressures of our material existence occupy our minds and don't leave much time for us to focus on things beyond our daily grind. Therefore, as Reb Noson explains, we recite blessings before partaking of the pleasures of this world. When we bless God, we focus on the eternal God and the eternal world, drawing that idea of sanctity into our physical acts (LH, *Betziat HaPat* 2:2).

Reb Noson encourages us to understand the power of one who utters a blessing. Before one recites a blessing, the item (that he is making the blessing upon) isn't complete; it is like it is not yet fully created. God created the world for His honor, as it states, "All was called [into existence] for My Name's sake; for My glory I have created it, I have formed it, and I have also completed it" (Isaiah 43:7; *Avos* 6:10). Therefore, before someone says a blessing and praises God for creating it, the creation wasn't yet completed. However, when a person recites a blessing, he completes and perfects the creation. It is as if he brings creation from potentiality to actuality, and he becomes a partner in the creation of the world (LH, *Birkhot HaRei'ach* 5:3).

Rebbe Nachman discusses a Kabbalistic concept called the *Noam HaElyon* (Supernal Pleasantness), which flows constantly

157 LM I, 54:1; see also LM II, 2:1.

and offers its blessings to everyone.[158] The reason we don't all feel this blessing is that we need a vessel with which to receive and hold this blessing. The vessel is formed by giving charity (LM II, 71:7).

Reb Noson explains that all pleasant senses in the world (such as the good tastes in food) come from the *Noam HaElyon* and we must return them to their source. We do so via the blessings. This is because blessings and all other forms of praising God are in themselves the *Noam HaElyon*. Therefore, through praises and blessings we return the sweetness and pleasantness of the world to their origin.

Reb Noson adds, "It is impossible to connect with God and to experience the *Noam HaElyon* without blessings and praises." With our praises we elevate the pleasantness of the world to their source, and we simultaneously experience and connect to the sweetness and supernal pleasantness of God Himself. This is referring to the sweet experience that people can feel when they praise God (LH, *Birkhot HaPeiros* 4:1).

158 The reference is to the exalted level of *Binah*. *NoAM* (נעם) carries the numerical value of 160, with the word itself adding up to 161. This is one of the expanded Names of God which is in *Binah*, and קסא equals 161; see Appendix.

CHAPTER 40

Minchah: The Afternoon Prayer

Rabbi Chelbo said in the name of Rav Huna, "A person should be very careful with the *Minchah* prayer. Even Eliyahu the Prophet was only answered at *Minchah* time" (*Berakhot* 6b).

Why does *Minchah*, the Afternoon Prayer, warrant special attention? The other prayers, *Shacharit* and *Maariv*, are recited at convenient times during the day: when people arise in the morning and when they finish their daily routine. But in the middle of the afternoon, people may get too involved with their business affairs and miss the time to pray *Minchah*. Therefore, our Sages warn us that we should be very careful about the *Minchah* prayer and make the effort to recite it within the allotted timeframe.

Tosafot asks, "Why is the Afternoon Prayer called "*Minchah*"? One may think that it is because a *minchah*-offering was brought at that time; however, the *Shacharit* service also had a *minchah*-offering, and we don't call the Morning Prayer "*Minchah*" (*Pesachim* 107a).

Tosafot answers that the prayer is called *Minchah*, for the afternoon when the *minchah*-offering is brought is the most auspicious time to attain Divine favor and for one's prayers to be answered. The Talmud says, "Be careful with the *Minchah* prayer, because even Eliyahu's prayers were answered specifically at the *Minchah* prayer" (*Berakhot* 6b). *Tosafot* explains that Eliyahu's prayers were answered when the afternoon *minchah*-offering was being sacrificed in the temple, a special time of Divine favor.

The Kabbalists teach that the day is divided into four quarters: from nightfall until *chatzos* (midnight); from *chatzos* until daybreak; from daybreak until noon; and from noon until nightfall. Furthermore, each twenty-four-hour period begins at nightfall, as the verse says, "It was evening, it was morning" (Genesis 1:5). The time when night sets in and darkness reigns represents *din* (i.e., judgment, constriction, chaos, or confusion). *Chatzos*, on the other hand, is a time of compassion and kindness, a time when God delights with the souls of the tzaddikim in the Garden of Eden. Those who arise at *chatzos* can receive an illumination of that kindness. This kindness descends throughout the night, and at daybreak, when the sun rises, this kindness spreads throughout the world.

This kindness remains until noon, when the sun begins to set. Noon is a precursor for the evening, when darkness again falls and *din* is present. Thus, *Minchah*, which is recited after noon, represents judgment (*Shaar HaKavanot, Drushei Minchah* 1). As a result, the Kabbalists disagree with what *Tosafot* teaches; apparently, *Minchah* is not a time of Divine favor after all. But the Kabbalists themselves answer this contradiction, saying that although during the weekdays, *Minchah* is a time of judgments, on *Shabbos*, *Minchah* is considered the greatest level of Divine favor.

Prelude to a New Creation

Expanding on the idea that *Minchah* is both a time of constriction and a time of Divine favor, Reb Noson compares each day to a new creation. In order for this new creation to take place, it must replicate the Act of Creation, which began with God constricting His light (*tzimtzum*) in order to create a "Vacated Space." This constriction was necessary because the light of God was ubiquitous and filled everything. Had God not constricted His light to make the Vacated Space, there would be no room for Creation to exist. Similarly, each day, as the sun passes its zenith, the minimizing of the light of the sun and the approaching darkness of night parallels the *tzimtzum*, which is the prerequisite for a new creation. Therefore, the time of *Minchah* represents the *tzimtzum* before the creation of a new day (LH, *Minchah* 4).

The Vacated Space is so-called because it seems to be void of Godliness. Indeed, God constricted His light from that space in order to "make room" for Creation. However, the truth is that no place can exist without Godliness to sustain it. Therefore, God's light must be in that void nevertheless. But if it is there, then it can't be called a Vacated Space! This is the paradox of the Vacated Space.

To understand the concept of the Vacated Space, a person needs to accept God's presence with faith (LM I, 64:2-3). Those who attempt to understand it intellectually can succumb to all sorts of heresies and philosophies that deny God's existence and ongoing involvement with the world. Prayer means that a person has faith in God to answer his requests. However, when there are constrictions that do not allow for answers, one must be very careful to exercise faith and not rely on intellectual reasoning.

This explains why our Sages instituted the Afternoon Prayer and advised us very strongly not to skip it. The afternoon is considered a time of greater judgment than night itself. Why? Because at night the darkness is total, while the afternoon still has some light. This means that the approaching constriction of light is actually the preparation for the entire next day. That constriction lasts but a moment, yet an influx of God's light fills the void and harbors the new day—the new creation! We understand from this that any challenges that we encounter are really the means for us to recognize the need for a "new creation" and prepare an appropriate response. That response is prayer, as we ask God to help us grow and do the right thing. This is the idea of the *Minchah* prayer.

On Shabbos, however, all judgments and constrictions become void. Therefore, *Minchah* on Shabbos afternoon is a time of great Divine favor when a person can attain great spiritual (and material) benefits.

The word *MiNChah* shares the letters of the Hebrew word for rest, *MeNuChah*. This connotes the sunset, a time when the sun is going to its "resting place" for the night. At that moment, the sun bows before God having completed its daily cycle. The commentaries note that we should learn from the sun how to be consistent in our devotions to God.

There are some who preface *Minchah* with a short prayer. "I thank You, God, that You allowed me to see the morning sun. May it be Your will that I see it set."

The prayers for *Minchah* include:

1. Reciting the Daily Offering and the *Ketoret* (as these sacrifices were brought before nightfall)
2. *Ashrey* (for the third time; see Chapter 16)
3. The *Amidah* (see Chapters 27-31)
4. *Tachanun* (see Chapter 33)
5. *Aleinu* (see Chapter 37)

The Patriarch Yitzchak established the Afternoon prayer of *Minchah* (*Berachot* 26b). Yitzchak corresponds to *Gevurah* (i.e., judgment and constriction). The afternoon, as it wanes, also represents constriction (as explained above).

Rebbe Nachman taught: There are people whose minds and prayers are blemished; they are in the mode of constriction. The constricted, blemished mind is when one harbors the attributes of anger and cruelty (and even displaced compassion). In contrast, a good mind, which produces proper prayers, is when one has compassion in its proper form. When a person's prayers are in the mode of constriction, his prayers will be captured by the Other Side. To counter this, we require a constricted prayer of a different nature—a holy prayer—that fools that Other Side, while only *appearing* to be constricted and blemished. A primary example of this is a "judgmental prayer," when a tzaddik prays by demanding things from God.

A judgmental prayer is seen as a demand from God, "as if it is due me." The prayers are not supplications (asking for God's compassion) but demands. These types of prayers are food for the Other Side as it represents challenges against God. Only a great tzaddik can recite a judgmental prayer, and when he does, his prayers are also swallowed up by the Other Side. This is because the Other Side seeks to swallow and capture any prayer that is in the form of constriction. But, as Rebbe Nachman describes it, the Tzaddik's prayer gets caught in the *Sitra Achara's* (the evil inclination's) throat, and he isn't able to swallow it. So as the *Sitra Achara* begins to reject the Tzaddik's prayer, all the souls and prayers that the Other Side already swallowed are rejected and freed as well (LM II, 8:2-3).

It is risky for the average person to pray in this brazen way. However, there are times when everyone prays holy prayers of constriction, and these prayers can have an effect, similar to the prayers of tzaddikim. For example, the prayers on Days of

Judgment, such as *Rosh HaShanah*. Even when a person prays pleadingly, begging for God's compassion—which that is how one should pray, since the day is a day of judgment—his prayer has a nature of a judgmental prayer. Another example happens every day by the *Minchah* prayer. Yitzchak represents *Gevurah* (i.e., judgment), and he established the Afternoon prayer (i.e., a judgmental prayer). Therefore, if we are careful with *Minchah*, we too can emerge from the realms of evil and even elevate the souls of others back to God.

Therefore, our Sages teach, "A person should be very careful with the *Minchah* prayer" (*Berakhot* 6b).

CHAPTER 41

Maariv: *The Evening Prayer*

Shacharit (the Morning Prayer) and *Minchah* (the Afternoon Prayer) are considered obligatory prayers. *Maariv* (the Evening Prayer) was established as an optional prayer,[159] but has since been made an obligatory prayer (*Tur, Orach Chaim* 235). The *Shelah* writes that it is very beneficial to join the day and night with Torah study and many synagogues have a short study period between *Minchah* and *Maariv*.

The Sages declared the Evening Prayer to be optional in order to teach us that even amid the darkest times, we must never give up hope in the power and potency of prayer. Rather, even in our darkest moments, when we feel God is not with us, we must make sure to arouse ourselves with a powerful yearning for God precisely at times like these. In this way, we awaken the desire to pray to God from within; we do something because we want to do it, not because we are commanded to. This is the reason for prayer: to arouse the desire in us to connect with God, even when we are not commanded directly (LH, *Tefillat Minchah* 7:82).

Reb Noson explains that nighttime parallels judgments and constrictions, which represent challenging times. Daytime represents brightness, expansion, and hope. The Patriarch Yaakov, who established the Evening Prayer, did so with the

159 *Berakhot* 27b; *Rambam, Hilkhot Tefillah* 3:7, 6:7; *Shulchan Arukh, Orach Chaim* 69:1.

understanding that even if a person feels trapped in the darkest moments of his life, where no solution seems evident, he can always find hope through prayer (LH, *Minchah* 7:82).

The ARI emphasizes the importance of closing one's eyes completely from the beginning of the Evening Prayer until the conclusion of the *Amidah.*[160] At night, the forces of judgment are free to roam the world and entice human beings to sin. We can overcome these forces by "closing our eyes" to the illusion that this world has any intrinsic reality. With our eyes closed, we can meditate on God's oneness and merge into the supernal unity that is entirely and utterly good. At that level, all judgments, sufferings, and afflictions, are automatically nullified. Reaching this level is the perfection of prayer; it is the goal and purpose of all existence (LH, *Tefillat Arvit* 4:2).

One is allowed to pray *Maariv* from nightfall (when three stars are visible) until daybreak. However, in extenuating circumstances, one can begin to pray *Maariv* from immediately after sunset, if necessary. Some people offer the following prayer prior to *Maariv*. "May it be Your will, God, that just as You took me out of darkness and allowed me to see light (the morning), so too, may I merit that You take me out of this darkness into light."

וְהוּא רַחוּם
He Who is merciful

The verse says about Jerusalem, "The righteous will dwell in it" (Isaiah 1:21). Rashi explains that the Daily Sacrifice in the morning (*Shacharit*) would bring forgiveness for those

160 *Shaar HaKavanot, Drushey Tefillat Arvit, drush aleph.*

sins committed at night, and the afternoon Daily Sacrifice (*Minchah*) would bring forgiveness for daytime sins. However, there is a gap of time between *Minchah* and *Maariv*. Therefore, it was instituted to say "*V'Hu Rachum*" (Psalms 78:38) to request forgiveness for any sins committed in the interim. The verse contains thirteen words corresponding to the Thirteen Attributes of Mercy, invoking the compassion of God.

בָּרְכוּ אֶת ה' הַמְבֹרָךְ

Bless God

The Midrash states that there is a certain angel in Heaven whose job is to oversee that the other angels bless God. During the day, the word *Emet* (truth) is displayed on its forehead, while in the evening, *Emunah* (faith) is engraved on its forehead. When we pray *Borekhu* it is a sign for that angel to switch signs and that reminds the other angels that their time has come to bless God.

The Blessings of the *Shema*

We are commanded to recite the *Shema* in the morning and at night as is written, "When you lay down and when you arise" (Deuteronomy 6:7). Furthermore, there is a verse that states, "Seven times a day I praise you" (Psalms 119:164). Based upon this verse our Sages learn that we recite seven blessings over the *Shema*: three blessings during *Shacharit* in the morning and four blessings during *Maariv* in the evening.

הַמַּעֲרִיב עֲרָבִים

He brings on evenings

The first evening blessing, *HaMaariv Aravim* (He brings on evenings), parallels the first morning blessing of *Yotzer*

Ohr (He creates light). This blessing speaks about the One God Who created light and darkness (see Chapter 19). It may appear as if night and day were created God forbid, by two separate deities. Therefore, we praise God for both to expressively state that both light and darkness come from the One God. This is the message of the *Shema*: declaration of our faith in One God, representing the truth of our faith and religion.

Rebbe Nachman teaches that in unity, there is truth. After all, there can only be one absolute truth (LM I, 51:2). Reb Noson expands on this idea, explaining that with plurality there is a chance for falsehood to rear itself. Therefore, although the blessings of the *Shema* speak of the plurality in creation, we praise and bless God in order to reveal—and make known to all—that all change, including changes in time, come from Him alone. For all change is rooted in His simple unity (LH, *Ribit* 5:46).

There is a vast difference between light and darkness. What is clear to one is misunderstood by another, and *vice versa*. Rebbe Nachman refers to light and darkness as the difference between good and evil. One must be very careful when discerning between the two. He cites the Midrash that Pinchas and Bilaam were both able to fly (Rashi on Numbers 31:6). Pinchas made use of God's Holy Name, whereas Bilaam's powers came from sorcery. Thus, we see that two people can do the same thing, but the difference between them is vast. We learn from this to be very discerning as we evaluate the acts and deeds we wish to perform (LM I, 234:1).

אַהֲבַת עוֹלָם
Eternal Love

The second blessing is based on the verse, "[God says,] I love you [Israel] with an everlasting love" (Jeremiah 31:2).

The love God has for every Jew is an eternal love that never is negated. It is as if God looks at every single Jew as if he is God's only child and He will never abandon that love! This blessing, too, parallels the second morning blessing which speaks of the eternal love that God has for the Jewish Nation.

Therefore, God, we will meditate on Your statutes... For they are our very life and the length of our days

We are asking to receive life through the Torah. As our Sages teach, "If one is worthy, the Torah becomes an elixir of life for him; if he is not worthy, the very same Torah becomes a deadly potion for him" (*Yoma* 72b). It is important to declare God's unity now as we prepare to say the *Shema* and to be included within it. We ask to be worthy that God's light, before it descends, be impregnated with blessing and life. Then we can be sure that it will be directed down to us as life and blessing (LH, *Kriat Shema* 4:10).

And we will rejoice in the teachings of Your Torah and Your commandments forevermore

The focal point of our Torah study is the joy with which we engage in *mitzvot*, because the true and perfect way to serve God is when we are happy when we perform the *mitzvot*. Joy is what creates the feeling of fulfillment and contentment (LH, *Piryah VeRivyah* 3:8).

At this point in the *Maariv* prayer we recite the *Shema* (see Chapters 21-26). The Talmud debates whether we should read the third passage of the *Shema* at night because the passage refers to donning *tzitzit* and the obligation of *tzitzit* is a daytime mitzvah. However, the Sages still obligate a person to say the complete *Shema* because the passage mentions the Exodus, which should be remembered at night, too. As Rabbi Elazar ben Azaryah said, "I am now as a man of seventy years, but I did not merit to have [this third passage] about the Exodus recited at night until Ben Zoma taught, '*All* the days of your life—including the nights.'" (*Berakhot* 12b).

Reb Noson explains that the Exodus from Egypt represents the exodus of each person from his personal exile, especially that of immorality. The Exodus in Egypt raised the Jews' level of morality and allowed them to attain a level high enough to be able to receive the Torah. Similarly, each person merits to attain high levels of morality and Torah by emerging from immoral thoughts and deeds.

The main harshness of this long exile is that we have fallen from our lofty levels of morality and have plunged into the depths of immorality. The evil inclination is constantly on the attack, and we often find ourselves trapped, with no hope of escape. Most importantly, even at nighttime, when things seem darkest and impossible to overcome, we must strengthen ourselves with the knowledge that God is with us, and He wants to illumine our lives with His light and to draw us close to Him. Therefore, we recall the Exodus with the hope that we will merit to emerge from our personal exiles and challenging moments (LH, *Yayin Nesekh* 4:21-22).

אֱמֶת וֶאֱמוּנָה כָּל זֹאת

True and faithful for us is all this...

The third blessing of the *Shema*, *Emunah kol zot*, parallels the third blessing of the morning *Shema*, speaking about the redemption from Egypt and all our other oppressors. This blessing also concludes with *Ga'al Yisrael* (He redeemed Israel).

During the daytime *Shema*, we declare that God is *Emet* (True) and bless God's attribute of truth. At nighttime, we declare that *Emunah* (faithfulness) is God's attribute. Rebbe Nachman explains that light corresponds to truth, which is obvious and clear unlike darkness, when we cannot see, and a person must rely on faith alone. When a person walks in the dark, he does not know what will come next. But faith is so powerful; it can carry a person as if he can actually see clearly—i.e., that which he believes in. Instead of "seeing is believing," it transforms the person who has faith into "believing is seeing" (LM I, 62:5).

הַשְׁכִּיבֵנוּ
Let us lie down

Hashkiveinu is the fourth blessing of the evening *Shema.* We are asking God to help us sleep peacefully and to be guarded from any danger that may occur when we are asleep. This is why the blessing concludes with "God, Who guards His nation Israel, forever." The reason we need this extra blessing is that at nighttime, the *mazikim* (demons and destroyers) are given freedom to prowl the world and wherever they can find a place to cause damage, they will inflict damages. When a person sleeps, he is said to be in a situation of "constricted consciousness," whereas a person who is awake can be aware of what is taking place around him. In a constricted state of consciousness, a person is subject to errors, mistakes, and damages. Therefore, we plead with God to protect us from damages while we are asleep.

Correct us through the good counsel that comes only from You

Rebbe Nachman explains that a person must say *Hashkiveinu* with great emotion and feeling from the very depths of his heart. This is a most precious prayer. We must always beg that God has mercy and grants us good counsel and advice, that we may be worthy of knowing what is right (*Rebbe Nachman's Wisdom* #238).

Remove the heavenly accuser from before us and from behind us

Rabbi Yitzchak of Atvotsk[161] teaches us not to become depressed from the phrases "From before us" (i.e., before we commit a sin) and "From behind us" (i.e., even if we have committed a sin). Rather we should turn to God anyway and not let the forces of evil distract us from serving Him.

Though one should take care never to speak between *Gaal Yisrael* and the *Amidah,* the insertion of the blessing of *Hashkiveinu* is not considered an interruption. That is because this fourth blessing is considered an extension of our prayer for redemption. When God slew the Egyptians, the Jews who were held up in their homes were constantly praying to God to protect them.

The *Maariv* prayer concludes with *Amidah* (see Chapters 28-32). The customs vary according to which *nusach* you pray. Ashkenazi Jews say *Aleinu* and then conclude with *Kaddish.* Most Sephardic Jews recite Psalm 121 and then say *Kaddish* before *Aleinu.* In the Land of Israel, those who pray according to *Nusach Sephard* recite the psalm, while those in the diaspora do not.

For those who say the psalm, the *Kaddish* is then followed by saying *Borekhu.* As with *Shacharit,* the custom is to say *Borekhu* for the benefit of those latecomers who might have missed the earlier *Borekhu.*

161 A Breslover chassid in pre-war Poland who was murdered in the Holocaust.

CHAPTER 42

Kiddush Levanah and Sefirat HaOmer

Kiddush Levanah – Sanctifying the New Moon

It was taught in the school of Rabbi Yishmael: "If the Jews only merited to greet their Father in Heaven just once a month it would be sufficient" (*Sanhedrin* 42a). Our Sages learn from this teaching that sanctifying the new moon is equivalent to greeting God in Heaven! Originally, God created the sun and the moon as equal luminaries (Genesis 1:16). The moon complained before God saying, "Two kings (i.e., the sun and the moon) cannot use the same crown." As a result, God diminished the size of the moon (*Chullin* 60b), causing it to wax and wane each month.

Unlike the nations of the world who count their years according to a solar calendar, the Jewish nation counts according to a lunar calendar. Therefore, Jewish festivals are calculated according to the lunar cycle, and the moon, representing the Jewish nation, is "celebrated" each month. Each month, as soon as the New Moon is visible in the sky, it is customary to say a blessing known as *Kiddush Levanah*, Sanctifying the Moon.

Ideally, the blessing should be said when the moon is clearly visible, but if it is a cloudy night, one may recite the blessing as long as the moon can be discerned through the clouds or at least an impression of the moon can be seen. The blessing can be said from the third day up until the fifteenth day of the Hebrew month.

It is customary, whenever possible, to say the *Kiddush Levanah* on a Saturday Night, as soon as Shabbos is over, because we are already wearing respectable clothes and it honors the moon, which represents the *Shekhinah* (Divine Presence) and *Malkhut*. The ARI explains that the reason for saying *Kiddush Levanah* on a Saturday Night is because that was the night that the Temple was destroyed and the *Shekhinah* descended into exile. Therefore, by sanctifying the moon on a monthly basis, we communicate to the *Shekhinah* that by the time of the redemption, all will be renewed, including *Malkhut*, the moon, and the Jewish nation.[162] Reb Noson adds that one of the reasons a New Moon is called *Rosh ChoDeSH* (ראש חדש) is because it shares the root of the word *ChaDaSH* (חדש), new, implying the power of renewal (LH, *Rosh Chodesh* 6:17).

The Blessing of *Kiddush Levanah*

This blessing contains references to the Creation and the entire solar system, which were placed in their positions to do the job of illuminating the world. Their function is to orbit the earth at specific intervals by which we can measure time. The blessing is mostly directed toward the moon's cycle, although God diminished the moon and made it smaller than He originally intended. The moon will be restored to its original status, but it still performs its daily cycle with joy and happiness.

To the moon it was said, it will renew

Just as the moon wanes and waxes, there will come a time when we will be redeemed from the suffering we endured throughout the long exile. Reb Noson writes that the life of a

162 *Pri Etz Chaim, Shaar Rosh Chodesh*, 3, p. 461.

person mirrors the phases of the moon which waxes and wanes constantly. Therefore, the blessing of *Kiddush Levanah* was instituted to show that the changes that occur throughout life are all from God (LH, *Ribit* 5:47).

Furthermore, the diminishing of the moon is a phase where it reaches its lowest point at the end of the month. However, exactly at that moment, it begins to renew itself! So too, this is a hint to each and every person that even in a person's lowest moments, there is hope for renewal, as in the blessing, "We will renew ourselves like the moon." Each month, as we bless the moon, it returns a bit to its original state and when *Mashiach* comes, the moon will be fully restored. Just as the moon is renewed each month, we believe that God will renew the Jewish nation. The power of renewal is within each and every one of us (LH, *Rosh Chodesh* 6:20).

כשם שאני רוקד (Just as I dance)

The first paragraph, *Barukh Yotzreikh* (Bless the creator), contains four praises to God, corresponding to the Four Worlds through which we ascend by performing the *mitzvot.* It is customary to dance when saying *Kiddush Levanah,* as a sign of the joy with which we perform the *mitzvot.* The next verse says that fear should descend upon our enemies. Just as we cannot touch the *Shekhinah,* so too, we pray that our enemies shall not be able to harm us. Reb Noson explains that the main way to rectify the blemish of the moon (the diminishing of the moon during its monthly cycle) is with joy, hence the practice of dance during *Kiddush Levanah* (LH, *Shabbos* 7:49).

דוד מלך ישראל חי וקים (King David lives)

King David represents *Malkhut,* the Kingdom of Holiness, which is signified by the moon. Just as the moon waxes and wanes, so too the Kingdom of David (*Malkhut*) became strengthened and then lost its power. Furthermore, just as the moon returns to its full glory month after month, God promises that the Kingdom of David will return to rule again, despite the lengthy exile.

שלום עליכם (Peace be unto you)

We continue the prayer by saying one to another, *Shalom Aleikhem,* which alludes to increasing friendships with joy. Despite the fact that the diminishing of the moon implies jealousy, assaults and accusations, we say *Shalom Aleikhem* to express peace. Furthermore, although we ask that our enemies refrain from causing us harm and that they be overtaken with immense fear, to our fellow Jews, we pronounce, "peace."

Rebbe Nachman teaches that the root of repentance is in *Rosh Chodesh*. Why? Because when God diminished the moon He said, "Bring a sacrifice for Me [too], for I diminished the moon" (*Chullin* 60b). Since God Himself asks for forgiveness on *Rosh Chodesh,* He placed the power of repentance into *Rosh Chodesh* (LM I, 10:9).

Sefirat HaOmer

During the period of the Temple there was a special mitzvah to bring a sacrifice known as the *Omer*. The sacrifice consisted of barley, and once offered, it allowed people to eat from the new harvests. It was brought on the second day of Pesach when we begin counting for a period of forty-nine days, until *Shavuot*. Today, in the absence of the Temple, we still count forty-nine days of the *Omer*, from *Pesach* until *Shavuot*. This is known as *Sefirat HaOmer* (Counting the *Omer*).

The Talmud teaches that there are fifty gates of *Binah* (understanding) (*Rosh HaShanah* 21b). Since God contrasts important concepts, we learn there are fifty gates of understanding and purity which parallel the gates of impurity as well.

As the verse says, "One to contrast the other" (Ecclesiastes 7:14). When the Jews were in Egypt, they descended to the forty-ninth gate of impurity. Had they remained in Egypt for longer, they would have fallen to the fiftieth gate of impurity, without hope for redemption. Therefore, God freed the Jews from Egyptian bondage before they could sink even further, and we celebrate the occasion on *Pesach*, the festival of freedom.

God promised the Jews that when they leave Egypt, they would receive the Torah (Exodus 3:12), but how could the nation receive Godly wisdom and sanctified teachings if they were steeped in impurity? Therefore, God enabled the Jewish nation to ascend from any impurities and enter the Gates of Holiness over the fifty days it took from leaving Egypt until receiving the Torah. Today, the mitzvah to count the forty-nine days of the *Omer* is meant to help us depart from the gates of impurity and to enter the gates of understanding (as the fiftieth day, *Shavuot*, represents the highest level of understanding.)

During the fifty days of counting the *Omer*, we take one step at a time as we ascend the spiritual ladder towards perfected *daat*, in order to receive the Torah on *Shavuot* (LH, *Pikadon* 4:4).

בָּרוּךְ... עַל סְפִירַת הָעוֹמֶר
Blessed ... to Count the *Omer*

When we count the *Omer*, we count both the days and the weeks. For example, "Today is eleven days, which is one week and four days in the *Omer*."

When counting the *Omer*, one should take care not to miss even a single day. If one forgot to count at night, then he can count the *Omer* during the day (but without a blessing). Afterward he can continue counting again, each night with a blessing. However, if one forgot to count an entire day, he should continue counting but without the blessing. In addition, since the days are counted at the onset of the night, in order for there to be "complete days," a person should wait a full twenty-four-hour period between counting (Leviticus 23:15). Therefore, one should count as early as possible after nightfall.

The period of the *Omer* is meant for us to take stock of our lives and examine the areas which require improvement. After all, these days represent the period where we emerged from "slavery and bondage" to actually become a 'free' nation, people who are able to control their lives and destiny. The ARI discusses the mystical intentions of the *Sefirat HaOmer* and its incredible impact upon our souls. He explains that every day there is a different type of Godly intellect which is given to us in order to prepare us to receive the Torah anew on Shavuot. The Counting of the *Omer* is a process to rectify and elevate *Malkhut.*[163]

Reb Noson points out that the mitzvah of the *Omer* was a sacrifice brought from barley (which is used more as animalistic food), as opposed to wheat (which is used more for human consumption). Why is animal fodder specifically used for this sacrifice?

We use barley to teach us that we should be like an animal—but in a holy way. That is, we should recognize the weakness of man's intellect and realize that the only true body of knowledge is the lessons of the Torah, so that a person accepts that his opinion is nullified before the view and the laws of the Torah. He accepts the Torah teachings without question because he recognizes the limitations of his mind and how distant he is from the true way of thinking. About such

163 *Pri Etz Chaim, Shaar Sefirat HaOmer*, 7, pp. 531-538.

people the verse says, "I am a fool; I don't know. I am like an animal" (Psalms 73:22).

Sometimes people transgress the rules of the Codes. They think that they are wiser than the Sages and can decide which laws are important and which are secondary. They can be too lenient or overly stringent. Erring in either direction means that a person thinks his personal opinion counts. Being an animal (in its correct way) means to humbly say, "I don't know anything. All I know is that if the Torah says to be stringent, I will do so; and if the Torah says to be lenient, I will do that. I am not wiser than an animal. Torah tells me how to think and how to act."

The purpose of counting of the *Omer* is to attain the correct form of being like an "animal." We distance ourselves from animalistic behaviors and drives, yet we attach ourselves to the awareness that only the Torah's mindset counts. When we follow that ideal approach, we will merit true intellect and perceive life and the world correctly.

Following a more simple, straightforward approach, Reb Noson explains that the mitzvah of counting the *Omer* is to teach us that each day of a person's life is set and counted and that for every day a person will have to account for what his actions were. No day is meant to go to waste. Therefore, we cannot truly accept the Torah — except if we accept that each day counts and we do our best to make the most of it (LH, *Pikadon* 4:5).

CHAPTER 43

The Bedtime Shema

God created man with the necessity to sleep. Sleep helps a person renew himself—both in body and mind. As Jews, our intention when sleeping is to rest in order to be refreshed and have strength to serve God. The verse states, "Know God in all your ways" (Proverbs 3:6). This includes mundane activities, such as eating and sleeping. Therefore, even when we sleep, it is considered as if we are serving God.[164] The Midrash teaches that the verse, "God saw it was very good" (Genesis 1:31), refers to sleep. With rest, a person can rise and serve God (*Bereishit Rabbah* 9:6).

Rebbe Nachman addresses the necessity of sleep by speaking about repentance and elaborating on how rest strengthens the intellect (LM I, 35:1-6). He explains that repentance entails returning an object to where it was taken from. *Chokhmah* is seen as the beginning and root of all Creation. Therefore, to repent, a person must return to the root of all things, to *Chokhmah*.

According to Rebbe Nachman, a person who possesses *Chokhmah* is consciously aware of God in all situations. Rebbe Nachman explains that one's soul and one's intellect are considered as one unit. So, the renewal of the intellect—i.e., renewal of the soul—is by means of sleep, as in the verse, "They are renewed every morning; abundant is Your faithfulness"

164 *Shaar HaKavanot, Drushei HaLailah* 4, p. 348.

(Lamentations 3:23). Therefore, while sleeping, the mentalities (i.e., the soul) enter into faith.

Reb Noson writes that the essential battle for Godliness takes place in the mind, which is being endlessly besieged by thoughts relating to extraneous wisdoms or evil desires. To repent and return to holiness, which in our context is returning to *Chokhmah,* one must wage a continuous and often wearying battle. Therefore, sleep is a necessity, as it enables a person to rest his mind and renew it (*Torat Natan* 35:3).

Reb Noson adds that a person does not need a lot of sleep because every hour spent sleeping is "time that never returns." Indeed, losing hours on too much sleep is worse than losing a great treasure, as it says, "There being no loss like the loss of time" (*Likutey Tefilot*). In fact, the same is true of time idled away, for the person who sits around wasting time is no better off than if he were sleeping (*Mishnah Berurah* 583:9). Rather, Reb Noson says, a person should sleep just enough to rest his mind, in order to possess greater energy to serve God. As for how much sleep is the right amount, it differs from person to person and within a person's lifetime. Therefore, as Reb Noson points out, the best thing a person can do is ask God to help him sleep just the right amount in order for him to maintain his health and well-being.

At night, when a person lies down to sleep, he should think about how his soul is in the process of leaving him and returning to the Master of all, for at night, everything in the world returns to its root and the forces of night (*kelipot*) take whatever is their due. Hence the soul returns to its root and the body lies dormant like a stone. During the night, the body attracts the forces of the Other Side, which render the hands impure, so that upon rising in the morning one must wash them (see Chapter 5). In addition, during the night, the souls of those who refrain from sin (i.e., the tzaddikim) ascend and return to their root in *Malkhut,* which is adorned by their good deeds.

Once the soul is renewed, it returns with new vitality (i.e., a person is reborn). The *Zohar* teaches that the renewal of the soul occurs not directly in *Chokhmah,* as one would imagine, since it is the root of everything, but rather through *Malkhut,* which supervises the soul's ascent. As the ARI teaches, when a person has sinned during the day, the *kelipot* restrain his soul from ascending and being renewed.

This is the reason that reciting the bedtime *Shema* before going to sleep is so important. The *Shema,* as a proclamation of our faith in God, has the power to vanquish the forces of the night and clear the way for the soul to ascend.[165] The time for this renewal is specifically at night (the time of *Malkhut*), when the *kelipot* reign. After reciting *Shema,* a person then goes to sleep so as not to be overwhelmed by these forces. While asleep, his soul ascends through *Malkhut* and reconnects to its root (i.e., *Chokhmah*) where it is renewed.

Reb Noson explains that "night" refers to more than just nighttime; it includes all those dark times in a person's life when a person is confused and otherwise mentally constricted. For when *Chokhmah* (i.e., an aspect of daylight) prevails, people know what to do (LM I, 1:2). But when a person is bewildered and his mind is overwrought (i.e., tired), he must go to sleep and renew his energies. Like the night, sleep is also conceptually a constricted mental state. As opposed to *Chokhmah,* which is clear knowledge, sleep corresponds to faith. Previously we mentioned that the difference between faith and wisdom is that faith only applies in those places where one cannot understand, where wisdom is lacking. Therefore, when a person feels overwhelmed by doubts and confusions, he must not resort to

165 *Shaar HaKavanot, Drushei HaLaylah* 5, p. 354.

his intellect (i.e., *Chokhmah*) to answer them. Rather, he needs to put aside his intellect and rely on faith.

Faith corresponds to the *Malkhut* of Holiness, the Kingdom of God. By accepting God's Kingship and Sovereignty, one displays his faith in God. The soul ascends to *Malkhut,* where it is scrutinized before being allowed to ascend further and reconnect to its root. Moreover, the greater effort a person puts into guarding one's mind from extraneous wisdoms and seeking true *Chokhmah* during the day, the greater the ascent his soul will experience when reconnecting at night to its root.

This is all the more reason to recite the *Shema* before going to sleep. As the *Shema* is our proclamation of faith in God, reciting it forges a bond between the soul and *Malkhut,* which is itself an aspect of faith. Thus, strengthening faith before sleep enables one to enter the realm of faith (i.e., *Malkhut*) with greater strength and receive a greater degree of renewal (*Torat Natan* #35:4-5). Reb Noson adds that this faith is innate to every Jew. It remains with him always—even when asleep and even when his efforts in serving God are "asleep." However, through this faith, his intellect is eventually renewed (when he awakes) so that he emerges from his confusion to recognize God with true *Chokhmah* and revitalized devotion (*Torat Natan* #35:6).

The importance of the *Shema* prayer

At night, when a person goes to sleep, his soul ascends on high. Since the soul is the guardian of the body, it leaves the body unprotected. Reciting the *Shema* thus serves as the protection for the person when he sleeps.

Our Sages speak about reciting the *Shema* before lying down to sleep. Even if a person already recited *Shema* in *Maariv,* he should recite the three passages of the *Shema* again. There are several variations of the bedtime *Shema* prayer, each equally acceptable. However, the most important sections are the *Shema* and the blessing, *HaMapil* (He Who makes sleep fall upon me). When a person sleeps his soul ascends and gives an accounting before the Heavenly Tribunal for his deeds of that day. The ARI writes that a person should confess before God over all that he might have done wrong during the day so that he is able to retire with repentance and become pure before he sleeps. After confession, a person can sleep comfortably knowing his soul will ascend to the correct place. A person should also forgive anyone who may have harmed or aggravated him during the day. After all, we are going before the Heavenly Tribunal; if you want them to be forgiving, we need to be forgiving as well (*Zohar* I, 201b).

The bedtime *Shema* has many benefits, as our Sages taught, "Whoever recites the bedtime *Shema* it is as if he is holding a double-edged sword in his hand! Whoever recites the Shema prior to sleeping, causes the *mazikim* (i.e., demons and evil spirits) to stay away from him" (*Berakhot* 5a). The ARI explains that reciting the bedtime *Shema* serves to "kill off" and remove the sparks from the Other Side. This *Shema* is the double-edged sword which can help repair any damage done by the *mazikim* and protect a person from further harm. This is not just a Kabbalistic teaching. Rashi comments on the verse, "He does not lay down until he eats of the prey" (Numbers 23:24) and explains that the Jewish nation does not lay down to sleep until he devours the *mazikim*. How? By reciting the bedtime *Shema*.

The Talmud derives this from the verses, "Let the devotees be *joyful in glory*, let them sing aloud on their beds. The great praises of God in their mouths, and a two-edged sword in their hand" (Psalms 149:5-6). To be "joyful in glory" refers to saying the *Shema* before going to sleep on their beds. Previously

(Chapter 25), we mentioned how reciting the *Shema* can help a person overcome his immoral thoughts (LM I, 36:4). The word, "glory" is connected to purity and morality (LM I, 11:3), and thus it refers to a person being able to sleep with purity and to have moral dreams.

The *Shema* protects from immorality

When we sleep, we fall from a state of awareness into a state of restricted consciousness. Not being aware of what takes place around us, we are exposed to the forces of evil. These forces bring about nocturnal emissions, the impurities of immorality, which lead to further distancing a person from God. Therefore, reciting the *Shema* prior to sleep is thus a very powerful tool in protecting a person from immorality.

The ARI writes that even if a person commits the worst types of sin, he does not create *mazikim* as terrible as those who have nocturnal emissions. One who does so creates *mazikim*, who envelop a person and cause suffering and problems. As the ARI explains, the blemish of wasted seed is a blemish of the mind — there is no other physical body involved. This seed, having nowhere to go, allows for bounty and blessing to go to the Other Side, who takes that blessing for itself. The result is that the seed, which could have formed a child, goes to the *kelipot* (forces of evil). Since seed is life-giving, it will eventually emerge as a living being, but in the realm of evil — neither moral, nor good. It is extremely difficult for such a person who has committed this sin to ever see the Divine Presence. Much repentance must be done in order to redeem those drops of semen (i.e., the sparks of holiness) which were given over to the Other Side.[166]

166 *Shaar HaKavanot, Drushei HaLailah* 7, p. 363-365.

Reb Noson explains further that when nocturnal emissions occur, they are a blemish of the *brit* (i.e., morality). Reciting the *Shema* is a protection from immorality, since there are twelve words in the *Shema* and *Barukh Shem*, which correspond to the Twelve Tribes of the Children of Israel. As they were tzaddikim, their merit helps to protect a person from a blemished *brit*. This is the reason we say, "Let my bed be perfect before You," in the blessing of *HaMapil*. The twelve tribes represent a "perfect bed," and since they were all tzaddikim, we pray that merit will protect us too. This is also why during the bedtime *Shema* we recite the verse, "Here is the bed of King Shlomo, sixty warriors surround it ... all hold swords, they are practiced in battle" (Songs 3:7). The sword refers to the double-edged sword that protects the person while he sleeps. They are "practiced in battle" which means they can hold their own in morality and guarding their covenants because they studied Torah and are well-versed in it (LH, *Kriat Shema al HaMitah* 1).

It is customary to conclude *Shema* with the verse, "In Your hands I deposit my spirit; You have redeemed me, God of truth, trust and faith." (Psalms 31:6), Reb Noson explains[167] that when we go to sleep, we deposit our spirit into the (bank of) *Emunah* (faith), which is referred to as "hands," as the verse says, "And his hands were faith" (Exodus 17:12).

167 LH, *Kriat Shema al HaMitah* 2.

PART IV

Shabbos and *Rosh Chodesh*

CHAPTER 44

Erev Shabbos: Preparation for Shabbos

Our Sages teach, "Whoever prepares for Shabbos will eat on Shabbos. But one who does not prepare for Shabbos, what will he eat on Shabbos?" (*Avodah Zarah* 3a). Throughout the Talmud and Codes of Law, we find many suggestions and laws that apply to our preparations for Shabbos.[168]

In the *Shema* we say, "Place these words of Mine on your heart." The *Zohar* points out that in the word for "place" (*VeSaMTeM* / ושמתם) alludes to the uniqueness of Shabbos. The acronym *SamTem* / שמתם stands for Shabbos (שבת), *Milah* (מילה, circumcision), and *Tefillin* (תפילין) and *Milah* (מילה) (cf. *Tikkuney Zohar*, Introduction, 2b). Each day a person must have two witnesses to testify to his relationship with God. During the week we don *tefillin* and we have our morality (the *milah*). But on Shabbos, since we do not don *tefillin*, Shabbos itself becomes our witness and the second reference to *milah* represents the tzaddik in us, our moral compass (LH, *Shabbos* 7:7).

The six days of the week correspond to the six *sefirot* of *Chesed, Gevurah, Tiferet, Netzach, Hod,* and *Yesod,* while Shabbos corresponds to the seventh *sefirah, Malkhut. Malkhut*

168 In our BRI publication, "*7th Heaven*," we have provided a thorough presentation of Shabbos, detailing the meaning behind those actions we make before the Shabbos Queen comes to grace our homes.

is beneath the other *sefirot,* yet how can it be that the six weekday *sefirot* are at a higher level than Shabbos? The answer is that the *Malkhut* seems to be lower, but it is actually higher than all the others.

When one experiences the attributes of the six *sefirot,* one has *daat* (intellectual awareness of God). By the seventh *sefirah, Malkhut,* there is no *daat* at all, only *emunah* (faith). Therefore, *Malkhut* is at a much higher level, for on Shabbos one attains the clarity that our intellect is limited and we don't really know anything about God. As a result, on Shabbos, we connect to God in the only realm that we truly can: in the realm of faith (LH, *Milah* 4:13).

It is a mitzvah to bathe in honor of Shabbos. When the Shabbos approaches, all the holy sparks ascend to heaven and the impure sparks, the *kelipot,* aspire to go up together with them. A "fire" from heaven descends in order to burn away the *kelipot,* to stop their ascent.[169] Our bathing in hot or warm water represents the fire that counters the forces of evil (LH, *Geirim* 3:24).

Shabbos is an established sanctity for it is every seven days without change. The holidays aren't so, for they are dependent on when the Jewish court declares the beginning of the month. This set sanctity of Shabbos parallels absolute truth. The unwavering Shabbos is the essence of truth, which represents the light of God Himself (LH, *Dayanim* 3:22).

The Shabbos Prayers

The Shabbos prayers are different than the weekday prayers. There is *Kabbalas Shabbos,* which contains psalms and prayers

169 *Pri Etz Chaim, Shaar HaShabbos* 3, pp. 384-385.

unique to Shabbos. Then there are the three *Amidahs* of Shabbos, each one uniquely designed for Shabbos. Shabbos morning we read the Torah and recite the additional prayer of *Musaf*. *Minchah* has its own unique presentations as well. In the following chapters, we will be examining the structure of these prayers in detail.

The Weekly *Parshah*

The Talmud says, "Whoever reads the Torah verses twice and its Targum once will merit to a long life" (*Berakhot* 8a-b). We understand from this that one should read the weekly *parshah* of the Torah twice and once more in the *Targum Onkelos* (Aramaic). However, if a person doesn't understand the Aramaic, he should read the *parshah* with Rashi (*Orach Chaim* 285), or in a language one understands.

Rebbe Nachman explains that there is "The Tree of Knowledge, good and bad." This refers to matters that are a mixture of good and bad. (Unlike *mitzvot*, which are entirely good, and sins which are totally bad, there are creations that are a mixture of both, i.e., the mundane). When one uses them for holy purposes, it elevates the sparks of holiness that were there and separates them from the bad.

One example of this principle is associated with languages. As Rebbe Nachman teaches:

> *Targum* is the Tree of Knowledge of Good and Evil for it stands between the holy language (*lashon hakadosh*, which is solely good and holy) and the seventy languages of the nations of the world (which are totally impure).

Rebbe Nachman explains that by reading the Targum after the Torah verses elevates the Aramaic wording into the holy language, which perfects the holy language. The bad that was there is separated from the good and is destroyed, which eliminates the influence of evil from the world (LM I, 19:4-6).

Shir HaShirim

There is a custom to recite the entire book of *Shir HaShirim* (Song of Songs) prior to the onset of Shabbos in order to awaken within us God's love for us and our desire to draw close to God. Our Sages call this book the "Holiest of the Holy" (*Yadayim* 3:5).

Saying *Shir HaShirim* protects us from the fire and punishments of Gehinnom. This is because there are 117 verses in *Shir HaShirim*, which is exactly the weekly quota of hours punishment is meted out in Gehinnom. So, we are protected from 117 hours of Gehinnom when we say the 117 verses of *Shir HaShirim* (*Taamei HaMinhagim* #256).

King Solomon authored *Shir HaShirim*. The Midrash teaches that *Shir* equals one, *HaShirim* (plural) equals two, and together it adds up to three times. King Solomon committed three errors: he took too many wives; he had too many horses; and he gathered too much money. The Torah specifies that a Jewish king is forbidden in these matters (Deuteronomy 17: 16-17). For each error, King Solomon was to receive the punishment of thirty-nine lashes. Three times 39 equals 117. Therefore, the 117 verses in *Shir HaShirim* were written to effect forgiveness for his errors. As our Sages teach, "He who sings to God about the wonders he lives in, merits to have all his sins forgiven."

Shabbos is considered one-sixtieth of the World to Come (*Berakhot* 57b). On Shabbos, the Song of the Future is revealed. This song is conceptually *Shir HaShirim*. The power of this song is that it can draw all the souls that have been distanced from God and elevate them back to God (LH, *Minchah* 4:12).

Psalm 107

We begin the Friday afternoon *Minchah* by reciting Psalm 107. This was instituted by the Baal Shem Tov to help elevate the fallen sparks which fell into the realm of the Other Side during the week. He wrote:

> It is well-known that there is nothing in the world that is without *nitzotzot kedoshot* (holy sparks). It is just that they are 'clothed' there in the mystery of *gilgul* (transmigration) [and hence, exile, entrapment, and subjugation to the forces of evil]. As a result, the *nitzotzot* require rectification through the deeds of human beings. On Erev Shabbos, however, they rise up from being trapped among the *kelipot,* and enter into the realm of holiness. This is why we say to these sparks, 'Praise and thank God who has done such a great kindness for you, by the power of the time of Divine favor embodied in Shabbos!' For through the power of the light of Shabbos that begins to shine into the world even before the sun goes down on Friday afternoon, they are allowed to return to their original strength."
>
> (*Baal Shem Tov al HaTorah, Yitro* #26)

The Talmud teaches (*Berakhot* 54b) that there are four categories of people who are required to publicly express thanksgiving to God (by saying the *HaGomel* blessing) as follows:

1. Those who safely complete a sea voyage
2. Those who traversed a desert
3. Those who were ill and recovered
4. Those who were imprisoned and were set free

Rebbe Nachman taught that the four who are "obliged to give thanks"—travelers on the sea, wanderers in the desert, the sick, and prisoners—are misfortunes of the soul and are alluded to in Psalm 107.

Type of misfortune	Verse in Psalm 107	Explanation
Sea travelers	They ascend heavenward, they descend to the depths (107:26)	This refers to those who travel through life and hints to the soul's struggles in life.
Wanderers	They wandered in the wilderness (107:4)	This refers to the soul that wanders about tired, hungry and thirsty in the wilderness, not knowing what it should do or where it should go to attain rectification and fulfillment.
Sick	Their souls abhorred all food (107:18)	This alludes to the sickness of the soul which has become so faint that even if given some spiritual food, it cannot tolerate eating it.
Prisoners	A person sits in darkness and is imprisoned in jail (107:10)	This refers to the soul who feels imprisoned by bad characteristics or attributes and/or life problems.

All these examples correspond to the soul which has much opposition, and many stand up against it. It suffers torment, affliction, great wanderings and unnatural misfortunes. But every time, God rescues it from all the misfortunes, and for this we are obliged to give thanks (LM I, 163).

Reb Noson puts Psalm 107 into a contemporary context as well. He writes:

> These four categories of people who must give thanks include every single one of us in all the various difficulties we experience ... and from which God rescues us. It is for this reason that we thank Him every day for all the miracles and wonders He does for His people at all times. Many of these miracles we actually see with our own eyes, and yet there are so many more of which we are not even aware. The main thing is to rejoice—even in the midst of our troubles—when we see all the many kindnesses and wonders He does for us each day, and to trust in Him and rejoice in His salvation.
>
> (LH, *Hodaah* 6:5)

Minchah

Following Psalm 107 we say the sacrifices, *Ashrey,* the *Amidah* and *Aleinu* as we do in every weekday *Minchah*. However, we conclude the *Minchah* without *Tachanun* since the next day is Shabbos.

CHAPTER 45

Kabbalas Shabbos: Receiving the Shabbos

At the onset of Shabbos, our custom is to recite the psalms of *Kabbalas Shabbos* (Receiving the Shabbos). This consists of six psalms, corresponding to the six weekdays. We next commence with the Friday Night Prayers, which consist of the *Shema* and its blessings, the *Amidah*, and *Aleinu*. The *Amidah* for Shabbos has seven blessings, corresponding to Shabbos, the seventh day. Moreover, having received the Shabbos Queen, we are compared to the groom who celebrates with *Sheva Berakhot* (*Taamey HaMinhagim* #262).

The six psalms recited in *Kabbalas Shabbos* (Psalms 95, 96, 97, 98, 99 and 29) are comprised of sixty-five verses, corresponding to the *gematria* of God's Name, *ADoNoY* (65=אדני). This Holy Name represents Kingship, *Malkhut*, which refers to the Shabbos Queen. To accept Shabbos, we praise God with psalms that speak of the elevation and revelation of God upon the entire world and refer to His *Malkhut* ascending.

Rebbe Nachman teaches that the evil forces cause forbidden thoughts and desires and prevent a person from clinging to God. Therefore, we subdue these evil forces when we reveal God's greatness (LM I, 25:4). Reb Noson notes that as we stand before Shabbos, the evil forces come and try to confuse our minds and prevent us from being attached to the holiness of Shabbos. These verses, which discuss the joyous revelation of God's kingship, subdue the challenges and obstacles that face us and enable us to enter Shabbos with a clear mind (LH, *Avodat Elilim* 3:17).

לְכוּ נְרַנְּנָה לַה'

Let us go forth and sing joyously to God

We begin *Kabbalas Shabbos* with the prayer of *Lekhu neranena laShem*. During the week, the forces of evil constrain us from serving God properly. At the onset of Shabbos, we say to these forces, "Go!" Now we are freed from restraints and can serve God without inhibitions (*Taamey HaMinhagim* #264).

Rebbe Nachman offers his unique insight:

> This is the great value of Shabbos. On the weekdays, outside forces rule. Thus, when a person performs a mitzvah, the evil forces draw sustenance from the "feet" of the mitzvah; for each mitzvah is an entire structure, in the form of a human being. As such, this particular mitzvah lacks the aspect of feet with which to ascend and go before the Holy One. The evil force has taken away the feet, as the verse says, "Her feet descend to death" (Proverbs 5:5). However, with the arrival of Shabbos and the elimination of the controlling outside forces, the feet of the mitzvah are returned. This is the meaning the verse, "If you return your feet because of the Shabbos" (Isaiah 58:13). Through Shabbos, your feet will be returned and removed from among the outside forces. Only then can the mitzvah ascend and go before God.
>
> God delights with each mitzvah, even if it was performed imperfectly and without good intention. Despite this, God has great pleasure from the mitzvah, like a father who has great pleasure when his son begins to walk. Even though his steps are not sure, the father is nevertheless delighted with his son. Likewise, the Holy One takes pleasure in each Jew whenever he performs a mitzvah, and the mitzvah walks before God (LM I, 139).
>
> Therefore, we begin the verses of praise at the beginning of *Kabbalas Shabbos* saying, "Go!" because the forces of evil no

longer have the power to restrain us nor our *mitzvot* from coming before God. All that pent-up energy of the weekdays that has prevented us and our *mitzvot* from rising before God has now been released and we can "sing joyously to God." Thanks to Shabbos, our *mitzvot* and good deeds can ascend directly to God.

מִזְמוֹר לְדָוִד...הָבוּ לַה' כָּבוֹד וָעֹז
Ascribe greatness to God

In this psalm, we find the phrase "God's voice" written seven times. This alludes to the Shabbos, the seventh day, for on this day we merit to a voice (*Berakhot* 29a). The verse says, "God's voice is over the waters" (Psalms 29:3). The commentaries point out that "water" implies movement and sound. When we say these praises of God, we should articulate them and make our voices heard.

This is the voice that directs us to God. Rebbe Nachman teaches that there are two kinds of food: spiritual and physical, and the two are not compatible. Either we eat for spiritual benefit and ascend the spiritual ladder, or we eat for physical pleasure and remain material beings (LM II, 8:1). On Shabbos, we merit spiritual food and spiritual ascension. This allows us to "hear" God's voice and find guidance for a spiritual life (LH, *Maakhaley Akum* 2:1).

Reb Noson explains "the waters" allude to awareness of God. The verse states (Isaiah 11:9), "The world will be filled with awareness of God like water covers the sea." When the Egyptians threw the male children into the Nile, they wanted to conceal and bury their awareness of God. Rebbe Nachman taught that the solution to reawaken one's awareness is to shout to God and to pray and study Torah in a loud voice. This is alluded to by the seven voices written in this Psalms about water (LH, *Giluach* 5:7).

The Psalm continues, "As during the Flood, God remains unchanged, and God will reign unchanged throughout eternity" (Psalms 29:10). Why is the Flood mentioned if Psalm 29 speaks about the Giving of the Torah (*Zevachim* 116a)? Reb Noson explains that Torah is compared to water (Isaiah 55:1). We learn from this that if the generation of the Flood would have repented, they would have been able to receive the revelation of the Torah. But since they didn't repent, they didn't have a vessel to accept Torah. Instead, the revelation of it came to them in the form of the Flood (LH, *Arvit* 4:18).

The ARI speaks of the impact of this psalm. There are eighteen mentions of God (YHVH), which correspond to the eighteen blessings that are said during the weekday *Amidah.* Furthermore, eighteen times the four letters of the Holy Name *YHVH* (18x4) equals 72, corresponding to God's Holy Name of Seventy-Two letters. And the eleven verses of this psalm parallel the final two letters of *YHVH* (וה), which is numerically equivalent to 11.

In addition, the 91 letters found in this verse parallel the combination of the two Holy Names of God: *YHVH* (יהוה, 26) and *ADoNoY* (אדני, 65), which are numerically equivalent to 91. Therefore, we learn that it is especially worthy to say this psalm with great joy.

אָנָּא בְּכֹחַ גְּדֻלַּת יְמִינְךָ

We beseech You

After the conclusion of the psalms, we recite the *Ana B'Koach* prayer. This paragraph contains God's Holy Name of Forty-Two letters. Shabbos is a "new creation."

לְכָה דוֹדִי לִקְרַאת כַּלָּה

Let us go out to greet the Shabbos Queen

Following *Ana B'Koach,* we say the *Lekha Dodi* prayer. The *Lekha Dodi* prayer was written by Rabbi Shlomo Alkabetz (c.1500-1576), a noted Kabbalist and author. This prayer became very popular around the world, with congregants singing these most incredible praises of God and supplications for redemption. The words are very moving and contain very deep Kabbalistic intentions about how we are able to elevate God's Name throughout the world.

The ARI used to go with his disciples out to the fields to greet the Shabbos Bride. This is based upon the Talmudic teaching (*Bava Kama* 32b) that Rabbi Chaninah would say, "Let us go out and greet the Shabbos Queen." Rabbi Yonah would wrap himself in his *tallit* and say, "Come, Bride! Come, Bride!" Since it is no longer practical to move the prayer service outdoors, later Kabbalists suggested we greet the Shabbos Bride in the synagogue.

The Moment of Acceptance

Following *Lekha Dodi,* we recite two more psalms: *Mizmor Shir LeYom HaShabbos* (A Song for Shabbos Day; Psalm 92) and *HaShem Malakh* (God is King, Psalm 93). Once these psalms are said, it is considered that the person accepts Shabbos upon himself. Others opine that by saying *Lekha Dodi* a person accepts Shabbos (*Orach Chaim* 261:4).

The ARI points out that the initial letters of *Mizmor Shir Leyom HaShabbos*—מזמור שיר ליום השבת are an acronym for *LeMoSheH* (למשה). This propitious moment of the acceptance of Shabbos has very important implications. At the exact moment when Shabbos begins, the fires of Gehinnom are extinguished and the wicked who suffer there are given a twenty-four-hour reprieve. At that time, Moshe, and the many righteous tzaddikim of all generations, enter into Gehinnom and begin taking out as many souls as they can (*Shaar HaKavanot, Inyan Mizmor Shir,* p. 49). It is recommended that during these Psalms, a person should bear in mind those members of his family who are deceased, as this is a propitious moment to elevate their souls to higher levels.

CHAPTER 46
Shabbos Maariv

KeGavna

Following *Mizmor Shir LeYom HaShabbos,* we recite *KeGavna,* a passage from the *Zohar* that describes the ascents of *Zer Anpin* and *Malkhut* on Shabbos. This passage speaks of the longing and yearning on Shabbos for a complete unity among the Divine Personae. Reb Noson writes that Shabbos represents yearning and longing, which depicts love, will, and desire for God. Because of the deep yearning for God that is revealed on Shabbos and through our prayers, we merit on Shabbos to the revelation of *Raava d'Raavin,* the Will of Wills, and achieve the level of *Atika Stima'a,* the highest of all levels (LH, *Dam* 1:7).[170]

The world is comprised of various types of creations, such as people, animals and plants. Every creation is different than the next, yet everything comes from one God. This is the message of *KeGavna,* for it discusses the unity of God, above and below. It is propitious to say this passage at the onset of Shabbos, when the diversity of the week merges into the unity that Shabbos represents (LH, *Perikah U'Te'inah* 4:22). *KeGavna* speaks about God descending onto His Throne of Glory and revealed as King once *Malkhut* is perfected in the mystery of unity, with *Zer Anpin.*

170 *Ra'ava d'Raavin*... Will of wills... In the Kabbalah, this refers to the highest level of the *Keter,* i.e., the greatest revelation of God's compassion.

הַשְׁכִּיבֵנוּ ... וּפְרוֹשׂ עָלֵינוּ סֻכַּת שְׁלוֹמֶךָ

Spread out Your Sukkah (canopy) of peace

After *Kabbalas Shabbos,* we say *Borekhu* and then pray *Maariv. Maariv* on Shabbos is similar to the weekday *Maariv,* with one difference: the conclusion of the fourth blessing, *Hashkiveinu,* ends with "Spread out Your Sukkah (canopy) of peace, the canopy of mercy, life and peace," whereas, in the weekdays we conclude the blessing with the words, "Safeguard our going out and our coming in."

The reason for the change is that on weekdays we travel around for business and require protection from the elements and from the unworthy people (e.g., thieves.) On Shabbos, the day itself guards us; therefore, we don't need to conclude the blessing asking that God guard us. It is sufficient that we request that God spread over us His canopy of peace.

Reb Noson explains the difference in detail: Too often, our efforts to build spiritual lives fall prey to the daily grind, especially to earning a living. We might intend to inject spiritual meaning into our jobs or professions, but the allures of career advancement and monetary gain cloud our spiritual vision. Try as we might to maintain high moral and spiritual standards, we find ourselves sacrificing our principles and ideals on the altar of success.

During the weekdays, we need an extra measure of protection to shield us from the enticements that would lure us away from spiritual living. Therefore, we conclude the *Hashkiveinu* passage in the weekday *Maariv* prayer with the request that God "safeguard our going out and our coming in" and acknowledge Him as the Protector and Rescuer of Israel. On the other hand, our devotions and prayers on Shabbos and

Festivals enable us to resist the allures of the marketplace and diminish their influence over us. Indeed, the all-encompassing holiness of sacred days is an effective shield to ward off the many impediments to leading a spiritual life. Thus, on Shabbos and Festivals, rather than concluding the *Hashkiveinu* passage with a request that God protect His people, we close with "Blessed are You, God, Who spreads His canopy (*sukkah*) of peace over us and over His entire people Israel."

Why is God's protection called a *sukkah*? The *sukkah*, our Sages tell us, symbolizes the Clouds of Glory that surrounded the Israelites when they journeyed through the wilderness. These clouds smoothed out their path and protected them from harm. When we declare that God "spreads His *sukkah* of peace," we affirm the superior protection from obstacles to spirituality that Shabbos and Festivals bring—the security and tranquility that we enjoy when sheltered under the all-encompassing canopy of God (LH, *Mekach U'Memkar* 4:16).

Sukkah of peace upon us and upon all Israel and upon Jerusalem

Why single out Jerusalem? Because of its centrality to the Jewish Nation, Jerusalem has been a focal point of strife and dissent among all the nations, not just the Jews. Therefore, we add a special mention of Jerusalem to be safe and protected (*Rabbi Eliyahu Chaim Rosen*).

וְשָׁמְרוּ בְנֵי יִשְׂרָאֵל אֶת הַשַּׁבָּת
The Jewish nation kept Shabbos

During the Six Days of Creation, God created the world *ex nihilo* (something from nothing), enabling nature to continue on its own. On Shabbos, He ceased to create *ex nihilo* and then created rest. Therefore, Shabbos is the testimony to God for having created the entire world. We say *V'Shamru* (Exodus 31:16-17) to declare that whoever observes Shabbos, Shabbos will guard over him. The verse says, "To make Shabbos for generations." Our Sages teach, "Were the entire nation of Israel to observe Shabbos twice, they would be redeemed immediately" (*Shabbos* 118b). Additionally, when one observes Shabbos, he is preparing his future generations to observe Shabbos. Thus, he hastens the redemption by causing the observance of Shabbos!

The first verse of *V'Shamru* has eleven words, which protect us from the eleven curses mentioned in Deuteronomy (27:15-26). In addition, the verse contains forty-three letters (גם, *GaM*) referring to the verse, "*V'af GaM zot*—even in the lands of the enemies I have not abandoned them" (Leviticus 26:44). Furthermore, there are twenty words in the following verse, "A covenant between Me and the Children of Israel," referring to the twenty generations before Avraham, when Shabbos was not observed.

The Three *Amidah* Prayers of Shabbos

The first three blessings of the *Amidah* (i.e., *Avos, Atah Gibor* and *Kedushah*) are similar to the weekday's *Amidah*. Afterwards we say, "*Atah Kidashta et Yom HaShivi'i*" (You have sanctified the Seventh Day). Interestingly, on Shabbos, each *Amidah* prayer is different from each other, (as opposed to the *Shemoneh Esrei* of each weekday, Festivals and Days of Awe, which all have the same seven blessings and the same order and words.)

These three different prayers represent the stages of marriage between Shabbos (the Bride) and God (the Groom). On Friday Night, we begin the blessing with "*Atah Kidashta*" (You have sanctified), referring to the "*kiddushin*" (the contract) between the bride and groom; on Shabbos morning, we say "*Yismach Moshe*" (Let Moshe rejoice), referring to the joy and celebration of the wedding party; and by *Minchah,* we say, "*Atah Echad*" (You are One), implying unity between the groom and the bride.

Another reason for the three distinct *Amidah* prayers corresponds to the three special *Shabbatot* for the world. The first is the Shabbos Bereishit, the very first Shabbos; the second parallels the Shabbos when the Torah was given (*Shabbos* 88a); while the third Shabbos expresses the great Shabbos of the Future at the time of the *Mashiach.* Thus, we find that Friday Night parallels the first Shabbos, for it begins with *Atah Kidashta* (You sanctified it at Creation); the morning *Amidah* states, "*Yismach Moshe*" (Let Moshe rejoice) for it corresponds to Moshe receiving the Torah; and the *Minchah Amidah* states, "*Atah Echad*" (You are One) for in the Future all will know that God is One (*Avudraham; Taamei Haminhagim* #317).

The ARI explains that on Shabbos all the worlds are elevated, level by level, and a unity is made between the Divine Persona. Friday Night corresponds to *Malkhut,* which begins its ascent to the upper persona; Shabbos morning corresponds to *Atika;* while *Minchah* time corresponds to when *Malkhut* is completely united with *Zer Anpin.* Thus, the prayers vary since each moment on Shabbos requires a different approach for the ascent of the universes and the Divine Persona.

You sanctified the Seventh Day. You established it as the purpose for which heaven and earth were created.

The true purpose of Creation is for God to offer goodness to His creations. Shabbos Day is a day of rest and enjoyment, especially when one connects to God and His eternal pleasures.

Rebbe Nachman explains that Shabbos is the purpose of creation because on this day we are given the ability to contemplate and to recognize God's wonders of creation. He says:

> Actually, this is a very amazing and awesome matter—that God created the entire creation in which there are any number of very many amazing and awesome things. 'How many are the works of God!' (cf. Psalms 104:24). Even in this world alone, God's wonders are countless. He created inanimate objects and vegetation, and so on. Who can fathom the greatness of God contained in the creations of this world, all the more so the other worlds?! And every single thing was created solely for the sake of the Jewish people. And the Jewish people themselves were created primarily for the sake of Shabbos, which is the ultimate purpose. Shabbos is the ultimate purpose for which heaven and earth were created.
>
> (LM II, 39)

Thus, we learn that everything created in the world certainly contains an aspect of the ultimate purpose. This is because each thing has a beginning and an end. The beginning is the place from which an object evolves until it materializes and forms into an image for which it was created. It also contains the concept of ultimate purpose and end, for which sake it was created. That ultimate purpose is so that the Jewish people are able to study deeply, know and comprehend the details of the creation—the *gestalt* of each thing's parts, shape, structure and form—and perceive in them God's greatness and serve Him through this.

You blessed it above all days.
You sanctified it above all other times.

Shabbos has a special level of sanctity that is not found in any other time of the year. Our Sages teach that "the blessing" refers to the *manna* which contained a double portion on Friday; and "sanctified it" refers to withholding the *manna* on Shabbos so that nation didn't have to go out and retrieve their daily portion (*Bereishit Rabbah* 11:2).

The Heavens and earth were completed.

While a craftsman is still working on creating a vessel, people know he is not finished. But once the craftsman completes his work and puts the vessel on display, everyone knows he is finished. So, too, for six days God was working on creating the world, but when He made Shabbos, He completed His work. Once God ceased to create, the entire world knew it had reached completion.

They will delight in Your Kingship.

This passage refers to the joy we should feel in participating in the ascent and revelation of God's Kingship on Shabbos.

Take pleasure in our rest.

This is the main blessing of the Shabbos *Amidah* and is repeated in all the *Amidah* prayers of Shabbos. Although we might not feel the spiritual pleasure of Shabbos, we ask that God accept our physical pleasure and enjoyment of Shabbos. Despite the fact that it is a day of rest from work, the pleasure derived is an outcome of not working.

We ask that we become sanctified by performing God's *mitzvot,* that our portion be in Torah, and that we receive God's goodness and His salvation. We also ask that our hearts be turned to God in purity. Rabbi Shimon bar Yochai taught that foreign and illicit thoughts can be compared to idolatry (*Zohar* III, 84a). Thus, we beseech God that we remain pure.

On Friday night, in the final sentence before the actual blessing, it says, "*v'yanuchu vah*" (וינוחו בה, she rests on it). Here the word "בה—on it" is in the feminine form. This is because Friday Night refers to the Feminine Principle, *Malkhut.* In the morning prayers we will find the phrase, "*v'yanuchu vo*" (וינוחו בו, he rests on it)—in the Masculine form, as it refers to *Zer*

Anpin, the Male Principle. And at *Minchah,* we find the phrase "*v'yanuchu vam*" (וינוחו בם, *they* [plural] rest on it)—since by that time they have achieved unity.

After the Amidah, we recite again *VaYechulu,* although we already said it once in the *Amidah.* It is repeated at this point since it is testimony that God created the world, and we are now giving witness to that publicly. An additional reason we repeat *VaYechulu* is that there are those who don't know how to pray the *Amidah.* Therefore, they can hear it when the *chazan* repeats the *Amidah* and fulfill the mitzvah of giving testimony (*Orach Chaim* 268:7).

Following *Vayechulu,* the *chazan* recites a blessing which is known as, "*Me'Eyn Sheva*" (one single blessing that compacts the seven blessings of the *Amidah*). The *Kallah* (bride, *Malkhut*) now receives the seven blessings that are customarily recited under the wedding canopy (*Pri Etz Chaim, Shaar HaShabbos,* 13, p. 417).

We conclude the evening prayer with Psalm 23, *Kaddish, Borekhu,* and then *Aleinu.*

CHAPTER 47

The Shabbos Evening Meal

שָׁלוֹם עֲלֵיכֶם
Welcome

Rabbi Yosi bar Yehudah said: Two angels accompany a person home from the synagogue on Friday Evening — one good and the other evil. If the person arrives home and finds the candles lit, the table set and his bed prepared, the good angel declares, "May it be His will that next Shabbos be the same"; and the evil angel, against his will, must say, "*Amen*." But if he does not find his home ready for Shabbos, then the evil angel says, "May it be His will that next Shabbos be the same"; and the good angel, against his will, must say, "*Amen*" (*Shabbos* 119b). This is the source for the singing of *Shalom Aleikhem,* welcoming the angels to one's home on Friday evening before we make *Kiddush.* We greet the angels who have come to our homes and to ask them for their blessings.

Mar Ukva said: When a person prays on Friday Evening and says "*Vayechulu*," the two accompanying angels place their hands upon his head and effect forgiveness for his sins, as the verse says, "May your sins be erased, your transgressions forgiven" (Isaiah 6:7; *Shabbos* 119b).

אֵשֶׁת חַיִל
A Woman of Valor

After *Shalom Aleikhem,* we sing *Eishes Chayil* (Proverbs 31:10-31). The chapter sings the praises of the Divine

Presence and of the Torah and speaks about the loftiness of the Jewish soul. According to *Metzudat David, Eishes Chayil* was written by King Solomon as praise to his mother who helped discipline him.

Eishes Chayil is comprised of the entire twenty-two letters of the Hebrew alphabet, paralleling the twenty-two channels of blessing which are opened and descend to us. Rebbe Nachman taught that all blessings for the weekdays are drawn through the sanctity of Shabbos. He said:

> Know! On Shabbos, eating is not at all for the sake of satiation, but rather that the six weekdays should be blessed, as is brought in the *Zohar* (II, 88a): 'As a result of Shabbos eating, all the six weekdays are filled with bounty and blessing.' For satiation is on Shabbos [and therefore, one wouldn't have to eat so much.] But on weekdays there isn't satiation because man is compared to a blind man, and a blind man is not satiated from eating (*Yoma* 74b). Our Sages tell us that during the week, man is busy, and his overly large strides removes the light from a person's eyes. That light is restored to him with Friday night *Kiddush* (*Berakhot* 43b). Thus it is that the main perfection of vision is on Shabbos. Therefore, that is the time of satiation, for satiation is a result of sight. This is the explanation of, "On this day we take small strides; we eat on it to bless three times" (Shabbos Table Song). That is, on Shabbos we take small strides, which keeps vision perfect, which in turn leads to satiation (i.e., blessings) (LM I, 276).

The Shabbos Meals

Rebbe Nachman said: Shabbos is like a lavish wedding. People are dancing and rejoicing with the greatest ecstasy. It is as if a man stands outside (looking in). He dresses himself in his best clothing and rushes to the wedding. He wishes to enter and join the festivities, but he needs great merit even to look in through a tiny crack (*Rebbe Nachman's Wisdom* #254).

One of the ways to join this "lavish wedding" is to eat, drink, and be merry at the Shabbos meals. After Adam sinned by eating from the Tree of Knowledge, eating became the central focus of mankind's existence. Though avarice and lust can be the stronger drives of a person's character, eating is unquestionably the main focus of a person's day. We conduct our lives around our meals: breakfast, the morning coffee break, lunch, afternoon tea, snacks, dinner, the evening cocktail or glass of wine, and so on. Rebbe Nachman calls gluttony, "the primary lust, since all other lusts receive their power and drive through it" (LM I, 62:5).

There are many decisions that surround eating: meat or vegetarian, macrobiotic or gluten free, dining out or dining in. We find in the Bible that a meal is referred to as "bread." For example, "The king seated Yonatan by the bread, to eat" (I Samuel 20:24). Reb Noson explains that the Hebrew word *LeCheM* (לחם, bread) shares the same root as *miLChaMah* (מלחמה, battle). Eating is an ongoing battle between the desire to eat in holiness and the urge to indulge in overeating and gluttony (LH, *Devarim Hanohagim BeSeudah* 4:22). Is there anything that can counter the physicality of eating and turn it into a spiritual experience? Yes—the Shabbos meals! Rebbe Nachman teaches that on Shabbos, eating is purely spiritual. It is entirely holy and rises to a place which is totally different from that of eating during the week (LM II, 17:2).

~

The source for eating three meals on Shabbos comes from the Torah, which states: Moshe said, "Eat it today, because today is a Shabbos to God. Today you will not find any manna in the field" (Exodus 16:25). Our Sages learn from the three-time repetition of the word "today" in this verse that one is obligated to eat three meals on Shabbos (*Shabbos* 117b).

Rebbe Nachman expands on this point by stating that each meal should be eaten for the sake of the day itself. Sometimes a person eats because he is hungry, and sometimes a person eats in order to prevent himself from hunger. But this doesn't apply on Shabbos. Rather, each of the three Shabbos meals should be eaten solely for the sake of Shabbos, not for what went on before or what will be afterward (LM I, 125).

Rebbe Nachman said that on Shabbos we have to increase food and drink because Shabbos eating is pure Godliness and pure holiness (ibid.). In addition, preparing special delicacies for Shabbos is the main way of honoring Shabbos. The food of Shabbos is very precious; it has a unique holiness. It is good to have plenty to eat on Shabbos. This alone can make up for having desecrated Shabbos (*Advice, Festivals and Seasons* #15).

Furthermore, Rebbe Nachman says that on Shabbos, eating is just as effective as fasting when it comes to defeating one's enemies. He points out the similarity between the words *ShaBboS* (שבת) and *lehaShBiS* (להשבית, putting an end to), as in the verse, "Putting an end to enemy and avenger" (Psalms 8:3). The chief enemy and accuser of the Jewish people is Esav, whose place is in the liver. The liver is full of blood (דם, *DaM*), and Esav is called the *aDMoni* (אדמוני, Red One) (Genesis 25:25). Our Sages also teach, "The liver is angry" (*Berakhot* 61b).

Rebbe Nachman explains that when a person eats, the liver is nourished first, and then the liver sends nourishment to the brain. Thus it is that on a day of eating, prominence and rule belong to the liver. From this "great accuser" (i.e., Esav), accusers are aroused that oppress a person who gets angry. But when a person fasts, the brain is nourished first, and afterward the brain sends nourishment to the liver. Thus it is that on a day of fasting, the liver is subservient to the brain, and prominence and rule belong to the brain instead. And when the liver—the chief accuser—is subdued, then all the enemies that are connected with the "liver" are subdued as well (LM I, 57:6).

Yet we needn't wait for a fast day to overcome our enemies, because we can accomplish by eating on Shabbos what we accomplish by fasting—namely, "Putting an end to enemy and avenger." For Shabbos eating is holy, and the verse says, "No stranger may eat of the holy" (Leviticus 22:10). The *Zohar* teaches, "All wrathful dominions and bearers of judgments—they all flee and depart from her, and there is no ruling power but *Malkhut* in all the world. Her (i.e., *Malkhut's*) face glows with heavenly lights" (*Zohar* II, 135b). Then the liver is subdued, and its power eliminated, as it says, "All wrathful dominions flee and depart" so that the mind grows great and illuminates the face, as it says, "Her face glows with heavenly lights." Then all is love, as it says, "O love of delight" (Song of Songs 7:7).

Simply put, the delight of eating on Shabbos brings an aura of illumination and clarity to one's mind and has the power to oppose and defeat one's enemies.

Eat to your heart's desire

There are three Shabbos meals: the Friday evening meal, the Shabbos morning meal, and the meal before sundown, also referred to as *Seudah Shelishit* (the Third Meal). These three meals correspond to the Patriarchs: Friday night corresponds to Yitzchak, Shabbos morning to Avraham, and *Seudat Shelishit* to Yaakov.

Our Sages state, "Whoever eats the three meals on Shabbos will be protected from three evils: from the birth pangs of *Mashiach*, from Gehinnom, and from the battle of Gog and Magog [Armageddon]." Moreover, "Whoever delights on Shabbos, [heaven] will give him a heritage without borders [an inheritance without parameters or delineations]." Furthermore, "By delighting on Shabbos, one is blessed with his heart's desires" (*Shabbos* 118a).

The delight of Shabbos is to eat to your heart's desire. The Talmud (loc. cit.) suggests that one can fulfill this delight on Shabbos with "a dish of spinach, a large fish, and heads of garlic," which were considered prestigious foods in that era. In other words, whatever makes you happy and satisfied, go for it!

Kiddush

The verse says, "Remember the Shabbos Day to sanctify it" (Exodus 20:8). Our Sages learn from here that one must declare the sanctification of Shabbos by reciting *Kiddush* over wine before the meal (*Pesachim* 106a; ibid. 117b).

Declaring the sanctity of Shabbos is one of the 248 positive *mitzvot.* We begin *Kiddush* with the section of *Vayechulu,* giving testimony that God created the entire world. The *Zohar* (II, 207b) says, "Whoever gives this testimony with joy and his willing heart, Heaven forgives all his sins." The *CHYDA* cites a law that a wicked person is forbidden to bear witness. However, one who gives testimony that God created the world, cannot, therefore, be a wicked person. Thus, his sins are forgiven (*Moreh B'Eztba* #143).[171]

We say *Vayechulu* Friday night three times: during the *Amidah,* when the *chazan* repeats it after the *Amidah,* and during *Kiddush.* As a result, we say the phrase, *BaYom HaShvi'i* (the Seventh Day) three times as well, each recital containing a distinct reference to *Malkhut,* the seventh of the lower *sefirot.* During the *Amidah* it refers to the ascent of *Malkhut* to the lower triad of the *sefirot* (i.e., *Netzach, Hod* and *Yesod*); Right after the *Amidah* it refers to the ascent of *Malkhut* to the second triad of the *sefirot* (i.e., *Chesed, Gevurah* and *Tiferet*); and during the *Kiddush* it refers to the ascent to the highest *sefirot* (i.e., *Chokhmah, Binah* and *Daat*). Thus, by our giving

171 The *ChYDA* is the acrostic of Rabbi Chaim Yosef David Azulai (1724-1806). One of the most prolific writers in Jewish history, he authored dozens of books on all types of teachings, from the simple explanation to deep Kabbalistic interpretations.

testimony to God's creating the world and sanctifying Shabbos, we elevate *Malkhut* to the highest level possible.[172]

The *Vayechulu* passage concludes with "*Bara ElohiM Lla'asoT*" (God created to do). The final letters (ברא אלהים לעשות) form the word *EMeT* (truth, אמת), depicting the seal of God which He placed into Creation.

We recite the *Kiddush* over wine because the wine represents the bounty and blessing that are given by Heaven to the Jewish Nation on Shabbos (*Zohar* III, 95a).

The word for wine in Hebrew, *Yayin* (יין), has the numerical value of seventy, corresponding to the seventy words in the *Kiddush*. There are thirty-five words in the opening passage of *Vayechulu*, and there are thirty-five words in the blessing, "*Asher Kidshanu*" (You sanctified us with Your *mitzvot*). Seventy is also the *gematria* of the word, *SOD* (סוד, secret), referring to the deep secrets and mysteries found in the Torah, from whence the blessings are drawn.

The Talmud says about wine, "If a person merits, then the wine will make him happy; if he is not meritorious, then wine will devastate him" (*Yoma* 76b). Reb Noson speaks about the merits (or "demerits") of drinking wine (and other alcoholic beverages). Reb Noson says that the *gematria* of wine (70) corresponds to the seventy facets of Torah.[173] One who drinks wine sagaciously, that is, in measure and in holiness — such as reciting *Kiddush* over wine — can merit to the seventy facets of Torah. On the other hand, one who is not careful and imbibes too much wine or does not drink in holiness, won't be able to merit the seventy facets of Torah.

172 *Shaar HaKavanot, Inyan Arvit Leil Shabbos,* pp. 71-72.

173 *BaMidbar Rabbah* 13:16; *Zohar* I, 47b; *Tikkuney Zohar* #32, p. 76b.

Furthermore, the nature of wine puts a person to sleep, referring to the spiritual slumber that many descend into. At the onset of Shabbos, we say in the *Lekha Dodi* prayer, "Awake, arouse yourself." Shabbos is a great opportunity to arouse yourself from the spiritual sleep you are in. There is a positive side to wine as well, as in the verse, "Wine makes glad the heart" (Psalms 104:15). When taken in measure, wine awakens a person to joy and positive thinking.

This is why we recite the *Kiddush* over wine. It is a reminder to awaken and arouse ourselves to celebrate Shabbos and come to recognize God (cf. LH, *Yayin Nesekh* 2:2).

Zemiros

In many ways, the Shabbos table can be compared to a formal meal, with its snowy white tablecloth, crystal goblets, fine serving ware, and lavish courses of tasty food and drink. However, unlike a formal meal, participants engage in spirited conversation and sing songs of joy and longing. These songs, called *zemiros,* were written hundreds of years ago by well-known Jewish composers. A Shabbos table without *zemiros* is like a body without a soul.

Rebbe Nachman encouraged his followers to sing many *zemiros* at the Shabbos meals. "Do not pay attention to any obstacles," he told them. "Others may be sitting at the table and not seem to have any desire to sing. Strengthen yourself and sing with joy. Conduct the Shabbos table in a happy mood. The main thing is Shabbos joy" (*Rebbe Nachman's Wisdom* #155).

The Rebbe's own Shabbos table exemplified the tremendous joy and holiness one can achieve on this day. Reb Noson testifies:

> The Rebbe's eyes would literally "glow like the sun and the moon" (from the Shabbos morning liturgy, *Nishmat*). This was

especially true on the holy Shabbos, when his eyes would shine and his face would glow. The Rebbe's great holiness and fiery bond with God on Shabbos were really something to see. There was the way he said *Kiddush* on Friday night and his customs at the table.

There was the awesome melody with which he sang *Askinu Seudata* and *Azamer BiShevachin*. There was the way he sang the other Shabbos table songs, such as *Kol Mekadesh, Menuchah VeSimchah, Eishes Chayil,* and *Me'Eyn Olam HaBa*. If you have not seen this, you have missed out.

Those who were at the Rebbe's table on Shabbos would be ready to bear witness that such a sight would never be seen again until the coming of the *Mashiach*. If all the seas were ink, it would still be impossible to describe even an inkling of the great beauty, awesome sanctity, intense awe, and sweet, pleasant, wonderful closeness to God that was there, with genuine humility. One could say that such a scene was never before witnessed. I am only speaking about our own meager understanding of what was taking place there. Beyond that, there were deep mysteries far above our understanding.

Before *Kiddush*, the Rebbe would take the cup in his hand and stand in absolute silence for a long time. All we could hear was a faint yearning sound coming from his lips as he reached the lofty spheres to which he ascended. Then the Rebbe would begin the opening words of the Kiddush in a wondrous chant: "*Vayechulu*" (*Rebbe Nachman's Wisdom* #169).

Rebbe Nachman said, "It is a good habit to inspire yourself with a melody. Song is an elevated concept. It can arouse your heart and draw it toward God. Even if you cannot sing well, you can still inspire yourself with a melody sung to the best of your ability even if you are alone or at home. The loftiness of melody is beyond all measure."

The Rebbe's tale of "The Seven Beggars"[174] alludes to the importance of melody. In the story, the unconscious princess is cured mainly through melody, through the ten categories of

174 *Rabbi Nachman's Stories* #13, the Sixth Day.

song. We learn from the story that the Divine soul in every Jew is a princess—a king's daughter. She is weary and faint because of her sins. She is held captive by an evil king and is shot with ten poisoned arrows. Only a great tzaddik has the power to enter every place where the soul has fallen and remove all ten arrows from her. In order to heal her, he must be able to discern all ten types of pulse. He must know all ten categories of song, for the soul's main cure is through melody and joy.[175]

Singing the Shabbos *zemiros* also mirrors the Rebbe's emphasis on simple devotions that draw the heart toward God. Reb Noson writes:

> Rebbe Nachman greatly loved the simple devotions of ordinary people, the uncomplicated, religious folk. He particularly loved anyone who could recite the many supplications and entreaties found in the thick prayer books, as is the way of the religious masses.
>
> The Rebbe would also repeatedly urge and exhort us to sing the Shabbos songs. And he would be stern and annoyed with anyone who considered himself too wise and therefore would not make the effort to sing the Shabbos songs or perform other simple devotions. For the essence of Jewishness is conducting oneself with complete straightforwardness and simplicity, without any sophistication. In fact, before contracting the severe illness from which he passed away (tuberculosis), the Rebbe himself always sang a great many songs each Shabbos (LM II, 104).[176]

175 *Rebbe Nachman's Wisdom* #273; see *The Water Castle*, by Breslov Research Institute.

176 The Breslov Research Institute has recorded many of the traditional Breslov melodies for the *zemiros* sung at the Shabbos meals, including Rebbe Nachman's own melody for *Azamer BiShevachin*. See our webpage for more details. Additionally, the Institute has produced a separate publication, "The Shabbos *Zemiros*" which contains all the *zemiros* of Shabbos and *Motza'ey Shabbos*, with translation and commentary.

CHAPTER 48

Shabbos Shacharit

The Shabbos morning *Shacharit* is generally similar to the weekday *Shacharit,* aside from several changes and additions. Between *Hodu* and *Barukh She'amar,* it is customary to add several psalms to the *Shacharit* prayers. The *Zohar* (II, 205a) teaches that these Psalms were added by the Members of the Great Assembly in honor of Shabbos. It states, "The Shabbos day is one of joy and arouses those Above as well as those below. One who dresses in honor of Shabbos and goes to the synagogue causes great joy Above which in turn envelopes them in Supernal light."

The additional psalms are:

Psalm	Verse	Explanation
19	השמים מספרים כבוד אל Dedicated to the Master of Creation	This psalm speaks of the Creation and of the Torah, which was given on Shabbos.
33	רננו צדיקים בה' You righteous be ecstatic in God	This psalm also mentions the Creation, with the verse, "With God's Name the Heavens were made."
34	לדוד בשנותו את טעמו לפני אבימלך About David when he acted differently before Avimelekh	This story happened on Shabbos; thus, it is included in the Shabbos morning prayers.[177]

177 *Taamei HaMinhagim* #309; see also *Pri Etz Chaim, Shaar HaSh*abbos 19, p. 429-430.

90	תפילה למשה איש אלוקים A prayer for Moshe, a man of God	This psalm alludes to the World to Come, with the verse, "Saturate us in the morning."
91	יושב בסתר עליון He sits in privately above	This psalm is known as the "Song of Incidence," a reference to its power to repel the forces of evil, which are made dormant on Shabbos.[178]
98	מזמור שירו לה' שיר חדש Sing to God a new song	This is the song that the cows sang when the Ark was returned to Bet Shemesh (1 Samuel 6:12).[179]
121-123	לדוד ברכי נפשי את ה' A song of Elevation	According to the ARI, each of these psalms refer to a specific rectification and elevation of *Malkhut*.
124	ברכי נפשי את ה' A song of Elevation	This psalm speaks of the Future Redemption. It is said on Shabbos since it alludes to that Day which will be completely Shabbos. That is, when the *Malkhut* of Holiness will finally be freed from all the *kelipot* which have tried to trap and destroy it.[180]

178 *Taamei HaMinhagim* #309; *Pri Etz Chaim* ibid.

179 When the Philistines returned the Ark, they sent it back on a wagon led by cows. The verse says, "*Vatashorna haparot.*" which is generally translated as "The cows took a straight path." But our Sages teach that *vatashorna* also alludes to that the cows themselves sang, they sang a new song to God; see *Avodah Zarah* 24b.

180 *Pri Etz Chaim, Shaar HaShabbos* 19, p. 429-430.

135	הללויה הללו את שם ה׳ Praise God's name	This psalm speaks of the greatness of God, of His awesome abilities and His powers of Creation and His authority.
136	הודו לה׳ כי טוב כי לעולם חסדו I thank God for the good, for He is forever kind	This psalm is referred to as the Great Hallel because it speaks of God disbursing livelihood to all His creations. The verse states, "Who remembered us in our lowly situations." Reb Noson quotes this verse often in his letters, thanking God that no matter what has happened to us He never forgot us. God remembers us always and takes care of us, even in the starkest situations.
92	מזמור שיר ליום השבת A song for the Shabbos day	This psalm is the Song of the Day for Shabbos, said with the next psalm after *Barukh She'amar*.
93	ה׳ מלך גאות לבש God rules…	This psalm is the Song of the Day for Friday. However, it also refers to the onset of Shabbos when God completed His work of Creation, thus it too is said on Shabbos morning (*Taamei HaMinhagim* #309).

הָאַדֶּרֶת וְהָאֱמוּנָה
Supreme Might and Steadfastness

The Kabbalists speak of this passage as being a song offered by the angels to God. From each word in this poem there are permutations of God's Holy Names.

נִשְׁמַת כָּל חַי

The soul of all living things

Pesukey d'Zimra follows its regular routine through *Az Yashir*, the Song of Deliverance, and then it is followed by the *Nishmat* prayer. When we begin to say *Nishmat*, we receive the *neshamah yeteirah* (the additional soul). *Nishmat* also speaks of the Exodus, similar to *Az Yashir*. Several communities have the custom to sing *Nishmat* since it praises God and singing on Shabbos elevates the Divine Presence.

הָאֵל בְּתַעֲצֻמוֹת עֻזֶּךָ

God is powerful and strong

Between *Nishmat* and *Yishtabach* there are several paragraphs added in the Shabbos morning prayers which also contain praises of God. In *Ha'El b'ta'atzumot* we praise God with the words, *HaGadol* (great), *HaGibor* (mighty), and *v'haNora* (awesome), which are references to Avraham, Yitzchak and Yaakov. We invoke their merit to enable us to praise God as King.

שׁוֹכֵן עַד מָרוֹם וְקָדוֹשׁ שְׁמוֹ

By the mouths of the upright, may You be praised.

Though God is ascendant Above all, He makes Himself available to those who seek Him. The verse says, "By the lips of the righteous, may You be blessed. In the speech of the devoted, may You be exalted. In the midst of the holy, may You be sanctified." The passage hints of the Patriarch, Yitzchak, and his wife, Rivkah. The initial letters of the Hebrew words *Yesharim* (**י**שרים, the upright), *Tzaddikim* (**צ**דיקים, the righteous), *Chassidim* (**ח**סידים, the devoted), and *Kedoshim*

(קדושים, the holy) spell the acronym *YitZChaK*, whereas the third letters of the Hebrew words *titRomam* (תתרומם, exalted), *titBarakh* (תתברך, blessed), *titKadash* (תתקדש, sanctified), and *titHalal* (תתהלל, praised) spell the acronym *RiVKaH*.

Both Yitzchak and Rivkah represent the awesome power of mitigating decrees. Yitzchak corresponds to severe judgments since he was scheduled to sacrifice his entire life for God. He was barren, indicating restraints and judgments. However, Yitzchak also represents the power of the Torah, since he is alluded to in the words "upright," "righteous," "devoted," and "holy," indicating the righteous who observe and uphold the Torah.

Rivkah, on the other hand, corresponds to the power of prayer since she is alluded to in the praises of God. It is specifically Rivkah's power of prayer that mitigates the severities of Yitzchak. Though she, too, was barren, the power of prayer is so great that it can mitigate the judgments.

Thus, the combination of Yitzchak and Rivkah—the interaction between Torah and prayer—can alleviate suffering and severities and reveal tremendous kindness and compassion (LH, *Matanah* 5:41).

וּבְמַקְהֲלוֹת רִבְבוֹת עַמְּךָ בֵּית יִשְׂרָאֵל

When the myriads of Your nation Israel gather

In the Future, when *Mashiach* comes, the nations will gather together. Then God's Name will be exalted throughout the world. One must pause for a moment when saying the words, "Your Name in every generation". The reason is because the next words are, "It is the obligation of all those created before You, God." If read without a pause, then the sentence would read, "Everyone's sins are before God." So, we try to avoid any condemnations.

הַכֹּל יוֹדוּךָ
All will thank You

Following *U'vmikhalot,* we say *Yishtabach* and *Borekhu* as we do every day. However, the opening passage to the *Shema* blessings on Shabbos morning is different than the way we begin the weekday blessings. It is more expansive, containing many more praises of God and fitting for the expanded Shabbos prayers. Several verses are similar, but there are additional verses praising God and declaring His uniqueness.

These verses are followed by a poem, *Eil Adon,* which states that God is Master over all creation. If it weren't for the Torah, comprised of twenty-two letters, the world wouldn't exist. Therefore, this poem is composed from the twenty-two letters of the Hebrew alphabet (*Taamei HaMinhagim* #314).

The first two stanzas contain ten words, corresponding to the Ten Commandments; the final stanzas contain twelve words, corresponding to the twelve constellations; and the remaining nine stanzas contain eight letters each, corresponding to the Holy Name of God of Seventy-Two letters (8x9=72). Seventy-two is also the *gematria* of *CheSeD* (חסד, kindness). The *Avudraham* combines both concepts and explains that due to the kindness of God, in His merciful act toward the Jewish Nation, He gave the Ten Commandments to the Twelve Tribes.

The *Zohar* (II, 205b) teaches that *Eil Adon* is an amazing and elevated song to God. There are groups of angels that accept and elevate this poem and invite the souls of those who have recited it to be with the tzaddikim in Gan Eden. The reason for the expanded words in *Eil Adon* (as opposed to the brevity of the corresponding prayer *Eil Barukh* during the weekdays) is that on Shabbos there are many blessings, and the greater expansion of these words spreads the blessings further. Thus, the added words in the poem *Eil Adon* are intended to radiate Godliness and blessing to a larger area.

לָאֵל אֲשֶׁר שָׁבַת מִכָּל הַמַּעֲשִׂים

For God Who rests from all creation

After *Eil Adon* we recite a passage that praises both God and the Shabbos. The *Kol Bo* explains that when God created the world, He created Ministers for each thing in Creation, which included appointing a Minister for Shabbos. Thus, the verse says, "On the Seventh Day, the Minister sat on his honored chair, and he clothed himself in beauty in honor of Shabbos." Realizing that honor should truly be given to God, the minister arose from his chair and told all to praise God. As it says, "The Seventh Day praised and said it is good to praise God" (*Anaf Yosef*).

The *Shacharit Amidah*

The remainder of the *Shema* blessings and the *Shema* itself are similar to the weekday prayers. The *Shacharit Amidah* consists of the same first three blessings of the weekday *Amidah* (see Chapter 29). In the *chazan's* repetition of the *Amidah,* it is followed by *Kedushah.*

Kedushah
Holiness

נקדישך (Sanctify God)

We are able to praise and sanctify God similar to the angels who praise and sanctify Him.

קדוש, קדוש, קדוש (Holy! Holy! Holy!)

Why do we repeat the word, holy, three times? The *Rambam* speaks of three worlds: the angelic world, the celestial (or solar system) world and this world.[181] Our sages teach that these three worlds are interconnected. Each blade of grass below has a star (solar system) above it; and above that celestial body, there is an angel who strikes that blade and tells it to grow" (*Bereishit Rabbah* 10:7). In *Likutey Moharan* (I, 9:2), Rebbe Nachman speaks of how prayer is the nourishment of all the worlds and that the person who prays and praises God provides sustenance to all of Creation! Therefore, we say the word, "Holy!' three times in order to evoke the blessings in all the worlds.

אז בקול רעש גדול (Then in a loud voice)

When we say "*Kadosh*!" the angels, too, gather and say aloud praises to God.

ממקומך מלכינו (From Your place)

On Shabbos, God's glory is elevated far beyond its regular place. Therefore, we say, "Blessed is God in His place" for no one can fathom the exaltedness of that place. However, that place is one of compassion. Therefore, we ask that God compassionately rule over us in His city, Jerusalem.

ועינינו תראנה (Our eyes shall see)

As it is written, "For eye to eye will see God's return to Zion" (Isaiah 52:8).

ימלוך ה' לעולם (God will reign forever)

Eventually we will see God's eternal reign over Zion and Jerusalem, *Amen*.

יִשְׂמַח מֹשֶׁה בְּמַתְּנַת חֶלְקוֹ
Moshe should rejoice with his portion

What is Moshe's portion? Moshe is called "Your faithful servant." The accolade is fitting for Moshe because it

181 *Yad HaChazakah, Yesodei HaTorah* 2:3.

says, "You placed upon his head a crown of splendor," referring to his face that shone with a heavenly glow when he descended the mountain with the Tablets (Exodus 34:29). And upon the Tablets were written to guard the Shabbos.

The Midrash tells that when Moshe was still a youth living in Pharoah's house he told Pharaoh that his slaves need a day of rest or they would die. Pharaoh agreed and told Moshe to set aside a day of rest for them, and Moshe chose Shabbos. Later, when God gave him the commandments which contained the mitzvah of Shabbos, Moshe rejoiced.

The passage states, "And the Children of Israel took off their ornaments at Mount Sinai. And Moshe took ..." (Exodus 33:6-7). What did the Jews take off and what did Moshe take? The ARI points out that when Moshe received the Torah, Heaven granted him one thousand lights. These lights are alluded to in the large letter *aleph* (א) which opens the Book of Chronicles (1, 1:1). When the Jews made the golden calf, these lights abandoned him and he remained with only one small residue of these lights, alluding to the small letter *aleph* at the opening of the book of Leviticus (1:1). Since Moshe did not sin, he did not lose these lights voluntarily. When the Jewish nation sinned with the Golden Calf, they lost their ornaments (i.e., lights), and these were given to Moshe to compensate for the thousand lights that he lost.[182]

וְשָׁמְרוּ בְנֵי יִשְׂרָאֵל אֶת הַשַּׁבָּת
The Jews keep the Shabbos

The word Shabbos, or Seventh Day, is mentioned three times in this passage, alluding to the three Shabbos

182 *Shaar Hakavanot, Inyan Mizmor Shir l'Yom HaShabbos*, p. 48.

meals. The juxtaposition of *v'shamru* following *Yismach Moshe* is that Shabbos is an exquisite present given to the Jews (*Shabbos* 10b), which they lost when the Tablets were shattered. Generally speaking, when one gets a great present and it gets lost and the gift is replaced, one says, "guard this carefully." Thus, it says, *v'shamru* (guard it) following *Yismach Moshe*.

וְלֹא נְתַתּוֹ ה' אֱלֹקֵינוּ לְגוֹיֵי הָאֲרָצוֹת
You did not give Shabbos to the nations

As mentioned earlier (Chapter 47), there are three special Shabbatot for the world: Shabbos Bereishit, the very first Shabbos; the Shabbos when the Torah was given; and the great Shabbos of the Future. Thus, there are three times mentioned here that God did not give Shabbos to the nations, nor to the idolaters, nor to the uncircumcised. It was given, with love, only to the Jewish people who were chosen by God.

Shabbos unalterably returns to this world once every seven days, just as it has done ever since the time of Creation. Even so, the Jewish people must actively participate in its manifestation. We alone have the power to welcome the holiness of Shabbos into this physical world. God "did not give it to the nations of the world;" we alone are charged with its observance. As the Midrash teaches: At Creation, Shabbos said to God, "You gave each one [of the days] a partner, except for me." God answered her, "The Jewish people will be your partner" (*Bereishit Rabbah* 11:8). The holiness of Shabbos is thus contingent upon each and every Jew (LH, *Shabbos* 7:11).

יִשְׂמְחוּ בְמַלְכוּתְךָ
They will delight in Your Kingship

This passage is referring to the joy we should feel in participating in the ascent and revelation of God's

Kingship (see Chapter 46). This passage is repeated in all three *Amidahs* of Shabbos.

רְצֵה נָא בִמְנוּחָתֵנוּ
Take pleasure in our rest

This is the main blessing of the Shabbos *Amidah* and is a constant in all the *Amidah* prayers of Shabbos (see Chapter 46).

שִׁיר שֶׁל יוֹם
Song of the Day

The last three blessings of the *Amidah* are similar to the weekday *Amidah*. After the *Amidah*, we say the song of the day that was sung by the Leviim. On Shabbos we say Psalm 92, which begins with "*Mizmor Shir L'Yom HaShabbos*," (a Song for the Shabbos Day; see Chapter 46).

The Torah states, "Remember the Shabbos day to sanctify it" (Exodus 20:8). The Sages say that this is a directive to count the days of the week according to Shabbos (*Mekhilta*, loc. cit.). During the week we say, "*Hayom yom [rishon] beShabbos* (Today is the [first] day of the Shabbos [week])," and so on. But on Shabbos the formula changes. We say, "*Hayom yom Shabbos kodesh* (Today is the holy Shabbos day)." Reb Noson explains that Shabbos is the foundation of the week and the source of all its sanctity, like the center stem of a seven-branched candelabra. Like the Menorah in the holy Temple, each branch of the week's candelabra turns inward, to face the center and be illuminated by the spirit of Shabbos. In this way, the sanctity of Shabbos illuminates all of time, as it has done ever since the beginning of Creation (LH, *Rosh Chodesh* 7:55).

CHAPTER 49

Shabbos Torah Reading and Haftorah

The Torah tells us that the river of Eden irrigates the Garden, as the verse says, "A river flows from Eden to water the Garden" (Genesis 2:10). Rebbe Nachman teaches that Eden hints to prayer and the Garden is the Torah (LM I, 8:7). This infers to the close relationship between Torah and prayer.

In addition, the verse, "No eye has seen it [Eden]" (Isaiah 64:3), applies to prayer; for prayer transcends nature, as it can wrought miracles and change the rules of nature.

The Garden (גן, *GaN*) refers to the Torah since its numerical value is 53, and the Torah is divided into 53 weekly *parshiyot* (sections). (There are actually 54 *parshiyot*, but *Nitzavim-VaYeilekh*, near the end of Deuteronomy, are often read together and thus are counted as one *parshah*.)

Rebbe Nachman teaches that prayer is the root of the Torah. Additionally, when we pray for something, this creates the potential, for now our wishes can potentially happen. But then we must study Torah to bring it into the realm of actual. After we study Torah, our prayers materialize and come to existence. Jewish souls grow in the Garden of Torah, like grass growing in a field. They need the irrigation from the river of Eden (i.e., prayer) to grow, so they can properly understand the Torah. In short, Torah and *tefillah* are two entities that must go together. Therefore, the custom developed to read the Torah during the prayers.

Originally, the custom was to read the weekly Torah *parshah* on Shabbos. Ezra HaSofer was one of the Members of the Great Assembly and helped build the second Temple upon his return from Babylon. He established the custom to read the Torah at Shabbos *Minchah*, and on Monday and Thursday mornings as well (*Bava Kama* 82a).

The primary time for reading the Torah is on Shabbos. During the week, people are busy with their livelihood. However, Shabbos is a day of rest, so people have the time to hear the Torah and learn their spiritual obligations. In the past, a spiritual leader would give a lecture on the weekly *parshah* so that the people (many of whom were unable to read) were advised of Torah lore and law (see Chapter 35).

Reb Noson explains that the main Torah reading is on Shabbos because on Shabbos we commemorate that God created the world, and our faith is attained through the Torah. Since the Torah was given to us by Moshe, the greatest prophet, there is the spirit of prophecy associated with the Torah.

Moshe and the Prophets of his time instituted the reading of the Torah on Mondays and Thursdays as well, so that the Jews shouldn't go more than three days without Torah. It was specifically the Prophets who established this custom because the spirit of prophecy infuses us with faith (LH, *Kriat HaTorah* 6:1-2).[183]

The verse says, "This is the book, the generations of Man (Adam), on the day that God created him" (Genesis 5:1). Reb

183 Moshe established the custom to read the Torah on Mondays and Thursdays and one person was called up to read the portion. Ezra extended the custom for three people to be called up and each one should read at least three verses (see *Bava Kama* 82a).

Noson explains that "this book" refers to the book of Torah. It was the blueprint of the world and thus every single person, from the time of Creation until the end of time, can find himself in "this book" — the Torah. The weekly reading of the Torah is divided into seven parts. The portion read during each specific week is the guide to the person for that week. Similarly, each individual portion of that parshah is meant to act as a guide for the person for that day. For example, the first reading parallels Sunday, the second reading parallels Monday and so on. Thus, the weekly parshah contains guidance and direction for a person the entire week. It is read in its entirety on Shabbos because Shabbos is the central and focal point of the week (LH, *Nesiat Kapayim* 5:27). Therefore, each person should study the weekly *parshah* and seek guidance from it.

The Codes (282:1) state, "[Shabbos morning] we take out the *sefer* Torah and seven people read from it." Each person says a blessing before and after a portion of the *parshah* is read, until the *parshah* is completed. Afterwards, a half *Kaddish* is recited.

Haftorah

After the reading of the Torah, we read a section of the Prophets called *Haftorah*. *Haftorah* was instituted at a time when the authorities banned the reading of the Torah, and the custom has remained. Reading from the Torah enabled us to receive faith to recognize God. When it was banned from being read publicly, the Prophets were read instead, because they also have the power to guide us properly and to instill in us faith in God.

The word *Haftorah* implies "an end," meaning the exile will come to an end when we accept the true leaders and tzaddikim and thereby attain perfect faith. In addition, the word *HaPhToRah* (הפטורה) also shares the root of the word *PeTeR* (פטר) *rechem*, indicating "a beginning." This teaches us that the tzaddikim guide us in making new beginnings each day and obtaining new resolves to keep the Torah (LH, *Kriat HaTorah* 6:26-27).

The person who is called up for *Haftorah* says the blessings on the Torah and the final few verses of the *parshah* are repeated. Afterward, he says the blessing on the Prophets (*Navi*). When reading the Torah was forbidden, seven people were called to say the blessings on the *Navi*, and each read at least three verses — a total of twenty-one verses. Today, only one person is called for *Haftorah*, while the custom of a minimum of twenty-one verses has remained.[184]

Removing the Torah from the Ark

As we open the Ark to remove the Torah, it is customary to say several verses. We begin with the acknowledgement of God by saying, "You have been shown, so that you could know, that God is the Lord, there is none like Him." We pray that God rebuild Jerusalem so His Kingship will be acknowledged by all.

Then we remove the Torah and say, "When the Ark traveled," followed by *Brikh Shmei*.[185] Following *Brikh Shmei*, the *chazan* then says three statements which the congregation repeats: "*Shema Yisrael*" (Hear O Israel), "*Echad Eloheinu*" (God is One), and "*Gadlu*" (Declare God's greatness). These three statements correspond to the three Patriarchs, to the *Kedushah* when we say "*Kadosh*!" three times, and to the three meals eaten on Shabbos.

184 *Orach Chaim* 282-283, see *Mishnah Berurah* 284:2. Where the *Haftorah* is a shorter idea related to the *Parshah*, then it may be less than twenty-one verses.

185 This passage is taken from the *Zohar* (II, 206a) where it states that when the Torah is taken from the Ark the Gates of Heavenly Compassion are opened and a person should recite this passage of *Brikh Shmei*.

The next passage, *"Al HaKol"* (Above all, May God's Name be blessed) teaches us that as much as we praise God, we haven't even begun to achieve the level that He is on for God is far more exalted above anything we can imagine. We ask that God's Name be sanctified through us and that we merit to see that which is beyond us — namely the salvation and redemption of the Future, as it says, "Eye to eye you will see when God returns to Zion" (Isaiah 52:8).

Reb Noson explains that the main Torah reading is on Shabbos. This is because on Shabbos we commemorate that God created the world, and this faith is attained through the Torah. The Torah was given to us by Moshe, the greatest prophet, and in the Torah there is the spirit of prophecy.

When the Jews went for three days in the desert without Torah, the Prophets instituted the reading of the Torah on Mondays and Thursdays. It was specifically the Prophets who established this custom because the spirit of prophecy infuses us with faith (LH, *Kriat HaTorah* 6:1-2).

This is why it is called *Haftorah*. The word implies "an end," meaning the exile will come to an end when we accept the true leaders and tzaddikim and thereby attain perfect faith.

As mentioned above, the word *HaPhToRah* (הפטורה) also shares the root of the word *PeTeR* (פטר) *rechem*, indicating "a beginning." This teaches us that the tzaddikim teach us to make a new beginning each day, new resolves to keep the Torah (LH, *Kriat HaTorah* 6:26-27).

יְקוּם פּוּרְקָן
May redemption come forth

After the conclusion of the Torah and the *Haftorah*, but before returning the Torah to the Ark, we say the prayer of *Yekum Purkan*. It's a prayer for the success and well-being of the community leaders, for those who support them and for the entire community. Since most of the community lived in Babylon at the time, the prayer was composed in Aramaic so it should be understood by all.

בִּרְכַּת הַחוֹדֶשׁ
Blessing of the New Moon

Once a month, on the Shabbos before *Rosh Chodesh*, it is customary to announce on which day the new month will fall during the upcoming week. Since establishing the New Moon was the first mitzvah the Jews as a nation were commanded when they left Egypt, we view it as a mitzvah that will hasten the redemption. In the prayer of *Birkhat HaChodesh*, we ask for a good life, a life of peace and consistent livelihood. We also recall the past salvations and pray for a blessed month and a speedy redemption from this present exile.

אָב הָרַחֲמִים
Compassionate Father

This passage was composed for the martyrs who were killed by the Crusaders in 1096 and 1106. The Crusades began when the English, French and German soldiers followed the call of the Pope to do battle with the Moslems who had conquered the Holy Land. The idea was to wrest control of the Holy Land from the "infidels." The history of the Crusades, which went on for several hundred years, offers no valid reason for any of the battles. Nothing but death and destruction emerged from these wars. But the Christians who went to battle against the Moslems nevertheless decimated the Jewish communities throughout Europe. They were burned alive, crushed by the sword and faced innumerable tortures because of the Pope's call to battle. This passage was composed as a prayer to remember those fallen—men, women and children who died sanctifying God's Name—and asks God to avenge their innocent blood.

אַשְׁרֵי יוֹשְׁבֵי בֵיתֶךָ
Happy are those who dwell in Your House

Before we return the Torah to the Ark, we recite the psalm of *Ashrey* for the second time during Shacharit. (We will recite *Ashrey* for a third time as part of the afternoon prayer.)

The five books of Psalms parallel the five books of the Torah. Moshe concluded the Torah with the words "*Ashreycha Yisrael*" (Fortunate is the Jewish nation) (Deuteronomy 33:29) and King David continues from that spot and begins the Psalms with the word "*Ashrey*" (fortunate). The Midrash teaches that King David used the word "*Ashrey*" twenty-two times in the Book of Psalms, paralleling the twenty-two letters of the Hebrew alphabet which were used for writing the Torah (*Midrash Tehillim*, Psalms 1).

Elaborating on this similarity between the Psalms and the Torah, Reb Noson shows that *Ashrey* is actually the key to fulfilling the Torah. Even when going through hard times, we should focus on the good we have and say *Ashreynu*—we are fortunate. We should rejoice in our great fortune that we were born Jewish and given the opportunity to observe the Torah and its commandments. This is why the Sages instituted the practice of reciting the *Ashrey* psalm three times every day. We also say in our daily morning prayers, "How fortunate we are, how good is our portion, how pleasant our lot, and how beautiful is our heritage" (LH, *Perikah U'Te'inah* 4:17).

Praising God enables us to endure the hardships despite the troubles (LH, *Perikah U'Te'inah* 4:12). Furthermore, praising God has the ability to turn a person's life around and to rescue him from his life problems (ibid.).

Returning the Torah to the Ark

After *Ashrey* but before embarking on the *Musaf* prayer, the Torah is returned to the Ark. The custom is the recite *Mizmor LeDavid* (Psalm 29) when the Torah is carried to be placed in the Ark. This psalm speaks of the Revelation at Sinai when the Torah was given (*Zevachim* 116a). Additionally, this psalm contains the word "*Kol*" (sounds or voices) seven times, corresponding to the seven *kolot* (sounds, prayers) that King David recited. These seven sounds parallel the seven blessings we find in the Shabbos *Musaf*.

CHAPTER 50

Musaf: Shabbos, Rosh Chodesh and Festivals

On Shabbos, *Rosh Chodesh*, and Festivals, we say an additional *Amidah* called *Musaf* between the regular *Amidah* and *Aleinu*. The word *Musaf* means "additional" and refers to the additional sacrifices which were brought on those special days (Numbers 28-29). Since the prayers parallel the sacrifices, this additional prayer, *Musaf*, was established accordingly.

Kedushah

The first three blessings of *Musaf* are similar to the weekday *Amidah* blessings, however when the *chazan* repeats the *Amidah*, the *Kedushah* is altogether different.

כתר יתנו לך (A crown will be given to You)

This refers to the fiery angels which stand before God and proclaim His greatness and loftiness (Isaiah 6:2-3). These fiery angels have six wings: two wings to conceal their faces so as to not look upon the Divine Presence; two wings cover their feet, concealing the "feet of the [golden] calf," so as not to arouse Divine anger; and two wings are used to carry the angel in its mission to exalt and praise God, saying "Holy! Holy! Holy! is He, the whole world is filled with His glory." Though the angels are in Heaven right near God, even they do not know His place, so they say, "Let the glory of God be blessed from its hidden place."

כבודו מלא עולם ... ברוך כבוד ה׳ ממקומו (The whole world is filled with His glory... Let the glory of God be blessed from its hidden place)

Rebbe Nachman teaches there are two types of Jews: those who think they are very far from God and others who think they have attained knowledge of God. To those people who feel distant, we must declare that "The whole world is filled with His glory," so they feel connected to God. On the other hand, to those people who feel privileged, we must declare, "Let the glory of God be blessed from its hidden place," so they realize that God is so great and lofty that no one can truly fathom Him, not even the angels who comprise His entourage. These opposing thoughts will draw people to continue serving God. Those who feel distant won't despair and give up because they know God is with them, while those who feel close and knowledgeable will discover that they still have a long way to go in God's service, and they won't be satisfied with their present level (LM II, 7:8).

שמע ישראל (Hear O Israel)

When it was forbidden for the Jews to recite the Shema, the Sages inserted the prayer in certain places in the prayers where it would not be noticed. One of those places was in *Kedushah*. When the decree was abolished, it remained in the Shabbos *Musaf Kedushah* to remind us of the miracle of the abolished decree and how Shema was said with self-sacrifice.

Musaf for Shabbos

The passage at the beginning of *Musaf, Tikanta Shabbos* (You ordained the Shabbos), contains all twenty-two letters of the *Aleph-Bet*, but in reverse order. The ARI writes that the inverted *Aleph-Bet* (from *Tav* to *Aleph*) in the Shabbos *Musaf* is meant to bring a great illumination to the intellects.[186] It then continues with the verse, מסיני נצטוו ציווי פעליה כראוי. The five beginning letters of these words have final letter counterparts in the alphabet. The commentaries point out that these *final* letter combinations refer to the *Final* Redemption. Since Shabbos is the key to the redemption, hence the insertion of this prayer in this manner on Shabbos *Musaf.*

Musaf for Rosh Chodesh and Shabbos *Rosh Chodesh*

When *Rosh Chodesh* falls on Shabbos, there is a different variation of the *Amidah. Atah Yatzarta* speaks of God creating the world and of God's everlasting love for us. The verse says, "God elevated us from all the languages." This refers to the seventy nations who each speak a different language. The language, *lashon hakodesh* (the holy tongue), is the language that God used when He "spoke" the world into existence (Rashi on Genesis 2:23).

Rebbe Nachman teaches that the holy tongue does not only refer to the Biblical Hebrew found in the Torah; it refers to any language which is kept clean from profanity, slander, falsehood, and the like. Each nation has its own evil desires and characteristics, which emerge in its speech. Anyone who keeps his speech clean will merit to ascend above these evil characteristics and attain a high spiritual level (LM I, 19:3).

In the account of Creation, God created two great luminaries (i.e., the moon and the sun) that were initially the same size. However, later on it states that the larger luminary (i.e., the sun) is to shine by day, while the smaller luminary (i.e., the moon) will shine at night (Genesis 1:16). What happened?

186 *Pri Etz Chaim, Shaar HaShabbos,* 20, p. 434.

At Creation, the moon complained that God had created two celestial bodies which radiated the same amount of light. The moon likened this to two kings sharing a crown and complained that this is never a good idea. In taking issue with God's plan, the moon exhibited haughtiness, for, in truth, the moon sought to gain prominence for itself. In response, God ordered the moon to make itself smaller. This is called "the humbling of the moon." God later sought to appease the moon, but it would not be pacified.

In the Torah reading portion for *Rosh Chodesh* it states, "A goat as sin-offering sacrifice *on My behalf*" (Numbers 28:15). It is as if God asked us to sacrifice a sin-offering to atone for His sin for diminishing the moon's light! On all Festivals we are required to bring the same goat sacrifice, yet only by *Rosh Chodesh* does it state the words, "*on My behalf.*" It is as if God wants to atone for His having diminished the moon (*Chullin* 60b; LM II, 1:14).

The New Moon thus signifies the day God introduced repentance to the world. Therefore, we find in the *Rosh Chodesh* liturgy that it is a time for forgiveness.

Rebbe Nachman expands this thought:

We see His compassion in that, for our benefit, He specified that *Rosh HaShanah*, the Day of Judgment, should fall on the New Moon. This is really a great kindness, for how could we be so presumptuous to ask for forgiveness from God? He was therefore kind to us and set the Day of Judgment, *Rosh HaShanah*, on the day of the New Moon, when God Himself, as it were, seeks forgiveness, as in "Bring an atonement offering on My behalf," which was said in connection with the New Moon (*Shavuot* 9a). And so we are not embarrassed to ask for forgiveness on the Day of Judgment, since He Himself asks for forgiveness then.

Because God Himself, as it were, did something for which He

is obliged to feel remorse, consequently we are not embarrassed to bring our sins before Him, to ask for forgiveness and feel remorse over them. For God, too, understands the feeling of remorse.

It is a very opportune time to pray on *Rosh Chodesh* for one's descendants. We learn this from the word for luminaries *MeORoT* (מארת, which lacks the letter *vav*, which translates as a curse). The lacking *vav* represents the blemished moon (Genesis 1:14). Rashi writes that the missing *vav* also hints to an illness that affects mostly children. Furthermore, the words (in the weekday *Rosh Chodesh Musaf*), *Kaparah L'khol Toldotam*" (forgiveness for all their descendants), spells out the word כלת (*KaLoT*) without the *vav*, hinting to the blemished moon as well. When the moon begins to wax on *Rosh Chodesh*, it is a rectification of the moon (LM I, 151). Therefore, since our descendants are connected to the new moon through the missing "*vav*," we learn that it is very beneficial to pray on *Rosh Chodesh* for one's descendants.

Musaf for the Festivals

Since the *Musaf* prayer parallels the sacrifices, we find that the individual Musaf prayer for each holiday (i.e., *Rosh Chodesh, Pesach, Shavuot, Sukkot, Rosh HaShanah* and *Yom Kippur*) all specify different types and amounts of animals to sacrifice.

Rosh HaShanah and *Yom Kippur* are days of repentance and days upon which God grants forgiveness, unconditionally, to anyone who asks for it, no matter what he did. The Three Festivals parallel the three patriarchs and invokes their merit to protect us. *Pesach* parallels Avraham; *Shavuot* parallels Yitzchak; and *Sukkot* parallels Yaakov.

All the Festivals contain prayers that we merit to return to Eretz Yisrael, our Holy Land, and merit to build the Holy

Temple, within which we can bring the sacrifices. We ask God to "gather us together from the exile and to bring us to Israel." The ARI teaches that this prayer is also a reference to "gathering in the broken shards and the sparks of holiness" which were scattered throughout the world. In addition, this is a propitious time to ask God for forgiveness for blemishing the *brit*.

Regarding the three Festivals, Rebbe Nachman taught that there are three negative characteristics that cover up and conceal our fear of God: avarice, gluttony and immorality. The way to rectify these three traits is through knowledge and awareness of God (i.e., *daat*). It is necessary to draw this *daat* into your heart, as it says, "Know it today and ponder it in your heart" (Deuteronomy 4:39).

Daat corresponds to the three mentalities (*Keter*, *Chokhmah* and *Binah*), the three regions of the brain (cerebrum, cerebellum and brain stem).[187] These also correspond to the three Festivals, for each Festival signifies a renewal of the mentalities, as a new intellect is drawn to rectify these three traits. In other words, on each of the three Festivals, one of the three traits is rectified. We must therefore take great care to honor the three Festivals and celebrate them fittingly, because it is through the *mitzvot* of the three Festivals that we merit rectifying these three traits.

On *Pesach* avarice is rectified, as it is written, "God granted the people favor in the eyes of the Egyptians, who lent them silver, gold and clothes" (Exodus 12:36). The Talmud teaches, "They lent them against their [the Jews] will" (*Berakhot* 9b). The Jews did not want to receive anything because the craving for wealth had at that time been rectified.

On *Shavuot*, when we received the Torah, immorality is rectified, as it says (*Niddah* 9a), "The [menstrual] blood

187 For more information on the connection between these *sefirot* and the brain, see *Anatomy of the Soul*, by Chaim Kramer, published by BRI.

decomposes and turns into milk," indicating that immoral passion ("hot, passionate blood") is transformed into a life-giving sustenance.

On *Sukkot* gluttony is rectified, because *Sukkot* is called "the Festival of the Ingathering" (Exodus 23:16), when one gathers in all types of food which were harvested in the summer. This represents rectifying the craving for food, for "there is no similarity between one who has bread in his basket and one who does not" (*Yoma* 74b; see LM II, 1:5).

We see that the three Festivals contain a remedy for the person's innermost cravings, and thus in the prayers on the three Festivals we can beseech God to grant us the wherewithal to conquer our evil traits and transform them into positive characteristics.

Rebbe Nachman teaches how the three Festivals have the power to reveal Divine Favor and Providence (LM II, 4:6). Each festival announces, proclaims and reveals Divine Will—that everything is governed solely by His Will—as in "an occasion proclaimed sacred" (Leviticus 23:7). On each festival, God performed awesome miraculous signs on our behalf; contradictions of nature that reveal Divine Will, proving that everything takes place through His Will and there is no determinism at all. *Pesach* recalls the exodus from Egypt; *Shavuot* recalls the giving of the Torah; and *Sukkot* recalls the envelopment in the Clouds of Glory. Therefore, through the Festivals, fear of Heaven is created.

However, we do not always hear the Festival's proclamation through which Divine Will is revealed. It depends on how much each person experiences the joy of the Festival and with which degree he feels and hears the festival's proclamation calling out and proclaiming Divine Will.

Conclusion of *Musaf*

We conclude the *Musaf* prayer with *Ein K'Eloheinu* and *Aleinu* as we do on weekdays. We also recite the *Ketoret*, which tells about the incenses that were brought each morning and afternoon in the Holy Temple. One of the incenses is a spice called *kosht* (costos) which in Aramaic translates as "truth." It is brought in twelve measures, corresponding to the Twelve Tribes. This teaches us that the Twelve Tribes must act truthfully. There is another spice called *kilufah* (aromatic bark) brought in three measures. This alludes to the merits of the three Patriarchs who represent the strength and power of the nation. Following the *Ketoret* we quote from the "Song of the Day," for each day of the week.

שִׁיר הַכָּבוֹד
The Song of Honor

Shir HaKavod, otherwise known as *An'im Zemirot,* is a liturgical poem of God of the highest order, which is why it is said only on Shabbos and Festivals. The idea is that since this song is so great, saying it during the weekdays would lower the value of such exalted praise. It should be said in a respectful manner, not rushed. The song brings joy to the soul so that it could attain great spiritual levels.

CHAPTER 51

Shabbos Minchah

The term used to describe Shabbos *Minchah* is *Ra'ava d'Ra'avin,* the "Will of Wills." (That is, the greatest level of the Will of God is revealed — a level of God's Divine Favor and love for the Jewish People.) It is the highest point of Shabbos where the *Partzufim* unite and the highest world, that of the *Keter* (will), is manifest and bestows untold blessings. It is why the custom of eating *Seudat Shlishit* (the Third Meal) together in shul became commonplace: it is a time for a special spiritual elevation, a time for an infusion of Torah, to try and internalize Shabbos into ourselves to carry us through the week.

Minchah begins with reciting the sacrifices as we do during the weekdays. *Ashrey* is then said, followed by *Uva L'Tzion.* There are several reasons why we say *U'va L'Tzion* by Shabbos *Minchah,* and not in the morning, as in the weekdays.

- There are many prayers Shabbos morning, and as to not overburden the congregation, it was moved to the afternoon (*Rokeach* #362; *Ta'amei HaMinhagim* #378).
- The *Uva L'Tzion* prayer contains references to the final redemption. Observing Shabbos brings about the Redemption. Therefore, we say it when we've almost completed keeping the Shabbos (*Ta'amei HaMinhagim* #378).
- Our Sages say (*Sotah* 49a), "The world is sustained by those who say *Uva L'Tzion.*" This prayer rouses God's compassion and removes the harsh judgment. This is the reason it's said every weekday morning. Shabbos morning, we don't

need to say it, because the world is already filled with God's compassion. But *Minchah* is at a time of judgment, even on Shabbos. We sweeten the judgments with *Uva L'Tzion* (*Ta'amei HaMinhagim* #380).

- Reb Noson writes that *Uva L'tzion* contains verses both in Hebrew and Aramaic indicating that we should bring the sanctity of holiness (Hebrew) into the mundane (Aramaic). It is similar to the ideal that Rebbe Nachman discusses (LM II, 2) of bringing the holiness of Shabbos to influence the weekdays. The afternoon is always associated with the next day. (A halachic hint to this is that we don't say *Tachanun* on the *Minchah* prior to a holiday, for although it is still a weekday, it is already like the upcoming holiday of the next day.) Similarly, *Minchah* of Shabbos is associated already with the upcoming week. Therefore, we say *Uva L'Tzion* during Shabbos *Minchah,* to effect the bringing of the sanctity of Shabbos to the weekday (LH, *Nesiat Kapayim* 2:end).

The Torah Reading

Ezra HaSofer established that the Torah should be read on Shabbos *Minchah* in order to prepare ourselves for the Torah portion of the upcoming week. We get a head start on Shabbos in case there are people whose work schedules prevent them from hearing the Torah reading on Mondays and Thursdays. (*Ta'amei HaMinhagim* #387).

Prior to taking the Torah from the Ark, the custom is to say the verse, "And I, my prayer is to You, God, at a time of will (compassion); God with Your great compassion, please answer with Your honest salvation" (Psalms 69:14). In other words, it is as if the Jews say before God, "even though we have eaten by the morning meal, we still come before You in prayer (i.e., we have not gotten drunk and removed our devotion to Heaven).

Shabbos *Minchah* is a time of Divine Favor; therefore, it is a time when all the prayers of Israel are accepted (*Sefer Chareidim* #71). Similarly, the *Zohar* teaches (II, 156a) that at Shabbos *Minchah* one is able to pray a perfect prayer because *ratzon* (the Will of wills) represented by *Keter* (compassion and mercy) manifests at this time.

There is another reason we say by Shabbos *Minchah* the verse "And I, my prayer is to You, God, at a time of will (compassion); God with Your great compassion, please answer with Your honest salvation" (Psalms 69:14). Prior to the final Redemption there will be nine months of terrible suffering. The final day of this suffering will be Shabbos — until *Minchah* — and then the salvation will come (*Ta'amei HaMinhagim* #381; 382).

The *Amidah*

As noted earlier, the three prayers of the *Amidah* for Shabbos are different from one another. The first three blessings of *Minchah* Amidah are similar to the weekday blessings. Then *Minchah Amidah* continues with "*Atah Echad*" (You are One) referring to the Future when God's Kingdom and Unity will be accepted by all.

אתה אחד ושמך אחד (You are One)

God is unique in that He is not made up of parts. He is ONE and He never changes.

מי כעמך ישראל (Who is like Your Nation Israel)

The Jews are God's chosen nation and He will never exchange them for any other nation. They are beloved by God for eternity. The Jews were the only ones to accept the Torah, so too, God chose the Jews as His nation.

The remainder of this passage speaks of the type of rest and relaxation that comes with observing Shabbos. It concludes with a prayer that we merit to acknowledge that Shabbos is a special gift from God and that by resting, we sanctify His Name.

צִדְקָתְךָ
You are just and merciful

Following the *Amidah,* the custom is to recite three verses of Psalms which speak of God's justice and mercy. We say these three verses, which declare God's righteousness, representing the three great tzaddikim who passed away by Shabbos *Minchah*: Moshe, Yosef and David.

Our Sages tell us that Moshe, Yosef, and David passed away by *Minchah* time on Shabbos. Why specifically then?

Reb Noson explains that Moshe, Yosef, and David passed away at the time of perfection in prayer. This is because the most perfect prayer is when one prays that he be able to keep the Torah. Besides praying for one's needs, the highest and most ideal prayer is when a person prays to succeed in God's service. This exalted form of prayer brings God immense pleasure.

Moshe gave us the Torah, so he represents Torah; David wrote Psalms, so he represents prayer, as it says, "I am prayer" (Psalms 109:4); and Yosef represents the tzaddik who connects the two, for he prayed to keep the Torah. Furthermore, if we add up the numerical value of these three tzaddikim (משה, יוסף, דוד), the total is 515, the same *gematria* as the word for prayer, *tefillah* (תפלה). Therefore, we learn that the combination of the three creates the most perfect prayer (LH, *Rosh Chodesh* 5:20).

The first verse, "Your righteousness is everlasting, Your Torah is truth" (Psalms 119:142), corresponds to Moshe. Moshe pleaded to be spared from death. God told him that if so, the Torah might seem false, since all mankind must die. Thus, "His righteousness is everlasting" and the Torah is a Torah of truth. The second verse, "Your righteousness extends to the highest heavens, You have performed great wonders, Who is like You?" (Psalms 71:19), parallels Yosef. Yosef passed away before his brothers because he displayed *ga'avah* (haughtiness) as a ruler. No human being can display haughtiness as if he can imitate God and do wonders. The third verse, "Your righteousness is like the great mountains; Your judgments are very deep; You protect man and beast" (Psalms 36:7), corresponds to David who asked God that he not pass away on Shabbos. God told him that he cannot take away from his son, King Solomon, even a moment of his time to rule, which was slated to begin on a Shabbos. This is a decree which cannot be changed, like the great mountains, deep and unfathomable, can't be moved.

We learn from *Tzidkadkha* that the Torah was given to us on Shabbos. The verse, "Your righteousness extends" contains ten words corresponding to the Ten Commandments; the verse, "Your righteousness is like great mountains" contains forty letters, paralleling the forty days in which the Torah was given; and the verse, "Your righteousness is everlasting" contains five words, corresponding to the Five Books of the Torah.

The *Anaf Yosef* comments that there are three major applications of faith: The existence of God, the belief of Torah from Heaven, and the concept of reward and punishment. In the verse, "Your righteousness...Who is like You?" we see that God exists and is seen. From the verse, "Your righteousness is everlasting, Your Torah is truth," we see that the Torah is from Heaven. And from the verse, "Your righteousness is like the great mountains; Your judgments are very deep; You protect man and beast," we understand that there is reward and punishment.

Reb Noson writes that Moshe passed away by Shabbos *Minchah*. The passing of the great tzaddik at the time of the manifestation of the Will is because the tzaddik can draw God's Light and Will down to us, who are on a much lower level, in a minimized form that we can receive. This enables us to connect with God and turn to Him in repentance. *TZiDKAdkha* is similar to *TZeDaKAh* (charity) because just as one would give charity to a poor man, Moshe disbursed knowledge of God to the Jewish nation, who were lacking that knowledge (LH, *Minchah* 7:*Roshei Perakim*).

Another reason we say *Tzidkadkha* at *Minchah* of Shabbos is because every Shabbos the souls in Gehinnom are given a respite, and by Shabbos *Minchah* they get ready to return to Gehinnom. At this time, they declare God's righteousness, pronouncing that they know that their punishments are just.

בָּרְכִי נַפְשִׁי
My soul blesses God

After *Minchah*, from the first Shabbos after *Sukkot* until just before *Pesach*, we read *Borkhi Nafshi* (Psalms 104). The psalm speaks of the Creation. After *Borkhi Nafshi* we say fifteen chapters of psalms which start with *Shir HaMaalot*. The story goes that when King David began digging for the foundation of the Temple, he dug until he breached the covering of the *tehom* (ocean depths). The waters began to gush out and threatened to flood the earth and destroy it. When King David recited the fifteen chapters of the *Shir HaMa'alot* (Psalms

120-134), the waters receded. This saved the World (i.e., the Creation). Therefore, we recite these Psalms right after *Borkhi Nafshi* (*Ta'amey HaMinhagim* #393).

פִּרְקֵי אָבוֹת
The Ethics of the Fathers

In the summertime, from *Pesach* until *Rosh HaShanah*, we say a chapter of *Pirkey Avos* each Shabbos afternoon after *Minchah*. Because summer is a time of leisure it was established to say *Pirkey Avos* to instill in people words of morality and fear of God. As a sign of respect for Moshe who passed away at *Minchah* of Shabbos, *Pirkey Avos* begins with the words, "Moshe received the Torah at Sinai and gave it over to Yehoshua" (*Ta'amey HaMinhagim* #394).

Reb Noson writes that it is customary to study *Pirkey Avos* during the days of the Counting of the *Omer* in preparation for the festival of *Shavuot*. We begin with the declaration that Moshe received the Torah from Sinai and transmitted it to Yehoshua who passed it on from generation to generation. This teaches us that the *tikkun* (rectification) of our individual and personal connection to Torah primarily depends on the true tzaddikim of each generation, all of whom received the Torah from the original source, Moshe (LH, *Birkhat HaPeirot* 5:14).

The Third Meal

After *Minchah*, we eat *Seudat Shlishit* (the Third Meal). The Talmud teaches that whoever eats the three meals on Shabbos is protected from three types of suffering: the suffering pangs prior to *Mashiach's* coming, the battles of Gog and Magog (Armageddon) and Gehinnom.

CHAPTER 52

Motza'ey Shabbos

Maariv

It is customary to recite Psalm 67 and / or Psalm 144 before beginning the *Maariv* prayer on Saturday night in order to extend the Shabbos by a few extra minutes. The fires of Gehinnom are rekindled Saturday Night, so by delaying the end of Shabbos, even for a few minutes, it gives respite to all those souls which must be returned to Gehinnom.

Similarly, it is customary to say the verse of *V'Hu Rachum* with a slow melody in order to extend the Shabbos as well. Furthermore, just as we sing *Shalom Aleikhem* to welcome in the Shabbos, we accompany the Shabbos Queen on her way out with song and joy as well. The verse states, "You will leave with joy" (Isaiah 55:12). When you leave Shabbos with joy, then your weekday will be infused with success.

The *Maariv* for *Motza'ey Shabbos* is similar to the weekday *Maariv* with the exception of *Atah Chonantanu* (You grant us knowledge) that is added to the fourth blessing in the *Amidah.*[188] After the *Amidah*, we say two additional passages: *V'ihi Noam* (May God's pleasantness be upon us) and *V'Atah Kadosh* (You are holy). *V'ihi Noam* (Psalms 91) is called, "The song of

188 *Atah Chonantanu* is a *Havdalah* prayer, distinguishing between Shabbos and the weekdays. If a person forgets to say it, he can rely on the *Havdalah* ceremony to be said over wine, spices and the candles. The *Havdalah* in the prayers allows a person to do work but he still cannot eat until the *Havdalah* ceremony. *Atah Chonantanu* was specifically placed in the fourth blessing of knowledge as our Sages say (*Yerushalmi, Berakhot* 5:2), "If knowledge is lacking there cannot be any differential between things."

pega'im" (the song that repels the damagers) as it contains verses of prayer to ward off evil and demons. We say this psalm Saturday night in order to ask God to save us from any damage this forthcoming week. Moreover, Moshe used *V'ihi Noam* to bless the Jews when they completed building the *Mishkan* (Sanctuary) in the desert (Rashi on Exodus 39:43).

וְיִתֶּן לְךָ
He will give you

After *Maariv*, some people have the custom of saying *V'Yiten Lekha*, either before *Havdalah* or after. *V'Yiten Lekha* consists of a collection of blessings found in the Torah, and we say this prayer as a means to draw blessing upon the new week.

The prayer begins with blessings for Avraham, Yitzchak and Yaakov, and then blessings for all of Israel. They are followed by verses from Isaiah which speak about God forgiving our sins. Then we say several sentences about the great joy that we will experience in the future.

There are three verses of redemption, three of transformation, and three mentions of peace. The three verses of redemption are: (1) King David said, "God redeemed my soul." (2) "The troops redeemed Yonatan, the son of King Saul" (1 Samuel 14:45). (3) "God's redeemed ones will return to Zion." The three verses of transformation are: (1) "You have transformed my mourning into dancing." (2) "God did not hearken to Bilaam and He transformed his curses into blessing." (3) "For I will transform their mourning into happiness." And the three mentions of peace are: (1) "Peace, peace to he who is far away and to he who is near." (2) Amassai said to David, "We are with you, son of Yishai. Peace to you…" (1 Chronicles 12:19). (3) "Long life! Peace to you" (1 Samuel 25:6).

Reb Noson explains that these verses help a person maintain the joy of the Shabbos as he enters into the hardships and the struggles of the week. The groups of verses are specifically in threes, referring to God's kindness in the past, present and future. The verses discuss redemption, transformations, and peace because God transforms our situation from bad to good and He redeems us from our struggles until our lives are filled with peace (LH, *Hodaa'h* 6:70).

The conclusion of *V'Yiten Lekha* is a quote from Rabbi Yochanan saying, "Wherever you find God's greatness, you will also find His humility" (*Megillah* 31a). The quote is meant to ensure us that no matter how distant we are from Him, He will always look upon us favorably. Therefore, we should never despair.

Havdalah

We mark the end of Shabbos and the beginning of the forthcoming week with the recital of the blessing of *Havdalah*. *Havdalah* translates as "differentiation" or "separation." It is a ceremony to show the separation between Shabbos and the weekdays. We say *Havdalah* over a cup of wine, recite a blessing over some fragrant spices and light a double-wick candle.

In *Havdalah,* we make the distinction between light and darkness, between the Jewish nation and the nations of the world, and between the seventh day (Shabbos) and the six weekdays. Additionally, it is meant for us to carry the sanctity of Shabbos into the week.

We specifically recite *Havdalah* over a cup of wine. Our Sages tell us that the Tree of Knowledge of Good and Evil was a grapevine (*Sanhedrin* 70a). Reb Noson explains:

> Shabbos represents the good (i.e., the sanctified), whereas the weekdays represent the side of evil (i.e., the unsanctified). Adam's

sin (of eating from the Tree of Knowledge) can be rectified by our taking a cup of wine and reciting a blessing over it, making the distinction between good and evil. Not only that, but if we are sincere in our efforts, we can even draw the sanctified into the unsanctified—we can bring the holiness of Shabbos into our weekdays (LH, *Maakhaley Akum* 2:12).

The *Havdalah* begins with verses of salvation which correspond to the three *mitzvot* we perform during *Havdalah* (i.e., wine, spices and candle). The verse, "I will raise up the cup of salvation," corresponds to the blessing we recite over the wine; the verse, "Behold! God is my salvation," corresponds to the spices; and the verse, "For the Jews there was light, happiness and joy," parallels the candle. Spices are considered salvation because just as they can help revive and restore a person, so too we trust in God that He will restore our special soul—the *neshamah yeteirah*[189]—which is forlorn when it leaves after Shabbos, and that we will see further salvations.

It is customary to spill a very little bit of the wine from the *Havdalah* cup. The Talmud teaches, "If in a house, wine is not poured [freely] like water, that house lacks a sign of blessing" (*Eruvin* 65a). The blessing that the Talmud is referring to is when people don't react angrily when someone accidentally spills wine in the home. If people can remain calm when wine is spilled, as if it was just water, then there is blessing in the home.

189 The *neshamah yeteirah* is an extra or added soul that is given to the person to enjoy Shabbos (*Beitzah* 16a). Rashi explains that a person is given an "expanded" heart to enjoy rest and his meals with joy.

CHAPTER 53
Hallel

The *Hallel* prayer consists of several chapters of Psalms (113-118) that specifically praise God. *Hallel* is recited on special days when we should be praising God, such as *Rosh Chodesh,* the three Festivals and *Chanukah.* The source for *Hallel* is the verse, "To make heard the voice of thanksgiving; and tell of Your wondrous works" (Psalms 26:7). This means we should declare the praises of God to all mankind (*Metzudat David,* loc. cit.) Rashi explains that this praise refers to the *Hallel,* which contains praises to God for the past, for the present and for the world of the Future (i.e., the era of the *Mashiach.*)

It is not appropriate to recite *Hallel* on *Rosh HaShanah* and *Yom Kippur* because we are in judgment. When the books of life and death are opened before God, it isn't the right time to joyously proclaim His praise. Although *Rosh Chodesh* is also considered a day of forgiveness, we say *Hallel* nevertheless. However, we shorten the *Hallel* by skipping two paragraphs. This is called half-*Hallel* (*Taamei HaMinhagim* #438). Another reason we say half-*Hallel* on *Rosh Chodesh* is that there is an opinion that saying *Hallel* on Rosh Chodesh is only a custom, not mandatory. Therefore, we compromise by saying half-*Hallel* (*Taamei HaMinhagim* #437). Hallel is said on the miracles that happened to the Jews before and after they entered the Holy Land. Thus, Hallel is not said on *Purim,* which took place in Persia.

We say the entire *Hallel* on *Shavuot, Sukkot* and *Chanukah.* However, on *Pesach* we only say the entire *Hallel* on the first day, and the remainder of the festival we say half-*Hallel.* Why?

Although the Jews were redeemed on *Pesach,* the Egyptians drowned by the splitting of the sea. The Talmud teaches that God said, "My handiworks are drowning, and you are saying *Hallel*?" (*Megillah* 12b). Therefore, we cut back and shorten the *Hallel* on the last day of Pesach. And since the last day of the Festival is greater than the Intermediate days, we shorten the *Hallel* in the Intermediate days as well.

According to the *Shelah,* another reason we say half-*Hallel* for most of Pesach is that although the Jews began to serve God after leaving Egypt, they weren't officially required to serve God until receiving the Torah on *Shavuot.* Therefore, we only say half-*Hallel* on the Intermediate and final days of *Pesach.*

CHAPTER 54
Afterword

The Siddur was composed by the Members of the Great Assembly through Divine Inspiration and a Spirit of Holiness. It would not be facetious to say that no matter how many commentaries there are on the Siddur and prayers, they couldn't even begin to explain the loftiness of the prayers.

What we have attempted to do in this book is to give the reader an idea of what the prayers mean on a simple level. Even more so, the commentary illustrates the reason for prayer (i.e., how uplifting it can be) and to understand that the greatness to which a person aspires is attainable.

God is Infinite. Therefore, His compassion is Infinite! Whatever we want, whatever we are seeking, be it material or spiritual, is His to give.

But do we really want to get those things or achieve that spiritual level? There's an old saying: Be careful what you ask for, you might get it! There is a well-known fable of King Midas who wanted everything he touched to be turned to gold. His wish was granted, but he could not eat or drink. He had to ask for that gift to be taken away.

Prayer is extremely powerful. If we place enough effort into it, we can and will see the answers to our prayers. So, what do we want? What do we *really* want?

The *Potency of Prayer* was written because many people asked me about prayer. They were confused about why we pray a specific prayer and say the same thing day after day, week after week, month after month and year after year. Our Sages who composed these prayers were filled with Divine Inspiration and covered the needs of each individual — for millennia to come — providing them with the tools of expression before God. It is up to us to learn from the prayers how to form our connection with God and how to eloquently express our innermost feelings before Him.

When we merit to understand how far-reaching our prayers are, when we merit to learn how to express our deepest feelings, then we will have learned the secret of life as King David says (Psalms 42:9), "Prayer to God is my life!" Prayer gives us the fortitude to live, to go forward in life despite the trials we go through.

My prayer is that along with my fellow brothers and sisters, that I, too, will merit to express myself before God and develop that coveted relationship, thereby understanding that I will always, through my prayers, have hope for a better life.

Glossary

Akeidat Yitzchak — The Binding of Isaac
Asiyah — The world of action
Atzilut — The world adjacent to God
Beis Hamikdash — The Temple
Beriyah — The world of Creation
Binah — Understanding
Chazan — The cantor who leads the prayers
Chesed — The *sefirah* of Lovingkindness
Chokhmah — The *sefirah* of Wisdom
Daat — Knowledge; the *sefirah* of Knowledge
Gehinnom — a place of punishment
Gevurah — The *sefirah* of Strength and Restraint
Halakhah — The codes of Jewish law
Hitbodedut — Self-seclusion
Hod — The *sefirah* of Splendor and Empathy
Kaddish — a prayer sanctifying a loved one or in between sections of prayer
Kavanah — deep concentration
Kelipot — forces of evil
Keter — The *sefirah* of Crown
Ketoret — An incense offering
Kohen — priest
Korbanot — sacrifices
Levi — Levite
Maariv — The evening prayer

Malkhut — The *sefirah* of Kingship
Mashiach — The future saviour
mezuzah — a piece of parchment placed on the door
Mincha — The afternoon prayer
Minyan — a quorum of ten men for prayer
Netzach — The *sefirah* of Victory
Nusach — variation of prayer
Raava d'Raavim — the will of all wills
ratzon — desire
Rosh Chodesh — the new month
Rosh HaShanah — the new year
sefirah (pl. sefirot) — ten distinct energies or characteristics from God
Segula — uniqueness
Shacharit — The morning prayer
Shattering vessels — a Kabbalistic teaching about how God created and formed the worlds
Shekhinah — The holy spirit
siddur — The Jewish prayerbook
Tamid — daily
Tefillah — prayer
Tiferet — The *sefirah* of Beauty and Justice
Tzaddik — a righteous person
tzizit — a four-cornered garment worn by men
Yesod — The *sefirah* of Foundation
Yetzirah — The world of Formation

APPENDIX A

The Sefirot Charts

THE ORDER OF THE TEN SEFIROT

כתר
KETER

חכמה
CHOKHMAH

בינה
BINAH

[דעת
DAAT]

חסד
CHESED

גבורה
GEVURAH

תפארת
TIFERET

נצח
NETZACH

הוד
HOD

יסוד
YESOD

מלכות
MALKHUT

THE STRUCTURE OF THE SEFIROT

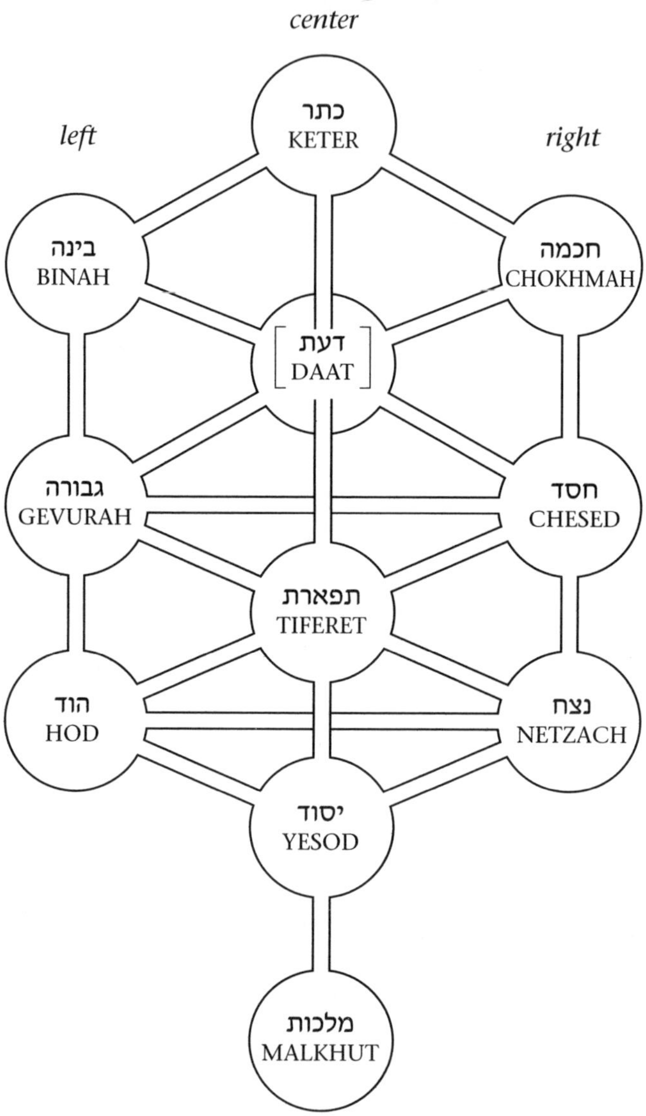

THE DIVINE PERSONAS (PARTZUFIM)

SEFIRAH		PERSONA
Keter		*Atik Yomin* *Arikh Anpin*
Chokhmah		*Abba*
	Daat	
Binah		*Imma*
Tiferet	Chesed Gevurah Tiferet Netzach Hod Yesod	*Zer Anpin*
Malkhut		*Nukva* of *Zer Anpin*

Alternative names for *Zer Anpin* and Malkhut:

Zer Anpin: Yaakov, Yisrael, Yisrael Saba, Torah, Written Law, Holy King, the Sun

Malkhut: Leah, Rachel, Prayer, Oral Law, Shekhinah, the Moon

LEVELS OF EXISTENCE

WORLD	MANIFESTATION	SEFIRAH	SOUL	LETTER
Adam Kadmon		Keter	*Yechidah*	*Apex of Yod*
Atzilut	Nothingness	Chokhmah	*Chayah*	*Yod*
Beriah	Thought	Binah	*Neshamah*	*Heh*
Yetzirah	Speech	Tiferet (six *sefirot*)	*Ruach*	*Vav*
Asiyah	Action	Malkhut	*Nefesh*	*Heh*

WORLD	PARTZUF	EXPANSION NAME	ORIFICE
Adam Kadmon	*Arikh Anpin*		Skull
Atzilut	*Abba*	*AB* = 72	Eyes (Vision)
Beriah	*Imma*	*SaG* = 63	Ears (Hearing)
Yetzirah	*Zer Anpin*	*MaH* = 45	Nose (Smell)
Asiyah	*Nukva*	*BaN* = 52	Mouth (Speech)

WORLD	INHABITANTS	T-N-T-A
Adam Kadmon	The Holy Names	
Atzilut (Nearness)	*Sefirot, Partzufim*	*Te'amim* (Cantillations)
Beriah (Creation)	The Throne, Souls	*Nekudot* (Vowels)
Yetzirah (Formation)	Angels	*Tagim* (Crowns)
Asiyah (Action)	Completed Forms	*Otiyot* (Letters)

THE SEFIROT AND YHVH

SEFIRAH	VOWEL POINTS	VOWELS ACCORDING TO KABBALAH	VOWEL POINTS OF YHVH	
Keter	*Kamatz*	*Kamatz*	*YaHaVaHa*	יָהָוָהָ
Chokhmah	*Patach*	*Patach*	*YaHaVaHa*	יַהַוַהַ
Binah	*Tzeirei*	*Tzeirei*	*YeiHeiVeiHei*	יֵהֵוֵהֵ
Chesed	*Segol*	*Segol*	*YehHehVehHeh*	יֶהֶוֶהֶ
Gevurah	*Shva*	*Shva*	*YeHeVeHe*	יְהְוְהְ
Tiferet	*Cholem*	*Cholem*	*YoHoVoHo*	יֹהֹוֹהֹ
Netzach	*Chirik*	*Chirik*	*YiHiViHi*	יִהִוִהִ
Hod	*Kubutz*	*Shuruk*	*YuHuVuHu*	יֻהֻוֻהֻ
Yesod	*Shuruk*	*Mloopum*	*YuHuVuHu*	יוּהוּווּהוּ
Malkhut	No vowel	No vowel	*YHVH*	יהוה

NUMERICAL VALUES OF THE HOLY NAMES

YHVH	=	26	=	יהוה
EHeYeH	=	21	=	אהיה
ELoHIM	=	86	=	אלהים
Adonoy	=	65	=	אדני

THE SEVEN SUPERNAL SHEPHERDS

Chesed (Loving-kindness)	Avraham
Gevurah (Strength, Restraint)	Yitzchak
Tiferet (Beauty, Harmony, Truth)	Yaakov
Netzach (Victory, Endurance)	Moshe
Hod (Splendor)	Aharon
Yesod (Foundation)	Yosef
Malkhut (Kingship)	David

THE SEFIROT AND THE HOLY NAMES

Keter (Crown)	*Ehyeh*
Chokhmah (Wisdom)	*Yah*
Binah (Understanding)	*YHVH* (*pronounced Elohim*)
Chesed (Loving-kindness)	*Eil*
Gevurah (Strength)	*Elohim*
Tiferet (Beauty)	*YHVH* (*pronounced Adonoy*)
Netzach (Victory)	*Adonoy Tzevaot*
Hod (Splendor)	*Elohim Tzevaot*
Yesod (Foundation)	*Shaddai, Eil Chai*
Malkhut (Kingship)	*Adonoy*

THE SEFIROT AND MAN

Keter (Crown, Will)	Skull
Chokhmah (Wisdom)	Right brain
Binah (Understanding)	Left brain
Daat (Knowledge, Awareness)	Middle brain
Chesed (Loving-kindness)	Right arm
Gevurah (Strength, Restraint)	Left arm
Tiferet (Beauty, Harmony)	Torso
Netzach (Victory, Endurance)	Right leg
Hod (Splendor)	Left leg
Yesod (Foundation)	Sexual organ (*brit*)
Malkhut (Kingship)	Feet

Alternatively: Chokhmah corresponds to brain/mind; Binah to heart
Alternatively: Malkhut corresponds to man's mate, or the mouth

HEBREW / ENGLISH TRANSLITERATION SCHEMA

Aleph	silent*	א
Bet	B	בּ
Vet	V	ב
Gimmel	G	ג
Dalet	D	ד
Heh	H	ה
Vav	V, O, U	ו, וֹ, וּ
Zayin	Z	ז
Chet	Ch	ח
Tet	T	ט
Yod	Y	י
Kaf	K	כּ
Khaf	Kh	כ, ך

Lamed	L	ל
Mem	M	מ, ם
Nun	N	נ, ן
Samekh	S	ס
Ayin	silent*	ע
Peh	P	פּ
Pheh	Ph, F	פ, ף
Tzadi	tZ	צ, ץ
Kuf	K	ק
Reish	R	ר
Shin	Sh	שׁ
Sin	S	שׂ
Tav	T	תּ

* The letters א and ע are "silent" consonants (with no English letter-equivalents) and are transliterated based on their accompanying vowel-point as A, E, I, O, or U.

HEBREW LETTER VALUES (GEMATRIA)

Aleph	א	1
Bet, Vet	בּ, ב	2
Gimmel	ג	3
Dalet	ד	4
Heh	ה	5
Vav	ו	6
Zayin	ז	7
Chet	ח	8
Tet	ט	9
Yod	י	10
Kaf, Khaf	כּ, כ, ך	20

Lamed	ל	30
Mem	מ, ם	40
Nun	נ, ן	50
Samekh	ס	60
Ayin	ע	70
Peh, Pheh	פּ, פ, ף	80
Tzadi	צ, ץ	90
Kuf	ק	100
Reish	ר	200
Shin, Sin	שׁ, שׂ	300
Tav	ת	400

APPENDIX B

The Exchanged Children

(*Rebbe Nachman's Stories* #11)

A Story by Rebbe Nachman of Breslov

Once there was a king who had a slave woman to serve the queen in the palace. (Obviously, a simple cook would not have access to the king. But this slave woman was a servant of low status.)

The time came when the queen gave birth. This slave woman also gave birth at the same time. The midwife exchanged the babies to see what would happen and how the situation would develop. She exchanged the infants by placing the king's son next to the slave and the slave's son next to the queen.

The two boys grew. The one who was assumed to be the king's son was given greater and greater status, continuing to advance until he became highly talented. The one who was assumed to be the slave's son but was the king's true son grew up in the slave's house. The two of them studied together in the same school.

The king's true son was called "the slave's son." Nevertheless, by nature he was drawn to the ways of royalty, even though he was raised in the slave's house.

Conversely, the slave's son was known as "the king's son." He was drawn by his nature to different ways to vulgarity and wildness, not to the ways of royalty. However, since he was growing up in the king's palace, he was raised in the royal manner and learned to behave accordingly.

Having a weak character, the midwife told someone the secret of how the boys were exchanged. One friend has another, and in the usual manner, the secret was passed from one person to another until everyone was speaking about how the king's son had been exchanged.

Of course, people did not speak about it openly, since they did not want the king to hear about it. They did not want the king to know about it since the king could not do anything. There was no remedy. He could not believe the rumor since it might be false, and he could not exchange the boys again. Therefore, the report could not be revealed to the king. Still, the people spoke about it among themselves.

Then one day someone revealed the secret to the "king's son," telling him that people were saying that he had been exchanged. "However," he said, "it is impossible for you to investigate this since it would be beneath your dignity. Besides, there is no way to ascertain the truth. However, I feel that it is my duty to inform you of this since there may be a rebellion against the king some day and the rebels' hand could be strengthened if they could claim that they are making the king's true son the king. I am speaking of the one whom they claim is the king's son in their rumors. Therefore, you must devise some sort of plan to do away with him."

The "king's son" began to persecute the father of the "slave's son" not realizing that he was really his own father. He was always looking for ways to do him harm. He caused him one evil after the other, trying to get him to emigrate together with his son.

As long as the king was alive, he the "king's son" did not have much power. Still, he caused the other father evil. But then the king grew old and died, and this slave's son inherited the kingdom. Then he sdid much greater evil to the father of the other son, causing him one evil after another. He would do it in secret ways so that people would not trace the evil back to him, since it would not be proper for the masses to realize what he was doing. Nevertheless, in his secret ways, he was able to cause the father much evil.

The father of the other son understood that the new king was doing him evil because of the rumors. He told his "son" who was actually the king's true son the entire story. He told him, "No matter what the truth is, I have great pity on you. If you are my son, I certainly have great pity on you. If you are really the king's son, the pity is even greater. He wants to destroy you completely, Heaven forbid! Therefore, you must get yourself far away from here."

The son thought this was terrible. But he did not have any choice since the king kept directing persecutions, one after another. The son therefore made up his mind to leave. His father gave him a lot of money, and he went on his way.

The king's true son was extremely upset at having been exiled from his land for no reason. He thought about his situation and tried to understand why he was being exiled. "If I am really the king's son, I do not deserve this to happen to me. And if I am not the king's son, I also do not deserve to have to flee for no reason. What have I done wrong?"

He felt that a terrible tragedy had happened to him and he began to drink and visit brothels. He wanted to spend his life doing nothing but getting drunk and following his heart's desires, since he had been exiled without reason.

The new king took over the kingdom with a firm hand. Whenever he heard people speaking and spreading rumors of the exchange, he would punish them harshly. He ruled with strength and arrogance.

One day, the king went hunting with his royal ministers. They came to a pleasant area where a river was flowing and stopped there to rest and stroll about.

The king lay down and began thinking about how he had exiled the other son for no reason. No matter what the truth was, it was not fair. If the other was actually the prince, then not only had he lost his position because of the exchange, but he had been exiled without reason. And if he was not the king's son, he also did not deserve to be exiled, since he had done nothing wrong.

Thinking about it, the king regretted the great wrong that he had done. But he did not know what to do for himself or what advice to follow. He could not speak to anyone to get advice. Worrying about this, he became quite depressed.

He told his ministers to go back; he had this concern and he did not feel like being on an outing. The entire group returned home.

When the king returned, he obviously had many other interests and concerns. He became involved with his affairs and soon forgot about the entire matter.

Meanwhile, the king's true son continued his activities and squandered his money. One day, he took a stroll by himself and then lay down to rest. He started thinking about what had happened to him. "What has God done to me?" he thought. "If I am the king's son, then it is certainly not right. And if I am not the king's son, I still don't deserve to be an exiled fugitive."

Then he began to look at the matter in a different light. "On the contrary. If it is so, if God can do such a thing, to exchange a king's son and all this should happen to him, is it right what I have done? Was it proper for me to act as I did?" He began to grieve and greatly regret the evil deeds that he had done.

Afterwards, he returned home and began getting drunk again. But since he had already begun to have thoughts of regret and repentance, these thoughts bothered him constantly.

One night he went to sleep and dreamed that there was a fair in a certain place on a certain day. He was told to go there and take the first job he was offered, even if he felt that it was beneath his dignity. When he woke up, the dream was firmly embedded in his thoughts. Sometimes a thought is immediately forgotten, but this dream was constantly on his mind. However, he felt that it was something very difficult to do, so he just got drunk again.

However, the dream recurred a number of times and disturbed him greatly. Once he was told in the dream, "If you want to have any pity on yourself, do as you have been told." He then realized that he had to obey the dream.

He went and gave all the rest of his money to his host. He also left all his fine clothing with his host, wearing only a simple merchant's robe. Thus, he went to the fair.

He arrived at the place and got up early to attend the fair. When he got there, he met a merchant who asked him, "Would you like a job?"

"Yes," he replied.

"I am driving some cattle," said the merchant. "You can work for me."

Because of the dream, he did not take any time to think the matter over. He immediately said that he would.

The merchant took him on and immediately gave him work to do. He ordered him around as a master would order his servants.

The king's true son began to appraise his situation. This type of work was certainly not befitting his station. He was a gentleman, and now he had to drive animals, walking on foot alongside them. Still he could not alter his decision.

The merchant was ordering him around like a master.

The young man asked him, "How can I drive the animals all by myself?"

"I have other drovers for my animals," replied the merchant. "You can work alongside them."

With that, the merchant gave him some animals to drive, and he brought them outside of the city. There the other drovers were gathered, and they all set out together.

The king's son helped to drive the animals while the merchant rode alongside on his horse. The merchant rode the horse cruelly with anger and arrogance and treated the king's son even more cruelly.

Seeing how cruel the merchant was, the king's son was very frightened. He was afraid that the merchant would strike him with his staff—he was so gentle that such a blow would surely kill him. He thus drove the animals with the merchant alongside them.

Finally, they came to a place, and they took the sack of bread that the merchant had given the drovers to eat. They also gave the king's son some bread, and he ate. Afterwards, they passed close to a very thick forest where trees were very close to each other.

Two of the animals that the young man was driving for the merchant strayed off. The merchant screamed at him, so he followed them to catch them. They ran further away, while he ran after them.

The forest was so dense and thick that as soon as he entered the forest, he was hidden from his companions. The more he chased the animals, the further they fled. He continued chasing them until he was deep in the forest.

He thought over his situation. "No matter what I do, I will die. If I go back without the animals, the merchant will kill me." He really thought that this was true; he was so afraid of the merchant that he was sure that he would be killed if he returned without the animals. "But if I stay here, I will be killed by the wild beasts in the forest. Why should I go back to the merchant? How can I confront him without the animals?" He was deathly afraid of his employer.

He continued chasing the animals, but the more he chased them, the more they fled.

Meanwhile, it became night. He had never before spent the night deep in the forest like this. He heard wild animals growling and decided, "I will climb a tree and spend the night there." All night he heard the sounds of wild animals roaring.

In the morning, he looked and saw his cattle standing right next to him. He climbed down from the tree, but when he tried to catch them, they ran further away. The more he chased them, the more they ran. The animals then found some grass and began to graze, but when he tried to catch them, they ran away again. He kept on chasing them, and they kept on running away.

He continued chasing them, and they continued fleeing, until they got deeper and deeper into the forest. They were so deep in the forest and so far from civilization that the wild beasts there were not afraid of man at all.

Night fell again, and when he heard the beasts roaring, he was very much afraid. Then he saw an immense tree. He climbed the tree, and when he got up in the tree, he found another person lying there. He was very frightened. At the same time, however, he was somewhat comforted, since he had found another person there.

They began questioning one another. "Who are you?" he asked.

"A human being. Who are you?"

"A human being."

"How did you get here?"

The king's son did not want to tell him what had happened, so he said, "Because of the cattle. I was tending cattle, and two animals strayed. This is how I got here."

He then asked the stranger he found in the tree, "How did you get here?"

"I came here because of a horse," replied the other. "I was out riding, and when I stopped to rest, the horse strayed into the forest. I tried to catch it, but it fled further and further, until I came here."

They decided to join forces and remain together. They spoke about how they would remain together even after they got back to civilization.

The two of them spent the night in the tree. They heard the wild beasts roaring and making a great noise.

In the morning, they heard the sound of loud laughter—"Ha ha ha!"—passing over the entire forest. The laughter seemed to spread all over the forest. It was such loud laughter that the sound made the tree tremble and shake. The king's son was very confused and terrified by the sound.

The stranger he had discovered in the tree said, "I am not afraid of this anymore. I spent a number of nights here already, and just before each day I hear this sound of laughter making all the trees tremble and shake."

The king's son was still very upset, and he said to his companion, "This seems to be a place of the dark forces. Such laughter is never heard in civilized areas. Who has ever heard laughter that resounds all over the world?"

It was then daybreak and they saw their animals standing nearby. The king's son's cattle were there alongside the stranger's horse. They climbed down and began to give chase, one after the cattle and the other after the horse.

The cattle fled further away, and the king's son ran after them as before. The stranger also ran after the horse, which ran further away. Eventually they were far from each other.

Meanwhile, the king's son found a sack of bread. This is surely very precious in the wilderness. He took the sack on his shoulders and continued after the cattle.

Suddenly he encountered another stranger. He was very frightened, but he was also comforted for having found another human being here.

"How did you come here?" asked the stranger.

He responded by asking the stranger, "How did you come here?"

"I?" replied the stranger. "My father and my father's fathers grew up here. But you? How did you come here? No one from a civilized area ever comes here."

The king's son was very confused. He realized that the stranger was not a human being. He had said that no one from a civilized area ever came here, and that his fathers had grown up here. He was obviously not a human being. Still, this stranger from the forest was behaving in a friendly manner and did nothing to harm him.

"What are you doing here?" asked the forest man of the king's true son.

He replied that he was chasing his animals.

"Stop chasing your sins," said the stranger. "These are not animals at all. They are your sins, and they are leading you around. But it is now sufficient. You have already received your punishment. Now you can stop chasing. Come with me, and you will attain what is coming to you."

The king's true son went with him, but he was afraid to speak to him and ask him any questions. He realized that the other was not a human being. Perhaps he would open his mouth and swallow him.

While he was walking after the forest man, he encountered his companion who was chasing his horse. As soon as he saw him, he signaled him, "This stranger with me is not a human being. Don't talk to him. Don't have any dealings with him, since he is not human."

The man with the horse joined them. He the king's son then whispered in his companion's ear, "This stranger is not human...," telling him everything he knew.

His companion the man with the horse stared at him and saw the sack of bread on his shoulder. He began to plead, "My brother! I have not eaten for days! Give me bread."

He replied, "Here in the desert, such pleas are of no avail. My life comes first. I need the bread for myself."

The other began to plead and beg. "I will give you anything I have."

The king's true son, however, realized that here in the wilderness no gift or bribe was worth as much as bread. He replied, "What can you give me? Here in the wilderness, what can you trade for bread?"

The man with the horse said to the man with the cattle, who was the king's true son, "I will give you my entire self. I will sell myself to you for bread!"

The man with the cattle decided to buy this stranger. He made up his mind that it would be a good bargain to buy a person for some bread. He bought the other as an eternal slave. The other made an oath and swore that he would be his eternal slave when they came back to civilization. The king's son would give him bread, and they would eat together from the sack until the bread was used up.

They followed the forest man. The man with the horse, who was now his slave, followed the man with the cattle, and the two of them walked behind the forest man.

Things were now somewhat easier for the king's son. If he had to lift something or needed something else done, he would order his slave to do it for him.

They followed the forest man until they came to a place of serpents and scorpions. The king's son was very much afraid. Out of fear, he asked the forest man, "How can we get across?"

"You think that's hard?" replied the other. "How can you get to my house?"

With that, he pointed to his house, which was standing in midair. "How can you get to my house?" he asked.

They went with the forest man, he brought them safely across, and then brought them into his house. He gave them food and drink and then went on his way.

The king's true son, who had been with the cattle, made use of his slave for all his needs.

Meanwhile, the slave was very upset. He had sold himself as a slave because he needed bread. He had only needed that bread for one hour, since he now had plenty of food to eat. For an hour's worth of food, he would now be a slave for the rest of his life. He moaned and sighed, "How did I come to such a state — to be a slave?"

The king's true son, who was his master, asked him, "What great status did you have before, that you are groaning now for having come to this state?"

He answered, telling him the whole story of how he had been a king, and that people had spread rumors that he had been exchanged as an infant. (The man with the horse was actually the king, who had been the son of the slave woman.) He related how he had exiled his friend. Then, one time, he had realized that it was an evil thing and had regretted it.

After that, he constantly regretted the evil deed and the great wrong that he had done to his friend.

Then one night he had a dream that he could rectify this wrong by abdicating his kingdom and going wherever his eyes would lead him. This would be an atonement for his sin, but he did not want to do it. However, the dream continued to disturb him and urge him to do it, until he finally decided to. He abdicated his kingdom and wandered around until he came here. Now he had become a slave.

The king's true son, who was the man with the cattle, listened to everything that the man with the horse, who was now his slave, said, and remained silent. He said to himself, "I will see what happens. Then I will make up my mind how to deal with him."

That night, the forest man came and gave them food and drink. They spent the night there. Before morning they heard the sound of the loud laughter, which made all the trees tremble and shake.

The slave persuaded the king's true son, who was his master, to ask the forest man the meaning of this.

The king's son asked the forest man, "What is this loud sound of laughter every day before morning?"

He replied, "This is the sound of the day laughing at the night. The night asks the day, 'Why is it that when you come, I do not have a name?' Then the day laughs with this loud laughter, and it becomes day. This is the significance of the sound of laughter."

The king's son found this very astonishing. It is a wondrous thing that the day laughs at the night. In the morning, the forest man once again went on his way while they remained there, eating and drinking. At night he came back and they ate, drank and spent the night.

That night, they heard the sounds of the beasts. All of them were making noise and roaring with different sounds. The lion roared while the leopard growled with a different sound, and the birds chirped and whistled with their own sounds. All of them made loud sounds, and at first the king's son and the slave's son trembled in fear. They were so afraid that they could not concentrate on the sounds.

However, they then began to concentrate, and they heard that it was the sound of music, an awesomely beautiful song. They listened more intently and heard that it was a very wondrous chant. It was a tremendous joy to hear it. All the joys in the world were like nothing—like absolute nothingness—compared to the wondrous enjoyment of listening to this song.

They discussed the situation and agreed that they would remain there forever. They had enough to eat and drink, and they could enjoy this wonderful delight, compared to which all other enjoyments were nothing.

The slave persuaded his master the king's true son to ask the forest man the meaning of this song, and he asked.

The forest man replied that the sun had made a garment for the moon. The animals of the forest realized that the moon does them a great service. Wild animals dominate the night, because sometimes they must enter an inhabited area. They cannot do this by day, so their main time is the night. By shining for them then, the moon provides a great benefit for them.

The wild animals therefore agreed that they would compose a new melody in honor of the moon. This is the melody that they were now hearing. All the animals and birds were singing a new song in honor of the moon's receiving a garment from the sun.

When they heard that this was a melody, they paid even more attention to it. They heard that it was a wonderful and beautiful song.

The forest man said to them, "Why do you find this so novel? I have an instrument that I received from my ancestors, who in turn inherited it from their fathers' fathers. This instrument is made with special leaves and colors. When this instrument is placed on any animal or bird, the creature immediately begins to sing this song."

The laughter was then heard, and it was day.

The forest man went on his way, and the king's true son went to search for the instrument. He searched the entire room but could not find it, and he was afraid to venture any further outside the area. The king's true son and his slave were afraid to ask the forest man to bring them back to civilization.

The forest man then returned and told them that he would bring them back to civilization. When he had brought them to a civilized area, he gave the instrument to the king's true son, and said, "I am giving you this instrument." Then, referring to the slave's son who had become king and was now a slave again, he said, "You will know how to deal with him."

"Where shall we go?" they asked.

The forest man told them that they should ask around and seek a land known as "The Foolish Land with the Wise King."

"In which direction shall we begin asking about this land?" they asked.

The forest man pointed out the direction and said to the king's true son, "Go there, and you will attain your greatness."

They set out and began their journey. They wanted very much to find a wild or domestic animal so as to try out the instrument, to see if it would produce the wondrous song, but they did not encounter any animals.

Then, when they had come closer to an inhabited area, they came across an animal. They placed the instrument on it, and it began to sing the song of the forest.

They continued traveling until they came to the land the forest man had described. There was a wall all around the land, with no means of getting in except through one gate. They had to walk several miles until they came to the gate through which they could enter the land. They walked around along the wall until they finally came to the gate.

When they came to the gate, the guards did not want to let them come in, since the king of the land had died, and his son was now the new king. The king had left a will declaring that although the land had previously been called "The Foolish Land with the Wise King," after his death it would be called "The Wise Land with the Foolish King." If a man came and was successful in restoring the land's name to "The Foolish Land with the Wise King," that man would be king.

No one was being allowed to enter the land unless he was prepared to undertake this. They therefore did not want the king's son to enter. They said to him, "Can you undertake the task of restoring the land's original name?" It was certainly impossible for him to attempt it. They therefore could not go in.

The slave urged the king's son to return home, but he did not want to, since the forest man had told him to go to this land and here he would come to his greatness.

Just then, another man arrived. He was riding a horse, and he wanted to enter the gate. However, the guards would not let him in for the same reason as before.

Seeing the stranger's horse standing there, the king's son placed the instrument on it. It began to play the wonderful melody of the forest.

The horse's owner asked very strongly that he sell him this instrument, but he refused to sell it. "What can you give me for such a wonderful instrument?" asked the king's son.

The horse's owner said, "What can you really do with this instrument? It has no real use. At best you can make a show and get a gulden. I have knowledge that is better than your instrument. From my father's father,

I have inherited the knowledge of how to understand one thing from another thing. No matter what someone says, through the tradition that I have, I can understand one thing from another. I have never revealed this to anyone in the world. But if you give me your instrument, I will teach you this knowledge."

The king's son decided that it would be wonderful to understand one thing from another. He gave the horse's owner the instrument, and the other taught him the method through which he could understand one thing from another.

Now that the king's true son could understand one thing from another, when he went to the land's gate, he understood that it would be possible for him to make an effort to restore the land's original name. Since he understood one thing from another, he understood that it would be possible, even though he did not know how or by what means. Nevertheless, understanding one thing from another, he understood that it would be possible.

He therefore made up his mind that he would tell them to let him enter, since he would make an effort to restore the land's original name. After all, what could he lose?

He spoke to the men who would not let anyone enter without making the effort, and he told them to let him in. He would make the effort to restore the land's original name.

They let him enter and informed the ruling ministers that a man had been found who was willing to make an effort to restore the land's original name. He was brought to the ministers of the land, and they told him, "You must realize that we are not fools, Heaven forbid. However, the late king was so extraordinarily wise that compared to him, we were all considered fools. It was for this reason that the land was called, 'The Foolish Land with the Wise King.' When the king died, his son took his place. He is also wise, but compared to us, he is not wise at all. The land is therefore now called the opposite, 'The Wise Land with the Foolish King.'

"The king left a will stating that when a wise person was found who could restore the original name to the kingdom, that person would be king. He ordered his son that when such a person was found, the son should abdicate the throne and let the wise person be king. This person would have to be so extraordinarily wise that compared to him, everyone else would be foolish. This man would be king, and then the name of the land would once again be 'The Foolish Land with the Wise King,' since compared to him, everyone else would be fools. Now you know what you are getting yourself into."

The ministers continued, "We have a test to see if you are so wise. There is a garden here which was left by the late king. All sorts of metal instruments grow in it, gold instruments and silver instruments. It is an awesome wonder. However, it is impossible to enter the garden. As soon as anyone enters it, he is pursued, and he begins to scream. He does not know who is chasing him, and he sees nothing. Still, he is pursued until he is chased out of the garden. Let us see if you are wise enough to enter this garden."

The king's true son asked them if the person who enters the garden is beaten in any way.

They answered, "Primarily, he is chased, and he does not know who is chasing him. But he flees in great terror." This is what they had been told by people who had entered the garden.

The king's true son went to the garden. He saw that there was a wall around it and an open gate. There were no guards there, since such a garden obviously did not need guards.

He went up to the garden and looked around. Next to the garden, he saw a statue of a man. He looked more closely and saw a tablet above the man. The inscription on it said that this man had been a king many centuries ago, and during this king's reign there had been peace. Before this king's reign there had been wars, and afterwards there had also been wars, but during his reign there had been peace.

He contemplated the situation. He already could understand one thing from another, and he understood that everything depended on this man. When a person entered the garden and was pursued, he did not have to run out at all. He only had to stand next to this man, and he would be saved. Furthermore, if this statue was stood in the middle of the garden instead of next to it, then anyone would be able to enter the garden safely. The king's son understood all this since he was able to understand one thing from another.

The king's son went and entered the garden. As soon as he was pursued, he walked over and stood next to this man, who stood just outside the garden. He was thus able to leave safely, without being harmed. Others who had entered the garden had fled in such terror when they were pursued that they had been injured. However, the king's son emerged safely and calmly since he had stood next to the statue. The ministers were amazed to see him come out safely.

The king's son then ordered that the statue be placed in the middle of the garden. When this was done, all the ministers were able to enter the garden. They entered the garden and went out in peace, without being harmed in any way.

The ministers said, "Nevertheless! Even though we have seen such a thing from you, for doing just one thing you do not deserve to get the kingdom. We shall give you one more test."

They explained, "The late king had a throne. The throne is very tall, and next to it stand all kinds of animals and birds carved out of wood. In front of the throne stands a bed. There is a table near the bed, and on the table stands a lamp.

"From the throne, well-trodden, walled paths go forth. These paths go forth from all sides of the throne, but no one knows the relationship of the throne to these paths.

"After the paths spread out for a certain distance, there is a golden lion standing by the first one. If a person comes near to it, it opens its mouth to swallow him. However, the path extends far beyond the lion. The same is true of the other paths extending from the throne. Thus, the second path extending from the throne is very much the same. Standing there is another type of wild beast, such as a leopard, made of a different metal. It is also impossible to come close to it. The path then extends beyond where it is standing. This is true of all the paths.

"These paths extend throughout the entire land. No one understands the meaning of the throne with all its details, nor the paths. This, then, will be your test. See if you can understand the significance of the throne and everything associated with it."

They showed him the throne and he saw that it was extremely tall. He went over to the throne and gazed at it. As he contemplated the throne, he realized that it was made of the same type of wood as the instrument that the forest man had given him. He gazed further and saw that a rose was missing from the top of the throne. If the rose were on the throne, then the throne would have the same power as the instrument, which would produce music whenever it was placed on any animal or bird.

Then he gazed even more and noticed that the rose missing from the top of the throne was lying at the bottom of the throne. He would have to take it and place it on top, and then the throne would have the same power as the instrument. The late king had devised each detail with such wisdom that no one could understand its significance until an extraordinarily wise person came along who would understand the concept. He would then know how to exchange and arrange all things correctly.

He then saw that the same was true of the bed. He understood that it had to be moved slightly from the place where it stood. The table also had to be moved somewhat, and the lamp likewise had to have its position adjusted. The birds and animals also had to be moved to different places. Thus, a bird would have to be taken from one place and set in another place. The same was true of all the animals. The king had cleverly disguised everything so that only a very wise person would be able to contemplate it and then rearrange it correctly.

The same was true of the lion which stood where the path emerged. It had to be stood in a different place. This was true of all the beasts on the paths.

The king's son gave instructions that everything be rearranged properly, to take the rose from the bottom and place it on top. Everything else was also rearranged in proper order.

All the animals and birds then began to sing a wonderful melody. Each one functioned properly.

The king's true son was then given the kingdom.

The king's son, who had by now been crowned king, then said to the son of the slave woman, "Now I understand that I am actually the king's son, and you are actually the slave woman's son."

This edition is dedicated in memory of
the very special, dear young man

Yerachmiel Daniel ז"ל
son of **Gedale נ"ו Fenster**

He was cleansed with great suffering and
left this world in cleanliness and purity.

May his soul be bound in the bond of
eternal life, and may he be a faithful advocate
on behalf of the Jewish People, that we soon
merit to see the Revival of the Dead,
in our days, with the coming of our
Righteous Redeemer, amen.

Dedicated by

Chaim Kramer
and
Breslov Research Institute

ni • Morning B
Amidah • Tachanun • Kriat HaTorah
essings • Minchah • Maariv • Kriat Shema
• Hallel • Modeh Ani • Morning Blessings
Amidah • Shabbos • Rosh Chodesh • Yom
r • Pesukey d'Zimra • Ashrey • Yishtabach
• Birkhat Hamazone • Blessings upon food
sh Levanah • Sefirat HaOmer • Shabbos
es • Barukh She'amar • Pesukey d'Zimra
ah • Yeridat Hashefa • Aleinu • Birkhat Ha
hema al Hamitah • Kiddush Levanah • Sef
orning Blessings • Sacrifices • Modeh Ani • M
rey • Az Yashir • Yishtabach • Shema • Am
azone • Blessings upon food • General Bless
firat HaOmer • Shabbos • Rosh Chodesh
rey • Az Yashir • Yishtabach • Shema • Am
ssings • Sacrifices • Barukh She'amar • Pes
Torah • Yeridat Hashefa • Aleinu • Birkhat
iat Shema al Hamitah • Kiddush Levanah
Morning Blessings • Sacrifices • Barukh S
Amidah • Tachanun • Kriat HaTorah • Ye
ssings • Minchah • Maariv • Kriat Shem